W9-AHY-782

ABOUT THE AUTHOR

For five decades, award-winning writer **Brad Steiger** has been devoted to exploring and examining unusual, hidden, secret, and otherwise strange occurrences. A former high school teacher and college instructor, Brad published his first articles on the unexplained in 1956. Since then he has written more than two thousand articles with paranormal themes. He is author or coauthor of more than 170 books, including *Real Vampires, Night Stalkers, and Creatures from the Darkside; Real Ghosts, Restless Spirits, and Haunted Places; The Werewolf Book; Conspiracies and Secret Societies*, and with his wife, Sherry, *Real Miracles, Divine Intervention, and Feats of Incredible Survival*. Brad's *Otherworldly Affaires* was voted the Number One Paranormal Book of 2008 by Haunted America Tours.

OTHER VISIBLE INK PRESS BOOKS BY BRAD STEIGER

Conspiracies and Secret Societies: The Complete Dossier
With Sherry Hansen Steiger
ISBN: 978-1-57859-174-9

Real Ghosts, Restless Spirits, and Haunted Places
ISBN: 978-1-57859-146-6

Real Miracles, Divine Intervention, and Feats of Incredible Survival
With Sherry Hansen Steiger
ISBN: 978-1-57859-214-2

Real Vampires, Night Stalkers, and Creatures from the Darkside
ISBN: 978-1-57859-255-5

Real Zombies, the Living Dead, and Creatures of the Apocalypse
ISBN: 978-1-57859-296-8

The Werewolf Book: The Encyclopedia of Shape-Shifting Beings
ISBN: 978-1-57859-078-0

ALSO FROM VISIBLE INK PRESS

Angels A to Z, 2nd edition
by Evelyn Dorothy Oliver and James R Lewis
ISBN: 978-1-57859-212-8

Armageddon Now: The End of the World A to Z
by Jim Willis and Barbara Willis
ISBN: 978-1-57859-168-8

The Astrology Book: The Encyclopedia of Heavenly Influences, 2nd edition
by James R Lewis
ISBN: 978-1-57859-144-2

The Dream Encyclopedia, 2nd edition
by James R Lewis and Evelyn Dorothy Oliver
ISBN: 978-1-57859-216-6

The Encyclopedia of Religious Phenomena
by J. Gordon Melton
ISBN: 978-1-57859-209-8

The Fortune-telling Book: The Encyclopedia of Divination and Soothsaying
by Raymond Buckland
ISBN: 978-1-57859-147-3

The Handy Religion Answer Book
by John Renard
ISBN: 978-1-57859-125-1

Hidden Realms, Lost Civilizations, and Beings from Other Worlds
by Jerome Clark
ISBN: 978-1-57859-175-6

The Religion Book: Places, Prophets, Saints, and Seers
by Jim Willis
ISBN: 978-1-57859-151-0

The Spirit Book: The Encyclopedia of Clairvoyance, Channeling, and Spirit Communication
by Raymond Buckland
ISBN: 978-1-57859-172-5

Unexplained! Strange Sightings, Incredible Occurrences, and Puzzling Physical Phenomena, 2nd edition
by Jerome Clark
ISBN: 978-1-57859-070-4

The Vampire Book: The Encyclopedia of the Undead, 3rd edition
by J. Gordon Melton
ISBN: 978-1-57859-281-4

The Witch Book: The Encyclopedia of Witchcraft, Wicca, and Neo-paganism
by Raymond Buckland
ISBN: 978-1-57859-114-5

Please visit us at visibleinkpress.com.

REAL MONSTERS,
GRUESOME CRITTERS,
AND BEASTS
FROM THE DARKSIDE

REAL MONSTERS, GRUESOME CRITTERS, AND BEASTS FROM THE DARKSIDE

BRAD STEIGER

VISIBLE
INK
PRESS

Detroit

Real Monsters, Gruesome Critters, and Beasts from the Darkside

Visible Ink Press®
43311 Joy Rd., #414
Canton, MI 48187-2075

Visible Ink Press is a registered trademark of Visible Ink Press LLC.

Most Visible Ink Press books are available at special quantity discounts when purchased in bulk by corporations, organizations, or groups. Customized printings, special imprints, messages, and excerpts can be produced to meet your needs. For more information, contact Special Markets Director, Visible Ink Press, www.visibleinkpress.com, or 734-667-3211.

Managing Editor: Kevin S. Hile
Art Director: Mary Claire Krzewinski
Typesetting: Marco Di Vita
Proofreaders: Sarah Hermsen and Sharon Malinowski

Cover image: Dan Wolfman Allen.

ISBN 978-1-57859-220-3

Library of Congress Cataloging-in-Publication Data

Steiger, Brad.
  Real monsters, gruesome critters, and beasts from the darkside / by Brad Steiger.
      p. cm.
  Includes bibliographical references and index.
  ISBN 978-1-57859-220-3
  1. Cryptozoology I. Title.
  QL88.3.S84 2011
  001.944—dc22
                                                                    2010024581

Printed in the United States of America

10 9 8 7 6 5 4 3 2

CONTENTS

CONTRIBUTORS

Thanks to the following gifted artists for contributing original illustrations and stories to this publication.

Ricardo Pustanio

Ricardo Pustanio is an enduring icon in the world of New Orleans Mardi Gras float design and local artistry. Today his phenomenal creative talents are witnessed by thousands upon thousands of locals and tourists who throng the streets of New Orleans each year to catch a glimpse of one of the oldest and most prestigious parades of the season, the Krewe of Mid-City. According to Ricardo, "The best is still to come!"

Born in New Orleans, Ricardo is the third son of local golfing legend Eddie "Blackie" Pustanio. When Ricardo was baptized, the famous "Diamond Jim" Moran was hailed as his godfather and all the major golfing pros who visited the elder Pustanio at his City Park Golf Course digs bounced little Ricardo on a famous knee at one time or another.

Like nearly every child brought up in the city of New Orleans, Ricardo was brought out by his parents to enjoy the pageantry and revelry of the great old-line Mardi Gras parades. These halcyon Mardi Gras days of his youth were Ricardo's first taste of the passion that would become the artistic pinnacle of his later career. During the 1960s Ricardo's entries won first place, and he rode with the King of Mid-City three years in a row: a true precursor of things to come.

The winner of many art competitions throughout his life, his earliest prize-winning work was created while Ricardo was still in Kindergarten. From an early age, Ricardo's work was distinguished with prizes and praise. Many are now in private art collections in New Orleans and across the United States.

Ricardo's special style has been very visible in his work on numerous backdrops and displays for the 1984 New Orleans World's Fair; several of his original pieces from that fair have garnered high prices at auctions throughout the United States and Europe.

Ricardo served Le Petit Theatre du Vieux Carre as technical director for its 1992 to 1993 season, during which he contributed his considerable artistic talents to the

Ricardo Pustanio building one of his popular New Orleans floats.

creation of scenery and backdrops for the season's major productions, including *West Side Story* and *The Baby Dance*, for which he created a giant 60 foot by 30 foot papier maché pyramid, one of the highlights of the season. Ricardo's set designs for the production of *King Midas and the Golden Touch* and *The Snow Queen* won him numerous awards.

In 1992 Ricardo also began his long association with William Crumb and the Children's Educational Theatre. His work on scenery and backdrops has toured with the company in 13 major productions across the United States, and he continues to contribute his talents to the organization to this day. Ricardo has also donated his time and talent to a number of nonprofit organizations, including the Save Our Lake Foundation and the March of Dimes.

Ricardo also displayed his talent with scenic design in some of the best-known, locally produced films in New Orleans, including *Angel Heart*, starring Mickey Rourke; *The Big Easy*, starring Dennis Quaid and Ellen Barkin; Anne Rice's *Interview with the Vampire*, starring Tom Cruise and Brad Pitt; and most recently in the much anticipated *A Love Song for Billy Long*, which stars John Travolta and was filmed on location in historic New Orleans.

Ricardo has conceptualized and designed numerous book covers and illustrations for major works of science fiction and fantasy: he was voted Best New Artist of the Year at world conventions held in New Orleans and in Amsterdam, Holland. Ricardo has also illustrated children's books, created portraits and artwork for private clients across the United States and Europe, and has to his credit three original action comic books, the illustration and design of the long-running International Middle Eastern Dancer magazine, and several decks of personalized Tarot cards.

Ricardo has said, in reflecting on his artist achievements, "I have paid my dues many times over the years and I am always in a constant state of expectation: I can't wait for the next challenge, the next thing to approach me. I am probably most proud of my work with the Krewe of Mid-City in recent years, because they have allowed me an unlimited palette to create with: the only limit is my imagination, and as you see, that has never had any limits!"

Ricardo Pustanio's hands have been busy creating artworks that have brought joy and pleasure to literally thousands of people over the years. It is no wonder that Ricardo has been named one of The Hardest Working Mardi Gras Artists in the City of New Orleans and in the history of Mardi Gras design.

Bill Oliver

Artist Bill Oliver is also a musician, composer, and award-winning song writer. His music is sometimes reflective and moody, and his compositions, like his art, often act as "sound photographs" that capture a moment of life and freeze it in time for further contemplation—even if that moment of contemplation involves a vampire, zombie, UFO visitor, or a werewolf.

Oliver resides in Vancouver, British Columbia, where he has nourished a life-long fascination for the paranormal, UFOs, the metaphysical, and all things esoteric, interests stemming from many personal experiences. His enthusiasm for pursuing the unknown brought him into personal contact and interview opportunities with experiencers in all aspects of the paranormal. These encounters have had significant influences on much of Bill's work.

Brad Steiger first became familiar with Oliver's exciting artwork when the Canadian won the Christmas Art contest on the Jeff Rense Program in 2005. In the art contest for Halloween 2006, Bill won honorable mention.

As the two men became better acquainted, Steiger was honored to learn that he had been one of Oliver's boyhood heroes with his work on the paranormal, the esoteric, and things that go bump in the night.

Bill Oliver

"To be reading one of Brad's classic books one day and being asked to do some art for one of his new books another is truly paranormal," Oliver said.

Visit Bill Oliver's website at http://www.boysoblue.com/.

Dan "Wolfman" Allen

Dan "Wolfman" Allen is the owner of Ronin Studio, where he has been perfecting his unique style of comic book art for many years. Wolfman also does incredible renderings of vampires, werewolves, and other assorted monsters in a very compelling and graphic manner. He is not really into the "superhero" genre that permeates the American comic book industry. Rather, most of his characters are more a part of the fantasy and sci-fi genre; his protagonists, while thought by some of their peers to be antiso-

Dan "Wolfman" Allen

cial or disreputable, continue to be themselves and try to rise above their superficial visages or reputations to solve a key problem, rather than trying to save the entire world.

Dan is also fascinated by Native American lore and shares both tribal and Viking blood in his genes. As much as possible, he attempts to follow shamanic teachings in combination with Christian philosophy. He has studied the paranormal and the mystical since he was a boy, and he has experienced many aspects of the so-called supernatural on a personal basis. Contact him at plan9motorsports@charter.net.

Tim R. Swartz

Tim R. Swartz

Tim Swartz is an Indiana native and Emmy Award-winning television producer/videographer. He is the author of a number of popular books, including *The Lost Journals of Nikola Tesla, Time Travel: A How-To-Guide,* and *Admiral Byrd's Secret Journey Beyond the Poles.* As a photojournalist, Tim has traveled extensively and investigated paranormal phenomena and other unusual mysteries from such diverse locations as the Great Pyramid in Egypt to the Great Wall of China. As well, he is the writer and editor of the Internet newsletter *Conspiracy Journal,* a free, weekly email newsletter considered essential reading by paranormal researchers worldwide. Visit his website at www.conspiracy journal.com.

Alyne Pustanio

Alyne Pustanio

Folklorist and occultist Alyne Pustanio is a New Orleans native whose roots go deep into the local culture; and it is from that proverbial "gumbo" that she draws her inspiration for most of her tales of terror and fascination.

A descendant of Portuguese and Sicilian immigrant families who trace their ancestry to European Gypsies, Alyne was exposed to the mysteries of the occult at an early age. Two great-grandmothers were gifted and sought out mediums and another relative is a verified psychic; however, Alyne credits her mother—an avid spiritualist—with inspiring her lifelong interest in the supernatural and unexplained.

These interests, combined with her avocations in folklore and history, result in a validity and passion that is immediately obvious in all her writings. Learn more at her website www.hauntedamericatours.com.

Pastor Robin Swope

Pastor Robin Swope

Pastor Robin Swope, who is known as the "Paranormal Pastor," has been a Christian minister for more than 15 years in both mainline and evangelical denominations. He has served as a missionary to Burkina Faso, West Africa, and ministered to the homeless in New York City's Hell's Kitchen. He is the founder and chief official of Open Gate Ministerial Services and a member of St. Paul's United Church of Christ in Erie, Pennsylvania. His website is http://theparanormalpastor.blogspot.com.

William Michael Mott

William Michael (Mike) Mott has been a creative director for a national toy and manufacturing company and a high-performance software company, an art director for a city newspaper, an artist/designer for Fortune 500 companies, as well as for an NSF Engineering Research Center, and has done work for a variety of clients on a freelance basis, such as book and magazine publishers. He is also a freelance artist and writer, and writes both fiction and nonfiction. His artwork and writing have appeared or been featured in many publications, such as *Computer Graphics World Magazine, DRAGON Magazine, FATE, NEXUS, World Explorer, Undaunted Press, Lost Continent Library Magazine*, and others. He has created artwork and graphic design for mass-market book covers, posters, brochures, packaging, CD-ROM covers and art collections, and digital/web-based media. And he has won several design awards, from regional Advertising Federation awards for printed material to awards for website graphics and design. His artwork has been featured in the exhibition "In Dreams Awake: Art of Fantasy" at the Olympia and York Gallery, NYC, 1988; at the 1987 World Fantasy Con, Con*stellation, the DragonCon 2001 art show, several one-man exhibits, and digital galleries in various venues. He also researches and writes on Fortean, folklore, comparative religion, and paranormal topics.

William Michael Mott

Mike is also the author of the satirical fantasy novel *Pulsifer: A Fable* and its sequel, *Land of Ice, A Velvet Knife*, both soon to be re-released in one omnibus edition from TGS Publishing, as well as the nonfiction books *Caverns, Cauldrons, and Concealed Creatures* and *This Tragic Earth: The Art and World of Richard Sharpe Shaver*. His pulp fiction anthology of fiction, verse, and artwork, *PULP WINDS*, featuring an introduction by Brad Steiger, has been recently published by TGS (www.hiddenmysteries.com). Mike can be reached at admin@mottimorphic.com and at mottimorph@earthlink.net. His website is www.mottimorphic.com.

Nick Redfern

Nick Redfern is the author of a number of books on cryptozoology, including *There's Something in the Woods; Memoirs of a Monster Hunter; Three Men Seeking Monsters;* and *Man-Monkey*. Originally from England, Nick lives with his wife, Dana, in Dallas, Texas, and only a stone's throw from the infamous Grassy Knoll. When he's not chasing monsters, you can usually find Nick playing music—very, very loudly. He can be contacted at his website www.nick redfern.com.

Nick Redfern

Donald Avery

Donald J. Avery was born in Tacoma, Washington, and has been a resident of Washington state for most of his life. He has been married to his wife, Peggy, for 31 years. Avery has a B.S. degree in business administration and a master's degree in public administration. He did a stint in the Marine Corps from 1966 to 1972. Most of his employment background centered around a

Donald Avery

Drs. Sharon and
Dave Oester

23-year period in which he was a city and county administrator. Don and Peggy retired in March 2010 after spending almost two years as assistant managers for a retirement community in Kennewick, Washington.

Drs. Dave and Sharon Oester

Drs. Dave and Sharon Oester began the International Ghost Hunters Society in 1996. They are the authors of 23 books. Their most recent, *Ghosts of Gettysburg: Walking on Hallowed Ground,* describes 50 of the most haunted sites on the famous Civil War battlefield. Dave and Sharon travel full time in their RV coach as they investigate the most haunted places in America. The Oesters' website is www.ghostweb.com. Their email address is ghostweb@ghostweb.com.

Eric Altman

Eric Altman's journey into researching the paranormal began at the young age of 10, when he watched the 1970s docudramas *Legend of Boggy Creek* and *Creature from Black Lake,* allegedly based on events that took place in the deep south of Arkansas and Texas. The two films inspired Eric to begin 27 years of research into the paranormal. His main interest is studying hominid creatures such as Bigfoot. Eric currently heads the Pennsylvania Bigfoot Society, a group of dedicated researchers who investigate encounters and sightings of Bigfoot in the "Keystone State." His official website is www.beyondtheedgeradio.com.

Eric Altman

Leslie Danielle Ferrymen

Leslie Danielle Ferrymen is a paranormal investigator from Franklin, Tennessee, who heads up The Franklin Ghost and Paranormal Investigation Team. Ms. Ferryman is very active in pursuing real urban legends and finding out what truth lies hidden in the stories told. Her 15- member group has investigated many haunted locations all over the United States since its founding in 2006.

Timothy Green Beckley

There always remains an audience eager to know the mysteries about the Hollow Earth. Timothy Green Beckley of Global Communications has made a sort of cottage industry out of his interest in the Inner and Hollow Earth theories, saving some old and rare books from obscurity and publishing up-to-date compendiums written by more recent researchers. His most popular titles dealing with this subject include: *Twilight, Hidden Chambers beneath the Earth* by T. Lobsang Rampa; *Underground Alien Bio Lab At Dulce: The Bennewitz UFO Papers; Admiral Byrd's Secret Journey Beyond the Poles* by Tim Swartz; *Best of the Hollow Earth Hassle* by Mary J. Martin; and *Finding Lost Atlantis Inside the Hollow Earth* by the late British writer Brinsely Le Poer Trench, the Earl of Clancarty. Beckley is also the publisher of *The Conspiracy Journal:* www.conspiracyjournal.com.

Timothy Green Beckley

Micah Hanks

Micah A. Hanks is a lifelong researcher of the unexplained who in his articles and written work has covered bizarre reports of Fortean oddities, including strange creatures, UFOs, historical mysteries, conspiracies, and mysticism from cultures around the world. He posts daily updated paranormal news on his website *The Gralien Report* (www.gralienreport.com), and is producer of the regional radio program *Speaking of Strange with Joshua P. Warren*. You can learn more about Micah at www.micahahanks.com.

Micah Hanks

Loren Coleman

Loren Coleman is one of the world's leading cryptozoologists. Certainly, he is acknowledged as the current living American researcher and writer who has most popularized cryptozoology in the late twentieth and early twenty-first centuries.

Loren Coleman

Starting his fieldwork and investigations in 1960, after traveling and trekking extensively in pursuit of cryptozoological mysteries Coleman began writing to share his experiences soon after his first expeditions. An honorary member of Ivan T. Sanderson's Society for the Investigation of the Unexplained in the 1970s, Coleman has been bestowed with similar honorary memberships of the North Idaho College Cryptozoology Club in 1983 (which was inspired by one of his books), and in subsequent years that of the British Columbia Scientific Cryptozoology Club, CryptoSafari International, and other global organizations. He was also a life member and benefactor of the International Society of Cryptozoology (now-defunct).

Obtaining an undergraduate degree from Southern Illinois University at Carbondale, Coleman majored in anthropology, minored in zoology, and did some summer work in archaeology. He received a graduate degree in psychiatric social work from Simmons College in Boston. Coleman was admitted to the Ph.D. programs, and took doctoral coursework in social anthropology at Brandies University and in sociology at the University of New Hampshire's anthropology/sociology department. His dedication to fatherhood made his decision to first raise his sons, teach, and write, an easy one.

Coleman's first cryptozoology magazine article was published in 1969, when he was 21 years old. His first book was published in 1975.

Today, Coleman has written more than 6,000 columns and articles, as well as over 30 books. He has appeared frequently on radio and television programs, and has lectured throughout North America, as well as in London and at Loch Ness. Coleman's cryptozoology columns, since the 1970s, have included "On the Trail" in the London-based *Fortean Times*; "Coleman's CryptoCorner" in *TAPS Paramagazine*; and "Mysterious World" in *Fate Magazine*, as well as regular contributions to *The Anomalist, San Francisco Chronicle, Boston Magazine,* and *Fortean Studies*. His unique signature column, "The Cryptozoo News," was published in *Strange Magazine* and *Mysteries Magazine,* and now appears as Coleman's blog at Cryptomundo.com.

Coleman has been both an on- and off-camera consultant to the Travel Channel's *Weird Travels*, the History Channel's *Deepsea Mysteries*, NBC-TV's *Unsolved Mysteries*, A & E's *Ancient Mysteries*, the History Channel's *In Search of History*, the Discovery Channel's *In the Unknown*, Discovery Science Channel's *Critical Eye*, the History Channel's *Deep Sea Detectives*, Animal Planet's *Animal X*, Discovery Kids' *Mystery Hunters*, Animal Planet's *Twisted Tales*, and other reality-based programs, such as *Current Affairs* and *Evening Magazine*. In 2000, he served as the senior series consultant to the new *In Search Of ...* program that was broadcast on the Sci-Fi Network. Read more at http://www.cryptomundo.com/lorencoleman.

Richard Senate

Richard Senate has been hunting ghosts since 1978 and has established a solid reputation for sense and sensibility in the field. He has visited over 200 haunted sites in northern California and the Southwest and authored many bestselling books on the subject of psychic research. He stresses that he is a normal person, but one with an obscure hobby. In the real world, Senate works for the city of Verona, California, where he manages three different historic sites as well as giving lectures at a local college His wife, Debbie, a gifted psychic, often joins him in his ghost hunts. You can email him at HaintHunter@aol.com.

Mary Croft

Mary Croft

Mary grew up in Toronto, Ontario, and moved to Hermosa Beach, California, where she ran on the beach and worked as a registered nurse. After a decade, she moved north to Petaluma, California, where her two boys, Colin and Casey, were born. Over the decades, Mary has remained fascinated by the power of the subconscious mind and all disciplines of energy and frequency healing. She then moved to Roswell, New Mexico, for the challenging experiences without which she would not have had the material to write—upon moving to Canmore, Alberta—her book: *How I Clobbered Every Bureaucratic Cash-Confiscatory Agency Known to Man: A Spiritual Economics Book on $$$ and Remembering Who You Are*. This book can be downloaded at www .SpiritualEconomicsNow.net/solutions/How_I_08.pdf, and her subsequent, related articles can be read on her blog: http://SpiritualEconomicsNow.net/.

Linda Godfrey

Linda Godfrey

As a professional artist, teacher, writer, and mother of two, Linda Godfrey has carved a niche for herself as one of the most respected authorities on anomalous animals and paranormal phenomenon in Wisconsin.

As the acknowledged expert on the creature knows as "The Beast of Bray Road," Godfrey has been interviewed on a plethora of television networks and programs that deal with bizarre creatures, such as *Inside Edition*, *Sightings*, Animal Planet, Discovery Kids and the SyFy channel. Godfrey has also been featured on AMC's exposé of the realities behind the werewolf film *Underworld* entitled *Fang vs. Fiction* and has recently been working with an Australian team producing a show for the Discovery Channel. Godfrey has also made numerous appearances on Godfrey has also made numerous appearances on *Coast to Coast AM*.

As a journalist, Godfrey was the first to break the chilling story of the horrific, werewolf-like monstrosity that is said to lurk in the shadow shrouded forests surrounding Elkhorn, Wisconsin's Bray Road.

Since then she has gone on to author three books: *The Beast of Bray Road, Tailing Wisconsin's Werewolf, Hunting the American Werewolf,* and *Lake and Sea Monsters (Mysteries, Legends, and Unexplained Phenomena)*.

Godfrey has continued to pursue her interests in the unknown and has gone on to investigate an array of unusual animals allegedly lurking in her home state. Next on her slate is the forthcoming *Beyond Bray Road*, which will continue her chronicle of this nefarious creature's exploits with numerous additional sightings and encounters as well as further exploration of possible explanations for the so-called "wolfman" phenomenon.

You can learn more about Godfrey and her work at http://twitter.com/lindagodfrey, http://www.beastofbrayroad.com/bloga.html, http://www.weird michigan.com, http://blogs.myspace.com/lindagodfrey, and http://lindagod frey.wordpress.com.

Dr. Franklin Ruehl

Dr. Franklin Ruehl

Dr. Franklin Ruehl holds a Ph.D. in physics (UCLA) and has a weekly column ("Weird Science") in the (San Bernardino County) SUN, has an online column ("Ask Dr. Ruehl") at tabloidbaby.com, and has published over 2,100 technical papers and popular articles in a wide spectrum of newspapers, magazines, and journals.

Additionally, he regularly lectures before various colleges, organizations, libraries, aerospace firms (such as Hughes, Lockheed, and ITT), and expos (such as the Whole Life Expo) and conventions (such as the Babylon 5 Con, Dr. Who Con, and Space: 1999 Con).

He has been a guest on television and radio talk shows, such as *Roseanne, Donahue, Mid-Morning L.A., Morning Edition, Tom Snyder Show,* and the *Michael Jackson Show*. He regularly appears as a guest expert on *EXTRA* and *Strange Universe*, and hosts his own segment, "The Dr. Ruehl Show," on *Weird TV*. Most recently he was a regular contributor to *A Current Affair*.

His UFO column is available at http://ufonews.tv/dr-franklin-ruehl-editorials/, and he can be reached at drruehl@yahoo.com.

Frank Joseph

Frank Joseph is the author of more than 20 published books about ancient civilizations and alternative spirituality. His latest title is *Gods of the*

Runes, Their Stone Age Roots and Original Meanings, from Bear & Company. He was the editor-in-chief of *Ancient American* magazine for 15 years from its inception in 1993. Today, Joseph lives with his wife, Laura, and Mystical Norwegian Forest Cat, Sammy, near the widest stretch of the Mississippi River in Lake Pepin, Minnesota. His website is www.InnerTraditions.com.

Sandy Nichols

Sandy Nichols

An alien abductee himself, Sandy Nichols is founder and president of ARG (Alien Research Group). A Brentwood, Tennessee-based organization for the study of alien abductions, ARG specializes in helping the abductee through all phases of the abduction phenomenon, especially in locating licensed counselors and certified hypnotherapist in their specific locale.

Nichols is also past coordinator for the *Tenn Files* website and magazine for the Memphis, Tennessee-based "Night Search" organization, and former update host for its radio program on WWOW 1430AM; a member of the "Night Search" X-Files coalition of Paranormal Researchers; and past contributing writer for the "Night Search" newsletter, Nichols has conducted numerous radio interviews with organizations such as the Heritage Radio Network and the "X-Zone," hosted by Rob McConnell.

Brent Raynes

Brent Raynes

Brent Raynes has been active in the UFO and paranormal fields since the early 1970s. He has written for *Fate* and other magazines, and in 1970 established *Alternate Perceptions Magazine*. Raynes is also the author of the book *Visitors from Hidden Realms and the Edge of Reality*. Learn more about him at www.mysterious-america.net.

INTRODUCTION: MONSTERS, CREEPY CREATURES, AND NIGHTMARISH BEINGS

In 2001, the Media Psychology Lab at California State in Los Angeles polled people across the United States from ages 6 to 90 in all ethnic groups to determine which movie monsters ranked as the favorites. According to the survey, the most frightening motion picture of all time for all groups was *The Exorcist* (1973), in which a demon possesses a young girl.

The favorite top ten monsters after *The Exorcist* were the following:

1. *Dracula*, with the majority of respondents favoring the 1931 version with Bela Lugosi as the blood-sucking count.

2. Freddy Krueger who uses razor-sharp metal talons on his fingers to attack teens in their dreams in *A Nightmare on Elm Street* (1984).

3. The Frankenstein monster, especially the original version in the Boris Karloff film (1931).

4. Godzilla, the prehistoric giant reptile that spews radioactive rays and stomps cities to rubble, who first appeared in the Japanese film *Godzilla of the Monsters* (1954).

5. King Kong, the giant ape from the original that features the Willis O'Brien stop-action figures (1933).

6. Chucky, the perverse, demonic murderous doll from *Child's Play* (1988).

7. Michael Myers, the masked murderer who is described in the film *Halloween* (1978) as the essence of pure evil.

8. Hannibal Lecter, the erudite, cannibalistic serial killer from *The Silence of the Lambs* (1991).

9. Jason, the unstoppable monster in the hockey mask from *Friday the 13th* (1980).

10. The multi-jawed, many-fanged extraterrestrial creature that terrorized the crew of a spaceship in *Alien* (1979).

Inspired by the Media Psychology Lab's poll of movie monsters, I decided to survey a number of cryptozoologists, paranormalists, psychical researchers, Forteans, and ufologists and receive their nominations for the Top Ten List of Real-Life Monsters—and thus I planted the seed for this present book.

Tie for First Place: Bigfoot and Mothman

Large apelike creature in the United States and Canada are known in the oral traditions of native tribes by such names as Bigfoot, Sasquatch, Wauk-Wauk, Oh-Mah, or Saskehavis. These creatures have also been described in the journals of early settlers and in the columns of frontier newspapers, but wide public attention was not called to the mysterious beast until the late 1950s, when road-building crews in the Bluff Creek area north of Eureka, California, began to report a large number of sightings of North America's own "abominable snowman."

The humanlike creature—whether sighted in the more remote, wooded, or mountainous regions of North America, South America, Russia, China, Australia, or Africa—is believed by some anthropologists to be a bipedal mammal that constitutes a kind of missing link between humankind and the great apes, for its appearance is more primitive than that of Neanderthal. The descriptions given by witnesses around the world are amazingly similar: height between six and nine feet; weight anywhere from 400 to 1,000 pounds; black eyes. Dark fur or body hair from one to four inches in length is said to cover the creature's entire body with the exception of the palms of its hands, the soles of its feet, and its upper facial area, nose, and eyelids.

In North America, the greatest number of sightings of Bigfoot have come from the Fraser River Valley, the Strait of Georgia, and Vancouver Island, British Columbia; the "Ape Canyon" region near Mt. St. Helens in southwestern Washington; the Three Sisters Wilderness west of Bend, Oregon; and the area around the Hoopa Valley Indian Reservation, especially the Bluff Creek watershed northeast of Eureka, California. In recent years, extremely convincing sightings of Bigfoot-type creatures have also been made in areas of New York, New Jersey, Minnesota, South Carolina, Tennessee, and Florida.

Most scientists remain skeptical about Bigfoot's existence, and the controversy rages on after 60 years.

The Mothman legend began in the 1960s. On November 15, 1966, two young married couples were driving through the marshy area near the Ohio River outside of Point Pleasant, West Virginia, when a winged monster, at least seven feet tall with glowing red eyes, loomed up in front of them near an abandoned TNT plant. Later, they told Deputy Sheriff Millard Halstead that the creature followed them toward Point Pleasant on Route 62 even when their speed approached one hundred miles per hour.

News of the mysterious encounter achieved local notoriety, and numerous other area residents added to the story with reports that they had also seen the giant bird-like creature near the same abandoned TNT plant. A few days later, Thomas Ury said that an enormous flying creature with a wingspan of 10 feet had chased his convertible into Point Pleasant at a speed of 70 miles per hour.

More witnesses came forward with accounts of their sightings, and the legend of Mothman was born. Although the majority of witnesses described the tall, red-eyed monster as appearing birdlike, the media dubbed the creature "Mothman" because, as writer John A. Keel noted, the *Batman* television series was very popular at the time.

Intrigued by the stories, Keel visited Point Pleasant on numerous occasions and learned about the bizarre occurrences associated with Mothman's appearance, including the eerie forecast that the Silver Bridge in Point Pleasant would collapse and many people would be killed as a result.

Number Two: The Jersey Devil

Some witnesses have said that the Jersey Devil that haunts the Pine Barrens in southeastern New Jersey is a cross between a goat and a dog with cloven hoofs and the head of a collie. Others swear that it has a horse's head with the body of a kangaroo. Most of the people who have sighted the creature also mention a long tail, and nearly all of the witnesses agree that the thing has wings.

People have been spotting the Jersey Devil in the rural area around southern New Jersey since 1735, which, according to local legend, is the year that it was born.

For well over 200 years, generations of terrified witnesses have claimed they have encountered the Jersey Devil. Although eye-witness accounts are reported every year, the most famous series of sightings occurred in January 1909, when hundreds of men and women claimed to have seen or heard the frightening creature. So many people refused to leave the safety of their homes that local mills were forced to shut down for lack of workers.

Number Three: Nessie-Type, Long-Necked Lake Monsters

Nessie, most often described as a long-necked monster resembling an aquatic dinosaur, has been seen in and near Loch Ness since St. Columba made the first recorded sighting in 565 C.E. Today, nearly two million tourists come to Scotland each year to see if they might obtain a glimpse and a photograph of the elusive beast.

Although Nessie is by far the most famous of all monsters inhabiting inland bodies of water, there are reports of equally large, equally strange aquatic creatures in lakes all over the world. In the United States and Canada, there are such familiar lake monsters as "Ogopogo" in the Okanogan Lake, British Columbia; "Champ" in Lake Champlain, New York; and "Memphre" in Lake Memphremagog, Vermont.

Number Four: Chupacabras

Named for its seeming penchant for attacking goats and sucking their blood, the chupacabras ("goat sucker") both terrified and fascinated the public at large when it first burst upon the scene in Puerto Rico in the summer of 1995. From August 1995 to the present day, the monster has been credited with the deaths of thousands of animals, ranging from goats, rabbits, and birds to horses, cattle, and deer. While some argue that the creature is a new monster, others point out that such vampiric entities have always existed and been reported by farmers and villagers in Puerto Rico and Central and South America.

Number Five: Werewolves/Shapeshifters

Native American tribes tell of bear-people, wolf-people, fox-people, and so forth, and state that in the beginning of human history, people were like animals and animals were more human-like. Stories of women who gave birth to were-creatures are common among the North American tribal myths.

Early cultures throughout the Americas, Europe, Asia, and Africa formed totem clans and often worshipped minor deities that were half-human, half-animal. Norse legends tell about hairy, human-like beings that live in underworld caves and come out at night to feast on the flesh of unfortunate surface dwellers.

The prefix *were* in Old English means "man," so coupled with wolf it designates a creature that can alter its appearance from human to beast and become a "man wolf." In French, the werewolf is known as *loup garou*; in Spanish, *hombre lobo*; Italian, *lupo manaro*; Portuguese, *lobizon* or *lobo home*; Polish, *wilkolak*; Russian, *olkolka* or *volkulaku*; and in Greek, *brukolakas*.

In the Middle Ages, large bands of beggars and brigands roamed the European countryside at night, often dressing in wolf skins and howling like a pack of wolves on the hunt. In the rural areas of France, Germany, Lower Hungary, Estonia, and other countries, these nocturnal thieves were called, "werewolves." The old Norwegian counterpart to werewolf is *vargulf*, literally translated as "rogue wolf," referring to an outlaw who separates himself from society.

Psychologists recognize a werewolf psychosis (lycanthropy or lupinomanis) in which persons so afflicted may believe that they change into a wolf when there is a full moon. Those so disturbed may actually "feel" their fur growing, their fingernails becoming claws, their jaws lengthening, their canine teeth elongating.

Number Six: Thunderbirds

The thunderbird figures prominently in the tribal traditions of many Native American tribes. To the Lakota of the American prairies, the thunderbird is an embodiment of the Great Mystery, the Supreme Being that created all things on Earth. While scholars over the centuries have attributed the Native American myths of the thunderbird to the reverence for the eagle, the largest of indigenous birds in North America, many people have claimed to have seen for themselves a great bird, far larger than the eagle, flying overhead. In fact, even in the nineteenth century, some witnesses claimed to have seen flying monsters that resembled pterodactyls, the winged reptiles that became extinct 65 million years ago.

Number Seven: Springheeled Jack

About the middle of November 1837, the lanes and commons of Middlesex, England, suddenly became places of dread. An eerie figure said to be possessed of supernatural powers was stalking the frightened villagers by night and effortlessly avoiding capture by the police. Because of this creature's ability to leap over tall hedges and walls from a standing jump. He was given the name "Springheeled Jack."

Close witnesses who encountered Jack face-to-face described him as being tall, thin, and powerful. A prominent nose stuck out of his pinched physiognomy and his ears were pointed like those of an animal. His long, bony fingers resembled claws.

Number Eight: Living Dinosaurs, Such as Mokele-Mbembe

For at least 200 years, stories have emerged from the swamps, rivers, and lakes of African jungles that there is a brownish-gray, elephant-sized creature with a reptilian tail and a long, flexible neck. The native people call it *mokele-mbembe* ("the one who stops the flow of rivers") or *emela-ntuka* ("the one who eats the tops of trees"). In 1980, Dr. Roy Mackal led an expedition into African swamps that are "Mokey's" hangouts and stated later that the descriptions of the beast would fit that of a sauropod, the giant plant-eating reptile that supposedly became extinct about 65 million years ago.

Number Nine: Flatwoods Monster

Kathleen May described the alien being that she and seven other Flatwoods, West Virginia, residents saw on September 12, 1952, as looking more frightening than the Frankenstein monster. A group of boys were at a nearby playground when they sighted a flying saucer emitting an exhaust that looked like red balls of fire. According to the boys, the UFO landed on a hilltop in back of the May house.

Gene Lemon, a husky 17-year-old, found a flashlight and said that he was going to investigate. About half way up the hill, Lemon directed the beam of his flashlight on what he believed to be the green, glowing eyes of an animal. Instead, the beam spotlighted an immense, humanlike figure with blood-red face and greenish eyes that blinked from under a pointed hood. Behind the monster was a "glowing ball of fire as big as a house" that grew dimmer and brighter at intervals.

Number Ten: Dover Demon

Whatever it was that William Bartlett and two other teenagers sighted from April 21 to 23, 1977, in Dover, Massachusetts, was real. The "thing" that has become known as the Dover Demon was seen by Bartlett as it crept along a low stone wall on the side of the road. It stood about four feet tall and carried its hairless, rough-textured body on two spindly legs. Its arms were also thin and peach-colored. The creature's huge, watermelon-shaped head was disproportionate in size to its relatively small torso, and it had two large, glowing, red-orange eyes.

Bartlett, who has made his career as a painter, told the *Boston Globe* (October 29, 2006) that he definitely saw something weird that night. "I didn't make it up," he said. "It's a thing that's been following me for years. Not the creature—the story."

In *Real Monsters, Creepy Creatures, and Nightmarish Beings*, we shall meet these frightening Top Ten fiends, devils, and monstrosities and many, many others. Be thankful that you can encounter them from the safety of your own home. Just ignore those shadows and strange noises that might occur while reading this book.

BIG CATS—PREDATORS OUT OF PLACE

When I was boy growing up in Iowa during the 1940s, I came to look forward during the winter months to the arrival of a curious guest—in addition to Santa Claus—who would faithfully visit our state. Santa, of course, was a welcome guest at our house on Christmas Eve. The other visitor was not at all welcome at any time. According to newspaper accounts, each winter a mysterious black panther somehow materialized among the snow banks and proceeded to frighten folks with its threatening growl and piercing yellow eyes.

Startled eye-witnesses from across the state sighted the beast near the mailboxes at the end of their lanes when they went to retrieve the day's newspaper and bills. Others spotted it running through the groves near their homes. Livestock was killed or mauled, victims of the black panther.

Each morning, my little sister and I had a very long lane to walk in order to be picked up by the school bus, and we kept a wary eye on our thick groves and apple orchards, hoping that we would never spot the big cat stalking us. During the winter months, it was nearly dark by the time the bus dropped us off to begin the trek back down the lane to the safety of our home. On each side of our lane, there were fields with fallen cornstalks awaiting next spring's plowing. A panther could easily crouch behind clumps of dried stalks, hungrily awaiting his prey.

Journalists had a wide variety of theories as to how a black panther could make its way to Iowa. Most common of these hypotheses was the obvious one: someone had obtained a panther as a pet and it had escaped when it reached its maturity. Pleas were made to whomever might know the origins of this dangerous creature to come forward and help provide clues to its possible whereabouts.

Experienced hunters suggested that a mountain lion (also called a cougar, puma, or panther, depending on regional preference) might easily have found its way down to Iowa from northern Minnesota, and they assured the populace that they would soon be able to hunt it down. Most people knew that cougars were not black, but others argued that the panther could be a freak of nature, turning black, rather than a cougar's typical tannish-brown color.

Big Black Cats Really Do Exist

Actually, a black panther is a kind of deviant cat from the norm of its kind. In South America, the black panther is actually a jaguar, whose typical markings are covered by an excess of the black pigment melanin. Although it has been rarely reported, black jaguars have been sighted in the southwestern mountain ranges of the United States. There are no substantiated sightings of black cougars. Apparently melanism never becomes dominant in the cougar as it does occasionally in the jaguar.

In the January 25, 2010, issue of the *New York Times*, Alan Rabinowitz, the president and chief executive of Panthera, a wild cat conservation group, responded to the recent announcement of the United States Fish and Wildlife Service that it would begin to take the initial steps toward mandating a jaguar recovery plan. The jaguar had been on the endangered species list in the United States since 1997, based on occasional sightings of the big cats crossing north over the United States–Mexico border.

Because natural jaguars are a rarity in the American Southwest, and are tracked closely by the U.S. Fish and Wildlife Service, is there some other explanation for the large cat sightings in that area (*iStock*)?

Rabinowitz pointed out that although the jaguar may have inhabited large sections of the western states in prehistoric times, the last documented sighting of a female jaguar with a cub was in the early 1900s. The Arizona Game and Fish Department reported one male jaguar desperately had attempted to survive in the harsh, dry region, but they concluded that he had been dead for quite some time.

Rabinowitz presented his argument that regardless of the few jaguars sighted crossing into the United States from the northernmost population of the cats in Sonora, the American Southwest is, at best, a "marginal habitat for the animals." Rather than waste any of the sparse federal funds allotted to the Fish and Wildlife Service to create a habitat for the jaguar, Rabinowitz stated that it made far more sense to help those countries in the "Jaguar Corridor," where thousands of jaguars flourish from Mexico to Argentina, to conserve the big cat's true habitat.

Because the Fish and Wildlife Service has been keeping a watchful eye on the handful of jaguars that cross the border between Mexico and the United States since the early 1900s, it is unlikely that sightings of jaguars can account for the twice-told winter tales of black panthers. Nor, if Mr. Rabinowitz's sage words are heeded, are we likely to see any black jaguars creeping into our livestock barns in the Midwest.

In addition to jaguars that fade their spots under darker hair, there are leopards with skin color containing a mixture of blue, black, gray, and purple—thus appearing "black"—but they are found in the dense forests of southwestern China, Myanmar, Assam, Nepal, and parts of southern India. Melanistic black leopards are thought to be more numerous in Java and the southern part of the Malay Peninsula than the spotted leopards. Interestingly, a female jaguar or leopard may give birth to spotted kittens along with black and albino siblings in the same litter.

Of course I knew nothing about melanistic mutations when I was a boy, nor did I realize that there were actually no species of big cats that were categorized as "black panthers," but I surely knew that any kind of cat as large as eye-witnesses described them did not belong in Iowa. Especially, perhaps, in the winter months.

As I became older and came to specialize in the investigation of such phenomena as ghosts, UFOs, monsters, vampires, zombies, and other strange creatures that go bump in the night, I discovered that out-of-place black panthers are not only sighted in Iowa during the winter months, but reports of big cats have come from nearly every state and province in North America.

On February 9, 2010, *Click Orlando* (http://www.clickOrlando.com/print/22506 062/detail.html) reported that a number of local residents had begun to feel nervous on their evening walks and noticed that they were being joined by bobcats, a feline about three feet in length and thirty pounds in weight. Spokespersons for Florida Fish and Wildlife said that bobcats migrate all over the state, and even though residents do not wish them to get in their homes or to attack their pets, it is not unusual to spot bobcats scavenging on the beach.

Interestingly, on that same date in February, three coyotes were spotting sprinting across the campus of Columbia University in Manhattan—that's Manhattan, New York, not Kansas. A few hours later, according to Andy Soltis of the *New York Post*, a coyote was seen sliding across a frozen lake in Central Park.

These are neat human interest stories that cause the reader to cluck his tongue in wonderment how the strangeness of out-of-place animals could come to be. However, bobcats in Florida and coyotes in Manhattan are in no measure comparable to sighting black panthers in Iowa or African lions in Indiana.

Mysterious Cougars and African Lions in Indiana

My friend and colleague Tim R. Swartz grew up in Indiana and he recalls that mountain lions have also been recorded in that state over the years, even though these large cats are believed extinct in the state.

"It is not unreasonable to suppose that some mountain lions could still live or migrate through some of the more unpopulated regions," Swartz said. "However, Indiana has had sightings of what appeared to be maned lions, animals indigenous to Africa, not the Midwest."

Here is an account of one such sighting that Swartz shared with me:

> On August 5, 1948 Deputy Sheriff Jack Witherby received a phone call from a man who reported that he and his family were fishing along the banks of Elkhorn Falls, in the extreme eastern part of the state. Suddenly, a large cat came running at the family, chasing them into their car. The cat lunged at the car, but then ran away along the stream bed. The cat was described as looking like an African lion with a long tail and a bushy mane around its neck and head.

> Deputy Sheriff Witherby examined tracks found at the scene and said they were "like nothing I have ever seen before in this area."

> A few days later two brothers, Arthur and Howard Turner, spotted two strange animals that they said looked just like African lions: "They were large headed, shaggy and brown in color."

The Big Vampire Cat of Bladenboro

In January 1954, experienced hunters by the hundreds arrived to trek through the swamp outside of Bladenboro, North Carolina, in search of the Vampire Cat that had been ripping people's prize hounds to bloody shreds.

The terror began on New Year's Eve, 1953, when Johnny Vause found two of his dogs "torn to ribbons and crushed." Everybody knew that there was no animal anywhere near the small mill town that could work such terrible carnage on two big and healthy dogs.

Within a few days, two more pairs of dogs were killed in a similar fashion, but this time it appeared that their blood had been drained by the thing that had killed them.

Chief of police Roy Fores informed Mayor W.G. Fussell that something mighty strange was going on near the swamp, and Fussell decided that the citizenry needed to be warned. If it were big healthy dogs being torn to ribbons then, how long would it be before the beast claimed its first human victims?

On January 5, 1954, the Wilmington *Morning Star* ran a front-page story warning that "Vampire Tendencies Found in Bladenboro's Monsters." That night people began to walk cautiously and look warily over their shoulders if they had to go out after dark.

There was no question that area residents were on edge, and numerous reports came in to the police and the North Carolina Wildlife Resources Commission demanding the capture or the killing of the Vampire Cat. Increasingly, people began to hear strange noises and to report shadowy figures moving near the swamp at night.

No one in the police force or the Wildlife Resources Commission denied that the witnesses were seeing something that they deemed out of the ordinary, but none of the official investigations yielded any hair, tracks, droppings, or any physical evidence of any kind. Some livestock was lost, but in each case when the authorities investigated the slaughter the deaths were quite obviously the result of attacks by feral dogs.

Newspaper reporters from around the United States descended on the small community, each journalist hoping to scoop the others with a photograph of the Great Vampire Cat. According to the people in the vicinity of Bladenboro, at least 1,000 hunters arrived to trek through the swamp. One of the men shot a large bobcat, and Mayor Fussell eagerly declared the dreaded monster slain and announced that the danger of attack by a vampire cat had come to an end.

Interestingly, today, over 50 years later, Bladenboro still celebrates "Beast Week," each year in recognition of the genuine terror that seized the community. A creature that was once feared as a "bloodthirsty shadow-dweller" now precipitates a "Boost the 'Boro Festival."

Hiram Hester, a former chairman of the festival, told Monica Holland (*The Fayette Observer*, March 16, 2008) that the beast was no longer an embarrassment to the townspeople. The people were now really excited about celebrating The Beast of Bladenboro.

The Beast of Bolivia

Still, though, there must really be *something* in North Carolina that delights in mauling large dogs. Paul Jefferson (of starnewsonline.com) reported on December 12, 2007, that a monster that local residents had called the Beast of Bolivia had returned to wreak havoc on their pets.

Shelby Sellers returned from work at the Brunswick County Government Center to find Rosie, his three-year-old pit bull, mauled, with claw marks and wounds on its hindquarters and paws. The veterinarian assured Sellers that Rosie would survive, but she was more fortunate than his neighbors, who reported that their two puppies had been killed.

It appeared that the Beast of Bolivia who had terrorized the region in mid-September had returned. At that time, three dogs had been found mauled by an unknown predator in the area of Midway, Brown, and Gilbert Roads.

Area residents had been completely unsatisfied with the efforts of the county's Animal Services department to identify the marauder. Some men came out to investigate the Beast's track, scoop up some droppings and other specimens, but there was no announcement of the analysis of these clues.

Those who had lost their dogs to the mysterious creature agreed with local animal experts who had pronounced the mauling of the dogs to be the work of a cougar or an unusually large bobcat. Others speculated that a lion or a tiger had escaped from the Faircloth Zoo, and the managers just didn't want to own up to their carelessness. The accusations against the zoo were silenced when authorities informed the citizenry that that particular zoo had been closed for 15 months and that all their animals had been shipped to other zoos.

In the meantime, attacks continued. While no one ever saw the Beast of Bolivia, some hunters theorized that the monster must have been a bear, judging from the size of the tracks.

The Beast Mangles a SUV

On April 2, 2009, it appeared that the Beast was still roaming around North Carolina, but it must have become enraged when people began keeping their dogs inside. The Gilliam family of Lincoln County came out of their home on Sunday morning to discover that some clawed creature had ripped their 2004 Saturn Vue SUV to pieces.

To their astonishment, the vehicle that stood in their driveway was scarred with scratches, bite marks, and gaping holes. The Beast had ripped through fiberglass and caused thousands of dollars in damage. The monster had even destroyed the brakes of the SUV.

The most frightening thing of all to Holly Gilliam was that all that destruction had taken place while the family slept. None of them had heard a thing while an unknown, unidentifiable beast had demolished their car.

Although experts were called and pictures of the damages were taken, no one claimed to have seen anything quite like the scratches and bite marks on the SUV. One investigator suggested that a very large bobcat had taken out some kind of peeve on the automobile.

Whatever it was, it had left muddy cat-like paw prints on the hood.

Eight-year-old R. J. Gilliam said that he could not imagine that anything could trash their SUV with only its claws and teeth. And if it could do that to a machine of metal, what could it do to him? He promised Mario Roldan, News Channel 36, WCNC that he would stay alert and on the lookout.

Two Large Black Cats Attack Father and Son in New York

In March 2009, Dorian Tunell and his eight-year-old son, Evan, were enjoying a pleasant bicycle ride in the woods near Tallman Mountain State Park in Rockland County, New York, when they sighted two very large black cats.

Tunell told his son to run to the road where the rock line was. Later, Evan said that he was so frightened of the two beasts that it was as if he were paralyzed.

Fortunately for the Tunells, the large black cats did not chase after them. Dorian Tunell said that the animals had bodies four or five feet long and had tails about three feet in length. Both of the cats stood about three feet tall.

Dorian Tunnel tells a frightening story of two huge black cats that chased after him and his son (*art by Bill Oliver*).

In Tunell's opinion, the cats looked like jaguars, but with shiny black hair instead of spots. Later, father and son directed park rangers to the spot where they had seen the big cats. The rangers located what appeared to be large paw prints and the remains of a deer. The fact that the black panthers had just fed may have saved Dorian and Evan Tunell from being their dinner.

According to the park rangers, not long before the Tunell sighting, a woman had called to report seeing two big black cats running along the Palisades Parkway.

Phantom Felids

In the November 28, 2009 posting of his Cryptomundo website (www.cryptomundo .com), Loren Coleman listed a number of "Phantom Felids" that had been sighted in Belgium, Australia, the United Kingdom, Canada, and the United States. In each instance, the witnesses claimed to have been startled and frightened by seeing the image of a large cat, a creature that had no geographical right to be where it was.

Coleman makes an interesting point that the Eastern Cougar in North America has become a semi-mystical creature, such as Bigfoot is in other sections of the United States and Canada. Although the cougar once thrived in great numbers in

Phantom Black Cats have been sighted in Belgium, Australia, the United Kingdom, Canada, and the United States (*art by Ricardo Pustanio*).

Ontario, the last living member of that feline tribe was sighted in 1938. About the same time, the cougar was declared extinct in that part of Canada.

The problem is that no one got around to informing the cougars that they had become extinct in Ontario. Over the past decade, Coleman reports, a number of reported and confirmed sightings have forced many wildlife experts to ponder if they should reconsider and pronounce the cougar "endangered," rather than extinct.

If one is determined to collected samples of DNA through hair and scat, solid evidence can be found to support the 500 eye-witness accounts since 2002 that have been made by farmers who claim that cougars have been munching on their livestock or of hunters who swear that the big critter that they spotted in the forests was no deer or large dog.

Black Panthers Invade Europe

In 2009, a black panther was reported on August 24 by hikers in the woods in the Meurthe-et-Moselle region of northeast France. Experts from the French Hunting and Wild Fauna Office found tracks that had been left by a very large cat, quite likely a panther.

Within a short period of time, more than a dozen sightings occurred of the black panther roaming throughout France. While some reports brought about jokes of too much wine or too lively an imagination, authorities found a sighting of the panther by a natural sciences teacher to be very credible.

By September, the mysterious, mercurial black panther had made its way to Belgium. On October 27, citizens of Luxemborg sighted the animal walking quite brazenly down the streets of a small community.

Luxemborg authorities took the reports seriously, sending out patrols with dog handlers and a police helicopter with a thermal camera. However, even such seriousness of purpose produced no physical animal to bring home in a cage.

With the exception of zoos, circuses, and the possibility of someone owning a leopard or tiger as a pet, there have been no big cats seeking prey in the forests of Europe since the cave lion (*Panthera leo spelaea*) became extinct about 2,000 years ago. Cave paintings have been found of this formidable creature, which, according to skeletal remains, appears to have been the largest lion that ever lived, reaching lengths of nearly twelve feet. This subspecies of lion lived as far north as Denmark, though probably existed more comfortably in southeastern Europe.

The United Kingdom's Beast of the Bay

Accounts of big cats, black panthers, and other feline monsters are seemingly reported more frequently in the United Kingdom than anywhere else on Earth. This fact seems all the more ironic since there have been no large cats in Ireland, Britain, Scotland, and Wales for over 10,000 years.

In the March 28, 2008 issue of the *Whitby Gazette*, Dave Holland and Liz Robb told the staff of the newspaper that they had watched the mysterious Beast of the Bay for 30 minutes while they were on holiday in the Whitby area. It was while they were walking to Danby Castle Farm when they saw the black beast about 200 meters away.

Holland said that he looked at the creature through his binoculars and determined that the animal was neither a large dog nor a black sheep. He described the beast as "black, with yellow eyes" and said that it walked with the gait of a panther. It appeared to have something in its mouth and seemed intent on settling down and enjoying its lunch. Holland and Robb got as close as they dared and watched the thing until it seemed annoyed by their surveillance and got up and walked off.

The staff of the newspaper stated that there had been numerous reports of the beast in recent weeks and that one man had even claimed to have seen the black panther walking with a young cub.

The Beast of Bretton

The Beast of the Bay is a newcomer on the scene of Black Cats in England compared to the Beast of Bretton, which has been sighted by hundreds of people over the years.

In June 2006, Jennifer Pratt was cycling along a footpath at Orton Mere heading toward Peterborough when she saw a black panther about 50 yards ahead of her. As she picked up speed and peddled past the creature, it looked up at her with large and yellow eyes.

Michelle Esposito contacted *The Evening Telegraph* in Peterborough after she spotted a large animal that she described as a large cat, like a puma, sprinting across the road.

Mark Williams, from Bretton, who has been tracking the Beast, said he can understand why people might think that witnesses who claim to see Black Panthers in England or Scotland are overly imaginative, but he stated that there were just too many sightings, many by police officers, to scoff them all away as mistaken identity of some other creature, such as a large domestic cat.

Chris Crowther, a sheep farmer who has 12,000 acres of land in the rugged area above Greenfield, is among those who keep a wary watch out for the Beast. In February, 2008, he found the first carcass near the Dovestone Reservoir. The lamb's coat had been torn off and all its bones picked clean. In June, he found another carcass, stripped of all flesh as before. It was then that he and other sheepherders began discussing the sightings that they had had of a "large black creature" near their flocks.

Crowther told Ken Bennett of the *Oldham Advertiser* that none of the farmers wished to cause people to become frightened, but it was his conclusion that "something really mysterious is happening here."

The farmers had agreed that no fox was to blame for their loss of sheep. It was more likely a predator the size of a puma that could do such damage. A member of the British Big Cat society had told them the number of such panther-like attacks on animals had been increasing.

On Christmas Day 2007, Howard Moody was cycling to work in the evening and was nearly knocked over by a large cat, three feet high and five or six feet long. Later, he told Stephen Briggs of *Peterborough Today* that he was certain that the creature was a puma. Moody said that he had got a really good look at the Beast. It all happened so fast, Moody commented, that he didn't have time to be frightened.

Briggs reported in the article that there had been several sightings of the Beast of Bretton in 2007 and in the years prior. In March 2005, Andrew Leatherland had encountered a huge black cat-like creature while walking in Castor Highlands.

Big Cat Hunters Claim the Creatures Are Indigenous to the British Isles

Peter Ross published an interview with Di Francis, one of the most persistent of all the big cat hunters in *NEWS.Scotsman.com* on December 2, 2009. Francis, a Londoner now living in Banffshire, is said to have pioneered big cat investigations in the late 1970s. During the winter of 1982, she camped on Dartmoor in the snow until she managed to take the first daytime photograph of a British big cat, a large black animal larger than a Doberman. She claims to have made six sightings since that time, some in Scotland.

Although many who have studied the subject grant that there may be black panthers and other large mammals mucking about in England, most of them believe that the beasts are the descendants of animals released by their owners following the introduction of the Dangerous Animals Act of 1976. Di Francis rejects this hypothesis and maintains that the large cat-like creatures are indigenous to the British Isles.

Weretigers and Other Large Cat-Men

Since this is a book about all kinds of monsters, we should not leave the subject of mysteriously appearing and disappearing large cats without mentioning the possibility of creatures from other dimensions popping into our own or the theory that some of these black panthers may be shape-shifters, skilled shamans or initiates of some secret magical society.

The Khonds are an aboriginal tribe of India who inhabit the tributary states of Orissa and Andhia Pradesh. Essentially, they are hunter and gatherers, but those who are land-owners and attempt some aspects of agriculture are known a Raj Khonds. The ancient traditions of the Khonds include a kind of voluntary shape-shifting which utilizes as its imagery a tiger deity.

Some years ago, an Englishman, whom we shall name Perkins, claimed that he had actually witnessed a Khond transforming himself into a weretiger and swore that his account was true. According to the Englishman, he had spent a good deal of time in India, especially among the Khonds and had frequently heard stories about the ability of certain individuals to transform themselves into tigers. When he persisted with a number of questions regarding such beliefs, he was informed that there was a place he could go to actually witness such metamorphoses.

Once Perkins had secreted himself at the designated spot in the jungle were such magic was alleged to transpire, he soon began to wonder if he had been played for a fool and was left to spend the night with snakes, wild boars, big cats, scorpions, and a host of other poisonous vermin. But as things turned out, he didn't have long to wait before the transformed tiger man appeared.

The individual was hardly what the Englishman had expected. Not at all fierce in appearance, the man was very young and almost feminine in his mannerisms. Once he reached the edge of the sacred circle, he knelt down and touched the ground three times in succession with his forehead, looking up all the while at a giant kulpa tree opposite him, chanting as he did so in some weird dialect that was unintelligible to the spying Englishman.

Suddenly the jungle seemed to become unnaturally quiet. For some reason he could not understand, Perkins was filled with a penetrating dread of the unknown. For a moment he wanted to turn and run, but he seemed unable to move. The silence was broken by an eerie half-human, half-animal cry, and there followed the sound of something very large crashing through the jungle.

Whatever the thing truly was, the Englishman saw it manifest before the young supplicant as vertical column of pure, crimson light about seven feet in height. The slim young man knelt before it and scratched a symbol of some kind in the circle and set within it a string of beads. As he began once again to chant, the column of crimson light shot forth a lightning-like bolt of energy to the beads, which instantly began to glow a luminous red. The boy put the beads around his neck, clapped his hands together, and began to chant in a voice that deepened and became more and more animalistic in tone. There was a shattering roar from the young supplicant's throat and the crimson column of light vanished.

And then Perkins beheld the young man staring directly at him from the circle, not with the eyes of a human, but with the yellow, glittering, malevolent eyes of a tiger thirsting for human blood.

Werewolves are familiar to moviegoers, but there is also such a thing as a weretiger (*iStock*).

The Englishman ran for his life toward a tree about fifty yards away. He could hear the tigerman growling behind him. When he reached the tree, the nearest branch was eight feet above him. Resigning himself to his fate, he slumped against the tree trunk as black, gleaming claws came toward him. Then, to his amazement and relief, the tigerman gave a low growl of terror and bounded away in the jungle.

Not bothering to speculate why the tigerman had spared him, Perkins ran as quickly as he could back to the village.

The next morning he learned that an entire family had been found in their home, mutilated, torn, and partially eaten. The horrible manner in which they had died indicated that a tiger had attacked them. Significantly, the Englishman learned through village gossip that they had been blood enemies of the young man that he had seen transform himself into a weretiger.

When Perkins asked a village elder why he thought the weretiger had spared him, the old man asked him for an exact description of where he stood when the beastman attacked. Listening carefully, the elder explained that Perkins had unknowingly sought refuge at a holy tree that bore an inscription of the name of the god Vishnu's incarnation. Merely touching the tree would protect anyone from attack by animals.

Perkins concluded his account by stating that he inspected the tree later that day and found upon it an inscription in Sanskrit. He never returned to that village again, but he swore that his witnessing of the weretiger transformation was true.

The Rites of Taigherim Summon Shape-Shifting Cat Demons

The rites of Taigherim consist of a magical sacrifice of cats that originated in old Scotland as a ritual to appease the subterranean gods. Beginning with the Christian era in Scotland, the rite was forbidden, but it still was performed in secret by sorcerers to invoke a special shape-shifting demon that would manifest as a very large black cat.

The rites themselves involved the systematic roasting of live black cats on a spit slowly turning over a fire. As each cat was dedicated to the demons of darkness, its terrible howls of pain were believed to summon a particular monster of demonic power.

After the cruel sacrificial rites had been conducted, small demons would begin to materialize in the form of black cats and match their cries with the yowls of the unfortunate true cats that were being roasted alive. As the sacrifices continued, celebrated by the screeching of the cat-demons, the sorcerer would at last behold the materialization of a frightful catlike creature of great size, much larger than a black leopard of the jungle. The appearance of the great demon signaled demonic acceptance of the sorcerer's sacrifices, and he was now permitted to make his demands of the huge black cat, whether it be the gift of prophecy, a bag of gold, or the ability to shapeshift into a wolf or black cat.

Attacked by a Werecat in the Shawnee Forest

On April 10, 1970, Mike Busby of Cairo, Illinois, was traveling on Route 3 to Olive Branch to pick up his wife.

About a mile south of Olive Branch on the dark, deserted road that parallels the edge of the Shawnee National Forest, Busby experienced car trouble. Grumbling his frustration, Busby got out of his car and popped open the hood.

He had not even had time to glance at the motor when he was distracted by a noise to his left. An incredible form, over six feet tall, moved in on Mike and hit him in the face.

Busby and his monstrous attacker fell to the highway. Dull claws ripped at his clothing, and Busby sought desperately to hold the thing's mouth open and at arm's length so its teeth could not tear his throat.

Busby was unable to clearly identify what it was that had seized him but he said later that he could feel something fuzzy around its mouth and that the thing's body hair was as short and wiry as steel wool.

"The thing kept letting out these deep, soft growls," Busby remarked. "Those sounds were unlike anything that I had ever heard."

After what must have seemed like an eternity locked in a death struggle, a diesel truck approached with bright headlights and the roar of a powerful motor—a combination of factors that frightened Busby's attacker back into the forest.

"It was a sleek, shiny black color," Busby said, "and it ran away with heavy, thudding feet."

John Hartsworth, the truck driver, reported that the thing that he had seen in his headlamps looked like some kind of "giant cat" until it had jumped off Busby and run into the forest on its hind legs.

A Phantom Black Cat

Lately Robin Swope, the Paranormal Pastor, has been doing *per diem* hospice work for a local hospital. He was delivering medication to a patient at the end of one

February in the middle of suburban Erie, Pennsylvania. There was quite a bit of snow on the ground from recent storms and the snow banks on the sides of the road were about two to three feet high.

Pastor Swope was traveling up a small hill …

Busby and his monstrous attacker fell to the highway. Dull claws ripped at his clothing, and Busby sought desperately to hold the thing's mouth open....

"… when I saw a dark shape slowly move across the street in front of me, two blocks ahead. It was about six or seven feet long and lurched like a quadruped with shoulders and hindquarters rocking. It passed in front of a few snow banks as it made its way across the street and eventually disappeared behind a house.

I arrived at the spot seconds later, and nothing was there. The creature was pure black, like a shadow being. I have passed by the same location at least six times since then at around the same time and am sure it was not an optical illusion. In fact, when I saw it I knew it was something not right. The head was not distinct, but the tail was long. It had an appearance of a phantom Black Cat.

Erie's Native American populace, the Eriez Indians, were called the 'cat' people by the Seneca and French. They dressed in panther fur, and there were accounts of some of the pelts being black. They were later eradicated/absorbed by the Seneca tribe, of which I have ancestry.

Was the phantom cat a residual haunting, a spirit from the ancient Eriez or a literal black cat to cross my path?"

BIGFOOT—
NORTH AMERICA'S KING KONG

In the spring of 1967, Carla, one of the English Department's student assistants, pulled a very reluctant young man into my office and insisted that he tell me what he had seen that weekend.

She introduced me to Bob, her boyfriend, but I acknowledged that we were already acquainted with one another. Although my principal teaching assignments were classes in creative writing and journalism, in 1963 I had also been an instructor in the Freshman English Core Program—where everyone, from future medical doctors to physics teachers, studied the classics of world literature. Bob had been in one of my classes, and even though he was a very polite and pleasant young man, he never made it a secret that he was a science major, concentrating on biology.

Although Dostoyevsky and Goethe may not have held an enormous amount of interest for him, when called upon in class, Bob's answers were concise and demonstrated that he had been paying attention. And now, four years later, in his senior year, his excited girlfriend was dragging him into my office and pressuring him to relate the details of an experience that he obviously he felt very awkward discussing. Finally, after a bit of coaxing from Carla and my assurance that I was no longer grading his work, he told a remarkable story—that weekend he had encountered a creature that was nowhere to be found in his biology texts.

He had been driving on Minnesota Highway 52 on his way to Decorah, Iowa. It was about ten o'clock in the evening, and he was a short distance from Rochester when his headlights picked up the form of someone crouching at the side of the highway. Bob's first thought was that someone might be injured or ill, and he pulled his car onto the shoulder of the highway only a few yards from the person to see if he might be of assistance. When the headlights caught the "someone" in full illumination, Bob saw that he had encountered something beyond his knowledge.

"I could see that its features were apelike," Bob told us. "There was no snout on its face. Its features were definitely humanoid, and its shoulders were heavy. The thing ran up the steep embankment to the shelter of the woods as easily as if it was running up a flight of steps."

Bob walked a few feet to the spot where he had seen the creature crouching and saw that the thing had been kneeling over a recently killed rabbit. Bob picked up the rabbit, and the thing standing on the embankment raised itself up to its full height and barked what sounded like a harsh cough of anger and protest. "It obviously thought that I was going to steal its dinner," Bob said, "and I wasn't about to argue with it. I dropped the rabbit and ran back to my car."

On his way to Decorah, Bob had time to ask himself a lot of questions in an attempt to explain away his impossible encounter. He decided that the creature could not have been a bear or a wolf—predators that would have been rare in southern Minnesota. "That thing had been crouching in a humanlike position," Bob said. "That was why I thought that I had seen a human being in trouble. When my car approached, it turned to look over its shoulder. The creature's head had definitely turned on a neck." Bob explained why such an action was strangely significant. As a biologist and an outdoorsman, he knew that neither a bear nor a wolf can look over its shoulder—they have to turn their entire bodies to see what is behind them.

"The thing that really capped it for me," Bob said, "was the fact that while it was running away from me, I saw well-developed buttocks. Buttocks are a distinctly human characteristic. No bears, wolves, or apes have buttocks. What I saw could only be described as a naked, hairy wildman!"

Bob was an intelligent young man. As his former English teacher, I could say without pronouncing any taint of disapprobation that he was not a highly imaginative student. Although always attentive, Bob's lack of participation in class discussions made it quite clear that he was a rationalist, a scientist, who was only intellectually respectful of the imaginative works of great literature—and who would not indulge in wild stories to entertain his buddies or his girlfriend.

The Man-Beast that Has Always Lurked in the Shadows

What Bob saw that night I believe to have been the same type of creature, the same kind of hulking man-beast that has always lurked in the shadows and seems always to have been with us. Over 25,000 years ago, the Franco-Cambrian artists may have been expressing their awareness of such creatures in the portraits of two-legged entities with the heads of animals that they painted on the walls of their caves.

Perhaps the earliest written record of a man-beast appears on a Babylonian fragment circa 2000 B.C.E. which tells the story of King Gilgamesh and his wolf-like friend, Enkidu. The Epic of Gilgamesh remains to date the oldest known literary work in the world.

Pieced together from 30,000 fragments discovered in the library at Ninevah in 1853, the story tells of Gilgamesh, the legendary Sumerian king of Uruk, and his quest for immortality. Deciding at first that he will be guaranteed a kind of physical immortality by fathering as many children as possible, Gilgamesh becomes such a sexual

Bigfoot greets visitors to the Cryptozoological Museum in Portland, Maine (*photo by International Cryptozoology Museum/Loren Coleman/Jessica Meuse*).

predator from whose advances no woman in his kingdom was safe. The goddess Aruru, troubled by the situation, forms the beastman Enkidu from clay and her spittle in order to create an opponent powerful enough to challenge Gilgamesh.

Gilgamesh soon learns of this powerful, hairy wild man, and he begins to have uncomfortable dreams of wrestling with a strong opponent whom he could not defeat. When Enkidu eventually arrives in the city, the two giants engage in fierce hand-to-hand combat. The king manages to throw the beast man, but instead of killing him, the two become fast friends, combining their strength to battle formidable giants. It is the jealous goddess Ishtar who causes the fatal illness that leads to Enkidu's death.

The hero finally abandons his search for immortality when the goddess Siduri Sabitu, dispenser of the Wine of Immortality to the gods, confides in him that his quest will forever be in vain—the cruel gods have decreed that all mortals shall die. Although the life of each human must end, the memory of the man-beast with whom our species struggles has never been extinguished.

There are many possible interpretations of the epic of Gilgamesh. Perhaps the saga lives in our collective consciousness as the memory of ancient struggles with Neanderthals and with other hominid species not yet discovered, species that were seemingly part human and part beast?

In 840 C.E., Agobard, the Archbishop of Lyons, declared the "giant people of the forest and mountains," as demons. He recorded that the wild men were stoned to death after being displayed in chains for several days. In his *Chronicles*, Abbot Ralph of Coggeshall Abbey, Essex, England, wrote of the discovery of the corpse of a "strange monster" whose charred body had been found after a lightning storm on the night of St. John the Baptist in June 1205. He stated that a terrible stench came from the beast with "monstrous limbs."

Villagers of the Caucasus Mountains have legends of a "wild man" that goes back for centuries. The Tibetans living on the slopes of Mt. Everest and the Native American tribes inhabiting the northwestern United States have their own stories of a giant man-beast. The Gilyaks, a remote tribe of Siberian native people, claim that there are creatures that are half-man, half-beasts that inhabit the frozen forests of Siberia and who have human feelings and travel in family units.

Do the appearances of the man-like beasts in our wilderness provoke our awareness that there are creatures essentially human in appearance that have survived for thousands of years and remain as our hidden cousins or even our ancestors?

Native Americans Have Known of Bigfoot for Centuries

Reports of Bigfoot-type creatures in California go back to at least the 1840s when miners reported encountering giant two-legged beastlike monsters during the gold rush days. Sightings of the Oh-Mah, as the native tribes called them, continued sporadically until August 1958, when a construction crew was building a road through the rugged wilderness near Bluff Creek, Humboldt County, and discovered giant humanlike footprints in the ground around their equipment. For several mornings running, the men discovered that something had been disturbing their small equipment during the night. In one instance, an 800-pound tire and wheel from an earth-moving machine had been picked up and carried several yards across the compound. In another, a 300-pound drum of oil had been stolen from the camp, carried up a rocky mountain slope, and tossed into a deep canyon. And in each instance, only massive sixteen-inch footprints with a 50- to 60-inch stride offered any clue to the vandal's identity.

When media accounts of the huge footprints were released, people from the area began to step forward to exhibit their own plaster casts of massive, mysterious footprints and to relate their own frightening encounters with hairy giants—stories that they had repressed for decades for fear of being ridiculed.

Some anthropologists, who take such accounts seriously, believe that Bigfoot may be a two-footed mammal that constitutes a kind of missing link between humankind and the great apes, for its appearance is more primitive than that of Neanderthal. The descriptions given by witnesses are amazingly similar. Height: six to nine feet. Weight: 400 to 1,000 pounds. Eyes: black. Dark fur or body hair from one to four inches in length is said to cover the creature's entire body with the exception of the palms of its hands, the soles of its feet, and its upper facial area, nose, and eyelids.

Based on the eye-witness descriptions of hundreds of reliable individuals who have encountered these monsters of the woods, it would seem that the creatures are more humanlike than apelike or bearlike. For one thing, these giants are repeatedly said by witnesses to have breasts and buttocks. Neither apes nor bears have buttocks— nor do they leave flatfooted humanlike footprints.

Common Bigfoot Sighting Areas

In North America, the greatest number of sightings of Bigfoot have come from the Fraser River Valley, the Strait of Georgia, and Vancouver Island, British Columbia; the "Ape Canyon" region near Mt. St. Helens in southwestern Washington; the Three Sisters Wilderness west of Bend, Oregon; and the area around the Hoopa Valley Indian Reservation, especially the Bluff Creek watershed, northeast of Eureka, California. Various Native American tribes have called the man-beast by such names as Bigfoot, Sasquatch, Wauk-Wauk, Oh-Mah, or Saskehavis. In recent years, extremely convincing sightings of Bigfoot-type creatures have also been made in areas of New York, New Jersey, Minnesota, Iowa, Indiana, South Carolina, Georgia, Tennessee, and Florida. Not to be out-done, Canadians began telling of their own startling encounters with Sasquatch, a tribal name for Bigfoot, that had been circulating in the accounts of trappers, lumberjacks, and settlers in the Northwest Territories since the 1850s.

An Encounter with the Bogwish?

Bill Oliver, who has contributed so much fine art to this book, is also an investigator of the UFO phenomenon in his native British Columbia, Canada. Back in the late 1990s, Oliver was checking out some sightings near Kitimaat Village, a native community of about 600 people, and he asked if there had been any Sasquatch reports in the area. One of the villagers said that he knew of a story of a man who had seen four during a hunting trip years before.

The man passed on the telephone number of someone who knew the story better, so Oliver called and spoke to an elderly man, Ken, who first asked Oliver why he wanted to know. Ken said that it was his grandfather who had done the shooting, and he had become irritated how the story had changed over the years since it happened. In particular, it disturbed him that people said his grandfather shot a Boqwish and that maybe this was an opportunity to tell it like it happened.

According to Bill Oliver's report:

In the spring of 1918, William Hall was out hunting for the family's needs with his good friend. In this case he was bear hunting eight miles west of Kemano in a small area known as Miskook/Miskuk (in native language), a small inlet on the Kemano

A display case at the Cryptozoological Museum in Portland, Maine (*photo by International Cryptozoology Museum/Loren Coleman/Jessica Meuse*).

River. He and his friend were joined by an elder whose job was to wait in the canoe and watch the supplies.

As William and his friend made their way through the terrain they came upon a split in the valley. It was here where they went separate ways. As the custom went, a wooden stake was pounded into the ground. Upon return, the first hunter would remove it and lay it on the path to let the other know he had safely arrived and to meet him down at the river's edge.

William, being the first to return, did so and started on his way back to the waiting elder. It was here on a small trail he came upon a group of four Sasquatch, or as known to the Kitimaat Indians, the Boqwish.

In absolute terror he started to run, but apparently blacked out. When he came to, he found himself on a large rock. The four Boqwish were below, reaching out and attempting to grab the startled hunter. In his own native tongue he spoke to them and said that he was not there to harm them but only hunting for food for his family. It was at this time that the aggressors seemed to back off, as if they understood. He made his way off the rock and began back to the river's edge where his partner had been waiting in the canoe. Along the way the creatures continued to follow him to the river and now the waiting elder also said, in his language, that they were not out to harm them. Again, seeming to understand, they left.

Upon getting into the canoe William Hall slipped into a coma that lasted four days. It was on the fifth day he awoke. It is well reported that accompanying the Bigfoot is a foul odor that fills the air whenever the creature is near. William had the same rancid odor permeating from his body until the day of his death, eight years later. So bad was the smell that he built a hut for himself to sleep in, so as not to offend his family. Since the day he came out of the coma, Ken said, "My grandfather could foresee the future." He displayed other traits of a psychic nature as well.

One night around the fire, William gathered the elders and chief to experience his newly acquired supernatural powers. He picked a salmonberry branch that was bare of any leaf or fruit, as it was now the fall, and walked past the chief who was seated. He displayed the branch and proceeded to walk around the circle of hot coals and fire. After the first time around he again stopped in front of the chief, this time displaying a freshly grown leaf, a second time around he displayed a large bud that upon the third encompass of the fire yielded a full rose. On the final two times around the elders he displayed an immature salmonberry and finally a large ripe berry that he placed in the chief's mouth.

Perhaps the most stunning display of William's powers came when he warned his people of a snake-like creature with bugs on it that would destroy their land. Twenty or so years later the ALCAN Project began. The "snake-like creature" was believed to have been the winding black highway put in and the "bugs" the many trucks that ride the road. His grandson also said William Hall picked the day of his death.

I find this story amazing in that it came from an offshoot of a hotline call regarding another matter. Had I not asked of any other reports this story would have remained in the village to be passed on down over the years. One wonders how many other villages and small towns have their share of amazing stories. I have been told also that the Sasquatch or Boqwish legend continues on in this part of British Columbia. In Ursala Channel, just a few miles away, the spring air is punctuated by the sound of yelping Sasquatch.

The Famous Patterson-Gimlin Bigfoot Photograph

On October 20, 1967, near Bluff Creek, north of Eureka, California, an event occurred over which Bigfoot hunters and skeptics have been arguing ever since. Roger Patterson and Bob Gimlin managed to film several feet of what appeared to be a female Bigfoot, thereby capturing one of the most famous and controversial strip of images in the world. The forest giant had pendulous breasts, and it looked back at the cameraman as it walked steadily toward a growth of trees. The creature appeared to be neither frightened nor aggressive, but it is obvious that it wished to avoid contact.

Some who viewed the film when Patterson and Gimlin showed it to expert woodsmen and scientists said that the creature in the filmstrip was over seven feet tall and estimated its weight at around 400 pounds. An immediate point of contention among some skeptics was how the Bigfoot walked away from the camera with a stride that appeared human. It left footprints seventeen inches long, and it had a stride of forty-one inches.

Patterson and Gimlin felt that they had at last provided the scientific community and the world at large with proof of Bigfoot's existence. However, other Bigfoot hunters and vast numbers of skeptics declared that the two men had merely tried to pull off a clever hoax. Many concluded that the alleged Bigfoot was nothing more than a partner of Patterson's and Gimlin's wearing a well-crafted "apeman suit."

Interestingly, Dr. John R. Napier, director of the Primate Biology Program of the Smithsonian Institution, was a bit more receptive to this filmed evidence for Bigfoot. After his examination of the Patterson-Gimlin film, Dr. Napier concluded that while he saw no evidence that pointed conclusively to a hoax, he did express some reservations about the exaggerated, fluid motion of the creature as it walked away from the two men. It was also Dr. Napier's opinion that the Bigfoot was male, in spite of the pendulous breasts, because of the crest on its head, a signature of male primates.

Dr. Osman Hill, director of Yerkes Region Primate Research Center at Emory University, stated that if the being in the film was a hoax, the costume had been incredibly well done.

Dr. Osman Hill, director of Yerkes Region Primate Research Center at Emory University, stated that if the being in the film was a hoax, the costume had been incredibly well done. Dr. Hill also stated his assessment that the Bigfoot in the filmstrip was hominid (humanlike) rather than pongoid (apelike).

Some skeptics swore that the gorilla outfit had come from the costume department for the motion picture *Planet of the Apes* (1968). However, technicians at the Documentary Film Department at Universal Pictures, Hollywood, agreed with the scientists' assessment and said that it would take them a couple of million dollars to duplicate the monster and its movements on the Patterson and Gimlin filmstrip. First, they stated, they would have to create a set of artificial muscles, train an actor to walk like the thing on the film, then place him in a gorilla skin.

The controversy over the film taken at Bluff Creek continued for thirty years. Then on October 19, 1997, the day before the thirtieth anniversary of the Patterson-Gimlin filming of Bigfoot and just prior to a release by the North American Science Institute announcing their analyses that the creature depicted on the film was genuine, stories appeared in the media once again claiming that John Chambers, the academy award-winning makeup genius behind such classic motion pictures as *The Planet of the Apes* had been responsible for creating the gorilla suit that had fooled Patterson and Gimlin and thousands of other Bigfoot believers. According to Howard Berger of Hollywood's KNB Effects Group, it was common knowledge within the film industry that Chambers had designed the costume for friends of Patterson who wanted to play a joke on the determined Bigfoot hunter. Mike McCracken Jr., an associate of Chambers, stated his opinion that he (Chambers) was responsible for designing the gorilla suit.

Interestingly, none of the individuals who had allegedly asked John Chambers to design a gorilla costume in order to hoax Patterson ever stepped forward and identified themselves. Chambers himself, who was living in seclusion in a Los Angeles nursing home when the story of the gorilla suit hoax broke, refused to confirm or deny the reports.

Roger Patterson died in 1972, never doubting that he had caught a real Bigfoot on film and swearing to all who would listen that the incident at Bluff Creek had been no hoax perpetrated by himself or Gimlin.

Chris Murphy, a Bigfoot researcher, told the *Sunday Telegraph* (October 19, 1997) that "very high computer enhancements of the film show conclusively that, whatever it was, it was not wearing a suit. The skin on the creature ripples as it walks."

Other Bigfoot experts have declared the Patterson-Gimlin film to be an authentic documentary of a genuine female hominoid. Two Russian scientists, Dmitri Bayanov and Igor Bourtsev minutely analyzed every movement of the female Bigfoot on the controversial film and concluded that it had passed all their tests and their criteria of "distinctiveness, consistency, and naturalness."

"Who," they ask rhetorically in their chapter in *The Sasquatch and Other Unknown Hominoids,* "other than God or natural selection is sufficiently conversant with anatomy and bio-mechanics to 'design' a body which is perfectly harmonious in terms of structure and function?"

In 2009, an outrageous rumor about a "Bigfoot Massacre" having taken place in which Patterson and Gimlin shot and killed the female Bigfoot and her family after following her back to her home in the forest began to make the rounds of the various Bigfoot hunting clubs and groups.

It has been only within the last few years that Bob Gimlin has begun appearing at Bigfoot conferences. At one such gathering in Texas in September 2009, Gimlin and respected cryptozoologist Loren Coleman shared a number of early morning breakfasts. Together, the two men spoke of their disappointment about what had happened with the Patterson-Gimlin film after the "human element" got involved. They agreed that human personalities had, unfortunately, "mucked things up," a sad fate that occurs to any field with strong egos and groundbreaking discoveries.

Loren Coleman, one of the world's most knowledgeable cryptozoologists, poses with a friend, the Cryptozoological Museum's eight-foot-tall, 400-pound Bigfoot, created by Wisconsin taxidermy artist Curtis Christensen (*photo by International Cryptozoology Museum/Joe Citro*).

They Interacted with Bigfoot for Nearly 20 Years

Don and Peggy Avery's Sasquatch experiences began as the result of an avid interest in the old gold rushes of the nineteenth century, particularly that of the Klondike, and continued sporadically for nearly 20 years. Don had read many books on the subject and had watched a number of television programs on the various techniques of prospecting. In 1989, Don and Peggy moved to eastern Washington where Don began his employment managing a small community. According to Don:

Somewhere along the line I became interested in dousing. I had carried a quartz crystal around with me for many years and I thought that I would attempt to invoke whatever ability I might have at map dousing for gold deposits. I purchased a Metsker's map of the region and triangulated on a sand bar some 55 miles to the northeast in the Snake River below the lower Granite Dam.

Several weeks later, Peggy and I drove to the area. We had never visited this locale before, and we wandered along the beach for quite some time, distressed by the ribbons of oil that we spotted in the sand. After about an hour of wandering around feeling like a fool, it dawned on me that I was staring at black sand and not oil tainted sand. I found a rich ledge a dozen yards inland and took some samples that I panned down. The effort revealed a flash of gold in the pan.

I was hooked. I subsequently made several trips to the area and wound up with a very nice gold button that I retorted from an amalgamation of mercury and hundreds of flakes of fine gold.

I subsequently read about the Liberty mining district in the Cle Elum area. It had been discovered by a group of Blewett miners heading over the pass in an effort to resupply in Cle Elum. This gold was crystalline wire, which is extremely rare. The nuggets found at the head of the creek that drains the area that I claimed held the largest nuggets ever found in Washington State. The heftiest of which was about 6 1/2 pounds. The miners lost the trail of this ancient deposit as the result of a basalt intrusion.

But logic dictated that a 6.5-pound nugget, shaped like a wing, would not tumble far from its source.

I hit upon a spot on a bench above the creek through dousing and soil sampling. I filed a mining claim in the summer of 1995 and fell in love with the area. It is like a slice of heaven; always peaceful, inviting, mysterious, and provides a strange sense of solitude. It is on a dead end, and very few people ever wander down the road. One man owns most of the mining claims on the creek, and he has dug up the head of the creek to its maximum extent in the last few years. This particular area is under the control of the Forest Service.

During the Veteran's Holiday three-day weekend in 1996, Peggy and I decided to stay a night in Ellensburg. It snowed that night, the first of the season. It was a wet snow about three to four inches. I parked down by the highway, loaded my pack onto my back and began the three-quarters of a mile walk into the claim.

Peggy decided to stay in the car and read a book. I made my way up the old mining road roughly half-way to my claim when I heard a guttural snarling sound coming from a short but steep embankment above the road and off to my right side. The sound was repeated every ten to twelve seconds and reminded me of the sound that a man might make just prior to vomiting.

The distance was about 70 to 75 feet. I could see something large and furry or hairy standing at the edge of the tree line. For the first time in many trips into isolated areas alone, I was armed. I stayed put, watching and listening for maybe 10 to 12 minutes.

I realized that it could have had me if it had wanted to. That was the key for me and always will be. Whatever it was, it was trying to intimidate me, not injure me.

I left the gun holstered and began to walk by it up the road toward my claim. I was very frightened, but I was not going to let it scare me off. It must have known me from prior trips into the area.

It was about 6'5" maybe 6'7". I'm 6'2" and I spent a long time trying to judge its height. I had never seen a bear or its sign in the area. This thing had no snout or conical ears. It was quite stout. I couldn't guess its weight, but it was substantial.

I worked the adit [entrance to an underground mine] of my prospect hole for about 20 minutes when I decided to return downhill to see if this creature was still around. I was getting hit with wet snow from the trees around me, and I knew my wife must be getting tired of waiting for me.

I had an old Kodak camera in my pack, but no film—and this is a big regret. As I approached the hillside, I could see it. The creature had moved about twenty-five yards along the bank closer to me and again began its guttural sounds. I watched this thing for at least twenty minutes that day. After returning to the car, I mentioned to Peggy that I thought I had seen a sick bear, only that it did not look like a bear or sound like a bear. I dismissed the experience from my mind. In late March of the following winter (1998), I stopped by and again walked the road. The snow had melted down to where the road was passable on foot.

I was amazed at what I saw. There were tracks in the snow made where no man could have any local logical reason to go. Some of these tracks were fairly old. But, they were all very large. Whatever it was, it appeared to follow a regular route, preferring to stay off the road. It also would come part way down one embankment and watch cars on the highway from behind a bush. I'm guessing that the night lights would attract it.

I began leaving celery and carrots, but I had no takers. I set up a camcorder to film the area around me while working the claim. No luck here either. I switched to apples, and I discovered that they love apples, especially the reds. I began to lose interest in the claim but I would leave apples in five selected places.

In July of 1999, while I was in the adit doing some clean up work, I heard the car door slam down below. Later, after arriving back home, I asked Peggy what had caused her to leave the car. She responded that she heard me call her by name.

I felt a chill, for I rarely call her by name. We discussed this issue at length. I still go numb whenever I think about it. In late March of 2000, I stopped by on my way to Tacoma. I had to get to my claim on snow shoes. The sun was out and the snow was very deep. I was several hundred yards below my claim near the basalt dike and a steep hill when I noticed very fresh tracks going from the stream across the road and up the steep hillside.

I could clearly see the toe imprints in the fresh snow, then the knee strike, and then another foot imprint. I was amazed that this thing could run in deep snow unaided. I tried to run up after it. I fell down and rolled into the ditch. I thought that I was going to drown in snow before I got back on my feet. It must have been only minutes in front of me.

Later that year in August, Peggy and I stopped by coming back from Leavenworth in the evening. It was about 7:00 P.M. We parked below the claim and exited the car. I had the camcorder in hand.

We could hear a holler or a high-pitched yell coming from down below us near the stream. It repeated roughly every ten seconds. We listened for quite some time, not knowing what to do.

> *I could clearly see the toe imprints in the fresh snow, then the knee strike, and then another foot imprint. I was amazed that this thing could run in deep snow unaided.*

I finally yelled a hello in its direction, and it fell silent. I climbed the hill to the adit. After a few minutes, I heard something stomp through the brush down below on the other side of the road. It came toward me, but it completely managed to escape me.

I did not even think to turn the camcorder on to record the sound. Over time, this thing has left me a sandstone block at one of my apple placement sites, and several handfuls of wood chips at another. The chunk of sandstone also gets moved around. I move it back, and it gets moved, again. We moved to Montana in January of 2002 to take a job managing a County. I really missed being able to visit the claim. I let it lapse—even though I got into the area and left apples once or twice a year. It was a twenty-hour round trip by car from where we lived near Kalispell, Montana, and we moved back to Washington in 2007.

I last made visual contact with the creature in October of 2008 when I attempted to sneak up on it while it was slapping a tree with a rock on the far side of the stream below my claim. In November of 2008 I visited my caved-in adit and again left apples for it. Downhill a few hundred yards where Peggy had parked the car, we began to hear a very strange noise. I've never heard anything like it. It also moved on the bank across and above the stream. It wasn't an elk, bear, deer, cat, rodent, or bird. We listened and watched for 15 to 20 minutes, and I frankly am not certain what it was. It was fast and curious, almost brazen. Over the nearly 20 years of our bizarre interaction, I have developed a few observations and opinions:

1. My wife thinks that it knows me and communicates because I feed it. I've left enough apples to claim it as a dependent.
2. They cannot walk quietly through the brush. It sounds more like an elephant.
3. It is territorial and works a regular route. The developments west of Cle Elum terrify me. Loss of habitat and more people wandering the woods does not bode well for them.
4. It picks me up at a considerable distance. Approaching the creature while concentrating on only positive thoughts is important. Leave your worries behind.
5. Pay attention, but don't think too much about your quarry.

Loren Coleman studies at the Cryptozoological Museum in Portland, Maine (*photo by International Cryptozoology Museum/Loren Coleman/Jessica Meuse*).

6. It is very quick and basically nocturnal. It knows when there is a camera mounted close by day or night.

7. I also think that it knew my car.

8. Sometimes I get the impression that I may be dealing with a phantom.

9. It has cognitive abilities that we only dream about. If it can call my wife, having not heard her called by name, then we are moved one step lower on the intelligence ladder.

Don Avery met a man in Walla Walla in the 1990s who did not believe in these creatures. He was from Houston and had recently arrived in the Northwest. "One day in the fall of 1993 he was parked on a dirt road up in the Blue Mountains when two of these creatures walked across the road in front of his pickup truck," Don said. "The Texan became an obsessed fanatic. He turned his home into a Sasquatch research center. He possessed some very interesting cast footprints, completely showing tendons. The prints were very large, larger than mine."

On another occasion, Don Avery received an email from a miner who lived about one and a half miles east of him. "He was totally intimidated by a large hairy thing that he saw on his claim," Don said. "This man was very frightened. I would be surprised if he ever went back."

Micah Hanks, author of *Magic, Mysticism, and the Molecule* (2010), remarked in a recent email to me that "Mankind's fascination with creatures that bridge the gap between humans and beasts has persisted for as long as we've been able to differentiate ourselves from what we label 'the animal kingdom.'"

"Still," Micah continued, "perhaps some of the most frightening creatures of this sort may not be natural at all, as rumors of experiments intended to create human-ape hybrids do exist outside the realm of fiction. The most famous (or infamous) reports of deliberate induced pregnancies with the intention of creating hybrids of this sort concerns the Soviet biologist Ilya Ivanovich Ivanov and his experiments with interspecific hybridization of animals beginning around 1926. Russian dictator Joseph Stalin reportedly told Ivanov that he wanted 'a new invincible human being, insensitive to pain, resistant and indifferent about the quality of food they eat.' The fact that such experiments have been hinted at, often conducted under the veil of secrecy, has led some to believe that reports of Bigfoot-like creatures may have a darker, more terrifying *scientific* background."

Two Ghost Hunters Meet Very Physical "Spooks"

More or less on a whim, I asked my good friends Dave and Sharon Oester, who started the International Ghost Hunters Society in 1996, if they had ever encountered any Bigfoot among the spirits, whose voices they record during their sessions with EVP (Electronic Voice Phenomena). I was quite surprised to learn that they had had three experiences with the Giant of the Forests. Two of the encounters we shall present herewith; the third, a bit later.

Dave and Sharon are the authors of 23 books, their most recent, *Ghosts of Gettysburg: Walking on Hallowed Ground* describes 50 of the most haunted sites on the famous Civil War battlefield. (The Oesters' website is www.ghostweb.com. Their email address is ghostweb@ghostweb.com.) Dave and Sharon travel full time in their RV coach as they investigate the most haunted places in America. I guess I shouldn't have been too astonished to learn that they had also encountered Bigfoot.

Shining Yellow Eyes in the Old Cascade Tunnel

The first experience, Dave said, happened at the Lost City of Wellington, Washington where they were going to hold a ghost conference investigation.

According to Dave:

Wellington was the site of a tragic train accident that occurred 100 years before on March 1, 1910, when an avalanche buried a passenger train and destroyed the railroad town. For unknown reasons the train foolishly moved out of the protective snow shelter and was buried under tons of heavy snow. A total of 96 people had their lives snuffed out from this killer avalanche.

A week before our scheduled ghost conference at Skykomish, Washington, we decided to check out the old Cascade Tunnel that is located just below Stevens Pass in the rugged Cascade Mountains. This is a high wilderness area and far removed from communities. We drove up to Stevens Pass and descended down the dirt road to the entrance of the old Cascade Tunnel. This 2.6-mile-long tunnel was abandoned in 1929 when a new tunnel was dug through the Cascade Mountains. We wanted to take some pictures for our website in preparation for the Ghost Conference.

It was a slow drive down as we had a Honda Accord that has a low ground clearance. We stopped by the edge of the tunnels and Sharon stayed in the car while I climbed down the bank to the entrance to the tunnel where I started snapping photos. A small stream ran out of the tunnel so I had to be careful to step on rocks to get inside the tunnel entrance, as I did not want to get my feet wet. I wanted to take some flash photos inside the tunnel so I walked until the light from the entrance was dim.

I had only gone about forty feet inside the tunnel when I noticed two glowing yellow eyes in the far end of the tunnel. I thought this must be an animal and continued snapping pictures when suddenly I noticed the glowing yellow eyes move back and forth as if the animal or creature was slowly moving toward me.

I realized that the eyes were glowing yellow and no natural animal eyes glowed like that. I then realized that the level of the glowing yellow eyes was over two-thirds the distance the top of the tunnel. This creature stood about nine feet tall relative to the height of the tunnel.

I immediately felt a strong desire to retreat to the safety of our car. I raced back to the entrance and up the hill to the car. I quickly got into the Honda and rolled up the windows. How silly of me to think glass would stop whatever was coming out of that tunnel.

As I sat in the car collecting my thoughts, I heard a loud heavy sound that sounded like something heavy hitting the ground at the front entrance to the tunnel. It sent chills up our spines and I realized that the rolled-up windows were no protection from this creature.

I had fears of the Honda not starting or of stalling. Too many horror films raced through my mind. I started the Honda and quickly retraced our route back to the main dirt road.

The next day we departed for home, stopped at Mt. Index, and chatted with a lady who reported someone had seen a Bigfoot a few weeks ago. I asked where, and her response was that it was near the Lost City of Wellington!

A week later, we held our Ghost Conference, and on Friday afternoon, many members had arrived and were standing around outside the Skykomish Hotel. We got into conversation about the activities for the weekend conference. When they heard

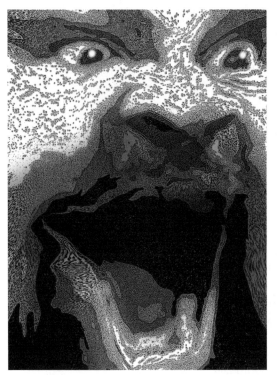

Do the appearances of the man-like beasts in our wilderness provoke our awareness that there are creatures—essentially human in appearance—that have survived for thousands of years and remain as our hidden cousins, or even our ancestors (*art by Ricardo Pustanio*)?

about the strange yellow eyes, six of the men wanted to see the place immediately.

We drove up to the old Cascade Tunnel site and parked near the same spot we had parked a week earlier. The six men climbed down the bank, waded across the small stream, and entered the mouth of the tunnel. Sharon stayed with the women who preferred not to hike down to the tunnel. I took along my night vision scope to see farther into the darkness of the tunnel.

We all walked into the tunnel about 40 feet and stopped. I looked through the night vision scope and again saw two yellow eyes staring back at me. I commented on seeing two yellow eyes, and everyone wanted to look through the night vision scope to see those eyes, so I passed the night vision scope to the first man who in turn looked through the scope and then passed it to the next man. Each of the men saw the same thing, yellow eyes that were moving slowly toward them. It did not take much for their courage to evaporate; suddenly the six brave men decided it was time to vacate the tunnel quickly.

We all ran back out of the tunnel and quickly climbed the bank and, jumping into our respective vehicles, drove madly for the open highway located about half a mile from the mouth of the tunnel. Yellow Eyes was real, and as far as we were concerned, the tunnel was his home and we would respect it.

The next day we conducted our investigation outside the tunnel and Yellow Eyes apparently respected our decision, as he never showed up to greet us. Today, the old Cascade Tunnel has collapsed and is now closed to the public.

Unseen Creatures Attacked with Rocks and Boulders

The Oesters' second experience with such a monster occurred appropriately at Bigfoot Canyon in Northern Utah and is told by Sharon:

Dave and I have always been interested in paranormal phenomenon, but this experience took place in 1990, long before we involved ourselves in ghost research. We had heard stories of Bigfoot, but we never dreamed our path would lead us into a remote canyon where we would experience Bigfoot firsthand. Although it has been eighteen years since this incident took place, it remains clear in our minds.

We had done some research into historic sites in Utah, where we were living at the time. We discovered that not far from where we were living in northern Utah there was a site where many stagecoaches had fallen into a steep canyon. It seemed according to records that the trail led dangerously close to a steep canyon, and if the driver was unaware of the location of the deep crevice in the ground, chances were good the coaches would end up at the bottom between the steep rock walls. Many coaches ended up at the bottom shattered, and many people perished. Rumor had it that gold coins and valuable items had never been recovered.

We decided to ask two of our friends to join us in a day of hiking to see what the canyon was all about. It was a blustery day with the wind howling, and remnants of past snow storms remained in nooks and crannies in the mountains.

Dave and I met our friends, Dave and Diane, at a café not far from our destination. The aroma of homemade cinnamon rolls and fresh brewed coffee filled the air. The sun was just rising over the mountains, and we looked forward to a day of hiking and exploring even though the weather was cold and stormy. The weather forecast promised sunny skies so we decided to proceed with our plans and headed farther into the mountains to find the mouth of the canyon.

We found the turn, parked our vehicles under old growth trees, grabbed bottled water, and started off on our adventure. We could hear water gurgling over the rocks in a stream nearby. The stream seemed to flow down the length of the canyon, but at that time most of the streambed was solid ice. The trees towered around us, and rocks formed solid walls that formed around the mouth of the canyon. It didn't look like much at first glance, in fact it didn't appear to be a canyon of any length or depth. Looks can be deceiving as we were soon to find out.

We walked side-by-side for a short time, but soon found we had to walk single file as the trail angled around rock outcroppings, rising and falling, narrow enough for only one person at a time. Mostly we walked in silence, listening to the sounds and stillness around us. There were birds here and there chirping in the treetops and a squirrel here and there but little else outside of the distant sound of the gurgling stream. There was no cold wind blowing; we had left that behind.

When the trail dipped down along the frozen stream and widened enough so we could rest and talk, we stopped and sat on boulders along the trail. It was cold and beautiful, and we felt as if we were a world away from civilization. We were four friends enjoying the beauty of nature, exploring an area of Utah history. It was exhilarating.

Though we had heard the sounds of birds chirping and water flowing as we walked along the trail, we realized that as we sat catching our breath, there wasn't a sound. The deeper into the canyon we'd hiked, the less the snow had melted under the cover of the trees. The canyon was heavily wooded; trees lined the top of the rock walls, which seemed to insulate the canyon from outside sounds.

We decided to go on, deeper into the canyon though we had been walking for quite some time. We were all curious as to how far the canyon went into the moun-

Dave and Sharon Oester (*photo courtesy Dave and Sharon Oester*).

tain and what we might see along the way. We had to walk slowly as the trail was steep and slippery in places where ice had formed. As we looked around and at each other we realized we all felt a bit uncomfortable though no one wanted openly to admit it.

When we finally did speak, we all agreed it was getting very eerie, and we all felt as though we were being watched even though we knew we were totally alone. We reasoned that maybe because all outside sound was blocked out and because we felt isolated from other people we felt the discomfort. No one really knew where we were if something were to happen.

Dave found a solid footprint in the partially melted snow, about eighteen inches long. There were signs of what could have been more prints, but little was left and only one print remained clear enough to identify. It was not the print of a bear, but something close to human with huge feet.

We slowed our pace to cross over some large rocks crossing the trail; Dave discovered a bone lying on the ground. He held it up and we all looked closely at it. It was fairly long and very unusual, unlike a human bone or that of any animals we had seen before. We felt very uncomfortable as though we were trespassing on private property and as we stood there, we started to look at our surroundings more closely to see if there were more bones or a carcass from a dead animal.

Dave turned and pointed down to the canyon floor below us, and there among the trees and snowy ground was what appeared to be a make-shift type of shelter. It was roughly put together with tree branches and leaves and if we hadn't looked closely, it would have blended in completely with the brush and terrain.

We immediately thought that someone had built a shelter because they had gotten caught in a snow storm. We looked closer and found no sign of life, no fire residue, or evidence of human presence. It was then we realized we might have found a Bigfoot lair in the middle of nowhere.

Dave had slipped the bone into his pocket as we had decided to take it with us to see if someone could identify it. As the decision was made, the first rocks started to fall. We thought that maybe an animal, a deer or elk was escaping from the canyon because it heard us talking.

That was a logical conclusion since we had heard no other sounds for quite some time. If it were a deer, climbing the canyon wall would have certainly knocked loose rocks out of place. We couldn't tell which direction the rocks were coming from but gave it little thought, as we were ready to head farther up the trail.

We started to turn to leave when the rocks started falling closer to us. They were also more numerous and larger than before. It seemed as though as we started to walk, the rocks started coming down harder and faster and they were getting bigger all the time. That couldn't have been a deer causing that to happen, and we hoped it wasn't the start of some type of rock slide!

We still could not tell which direction the rocks were coming from, only that it seemed they were coming down all around us now. It seemed they were not only warning us, but they were preventing us from leaving. We had to have hiked two miles up into the canyon and there was one way out. It was slow going at best along a narrow, slippery trail. We hoped that we didn't have to run from whatever was out there that remained unseen.

The rocks had turned into boulders coming down from above us and we didn't know what to do about the situation.

"Dave, the bone, they want us to leave the bone," I said. It was the only thing that could have created such a stir.

Dave took the bone out of his coat pocket and placed it back where we'd found it.

A family discovered this deer behind their house. Its foot lodged in a tree, the animal's head bore welt marks as if it had been bludgeoned, and its belly had been ripped open. How it died remains a mystery (*photo courtesy of the Pennsylvania Bigfoot Society*).

Whatever had made that footprint was now hurling boulders at us from an unseen place—and it meant business. Dave suggested that we all focus our thoughts on our intentions, "We meant no harm and will leave the bone where we found it."

Maybe we could let whatever was angry with us know our intentions telepathically. There was little else we could do, and we all felt we were in danger. We also felt there was more than one "creature" and our actions were closely scrutinized and had been for a while. None of us had encountered anything such as this before so all we had to go by to rectify the situation was our gut feelings.

When the bone was returned to where Dave found it, and we stepped away, the rocks and boulders stopped completely. The canyon was silent once again, and we made our way out of the canyon without further incident.

We discussed what happened many times, but always came to the same conclusion. It had to be that we stumbled into a lair and the encounter was with Bigfoot. It could have ended badly, but rather ended up as an experience to share. We'll never forget it.

Bigfoot in the Keystone State

Eric Altman's journey into researching the paranormal began at the young age of 10 when he watched the 1970s docudramas Legend of Boggy Creek *and* Creature from Black Lake, *allegedly based on events that took place in the deep south of Arkansas and Texas. The two films inspired Eric to begin 27 years of research into the paranormal that he has undertaken with the utmost seriousness. Eric has an interest in spirits, haunted locations, UFOs, and the paranormal in general. However, his main interest is studying hominid creatures such as Bigfoot. Eric currently heads the Pennsylvania Bigfoot Society, a group of dedicated researchers who investigate encounters and sightings of Bigfoot in the "Keystone State." Although Eric has never had a face-to- face encounter with a hominid creature, he hopes through persistent research and ongoing investigations either to prove or disprove these creatures' existence. (Eric and the Pennsylvania Bigfoot Society can be contacted through the group website at www.pabigfootsociety.com or by email at bigfootboy_2000@yahoo.com.) Eric also co-hosts an internet talk show entitled "Beyond The Edge" and is the chairman for the annual East Coast Bigfoot Conference that takes place in Pennsylvania.*

When I asked Eric for a case currently under investigation, he told an interesting story involving a family and the discovery of a dead deer that appeared to be the victim of a Bigfoot. According to Eric:

In the small town of Wysox, Pennsylvania, a family was visited by some unusual but violent being(s) on the night of July 4, 2006. The family had returned from a family outing, and as they were walking from the car to the house, they began to hear loud screams coming from the wooded area behind their home. What they heard not only puzzled them, but frightened them as well.

They heard screams coming from three different locations in the large forested area behind their home. They own several hundred acres of forest behind their home, and somewhere, around 11:00 P.M. there were three "things" in the forest screaming.

One animal or being would scream. A few moments later, something would respond in kind with a loud scream. Within what seemed another few moments, another shrill answer would respond in kind with yet another scream coming from another location in the wooded acreage.

This calling and answering occurred for over 15 minutes before the family went into their home.

The next day, the children of the family decided to explore the woods to try to determine what or who may have been responsible for the sounds they heard coming from the wooded area behind the home. What they found would not only shock the family but the researchers involved in the investigation.

The family discovered a dead deer. The animal was found with its right front leg wedged tightly in the "Y" of a small tree. How it got there in that position was a mystery.

But the bizarre occurrence doesn't end there. The deer appeared to have bloody welts on the top of its head as if it [had been] beaten by a blunt object. The deer also was ripped apart from the midsection back. A large hole was ripped in the side and underbelly of the deer, and its right rear leg was missing.

The method of the deer's brutal death was accompanied by the discovery of a large bloody rock found not far from the animal, along with several large human shaped impressions in the ground which led the family to speculate that a "Bigfoot" or similar type creature was responsible for the death of the deer.

> *The method of the deer's brutal death was accompanied by the discovery of a large bloody rock found not far from the animal, along with several large human shaped impressions in the ground....*

The family also found several broken trees and branches in the area. They also found several trees ripped out of the ground with the roots still intact.

Upon contacting our group, our researchers visited the location about eight days afterwards to look at the deer. It was still there; no other predators had touched it, and the evidence of the tracks and so forth were still there.

During our investigators' visit with the family, our researchers heard the screams the family had heard on that first night, July 4th. Although the person/creature responsible for the screams and the brutal death of the deer was never seen or discovered, some of the circumstantial evidence leads to the possibility of a Bigfoot being the culprit. Unfortunately, by the time our researchers arrived, there was no fresh evidence to collect to be tested. The weather and elements had contaminated the tracks, deer, the tree, and the rock.

Compelling Evidence from a Bigfoot's Mud Bath

In his book *Sasquatch: Legend Meets Science* (2007), Jeff Meldrum, who works in the Department of Biological Science at Idaho State University, states that it is not simply a matter of believing in Bigfoot, but it is using scientific evidence to prove his existence. No history is without myth. No myth is without history. Unfortunately, a large number of his fellow faculty members are not enthusiastic about Meldrum's quest for Bigfoot and feel that his research is an embarrassment to the college.

Meldrum forges onward. On September 22, 2000, he was among a team of fourteen researchers who had tracked the elusive Bigfoot for a week deep in the mountains of the Gifford Pinchot national forest in Washington state. There, in a muddy wallow near Mt. Adams, the team found an extraordinary piece of evidence that could end all arguments about whether or not the mysterious creature exists. It was here that they located an imprint in the mud of Bigfoot's hair-covered lower body as it lay on its side, apparently reaching over to get some fruit. Thermal imaging equipment confirmed that the impression made by the massive body was only a few hours old.

The team of Bigfoot hunters who discovered the imprint—Dr. LeRoy Fish, a retired wildlife ecologist with a doctorate in zoology; Derek Randles, a landscape architect; and Richard Noll, a tooling metrologist—next made a plaster cast of what appeared to be impressions of the creature's left forearm, hip, thigh, and heel. More than 200 pounds of plaster were needed to acquire a complete 3.5 × 5 foot cast of the imprint. Dr. Meldrum stated that the imprint had definitely not been made by a human who had improbably crawled into the mud wallow.

On October 23, Idaho State University issued a press release stating that a team of investigators, including Dr. Meldrum; Dr. Grover Krantz, retired physical anthropologist from Washington State University; Dr. John Bindernagel, Canadian wildlife biologist; John Green, retired Canadian author and long-time Bigfoot hunter; and Dr. Ron Brown, exotic animal handler and health care administrator, had examined the plaster cast obtained from the mud wallow and agreed that it could not be "attributed to any commonly known Northwest animal and may present an unknown primate."

According to the university press release, after the cast had been cleaned, "extensive impressions of hair on the buttock and thigh surfaces and a fringe of longer hair along the forearm were evident." In addition, Dr. Meldrum, associate professor of anatomy and anthropology, identified what appeared to be "skin ridge patterns on the heel, comparable to fingerprints, that are characteristic of primates."

While the cast may not prove without question the existence of a species of North American ape, Dr. Meldrum speculated that it "constitutes significant and compelling new evidence that will hopefully stimulate further serious research and investigation into the presence of these primates in the Northwest mountains and elsewhere."

A Scientist's Quest to Find the Elusive Bigfoot!

My long-time friend and associate Dr. Franklin Ruehl told me that among the most impressive pieces of recent evidence for Bigfoot that he had examined is a three-minute videotape shot on Saturday morning, April 16, 2005, just after dawn, by Bobby Clarke, a bargeman on the Nelson River in northern Manitoba in the Cree Indian community of Norway House. He sighted and videotaped what he described as "a big black figure" on the opposite side of the riverbank approximately 750 feet away.

Dr. Ruehl was willing to dismiss the possibility of a hoax because Clarke waited several days before going public with his film, wanting to avoid publicity. On May 4, 2005, Dr. Ruehl analyzed the video for the TV program, *A Current Affair*. While the image was blurred to a certain degree, Dr. Ruehl endorsed it as having a high coefficient of credibility. Indeed, if it had been too perfect, one would wonder if it might have been choreographed with someone in a costume.

The very next morning after he had analyzed the film, Dr. Ruehl received a phone call from the show's producer, Burt Kearns, inviting him fly up to Canada to personally investigate the case.

According to Dr. Franklin Ruehl:

> At first, I demurred as I am a stereotypical wimp, not a wilderness hunter! But, at breakfast, my mother encouraged me to give it a go.

> Early the next morning, I found myself on a plane headed for Manitoba, along with segment producer Brett Hudson and chainsaw artist Cherie Currie (who was going to carve an image of the creature out of local wood). On the final leg of the flight, as we journeyed from Winnipeg to Norway House, I was most impressed with the dense forestation on all sides, the left, the right, the north, east, south, and west … you could easily have had 100 such creatures concealed within.

> Soon after arriving, we met with Clarke, who impressed me with both his sincerity and knowledge of the region. Then, accompanied by two Cree guides, we made our first excursion into the brush in the area where the video was shot. I was struck with the awareness of just how difficult it would be to track and chase one of these creatures down. We were truly in Bigfoot country!

Dr. Franklin R. Ruehl is a physicist, anomalist, ufologist, author, lecturer, and television host and producer (*photo by International Cryptozoology Museum/Loren Coleman/Jessica Meuse*).

Every step of the way, our path was encumbered with mud holes, bramble bushes with thorns, and branches of all sizes. My immediate conclusion was that it would be very dangerous, very difficult, to pursue a creature if he indeed does exist there, a creature which knows its way around and may have evolved heavy foot and lower-leg padding to easily navigate through such terrain.

While our team did not find Bigfoot, we did uncover a significant amount of secondary evidence. For instance, in what may have been a Bigfoot feasting field, we found bird bones that had their feathers peeled off before being eaten, something a bear or other predator, for example, would not do—but perhaps an intelligent primate, such as a Bigfoot, might take the time to more carefully prepare its food.

The locals continued to bring us sophisticated digital photos of possible Bigfoot footprints. Indeed, one contingent even delivered a large box of dirt with the footprint embedded within.

Moreover, as word spread that we were investigating Bigfoot, I was being inundated by calls from other areas of Manitoba about sightings and footprints. One woman with whom I spoke definitely impressed me with an account of a Bigfoot suddenly materializing near her home, again suggesting that this was the time the entity was awakening from hibernation.

One hair was recovered from the area and subsequently analyzed by a technician with the Royal Canadian Mounted Police (RCMP). His conclusion that it was of indeterminate origin, but he kept open the hope that it was indeed from Bigfoot.

A legitimate question raised by skeptics that needs to be addressed is why no Bigfoot cadavers have yet been recovered.

I point out that while birds, squirrels, and other creatures are dying all the time in the forest, we virtually never see their corpses as a variety of predators tend to feast on such remains, with microscopic scavengers ingurgitating whatever is left behind. And, with Bigfoot, we may well be dealing with an intelligent entity that may carry off its dead, hiding or even burying those remains.

In conclusion, I arrived in Norway House as a believer in Bigfoot, and my belief has been strengthened by what we uncovered in such a short amount of time. I submit that it is just a matter of time before we have absolute confirmation that Bigfoot exists! No doubt about it whatsoever!

Other researchers have pointed out that Mother Nature keeps a clean house. The carcasses of the largest forest creatures are soon eaten by scavengers and the bones are scattered. Zoologist Ivan T. Sanderson suggested that if these beings are members of a subhuman race, they may gather up their dead for burial in special caves. Others remind the skeptical that it is not unusual for certain of the higher animals to hide the bodies of their dead. Accounts of the legendary "elephants' graveyard" are well-known; and in Ceylon, the phrase "to find a dead monkey" is used to indicate an impossible task.

How the Nantiinaq Closed Down
Two Alaskan Communities

On the southern-most tip of Alaska's Kenai Peninsula there once was a thriving little community named Port Chatham. Through the centuries, the village had offered friendly hospitality to strangers. When Captain Nathaniel Portlock visited the place on his 1786 Alaska expedition, he and his men were made to feel welcome.

In the mid-1930s, strange and terrible things began to happen to the people of Port Chatham. The Nantiinaq ("big hairy creature" in the native Sugt'sun) had become bolder and had begun to terrorize the villagers. Sometimes they would even come into the village and hurt people. Some witnesses swore that the Nantiinaq were led by the spirit of a woman dressed in flowing black clothes who would materialize out of the cliffs and summon the Nantiinaq.

A logger was killed instantly when he was struck from behind with a piece of log-moving equipment.

A gold prospector who was working his claim disappeared one day and was never seen again.

A sawmill owner saw a Nantiinaq on the beach, tearing up the fish traps that had been set.

By about 1936, the people of Chatham left the village en masse. They abandoned their houses, the school, everything, and vacated their once peaceful town to move to Nanwalek.

In the early 1900s, the town of Portlock, named for Captain Nathaniel Portlock, was established as a small cannery town. In 1921, a U.S. post office was opened, and the town appeared to be prospering. The population was made up largely of natives of the region who were mostly of Russian-Aleut heritage and who had lived in peaceful interaction for decades.

Sometime in the early 1940s, the same kind of strange occurrences that drove people out of Chatman in the past began to happen in Portlock. Men who worked at the cannery began to disappear. Some would go hunting for Dall sheep or bear and never be seen again.

Reports of sighting the Nantiinaq became common. So did the reports of mutilated and dismembered human bodies floating in the lagoon.

> *In the mid-1930s, strange and terrible things began to happen to the people of Port Chatham. The Nantiinaq ... had become bolder and had begun to terrorize the villagers.*

Hunters tracking signs of moose would suddenly find the tracks of the great animal overlaid with giant, human-like tracks over those left by the moose. Signs of a struggle in the snow were mute testimony that a giant human had slain the huge moose. Then the only tracks remaining were the monstrous, manlike tracks heading back toward the fog-shrouded mountains.

As with the people of Port Chatham before them, the residents of Portlock moved en masse, leaving their homes, the school, and the cannery. In 1950, the post office closed.

Naomi Klouda of the *Homer Tribune* (October 26, 2009) interviewed Malania Kehl, the eldest resident in Nanwalek, who was born in Port Chatham in 1934 and who remembers how the entire village left everything behind to escape the Nantiinaq. It was her uncle who had been killed with the piece of logging equipment. Once the people of Port Chatham left their community, Malania said, the Nantiinaq stayed far away from them and left them in peace.

According to Sugt'stun culture, the Nantiinaq may once have been fully human, but now, through some events not understood, he is a different kind of creature—half-man, half-beast.

BLACK DOGS
THAT HERALD DISASTER

According to an old story often told in England, there was a terrifying thunderstorm that descended on Bungay on Sunday, August 4, 1577. The storm transformed the day into a darkness, rain, hail, thunder, and lightning beyond all imagining. Fearing the worst, a number of the townsfolk had gathered in St. Mary's Church to pray for mercy.

As the lore tells it, it was while the people knelt in fear and prayed for deliverance, that a large black Hell Hound manifested suddenly in their midst. Without any challenge from the cowering congregation, the massive black hound charged many members of the church with its terrible claws and large fangs. According to a verse taken from a pamphlet published by Rev. Abraham Fleming in 1577: *All down the church in midst of fire, the hellish monster flew.... And passing onward to the quire, he many people slew.*

After the Hell Hound had finished ravishing St. Mary's Church and chewing up a good number of its members, tradition has it that the creature next appeared in Blythburgh Church. Its appetite for human flesh had merely been whetted by its attack on the people of Bungay, for it viciously mauled and killed more churchgoers at Blythburgh.

According to the accounts of the Hell Hound's attack at Bungay, the beast used more than its teeth and claws to kill. Fleming testified that in some instances, the monster wrung the necks of two churchgoers at the same time, one victim in each of its paws as it stood upright.

At Blytheburg, the Hell Hound burst through the church doors, ran into the nave, and then dashed up the aisle, killing a man and boy. In addition to leaving bodies strewn about before it departed the church, the monster left numerous scorch marks about the church—marks, which people swear, can still be seen to this day.

Tales of Black Hell Hounds seem to abound in the British Isles. Below, popular author and researcher Nick Redfern recounts a number of ghostly dogs that haunt British woods. Redfern can be contacted at his blogs: http://www.ufomystic.com and http://monsterusa.blogspot.com.

Phantom Hounds of the Woods

BY NICK REDFERN

In his definitive book *Explore Phantom Black Dogs*, English author and researcher Bob Trubshaw wrote: "The folklore of phantom black dogs is known throughout the British Isles. From the Black Shuck of East Anglia to the Mauthe Dhoog of the Isle of Man there are tales of huge spectral hounds 'darker than the night sky' with eyes 'glowing red as burning coals.' The phantom black dog of British and Irish folklore, which often forewarns of death, is part of a world-wide belief that dogs are sensitive to spirits and the approach of death, and keep watch over the dead and dying. North European and Scandinavian myths dating back to the Iron Age depict dogs as corpse eaters and the guardians of the roads to hell. Medieval folklore includes a variety of 'Devil dogs' and spectral hounds."

And while the image that the devil dog or phantom hound conjures up is that of a sinister beast prowling the villages and towns of centuries-old England, it is a little known fact outside of students of the phenomenon that sightings of such creatures continue to surface to this very day.

According to the accounts of the Hell Hound's attack at Bungay, the beast used more than its teeth and claws to kill.

Interestingly, one area that seems to attract more than its fair share of such encounters is a sprawling mass of dense forest in central England known as the Cannock Chase—a strange and eerie location that has also been the site of numerous encounters with UFOs, Bigfoot-like entities and strangely-elusive "Big Cats." Indeed, among the folk of the many small villages that sit on the fringes of the Chase—or that, in some cases, can be found deep within its wooded depths—tales of the diabolical hounds of hell are disturbingly common.

Late one evening in early 1972, a man named Nigel Lea was driving across the Chase when his attention was suddenly drawn to a strange ball of glowing, blue light that slammed into the ground some distance ahead of his vehicle, and amid a veritable torrent of bright, fiery sparks. Needless to say, Lea quickly slowed his car down; and as he approached the approximate area where the light had fallen, was shocked and horrified to see looming before him, "the biggest bloody dog I have ever seen in my life."

Muscular and black, with large, pointed ears and huge paws, the creature seemed to positively ooze menace and negativity, and had a wild, staring look in its yellow-tinged eyes. For twenty or thirty seconds, man and beast alike both faced each other, after which time the "animal" slowly and cautiously headed for the tall trees, never once taking its penetrating eyes off of the petrified driver. Somewhat ominously, and around two or three weeks later, says Lea, a close friend of his was killed in an industrial accident under horrific circumstances; something which Lea believes—after having deeply studied the history of Black Dog lore—was directly connected with his strange encounter on that tree-shrouded road back in 1972.

Throughout the British Isles, there are tales of huge spectral hounds "darker than the night sky" with eyes "glowing red as burning coals." The phantom black dog of British and Irish folklore, often forewarns of death (*art by Bill Oliver*).

In the early to mid 1980s, reports began to surface from the Cannock Chase of something that became known as the "Ghost Dog of Brereton"—a reference to the specific locale from where most of the sightings originated. Yet again, the dog was described as being both large and menacing, and on at least two occasions it reportedly vanished into thin air after having been seen by terrified members of the public on lonely stretches of road late at night.

In direct response to an article that appeared in the *Cannock Advertiser* newspaper during the winter of 1984–85 on the sightings of Brereton's infamous ghost dog, a member of the public from a local village wrote to the newspaper thus:

"On reading the article my husband and I were astonished. We recalled an incident which happened in July some four or five years ago driving home from a celebration meal at the Cedar Tree restaurant at about 11:30 P.M. We had driven up Coal Pit Lane and were just on the bends before the approach to the Holly Bush when, from the high hedge of trees on the right hand side of the road, the headlights picked out a misty shape which moved across the road and into the trees opposite."

The writer continued:

"We both saw it. It had no definite shape seeming to be a ribbon of mist about 18 inches to 2 feet in depth and perhaps 9 or 10 feet long with a definite beginning and end. It was a clear, warm night with no mist anywhere else. We were both rather stunned and my husband's first words were: 'My goodness! Did you see that?' I remember remarking I thought it was a ghost. Until now we had no idea of the history of the area or any possible explanation for a haunting. Of course, this occurrence may be nothing to do with the 'ghost dog' or may even have a natural explanation. However, we formed the immediate impression that what we saw was something paranormal."

Possibly relative to the tale of the ghost dog of Brereton was the story of a man named Ivan Vinnel. In 1934, as a twelve year old, he had a strange encounter in his hometown of nearby Burntwood. The sun was setting and Ivan and a friend were getting ready to head home after an afternoon of playing hide-and-seek. Suddenly, however, the pair was stopped dead in its tracks by the shocking sight of a ghostly "tall, dark man," who was "accompanied by a black dog" that had materialized out of a "dense hedge" approximately ten yards from the boys' position. Both man and beast passed by in complete and utter silence before disappearing—quite literally.

Ivan later mentioned the incident to his uncle, who then proceeded to tell him that he, too, had seen the ghostly dog on several occasions as a child. It was always in the same location: on the old road that stretches from the village of Woodhouses to an area of Burntwood, near the town's hospital. As with the majority of black dog legends from all across Britain, this particular ghostly animal would always faithfully follow the same path and walk the same stretch of road before vanishing as mysteriously as it had first appeared.

And weird reports from the Cannock Chase of out-of-place dog-like beasts continue to surface to this very day.

It was in late June 2006 that all hell metaphorically broke loose, when reports flew around the people of the Cannock Chase to the effect that nothing less than a fully-grown wolf was roaming the area. Early on the morning of June 28, motorists on Junction 10A of the M6 Motorway near Cannock jammed Highways Agency phone-lines with reports of a "wolf-like creature" that was seen "racing between lanes at rush hour." Motorists stared with utter disbelief as the three-foot-long beast, described as "grayish-black," raced between lanes, skillfully dodging cars, before leaping for cover in nearby trees.

Highways Agency staff took the reports very seriously, but concluded that the animal was "probably a husky dog." However, a spokesperson for Saga Radio—the first media outlet on the scene—said in reply to the statement of the Highways Agency: "Everyone who saw it is convinced it was something more than a domestic dog. I know it sounds crazy but these people think they've seen a wolf."

The local newspaper, the *Chase Post,* always quick to report on mystery animals seen in the vicinity of the dark woods, stated on July 6 in an article titled *Great Beast Debate on Net* that: "Internet message boards are being flooded with debates on our front-page revelation last week that a 'wolf-like' creature was spotted by dozens of motorists on the M6 hard-shoulder."

The *Chase Post* further noted that: "Our own website has been thrown into overdrive by the story, which received around 2,600 hits from fans of the unexplained across the globe in the last week alone."

While the affair was never ultimately resolved to everyone's satisfaction, the final words went to the Highways Agency, who said: "We have received a number of reports that the animal was captured. But we don't know where, who by, or what it was."

Perhaps the event had indeed been due to the mistaken sighting of an escaped Husky; however, that does not in any way come close to explaining the eerie encounter of Jim Broadhurst and his wife that occurred while the pair was out for a morning stroll on the Cannock Chase, only days before the events of June 28.

Broadhurst stated that he and his wife had seen at a distance of about one hundred and fifty feet, what looked like a large wolf or "a giant dog" striding purposefully through the woods. Broadhurst added that fear gripped the pair when the creature suddenly stopped and looked intently and menacingly in their direction. That fear was amplified even further, however, when the beast reportedly, and incredibly, reared up onto two powerful hind legs and backed away into the thick trees, never to be seen again. The Broadhursts, unsurprisingly, fled those dark woods—and have not returned since; fearful of what they believe to be some form of "monster" lurking deep within the mysterious depths of the Cannock Chase.

Interestingly, and certainly unfortunately, in the weeks that followed their sighting, the Broadhursts were cursed with a seemingly never-ending run of bad luck and disaster that did not abate until well into September of that same year.

Whether they are the precursors to doom and tragedy; ancient and paranormal entities that are somehow connected with the realm of the dead; or the spirits of long-deceased animals that have returned to watch over the living, it seems that the phantom black dogs of Britain's Cannock Chase are here to stay.

The Black Dogs Have Many Names

Researcher Theo Brown has divided the phantom black dogs into three separate categories: 1) a shape-shifting demon dog; 2) a large black dog about the size of a calf with dark shaggy fur; 3) a dog that manifests in association with particular ancient festivals in various parts of the country.

Unexplained Mysteries (theunexplainedmysteries.com/phantom-dogs.html) discovered different names for the black dogs that bring death and disaster in different counties. Among the fearful names are Bogey Beast, Lancashire; Black Shuck, East Anglia; Cu Sith, Highlands (dark green in color, rather than black); Gurt Dog, Somerset; Hairy Jack, Lincolnshire; Mauthe Dog, Scotland; and Padfoot, Yorkshire.

The Black Shuck

It would seem after some study of the Hell Hound that its most common name is the Black Shuck, a truly massive dog that bodes no one any good. The Vikings brought the legends of the giant black dog to Anglia. As if the Vikings suddenly appearing on the beach one morning with their savage war cries that firmly announced their intent to raid one's village were not terrible enough, the sea wolves left warnings of the Black

Black dogs go by many names, including Bogey Beast, Black Shuck, and Hairy Jack (*iStock*).

Shuck behind them to keep the villagers in a state of constant fear. This gigantic dog had glowing red or green eyes, and anyone who saw it was doomed to bad luck or death. "Shuck" likely comes from the Old Norse word "scucca," a hairy demon.

It is my own opinion that the Black Shuck is another manifestation of Fenrir, the large and terrible wolf, who is the eldest child of Loki and the giantess Angrboda. Fenrir is so strong and so threatening to the other Norse gods that they bound him with chains, which he easily broke. Finally, mountain elves created a magic chain which has managed to keep Fenrir imprisoned. All who know of Fenrir fear him, for on the day of Ragnarok, when the final destiny of the Norse gods will be decided, Fenrir will shatter the magic chain and join the giants in their battle against the gods. The Black Shuck, then, inspired the Vikings to become as wolves when they attacked others and to leave behind warnings to all people that the image of Fenrir is to be feared.

Terror and Death Brought by the Black Dogs Seems Endless

On January 14, 1971, a large, black dog received the blame when six hogs and three dogs were found slain, mutilated, and partially eaten at two farms a short distance east of Waterloo, Iowa.

The tracks found at the scene of the slaughter puzzled authorities. Some experts insisted that the prints were those of a large mountain lion that had somehow found its way to Iowa.

Later three lawmen reported that they had sighted and trailed a large black dog that they believed had been responsible for killing the nine farm animals, but the savage animal had easily escaped the hunt. "He was an extraordinarily big dog, and pretty fast, too," said Walt Berryhill, a La Porte City police dispatcher. "We saw him jump over fences."

Then, just as suddenly as they had begun, the attacks of the great black dog ceased. After a month had gone by, the black large dog with the voracious appetite had ceased to sample any more plump Iowa livestock. Could the monster have found its way back into the dimension from whence it had come?

Farmers in the Midwest often encounter unidentifiable footprints left by unknown animals that have mauled their livestock—then disappeared without a trace. The fact that so many farmers find their dogs slain with necks and backs broken may be an example of the creatures' powerful ability to defend itself, rather than a quest for fresh meat.

The Campeche Beasts—Lafitte's Black Hounds from Hell

According to Leslie Danielle Ferrymen, an unidentified animal found dead in Galveston Island on September 1, 2008, is believed to be one of the Campeche Beasts, a pack of large black dogs that are said to date back to the time of Jean Lafitte (c. 1776–c. 1826), the notorious pirate. Residents of the small island have been hearing "chilling animal cries" since 1891, with sightings of a monstrous animal with glowing red eyes that apparently mated with a Doberman and a Rottweiler before it died.

The Campeche Devil Dogs

Leslie Danielle Ferrymen is a paranormal investigator from Franklin, Tennessee, who heads up The Franklin Ghost and Paranormal Investigation Team. Ms. Ferryman is active in pursuing real urban legends and finding out what truth lies hidden in the stories told. Her 15-member group has investigated many haunted locations all over the United States since its founding in 2006. Her account below originally appeared in Haunted America Tours *and is reprinted with the permission of Leslie Danielle Ferrymen.*

A pack of twelve dogs from hell is said to have been born in the eye of a hurricane during Pirate King Jean Lafitte's time on the Island. The Voodoo Queen who performed the ritual that spawned the dogs is said to have died as the last evil pup was born, thus infusing her eternal black powers into the pack. The pups were cross bred from a large Spanish or European black wolf and an evil bitch dog that Lafitte owned.

Some tell the story that the twelve black dogs were bred for hunting down unsuspecting thieves, travelers, and interlopers. Other tales tell that the evil Pirate King claimed the hounds have brought home to him each night multiple heads, hands, and human penises. These bloody trophies came from the people who tried to steal his treasure, his belongings, or his woman.

Jean Lafitte was a privateer in the Gulf of Mexico in the early 19th century. (He often spelled his [name] Laffite.) Lafitte is believed to have been born either in France or the French colony of Saint-Domingue. By 1805 he operated a warehouse in New Orleans to help disperse the goods smuggled by his brother Pierre Lafitte. After the United States government passed the Embargo Act of 1807, the Lafittes moved their operations to an island in Barataria Bay. By 1810, their new port was very successful.

The Pirate King is said by some to have been involved with the powerful forces of black magic and Voodoo-Hoodoo practices. After being run out of New Orleans around 1817, Lafitte relocated to the island of Galveston, Texas, establishing a "kingdom" he named "Campeche." In Galveston, Lafitte either purchased or set his claim to a lavishly furnished mansion used by French pirate Louis-Michel Aury, which he named "Maison Rouge." The building's upper level was converted into a fortress where a cannon commanding Galveston harbor was placed.

Around 1820, Lafitte reportedly married Madeline Regaud, possibly the widow or daughter of a French colonist who had died during an ill-fated expedition to Galveston. In 1821, the schooner *USS Enterprise* was sent to Galveston to remove Lafitte from the Gulf after the captain of one of the pirates attacked an American merchant ship. Lafitte agreed to leave the island without a fight, and in 1821 or 1822 departed on his flagship, the *Pride*, burning his fortress and settlements and reportedly taking immense amounts of treasure with him. All that remains of Maison Rouge is the foundation, located at 1417 Avenue A near the Galveston wharf.

While Lafitte and his brother Pierre were engaged in running the Galveston operation, Lafitte demanded that a voodoo queen give him an army of dogs to guard his Island retreat. He reportedly maintained several stashes of plundered gold and jewelry in the vast system of marshes, swamps, and bayous located around Barrataria Bay. Other rumors suggest that Lafitte's treasure sank with his ship, the *Pride*, either near Galveston or in the Gulf of Mexico during an 1826 hurricane. It is most commonly said that Lafitte buried his treasure on Galveston Island, and in each location a large black devil dog from his pack of 500 dogs is said to guard it. When Lafitte left the island he left only twelve of the largest and meanest of his supernatural black dogs.

The dogs are said to possess supernatural powers that defy explanation. If you are on Galveston Island, be aware of the shadows day and night, for you might be followed by the dogs of Campeche where ever you go.

The dogs are more [than] able to become just shadows and are said to track anyone who might have strange or covert intentions. Many locals will tell you they will closely follow any stranger[s] on the Island until they leave.

The black dogs are known to breathe heavily on the necks of those who have no good on their minds. One recent tale tells of a tourist who said that she was chased back to her hotel by a large black beast.

Lafitte's Black Hell Hound Devil Dogs are also said to haunt New Orleans, Barataria, and anywhere Lafitte set foot in his lifetime. Some say the shadows of these dogs can be seen in the waves that crash ashore along the Gulf of Mexico.

Black Dogs Are No Respecter of Persons

Seemingly, Black Dogs as portents of evil can manifest anywhere. In 1990, Sherry and I were speaking with the actor Clint Walker about his near-death experience

There is no love in a Black Dog's eyes for the human race (*iStock*).

during a skiing accident in 1973. Walker was a large man, standing six-foot-six, a strapping leading-man who played the strong, silent hero in such motion pictures as *The Dirty Dozen* (1967), *The White Buffalo* (1977), *Yellowstone Kelly* (1959), and *Night of the Grizzly* (1966). Clint was probably best known as "Cheyenne Bodie" in the popular *Cheyenne* series that ran for eight years on ABC television network.

Walker was just learning how to ski when he fell on the sharp end of a ski pole with such force that the sharp tip pierced his breastbone and moved through his heart. Soon Clint's true self was not merely floating above is body, he was rising outward into the universe. He saw that time was an illusion and that the body was just a vehicle, a garment that we put on for a while. The soul, however, could not be destroyed.

Two doctors had pronounced Clint dead before a third physician who just happened to be passing through the room, taking a shortcut to somewhere else, believed that he saw a flicker of life in the body lying on the gurney. Clint remembered going down a long tunnel while the doctor worked on his heart, and he recalled his recovery being pronounced a medical miracle.

When he left the hospital, Clint Walker realized that with discipline he could learn to master his thoughts and move closer to the image of true love. He knew that he had his own inner guidance, but that there would be times of testing—and sometimes the power of good could attract the counterbalance of evil.

Five years later, Clint was told that he must have surgery to remove excessive scar tissue that had grown up around the old ski pole wound. Once again, he said, he traveled down the long tunnel with the misty faces and the mumble of voices. Once again, he asked God to allow him to live.

Walker never stayed in a hospital any longer than he had to, so he was home convalescing within a few days. By his second day at home, he was out walking in his yard. By the third day, he was walking down the road toward his mailbox, weak but glad to be alive.

The rugged actor lived at that time in a remote canyon off Mulholland Drive, and he was walking on a dirt road when he saw a large black dog some fifteen feet away. Feeling full of good cheer, he said hello to the dog.

"The dog stared at me in this very eerie manner, and then, suddenly, there were three other dogs with him," Clint recalled. "I knew that they were about to come for me. I scooped up a rock in each hand, being careful not to rip open my stitches from surgery, and I was barely standing upright again when they were on me."

Fighting against his own weakness from the surgery, Walker managed to kick one of the dogs under its chin and send it sprawling. He pelted another with a rock. With angry growls and yelps, the vicious, growling dogs beat a retreat.

He was about three-quarters of a mile from his home, facing a walk up a long, curving driveway. "That's when my inner voice said loud and clear: 'Get a club. They're waiting for you!'" Clint found a thick branch and began to walk in anticipation of attack.

"Sure enough, when I went around a curve, they were waiting for me in the road. They were strange-looking dogs, like dogs I had never seen before."

The brandishing of the club and a few well-aimed rocks sent the mysterious black dogs back to whatever dark den had produced them. Once he was safe again in his house, Walker felt the unpleasant memory rush of a nightmare that he had experienced the night before.

"It was a nightmare that wasn't a nightmare," he said. "It was a dream, I know, but it was also very real. A devilish face was grinning at me, and I knew the only way to whip it was with willpower, so I said, 'I reject you in the name of Jesus Christ.' I repeated that rejection and kept my will strong against it. There are evil forces, you know," Clint Walker said. "I have learned that this is so, and we must stay strong against them and not give them power over us."

BOGEY MAN—HE DOESN'T JUST LIVE UNDER YOUR BED

Every culture has its "Bogeyman," a fearsome creature that will come to get all little children who misbehave—or especially, won't fall right to sleep at night. Consequently, a great majority of children in the English speaking world are kept awake at night, fearing the Bogeyman is in their closet or under their bed.

Perhaps parents would be a bit more circumspect about using the threat of the Bogeyman if they truly understood the origin of the term. In the old folklore and legends, the Bogey was a shape-shifting demon that dwelt in the bogs. From time to time, he made his way into the rural homes and villages and was only too pleased to capture the souls of children.

The Native Americans are also well aware of the Bogey. However, they seem to be more protective of their children. Rather than setting the monster on their wee ones, they have devised special masks and dances to frighten the Bogey away from the village children.

Who's Afraid of the Big Bad Bogey Man?

Peter told me that when he was a kid, eight or nine-years old, he was playing hide and seek with his cousins in their parents' house. It was daylight, he emphasized. He was wide-awake and not dreaming.

Then, in Peter's own words:

I slipped upstairs, thinking that maybe my younger cousins wouldn't think to look for me on the second floor. I slid under the bed that was in the single room that occupied the guest room. Great! This was a fantastic hiding place!

After one of Brad Steiger's international broadcasts on "The Bogey Man in the Closet at Night," Eugenio, an artist from South America, sent Brad this imaginative drawing.

A few minutes later, I heard someone mount the stairs. I held my breath and listened. It wasn't one of my cousins. The stairs creaked as if whoever was climbing them had some weight to him or her. This had to be an adult. Great, I assumed, I'd get in trouble now.

I followed the creaking sound as it grew louder. I couldn't really see the stairs from where I was.

Lying quietly, I watched from my hiding place as two legs strode from the area of the stairs. They were clad in grey dress pants … but the feet were bare and clawed … big, black claws … and covered with grey hair.

I think I forgot to breathe at that point. I heard a loud "sniffing" noise. I'm not sure where I got the courage to crane my neck and look up, but I did. And when I did, I saw what was very likely, the most unusual sight of my life—even until this day.

It wore a shirt and a bow tie, and its hands were hairy and clawed, just like its feet. And it had a wolf's head! Swear to God. This thing, whatever it was, seemed to be the living, physical embodiment of "The Big Bad Wolf" from fairy tales. It stood, looming over the bed, and sniffed.

I bit my tongue, because I sure as heck knew what would happen if I screamed. I closed my eyes, tighter than I'd probably ever closed them before, and I prayed silently.

And when I opened them again, it was gone. I didn't leave my hiding place for a long, long time. And when I finally did, I told no one about this, as I knew no one would believe me. So, here it is for the first time ... I'm telling you.

I told Peter that he had shared a really great story. Off the top of my head, I had two thoughts for him to consider:

1. The entity probed your young mind and pulled out the image of the Big Bad Wolf from your knowledge of fairy tales and animated cartoons.

2. The entity, being of a horribly negative nature, may manifest in our dimension in a grotesque appearance. In this case, it manifested as a werewolf, a man wolf, yet with an offbeat touch—the bow tie.

Peter thanked me for my quick reply, and replied that he had given this incident a lot of thought over the years and he realized that there were some odd points:

1. It was an isolated incident (I didn't spend my childhood seeing The Big Bad Wolf or any other fairy tale denizens, for that matter).

2. The entity certainly wasn't what I pictured as a "werewolf" at that point in time. Aside from the clothing, this was like something out of the movie *The Howling* which wouldn't be around for another decade or more. I'd guess my mental image of "werewolf" would have been of the Lon Chaney variety at that time in my life. So, whatever it was, it either simply looked like it really appeared to me, smashing bow-tie and all (yes, the bow-tie bothers me a tad, a bizarre little detail to say the least). Or, as you suggest, the creature pulled a "Big Bad Wolf" image from my own psyche.

3. If, in fact, it did pull information from my subconscious, that would indicate that it knew I was in the room. If it knew I was in the room, why did it act as if it didn't? My take on this is it was simply, literally trying to scare the hell out of me. It did its job well, but I'm not certain I understand the reasoning behind this, unless it was feeding off of the fear I was projecting or some such pseudo-scientific babble.

4. I have also greatly pondered the creaking of the stairs and what seemed to be the entity physically coming into the room. Again, as a supernatural entity, it didn't *need* to do this, unless, of course, it was building up my inner fear to, essentially, "milk all it could" from me. I don't, for a second, assume this was something physical, even though it behaved as such.

5. What the heck was it doing in my cousins' house? It's not something that, as children, was discussed among us, it was simply "there," in broad daylight, pretty darned bold for something akin to this thing, wouldn't you say? And no one ever mentioned seeing anything like it later. Is it possible it was "just passing through"? (Of course, I never talked about it to anyone else, so I prob-

ably shouldn't assume anyone else would have told me if they'd had similar experiences.)

6. It went away when I prayed. I believe my prayer was something very much like, "God, please make it go away....." I don't know if this is a significant point or not. Maybe it'd already done it's duty and simply left when I had my eyes closed, not being affected by the "praying" that my eight-year-old brain could muster at all. But, at that point, I put a real significance on the fact that it was gone after I prayed.

Okay, here's what I've come up with. Could this have literally been a "Boogie Man"?

I've considered this for years, what if *this* is what children fear when they're in the dark or alone in an unfamiliar place. Maybe I'm getting a little too Stephen King-ish, but I've often wondered if what I saw wasn't some sort of entity who's assigned "job" was to frighten small humans. Aside from the "daylight" element of the encounter, it had all the earmarks of a classic bedroom night-visitor.

He Awakened to See a Monstrous Little Bogey Man

Don had a lot of incidents with the Bogey Man in which he would wake up with the blanket pulled over his head and having the sensation of something sitting on his stomach and punching him in the ribs.

But the incident that chills him to this day is that awful night when he was sleeping on his side and awakened to see a monstrous little Bogey Man crouching beside his bed.

According to Don:

❝It was small and thin and it had wings. The skin looked black and gray, spotted with small shiny spots that looked like mica. I could see the veins in its head and hand. It had cat-like ears. I screamed and swung at the being."

And now comes the bizarre Warner Brothers cartoon aspect of the visitation, similar to Peter's. After Don's father entered the bedroom, turned on the lights, and comforted his son, he left the lights on in the room to keep the Bogey Man away. A few minutes later, Don's stepmother came into his room to check on him. When she left the bedroom, however, she turned out the lights.

"Instantly, a large cartoon-like figure appeared behind her as she closed the door. I am not pulling your leg! It was a typical cartoon of Satan with bright red skin, complete with pitchfork, standing in polka dot underwear. I screamed; my stepmother screamed; and both of my parents came in my bedroom once again to comfort me.

"My impression after all these years is that the winged creature was real, and the fearsome cartoon-like figure was an hallucination created by the being. The thing that bothers me is that I had no previous reference as far as the being was concerned, and it seems difficult to fathom how my mind could have created it as an hallucination."

Martha Learned Not to
Put Her Hand Under Another's Bed

Martha was another who learned as a child that hiding "under the bed" might not be the safest place to hide while playing hide and seek:

I was at my friend's house for a party, and we were in her basement just having a good time. Then, my friend decided we should all play a game of "hide and seek" in the pitch-black darkness.

I had no objection; in fact, I had fun doing these types of things. So then we shut all the lights off and began. I was picked to be "it." I could hear all my friends scurry off into various nooks while I fumbled around after the muffled noises. I searched for a long time. I had looked everywhere—except for one room ... an especially dark room. It was my last resort. My friends had to be there.

I started to walk down the hallway, feeling against the walls. I entered the doorway, and I had this amazingly bad feeling in my stomach. I felt like going into the room would just be horrible, but as uncertain as I was feeling, I did it anyway.

I walked in and discovered that this room was a spare bedroom. I knew there was a bed, and I assumed my friends were underneath it and ready to freak me out. So I thought, "Better just get it over with...."

I reached under the bed and began to feel around a bit. That's when it happened. This enormous spark occurred under the bed. I could see its brightness. And it was loud, too. The shock vibrated through my whole body.

I immediately began to pull back my hand, but it was stopped. Something grabbed my arm! It started to pull me under the bed. Luckily, I was able to retrieve control of my arm and ran from the room. I screamed for my friends and they popped out and turned on the lights.

And they did NOT come from the room. They came from the totally other side of the basement, and there was no way they could have sneaked past me. We went back to the room, flipped the lights on and checked under the bed. NOTHING.

Martha immediately began to pull back her hand, but it was stopped. Something grabbed her arm! It started to pull her under the bed (*art by Ricardo Pustanio*).

The Awful Man in His Bedroom Has Never Left Him Alone

Kevin M. is a single man who lives alone and who has been unable to form any lasting relationships or to hold down any jobs for more than a few months. He is not ashamed of the way things are in his life, for he feels the circumstances that he finds himself in are not of his making and he feels no guilt for the person he is.

His problems began when he was a child and a man began to appear in his bedroom at night.

As Kevin tells his story:

My parents entered the room when I would scream that there was a man in my room. I remember feeling puzzled as to why this man was there and could not be seen by my parents. This man frightened me, and I would often cry out due to fear.

On one occasion, I remember this man coming over to my bed and peering down at me. We both made eye contact, and it slowly dawned on him that I could see him. This seemed to cause a mild panic in the man, and from that night on, he would often come over to me and try to talk with me—which just had the effect of scaring me stupid, and I would yell for my parents. As soon as my parents would come into the room again, the man would back away. All I could say to my parents was that there is the man that I don't like.

Of course my parents looked about, saw nothing, and assumed it was a bad nightmare. This continued for quite some time, and I was eventually moved from that room to sleep in my parents' room. Here, I always slept well.

The episode of the man in my room was totally forgotten until I reached my early- to mid-twenties when I started to receive severe spirit contact. During a discussion with my mother, she said that she recalled my man-in-the-room experience. She also added an explanation for it. It turns out that the cottage in which we were living had a previous tenant, an old man with a walking stick, who was disabled and lived most of his later years in the same room as mine. Because of this man's disability, he would often tap or bang his walking stick on the bedroom floor to get the attention of relatives down below. This man had passed away some years before our tenancy of the cottage.

My parents would often hear this banging in the house, which would seem to come from upstairs but whenever they went to investigate, it stopped. They just assumed that it was a water pipes. Now, as I learned of the deceased/disabled man and the knocking on the floor of his walking stick, we started to put two and two together and realized that the man I saw in my room and the knocking heard in the cottage were from the same source: The disabled man, desperately wanting someone to answer his signal for help.

Patrick's Encounters on Cape Cod

Patrick M. relayed a number of remarkable encounters with the "Boogey Man." Although he was old enough to deal rationally with his night time visitations, they were nonetheless unsettling:

In the mid- to late-1980's while at my aunt's house in Cataumet on Cape Cod, my mother, who knew I had an interest in ghosts, bought a book for me called *New England's Ghostly Haunts* by Robert Cahill. Later, alone in the house, reading the book on the sun porch, and grown fairly nervous by what I was reading, the window behind me slammed shut and nearly caused me to leap out of my skin.

Now, this is a three-foot by two-foot window which opens outward and is secured by a hook-and-eye latch. It may have been a coincidence, but in light of what happened later, may not have been.

Either that night or the next I was upstairs in my bedroom reading another book (the Cahill book is short and I'd finished it off in one go). I was sitting on the bed, with my back against the wall and my legs hanging over the side, when I thought I felt movement. I stopped reading and looked to see if the bed was moving and, indeed, it was. It was going back and forth slowly at first and steadily grew more violent so that eventually the headboard was banging against the wall.

Thinking it was one of my brothers playing a joke on me, I leaned over to look under the bed, about to say, "You jerk, cut it out!" I got as far as saying, "You…!"

As soon as I looked under the bed, I saw that nobody was there and the bed instantly stopped shaking. I felt the blood drain from my head with the sudden understanding of what had just happened.

To give a quick overview of that house, these things happened to me there over the years:

A) I was once awakened in the middle of the night by a woman's voice in a darkened room. She seemed to say *"Pot pot, ahlen ahlen, pot pot, ahlen ahlen."* It makes no sense, but that's what I heard. I turned the lights on, but saw nothing.

B) At another time, my clock radio made terrible screeching static noises at night as I was trying to sleep. This would only happen as I was about to drop off and stop as soon as I woke up again. It probably happened a half dozen times.

C) Similarly, one night I heard footsteps of someone outside my bedroom door. It wasn't the sound of heavy walking, but the squeak of feet on a hardwood floor. Again, this sound would come as I was about to drop off to sleep and would stop when I awoke.

D) Awake in the living room after everyone had gone to bed, I heard a woman's voice and music playing upstairs. I went to the foot of the stairs and listened for a while and then went back to watching TV. My aunt came down about twenty minutes later, and I asked her who was playing the music—and she said, "Music?" She hadn't heard anything. I found out the next day that nobody had even brought a radio.

An aside on the house: For the longest time I thought that it was related to the serial killer Jane Toppan, who murdered four people in 1901 at a house around the corner. In fact, the next street is called Mystery Lane after these murders. This would have been Alden Davis, his wife, and two daughters. I did some property research and found that Alden Davis had once owned the land my aunt's house is on, a part of the Cataumet Grover and Shore Company, but it was apparently sold before a house was built on the property in the 1870s or 1880s.

> *As soon as I looked under the bed, I saw that nobody was there and the bed instantly stopped shaking. I felt the blood drain from my head with the sudden understanding of what had just happened.*

Curiously enough, Davis had once followed a preacher named Charles Freeman who, in the 1870's, heard the voice of God speak to him and tell him that he had to sacrifice a member of his family. The next night, God told him which one would have to be sacrificed: it was to be his youngest daughter. Freeman murdered her, believing that she would be brought back to life in three days.

Instead, Alden Davis's surviving daughter told her boyfriend, who happened to be a local police officer, and Freeman was arrested. One of my older brothers pointed out that the voice I heard in the bedroom said *Pot and Ahlen*, which is almost my first name and Davis's first name. (Is any of this related to me? Who knows?)

We go to my aunt's house on Cape Cod every Thanksgiving. Just before Thanksgiving 2005, the day before we were set to arrive, my aunt drove down from her condo in Boston to get the house ready. She pulled in and walked to the front door, only to find it slightly ajar. A set of her house keys sat on the front stoop. She has no idea where this spare set of keys came from. She entered the house and had a look around and eventually found, in the bedroom I normally stay in, a screech owl, which had made a mess of the place.

She called the police, who called animal control. The guy from animal control went in, opened a bedroom window, and told her that the owl would leave when it got dark, which it did. Nobody has any idea how any of this happened, but I began to wonder if there wasn't something more to it. I did brief research on owl symbolism and found that it symbolizes a) evil or b) wisdom, the ability to see in the dark.

I'm not sure if this is a symbol or just a wild, bizarre coincidence. Her house, by the way, was in no way burglarized.

In February of 2006, I had a strange week. It started off one night when I was watching TV in the basement and thought I saw something flying around. It looked kind of like a bug, but since it was the height of winter, I didn't think it likely that it could have been one. I got my digital camera and tried to snap a picture of it.

Only one picture is at all strange, showing a glowing green ball about the size of a quarter. The next morning, at about 5:00 A.M., I was walking from my bedroom to the bathroom when I thought I heard a clear whisper in my ear say, "*Paaat!*"

My response was to say, aloud, "Pssh! Yeah, right!" and I went on to take a shower.

Later, that night, while in bed, I heard the whisper again. I turned on my computer, downloaded a quick audio clip of forest noises and played it in a loop so I could get to sleep.

The next night, I set up a radio and had it play loudly while I went to sleep so that I wouldn't hear any whispering. When I awoke in the morning, I found that the radio had been switched off (it's very low-tech and couldn't have switched off by itself).

That night, I figured I'd try to catch something on video and set my radio up the way I'd done it the night before, but pointed my Sony Handycam at it. But to no avail. The radio was still playing the next morning.

Finally, I'd had enough. I felt that there was something in my house and wanted to get to the bottom of it. I have a digital voice recorder and decided to try to get some EVPs [Electronic Voice Phenomena]. I made a few recordings and what I got put me at ease (somewhat).

On one recording you can hear my voice and then what sounds like a few men chanting, a quick series of percussion sounds, and a woman's voice saying "be strong" or "be cool" or something. In any case, it's a definite musical composition. It's not anything I would associate with a ghost. I listened to the recordings over and over and finally grew calm. My nervousness left me. I said aloud to the room, "You guys are just messing with me, aren't you?"

Whatever seemed to be in my house left and I haven't felt a presence since.

The Nasty Boogy Man with the Belt Nearly Killed Bobby

In June 2004, I received a very disturbing letter from a teenager named Lisa who said that she and her parents first noticed something was wrong when her little brother, Bobby (age 6) started to get bruises and cuts on his arms and legs.

In Lisa's account of the frightening and painful encounters:

We would ask Bobby what was wrong, and he would say, "That man who comes into my bedroom hits me with a belt."

Mom would roll her eyes and clean the cuts. Then one night, when he went to bed he acted scared, and he asked Mom to sleep with him. Mom told him no, but she turned on the night light.

The next morning when Bobby got up, he had a cut below his right eye. Mom figured he scratched himself, so she cut his fingernails.

Then a week later, he got a large bruise on his back. It covered both his shoulder blades. It really hurt him, so Mom took him to the doctor to see if he had something wrong with him. The doctor asked if he had a babysitter or someone we didn't know very well watching him, because the bruises were probably from a beating, since he had so many of them.

They would ask Bobby what was wrong, and he would say, "That man who comes into my bedroom hits me with a belt" (*art by Ricardo Pustanio*).

Mom never had anybody baby-sit us, and she told the doctor this.

On a Monday, Mom woke Bobby for school. He said his arm really hurt, and he started screaming.

Mom rushed him to the hospital. His arm was broken. I learned from a neighbor while Bobby and Mom were in the hospital that a man used to live in that house in the 1960s with his two sons and daughter. They were all under seven years of age. He beat them, and one, the older son, even died from a beating. He was arrested, and killed himself in jail.

The younger boy and girl still lived in the neighborhood. I went to school with one of their children, and I went over to visit. When Mom came to pick me up, the daughter noticed Bobby's broken arm. She asked Mom what happened, and Mom told her of the strange things that had been happening in Bobby's room.

The girl got a look of terrible fear on her face. She advised Mom to move away. She said she didn't know about ghosts, but she was sure Bobby was in danger.

The neighborhood was going to the dogs anyway, so we decided to move. We heard that a few months later that a family had moved in with a month old baby. The next day, the baby was found dead in its crib. It had a huge cut across its chest, and a bruised face. I guess you couldn't even recognize the baby.

The parents were tried for child abuse and the death, but no evidence was ever found that they did anything to their baby so they were released.

I am nineteen now. I was about ten years old when all this went on, but I remember enough to know that the ghost of that terrible man was abusing my brother.

The Creature at the Foot of Her Bed

BY JANNICE FADLEY

"It was a very bright moonlit night," Jannice said. "I was in my bed and wide awake enjoying the moonlight. Everyone else was asleep. The moon was directly in line with my large window which had no curtains on it so my room was bright enough to read by. This window was at the foot of my bed to the left. Next to it on the wall facing my bed was another large window with no curtains. To

the right of the end of my bed was the opening into my room. There was no door. My room had been added on and opened into my brothers' room."

Here is Jannice's recollection of the nightmarish encounter:

It is a straight line of doors from the outside door to my brothers' door to my door opening. It is very easy and quick to move from outdoors to my room. The outside door was never locked. We lived in the country, and all the neighbors were either friends or family.

I had a bad feeling come over me as I was laying down in my bed. I heard the outside door open and close softly. I heard someone walk across the living room into my brothers' room and then into my room. I was laying down so I could not see the end of my bed. I was too terrified to look. I knew something horrible was standing there. I do not know how long I laid there too scared to look. I finally could not stand it anymore and sat up in bed.

It was not a person at all. I sat there frozen looking at it standing in the bright moonlight right at the end of my bed. It was inches from the end of my bed. Its body was facing the window to the left of the end of my bed and it was hunched over as it was taller than my low ceiling. Its hideous face was turned towards me with its arms held as if creeping. Its body was covered in hair that looked dark.

It was glaring at me. I could feel it was furious with me for not submitting to them. I thought it was going to kill me. I tried to scream but I could not make a sound. I was trapped in my bedroom with a hairy monster that hated me and wanted me dead.

I did what any little girl would do. I lay back down and covered my head expecting to be killed at any moment. I heard it go back out of my room, through my brothers' room, across the living room and back out the door. I still could not make a sound.

When I finally got my voice back, I screamed for my mom. She asked what was wrong from her bed and I hysterically told her what I had seen. She told me it was a dream and to go back to sleep.

I did not go back to sleep.

It was not a dream.

She did not even come to calm me down. I never trusted her after that.

DEMONS FROM THE DARKSIDE

Recently my friend and colleague cryptozoologist Paul Bartholomew of White-hall, New York, informed me of a terrifying experience that a National Guardsman had undergone in the fall of October 1987. Because of his fear of the laughter barrier, he had waited 20 years to share his nightmarish encounter.

The guardsman had been awakened one night by the sound of his kitchen door being slammed open. He heard furniture being tossed around his living room.

Picking up a baseball bat to defend himself, he decided to go downstairs and rout the intruder (or intruders), the guardsman found that the uninvited visitor had ascended the stairs to confront him in his bedroom.

The guardsman found himself paralyzed, unable to move, as his descent was blocked by a six-foot-five inch, 300-pound entity that had red-glowing eyes and that smelled like rotten eggs.

The guardsman, being a religious man, shouted out a prayer—and the creature vanished.

Overcome by the bizarre and frightening circumstances, the guardsman collapsed back on his bed and awakened in the morning wondering if he had just experienced the worst dream of his life.

When he went downstairs, however, he found the front door wide open and his furniture either broken or thrown about from room to room.

Over twenty years later, the guardsman wondered aloud to Paul Bartholomew if he had encountered an angry Bigfoot or a malicious demon.

In essence, the guardsman had expressed a persistent enigma that often arises when one is monster hunting: Are there times when we encounter an entity that has intruded into our reality from a world unseen?

Monsters or Demons … or Both?

The folklore of Tibet includes numerous accounts of malignant, shape-shifting demons that lurk near trees, rocks, lakes, and many other places to seize men and animals and suck away their vital breath and life force. One of the most vicious of these entities is the Thags yang, a demon that can appear as a tiger, a man, or a weretiger. The terrible Thags yang follow those travelers who are not sufficiently protected by strong spiritual beliefs and drain their life essence from them. They also lurk near villages, seeking out the weak and the foolish who do not utter their prayers of protection.

> *The guardsman had been awakened one night by the sound of his kitchen door being slammed open. He heard furniture being tossed around his living room.*

Could our guardsman from New York have come face-to-face with such a being? Could his home have been invaded by a demon that could appear as a Bigfoot-type creature?

How a demon is defined is determined in large part by who is framing the definition.

When Socrates spoke of consulting his "daimon," he was not referring to an evil spirit or a fallen angel, but to his tutelary spirit. The ancient Greeks believed that everyone had an attendant entity to which he or she might turn for advice in dealing with life's problems.

The Romans called their "daimon," their guardian angel, a "genius," which could also be interpreted as roughly analogous to the soul.

Since those days of antiquity, however, most people would call Socrates's "daimon," a spirit guide; a "genius" is a mortal human being of high intelligence; and a "demon" has through millennia of the Abrahamic religious come to refer to the fallen angels who rebelled against the Creator and who seek to work harm against humankind.

While, indeed, there may well be fallen angels, demons are not members of that rebellious band of entities.

The Pattern Profile of a Demon

Demons are inhabitants from another dimension, another plane of being. They have never been angels and they have never been human—although they may adapt the trappings of a ghost of a dearly departed one if it will serve their ultimate purpose—which is to prey upon the human soul.

Demons are the ultimate shape-shifters, for they can manifest in any form they choose. They are unlikely to appear as slit-eyed, reptilian monsters, however, for then they would be easily recognized as evil-doers. They are more likely to appear to their potential victims in as an attractive, seductive, and alluring a manner as possible.

The main task of demons is to disseminate errors among humankind and to deceive mortals into committing evil deeds, which, in turn, "feeds" them. The Middle Ages in Europe was a devil-infested period, and perhaps the demon horde's greatest accomplishment lay in deceiving officials of the Church that there were millions of witches, werewolves, vampires, and other shape-shifters that required the torture chamber and deserved death by burning at the stake.

Throughout the centuries, the wisest priests among their flocks have acknowledged that it is very difficult to develop an adequate litmus test that will unfailingly distinguish between good angels and bad ones. Unless one is pure in heart, mind, and soul, it is an exceedingly complex task to discern accurately the true nature of spirits. It is generally known that good spirits will never attempt to interfere with our free will or possess our physical body. And, on the other hand, it is acknowledged that demons, the evil ones, desire the physical body of the human. In fact, they must have it in order to experience earthly pleasures and to work spiritual harm against other humans.

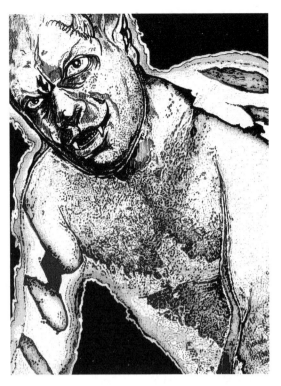

Demons are inhabitants from another dimension, another plane of being. They have never been angels and they have never been human (*art by Ricardo Pustanio*).

The Demonic Power of Illusion

Demonic entities are credited with will and intellect that are directed toward evil as they exert their malevolent powers. When these evil spirits penetrate the world and the circumstances of human life, they conceal themselves in every aspect of earthly existence. When it serves their purpose, they may assume the form of a lovely woman or a handsome man to seduce a confused human. These entities are succubi (the voluptuous and mysterious female night visitors) and the incubi (the buff and virile male lovers who disappear after planting their demon seed.) Artist and illustrator Wm. Michael Mott speaks to this demonic power of illusion very well in his superb Caverns, Cauldrons, and Concealed Creatures:

As of late, conspiracy and UFO literature alike abound with similar accounts [of entity/human sexual intercourse], the only difference being that most of the reptilian seducers or rapists are male, and the human victims are female. Often, these accounts also involve abduction to underground bases or caverns, cavern-worlds, or close proximity to a cave or cavern in which the rape takes place.

Another version of the succubus or incubus attack or rape occurs when the percipient awakens fully (at least mentally), can see and feel, but can't move a muscle.

Medical science refers to all such cases as sleep paralysis, and states that the condition is due to an awakened mental state, while the body is still asleep, or the person is in a hypnogogic state.... Often these incidents are accompanied by waking dreams or hallucinations, in which the victim feels, senses, or sees someone or something else in the room or beside the bed, or even feels a bodily or electrical pressure or weight descend upon them. A few female victims have reported actual physical intercourse with an unseen entity or group of entities, and this has, according to them, led to rape by invisible presences at later times, when alone and fully awake.

Some see a psychological connection or cause to the latter type of supposed "hallucination," often arising, in theory, from childhood trauma or molestation. But not all experiencers have such a thing in their chest of childhood memories or secrets. Some victims have noted that the emotion of fear increases the severity and frequency of the attacks, while praying to God for deliverance halts them, or ends the phenomenon completely. Rather than a hallucination, this would seem to indicate a conflict with the unseen, operating on the terms of the spiritual world.

This calls into question the nature of this intrusive reality, and its intrusive, abusive inhabitants. Some evidence indicates a physical reality that requires blood, seminal matter, sperm and ova, and perhaps an ongoing ritualistic pattern of inflicting pain, fear, desire, and even servitude, for purposes of emotional or energy vampirism and behavioral conditioning. Folktales and mystical traditions are filled with accounts of these beings, and their ability to shape-shift, as well as alter their forms, from seemingly 'fleshly,' to barely substantial or opaque, to absolutely transparent or invisible.... The apostle Paul may have been alluding to this in Ephesians 6:12, when he named a hierarchy of enemies who oppress and victimize mankind, and oppose the will of their Creator (items in brackets are mine—W.M.M.):

> For we wrestle not against flesh and blood, but against principalities [fallen angelic types and kingdoms], against powers [fallen angels], against the rulers of the darkness of this world [the unseen predators under discussion here, as well as possibly those human beings who interact with or serve them], and against spiritual wickedness in high places [the etheric and ufological connection, which has been often noted by researchers].

Visitors from the Unseen World

When we consider all of the remarkable discoveries in physics in the last few decades, acceptance of the world of the unseen should have been made much easier. The invisible reality of quarks and atoms and molecules and electrons that form our very existence are now able to be seen with the powerful microscopes and telescopes that can penetrate and examine both the inner space and the outer space that have for centuries been withheld from mortal eyes. The reality of the unseen spirit world should no longer require a great stretch of imagination or a mighty leap of faith. It simply needs to be better identified and understood.

When we speak of spirit, we are speaking of something that is eternal, nonmaterial, and beyond time and space. Spirit is unchangeable, enduring, and above the laws of nature.

Matter, on the other hand, is ephemeral, transient, material, subject to change in space and time.

Regardless of the theories of quantum mechanics or the large numbers of serious scientists beginning to theorize about ten or more planes of reality, for the great majority of contemporary humanity accounts of demons are found only in grisly novels that depict vicious serial killers or in eerie horror stories that tell of tormented men and women who hear voices that order them to kill their victims in horrid ways. And, of course, there are the blockbuster movies that depict ingenious mass murderers who dissect and digest parts of their victims with fine wine and fava beans while they make fools of the authorities.

All of these grim depictions of the criminal mind are devised to cause a shudder of primal fear within the reader or the viewer, but the effect is temporary. The book is ended. The theater lights come up. One can sigh, perhaps even chuckle wryly at the author's or screenwriter's rather perverse imagination, for these vivid works of fiction and cinematic chillers are just that—made up stories. We are relieved to put the book aside or leave the theater, knowing that the monsters that these tales portray are not real. They are only creatures born somewhere in the darkside of a writer's psyche.

There are, however, tortured individuals in real-life who heed fiendish commands to kill. There are men and women who really hear demon voices that demand unquestioning obedience.

Those possessed by demons are truly human monsters, willful agents of death, who practice ritual slayings, human sacrifice, and large scale slaughter of innocent victims.

These disciples of murder and mayhem are very real.

And so are the demons who scream at them relentlessly to do their awful bidding and kill without mercy.

Demons Are Real

By now many readers are saying to themselves that they have certainly heard of demented people who claim that demonic voices told them to

Demonic entities are credited with will and intellect that are directed toward evil as they exert their malevolent powers. When it serves their purpose, they may assume the form of a lovely woman or a handsome man to seduce a confused human (*art by Dan Wolfman Allen*).

commit murder. Bu these individuals are sick. Demons are not real. These human monsters are insane, but they are not actually possessed. Demon possession in this day and age? That kind of thinking is a superstitious throwback to the Middle Ages.

Here is what Dr. Morton Kelsey, an Episcopal priest and noted Norte Dame emeritus professor of theology, has to say about that old "superstitious" belief: "Most people in the modern world consider themselves too sophisticated and too intelligent to be concerned with demons. But in thirty years of study, I have seen the effect of demons upon humans."

Dr. Kelsey maintains that demons are real and can invade the minds of humans. Demons are not the figment of the imagination, but are negative, destructive spiritual forces that seek to destroy the possessed host body and everyone with whom that person comes into contact.

All right, you say, but Dr. Kelsey is a priest, a theologian. He's supposed to believe in demons.

Then take into serious consideration the comments of Dr. Ralph Allison, retired senior psychiatrist at the California state prison in San Luis Obispo:

> My conclusion after thirty years of observing over one thousand disturbed patients is that some of them act in a bizarre fashion due to possession by spirits. The spirit may be that of a human being who died. Or it may be a spirit entity that has never been a human being and sometimes identifies itself as a demon, an agent of evil.

Dr. Wilson Van Dusen (1923–2005), a university professor who served as chief psychologist at Mendocino State Hospital, boldly stated his opinion that many patients in mental hospitals are possessed by demons: "I am totally convinced that there are entities that can possess our minds and our bodies," he said. "I have even been able to speak directly to demons. I have heard their own guttural, other-world voices."

And all too often, those hellish guttural voices commanded their possessed hosts to kill, to offer human sacrifice to Satan.

In a report released by the American Psychological Evaluation Corporation, Dr. Andrew Blankley, a sociologist, issued alarming statements about the rise in contemporary sacrificial cults, warning that society at large might expect a "serious menace" to come. According to Dr. Blankley, human sacrifice constitutes an alarming trend in new religious cults: "Desperate people are seeking dramatic revelation and simplistic answers to complex social problems. They are attracted to fringe groups who provide the ritualistic irrationality that they crave. In the last ten years, fringe rituals often include the sacrifice of a human being."

Need more proof than a sociologist's alarming report?

A Gallup Poll taken in 2001 stated that 41 percent of North Americans believed in demons. In 2007, the Pew Poll found that the number of those who recognized the power of demons had risen to 68 percent and that many individuals surveyed claimed an actual encounter with such an entity.

Dr. Al Carlisle of the Utah State Prison System estimated that between 40,000 and 60,000 humans are killed through ritual homicides in the United States every year. In the Las Vegas area alone, Dr. Carlisle asserts, as many as 600 people may die in demon-inspired ceremonies each year. Mutilated bodies of hitch-hikers and transients are being found in forested regions, beside lonely desert road, and alongside river banks—their hearts and lungs removed, strips of flesh slashed from their bodies.

Devil-worshipping rites are being held in our state and national parks. Blood is mixed with beer and drunk by all participants.

Devil-worshipping rites are being held in our state and national parks. Blood is mixed with beer and drunk by all participants. Human bone fragments, teeth, and pieces of flesh are discovered in the ashes of campfires.

Bikers, arrested on other charges, confess to being part of a nationwide kidnapping ring that captures virginal young men and women for sale to satanic cults both here and in Europe. The youthful victims are marked for human sacrifice.

The terrible power that drives and compels those obsessed with sacrificial murders is something so much more insidiously evil and complex than can be created by the distortion of creeds, ecclesiasticisms, or belief structures. The monstrous voices that command men and women to kill others are not those of mortals.

A Demonic Line-up of Those Who Obeyed Their Orders to Kill

Demon voices—whether you prefer to identify them as symbolical of some strain of psychopathology or as literal perverse and evil entities—can utter the command to kill to a quiet, conventionally-reared individual just as readily as to a disheveled disciple of the iconoclastic. However one wishes to identify these Parasites of the Spirit, they have the ability to sense and to seize the moments of vulnerability in the strongest of men and women. They possess the uncanny power of knowing the precise moments when even the most righteous can be tempted, when even the most devout can be led astray, when the most disciplined moralist may be seduced. Here are a number of cases of men and women possessed by demons and commanded to kill:

- On January 5, 1990, authorities searching an Ohio farm commune found the slain bodies of a family of five—all victims of human sacrifice. Jeffrey Lunden, a self-declared prophet of a new religion, had decreed the sacrifices necessary to persuade the "forces" to present the cult with a magical golden sword.

- Daniel Rakowitz couldn't quite understand whether or not the voices said that he was actually Jesus reborn, but he knew that they were insistent that he was a messiah. The voices also told him to form a new religion to be named the Church of 966. To ensure his messiahship, in September of 1989, he sacrificed his girlfriend.

- Once they had accepted Satan as their savior, heavy metal, grass, and sex parties just weren't enough. Soon the demon voices ordered Terry Belcher, the young high priest of the cult, to sacrifice Theresa, one of his followers, in January 1988.

The Devil's Dossier on the U.S. Presidency is a frightening one:

- When John Wilkes was but an infant in his crib, Asia Booth had a horrid vision of her son being one day transformed into a monster—but it is unlikely her prophecy revealed that he would assassinate President Abraham Lincoln.

- On the morning of July 2, 1881, Charles Guiteau could no longer resist the demon voices that commanded him to kill President James Garfield. The President clung to life through the agony of a long summer before yielding to the assassin's bullet in his back. Guiteau was relieved that he had fulfilled his mission. He went to the gallows confident that the demon he hailed as "Lordy" would take care of him in the afterlife.

- Lee Harvey Oswald was obsessed with his fears that "devilmen" would usurp all earthly governments. President John Fitzgerald Kennedy served as a kind of sacrifice to keep them at bay.

- Sirhan Sirhan's legal defense in his trial for the murder of Robert Kennedy strongly considered arguing that he had been possessed by the fanatical spirit of a dead Arab nationalist.

- Squeaky Fromme, one of Charles Manson's family, received mental instructions from her imprisoned master to murder President Gerald Ford on August 5, 1975.

- John Hinckley was literally possessed with the impulse that the assassination of Ronald Reagan would somehow impress a young actress.

- On January 11, 1990, the Secret Service arrested John S. Daughetee, a medical school dropout, who was acting under the orders of his "voices" when he robbed eight banks to finance his assassination attempts on Presidents Reagan and Bush.

The list of demon-inspired killers goes on:

- Earle Leonard Nelson was a quiet boy, an avid student of the Bible, who aspired one day to be a minister. And then there was the accident, the blow to the head that unleashed the terrible voices that commanded him to kill all the Jezebels of the world. Somehow equating hardworking landladies with prostitutes, Nelson became the "Gorilla Man" who strangled 22 female victims before he was captured and the demonic voices were silenced.

- The voices told Herbert Mullin that California was about to be destroyed by a cataclysmic earthquake and a giant tidal wave unless he immediately began sacrificing human life to Satan. The voices nullified Mullin's squeamishness

The worship of the horned image of Satan has been a trait among a number of serial killers (*iStock*).

by declaring that the sacrificial victims would actually be grateful for being given the opportunity to serve the greater good of California. Before he was stopped on February 13, 1972, Mullin had sacrificed thirteen victims and, in his mind, had become the Savior of California.

- Albert Fish killed and ate between eight and fifteen children, castrated a large number of small boys, and molested more than 100 children during the course of a long criminal career. Among his perversions: he was the writer of obscene letters, a coprophage (eater of excrements), a pedophile, a masochist who inserted needles into his body, a sadist, vampire, cannibal, and lust-murderer. All was well in Fish's worldview, however, because the voices had informed him that he was the new messiah, come to be an instrument of God's vengeance upon a sinful and depraved humanity. When he was executed in 1935, he displayed no fear, seeming to take an interest and even pleasure in the operation of the electric chair.

- In October 1981, Satanic High Priest Robin Gecht and three of his followers were arrested following a series of grisly cannibalistic murders in Chicago. Gecht heeded the demonic voices that ordered him to conduct elaborate sadistic rituals of mutilations and the eating of the flesh of their female victims.

- When the jury passed sentence on Richard Ramirez in 1985, he was convicted of twelve first-degree murders and 30 other major offenses of rape and burglary. Throughout his trial, the infamous "Night Stalker" flashed the devil's pentagram scratched into his hand or placed his fingers to the side of his head to fashion demon's horns. Defiantly, he declared his worship of Satan.

- In 1977, young Jimmy Riva began to hear the voices that told him to haunt graveyards and to kill small animals and drink their blood. Eventually, on a cold, rainy day in April 1980, the demon whispers pronounced him a vampire who would gain strength from drinking his grandmother's blood.

- In May 1983, Michael and Suzan Carlson went on trial in San Francisco for obeying their demonic visions to hunt down and kill three victims that the voices identified as witches that must be slain to set California right.

- While other households in the Queens district of New York watched the Thanksgiving Day parade on November 22, 1990, Joseph Bergamini honored the satanic promise that he was immortal by stabbing and killing his mother and wounding his father.

- As a teenager, Mark David Chapman had experienced a vision of Jesus which led him to become an advocate for the common man. When the visions later revealed the popular idol John Lennon was no longer a working-class hero, but a prosperous businessman, the voices decreed that the former Beatle must die on the night of December 8, 1980.

- In June 1988, Jason Rose and John Jones were indicted for the ritual sacrifice of nineteen-year-old Melissa Ann Meyer. The two Satanists cast their own fate in the form of life imprisonment when it was revealed that they videotaped their human sacrifice.

- Inspired by the vampire movie *Lost Boys*, Tim Erickson and other Minnesota teenagers decide to form a vampire cult in March 1987. They murdered a drifter and drank his blood.

- July 1991, Jaime Rodriguez is convicted and sentenced to life for beheading a teenage runaway as a sacrifice to Satan. He also severed all of her fingers to wear as a charm around his neck. Augustin Pena, a fellow Satanist, kept the girl's head in his refrigerator.

- April 1994, Carey Grayson and three others murdered a female hitchhiker in Birmingham. Police say the victim was mutilated in an apparent ritual that involved cannibalism.

- May 1996, three Satanists in San Luis Obispo tortured and murdered a fifteen-year-old girl. The demon-possessed tell arresting officers that they hoped the sacrifice of a virgin would put them in good with Satan.

- September 1997, a teenager in Kobe, Japan, claimed that an evil spirit possessed him when he bludgeoned to death a primary school girl and killed and decapitated an eleven-year-old boy.

- January 1998, Charity Miranda, a 17-year-old cheerleader from New York, was killed by her mother who feared that the girl was possessed by demons. The teenager's sisters witnessed the murder and chanted and prayed over Charity's body.

- October 2000, Brandi Blackbear, a 15-year-old Oklahoma high school student, was suspended for fifteen days for casting a spell on her teacher and causing her to become ill.

- January 2008, Lawrence Douglas Harris, Sr., murdered his two stepdaughters in their Sioux City, Iowa, home after an ill-performed ritual caused the casting of a spell to go bad.

DINOSAURS THAT LIVE AND PROWL IN THE JUNGLES

"**T**he place is called Dafara. It is an anomaly in the flat landscape that stretches for miles in all directions in Africa. It is as if the earth collapsed here, like God punched a hole in the ground and the darkness came flooding in," Pastor Robin Swope recalled. Today, he is known as the Paranormal Pastor (http://theparanormalpastor.blogspot.com/); in that time, he was Pastor Swope, serving as a missionary in a remote region of Africa.

Do Not Go in the Water or the God Will Eat You Alive!

BY PASTOR ROBIN SWOPE

The local missionaries call it "The Rocks," because the 100-meter diameter hole in the earth is edged by sharp shale cliffs. There is a single trail that leads through the dense foliage to the bottom of the ravine that gently angles down into a scene that is both otherworldly and frightening.

The first thing you notice is the stench. It is a dank putrid odor of blood, bile, and rotting gore that permeates the entire valley. It is the odor of death.

The second thing you notice is the blood. At first glance it looks as if the entire floor of the ravine is covered in dark, thick blood. Every rock has been used to carve the animals that have been brought down the path for sacrifice, and it is not only covered in the thick fluid of life but indistinguishable pieces of flesh and bone that lay scattered about as evidence of the hecatomb butchery that befalls the victims of the sacred god—a god that dwells in the dark recesses of the watery abyss that dominates the center of the chasm.

The entrance to the Dafara chasm is permeated by the rank smell of blood and rotting flesh, according to Pastor Robin Swope (*photo by Pastor Robin Swope*).

The murky pond is roughly kidney-shaped and covers an area just slightly smaller than that of an Olympic-sized pool. How deep it is, no one can know since the fertility god that abides here is no idol made out of wood or stone. No, the fertility god that demands the sacrifice of highly prized livestock is a living creature. A flesh-eating aquatic creature of shocking proportions that lives in a small lake far from any other source of fresh flowing water.

The dark creature is rumored to have grown to such enormous size not only because of its taste for raw flesh, but also because of the occult forces which it allegedly wields. The villagers of Koro and the surrounding area flock here so that their infertile women may bear healthy offspring. Famine has decimated the area population, and the infant mortality rate is close to 10 percent.

The nationals struggle to eke out the most meager of existence. Yet they offer up what sometimes is their only source of protein in order to procure the healthy birth of a child. They believe if they do not sacrifice to the god in the water, they risk not only the loss of their children that are still in utero, but they flirt with the chance that they themselves might become sterile. If that curse should be upon them, any hope for any offspring will be denied them forever. They live in darkness and fear, enslaved to the power of the behemoth beneath the water of Dafara.

The place where animals were sacrificed in Dafara for the god that dwells at the center of the chasm (*photo by Pastor Robin Swope*).

It is a fear that also lives in legend. You cannot go in the water of Dafara. The god will eat you alive.

Such was the fate of the first Western explorer who happened upon the site in the middle of the nineteenth century. It is rumored that he scoffed at the natives' superstitions and dove off the cliffs into the milky water of the pool.

He never surfaced.

Days later they found his bones along the shore.

I witnessed the creature at Dafara in the summer of 1986. I was on a missionary tour in the city of Bobo Dioulasso, and some of the long-term missionaries wanted me to take a look at the site.

As the Africans approached the water's edge they offered pieces of flesh by throwing them into the cloudy water.

Silently, a large hump broke the surface. Its skin was smooth and black without any noticeable dorsal fin. The creature's back rose out of the water until the enormity of its size could be revealed.

At the time I estimated it to be the size of a large couch that was in the lobby of the missionary station where we were currently residing. It was about seven feet long. I saw no other feature on the animal, neither eyes nor mouth—just the large hump and the splashing about of something a few inches away from it where the meat had been thrown.

After it had finished a small chicken, the ebony mass submerged and we did not see it again.

On the way up the path to our Rover, I asked our host what exactly it was that we had just seen lurking in that murky water. He said he had no idea. He had been stationed there for almost ten years, and he had never had the opportunity to actually see anything more than what we had just beheld ourselves.

"It's some kind of fish I think," he finally gave an opinion. "But I have never seen one that large."

If it was a fish, I asked him how in the world it got there. The nearest river, the Upper Volta, was over 50 miles away. He gave me an odd look that told me he thought it was beyond any rational explanation.

What was that enormous creature in the ravine's lake?

Some supernatural being that offered fertility as a reward for being well fed?

Or an unknown local creature that for some reason had become trapped in this remote location and spawned a population that had grown to enormous size?

Quite honestly, the only aquatic creature that can grow to even close that size is the African Catfish, *Heterobrachus bidorsalis*.

They are common in the areas of the Upper Volta, and they do grow to a great size. A photo was once sent to me by a Missionary friend stationed in Burkina Faso showing his kids feeding some African Catfish at a pond by the Volta.

The only problem is that the African Catfish only grows to 1.5 meters. The ones in the picture were about four feet long, falling in line with the average length.

Could it be that in the distant past a group of *Heterobrachus bidorsalis* might have found its way to the ravine through a long dried up tributary of the Upper Volta? Did the constant attention from the local cultists cause them to grow to such enormous size? Or are there more sinister forces at work deep below the surface of the lake at Dafara?

The missionaries and locals have no idea.

They just make sure that they never go for a dip in the pond.

The Search for Mokele-Mbembe, Who Stops the Flow of Rivers

For over 200 years, stories have emerged from the swamps, rivers, and lakes of African jungles that there is a brownish-gray, elephant-sized creature with a reptilian tail and a long, flexible neck. The native people call it "Mokele-mbembe" ("the one who stops the flow of rivers") or "emela-ntuka" ("the one who eats the tops of trees").

In 1980, Dr. Roy P. Mackal, a distinguished biochemist, engineer, and biologist, who has spent most of his academic career at the University of Chicago, led an expedition into African swamps that were said to be "Mokey's" hangouts. After numerous interviews with the native inhabitants and with those who had seen the creature in the rivers, Dr. Mackal stated that the descriptions of the beast would fit that of a sauropod, the giant plant-eating reptile that supposedly became extinct about 60 million years ago. In 1987, Dr. Mackal's *A Living Dinosaur? In Search of Mokele-Mbembe* was published, indicating his dedication to investigating reports of "impossible" creatures.

J. Richard Greenwell (1942–2005), an expedition member from Tucson, reported his discovery of huge tracks that led into the Likouala River. In his opinion, no animal smaller than an elephant could have left such a path through the thickets near the river, and, Greenwell noted, elephants always leave an exit trail when they leave a river. Whatever left these massive prints made no such sign of an exit, which may indicate that Mokey is a marine, as well as land, creature.

The Likouala swampland, Mokey's hangout, is twice the size of Scotland, and thick with venomous snakes and disease-bearing insects. Even something as large as the Mokele-mbembe is said to be, it would not be easy to find it.

In September 1981, Herman Regusters (d. December 19, 2005) an aerospace engineer from South Pasadena, and his wife, Kia, became the first Westerners to reach Lake Tele, Congo. On November 28, they claimed to have seen and to have photographed a dinosaur-like animal in a remote African lake. Mrs. Regusters said that the gigantic reptile was dark red with a long, thick neck, and longer than two hippopotamuses. Unfortunately, the photograph taken by the Regusters was judged by others as being rather fuzzy, and their tape recording of the "roaring trumpeting noise" heard frequently around Lake Tele, was impossible to identify.

Although the beast was said most often to be herbivorous, it also used its great tail to assist in tipping over an elephant or a hippopotamus.

In 1986, Rory Nugent was in the Likouala Swamp near Lake Tele when he saw a long, thin neck come up out of the water. The creature gave every appearance of being a dinosaur. Nugent immediately took two photographs of the monster before it submerged.

Nugent's moment of triumph was dashed when he was stopped from re-entering his canoe by the rifles of his guides. They ordered him to destroy the film or they would take the camera from him. Angrily, they made their point perfectly clear that if he did not do so at once, the great creature would pursue them and kill all of them before they could leave the lake.

Reluctantly, Nugent yielded to their demands. He was well aware that the Mokele-mbembe was extremely aggressive and had been known to flip over canoes with its tail, then chomp down on the occupants with its huge teeth. Although the beast was said most often to be herbivorous, it also used its great tail to assist in tipping over an elephant or a hippopotamus.

Dr. Bill Gibbons, a zoologist who specializes in attempting to track down new species and has tracked the Mokele-mbembe, told the (London) *Sunday Times* [June 3, 1999] that he is certain that Mokele-mbembe exists. According to Dr. Gibbons, cryptozoologists had heard reports that hunters from the Kabonga tribe had killed a Mokele-mbembe and had tried to eat it. Its flesh proved inedible and the carcass was left to rot and be gnawed and pecked at by scavengers.

In 1996, zoologist Professor Michelle Gupton told the British press that she was attacked by a huge water monster as she investigated the shoreline of Lake Tele. According to Ms. Gupton, the brownish-gray creature about the size of an elephant suddenly rose out of the waters of the lake right in front of her. Awestruck, she reached out to touch its smooth skin.

That was a nearly fatal mistake on the part of the zoologist. The monster snapped at her with its huge teeth, slashing out a foot-long slice of skin on the side of her stomach.

Ms. Gupton said that she passed out from the pain and was later rescued by members of her party who had been searching the surrounding jungle for signs of Mokele-mbembe. She was rushed to a hospital where her wound was treated. In her considered opinion, her experience proves that dinosaurs are far from extinct.

An Extinct Serpentine Monster
Who Nearly Grabbed a South Dakota Farmer

In the mid-1930s, a high school student at Frederick, South Dakota, Don Neff, found some strange looking teeth on the banks of the Elm River. After doing some investigating, the inquisitive student found the remains of a giant 28-foot marine lizard buried in the shale and mud along the river.

When brought to his attention, Professor James Bump, director of the museum of the State School of Mines, in Rapid City, South Dakota, said that the remains had probably been there for "several million years." Professor Bump had his degree in metallurgy, but as director of the museum, he was becoming increasingly interested in the discovery of such fossils as the high school boy had brought to him. Bump's first estimate of "several million years" for the marine creature was later revised when the species was identified as a mosasaur, which had been supposedly extinct for 130 million years.

Prof. Bump's excavation was considered a great archeological find, and in 1940 he and his associates made an important collection of Whitneyan fossils from south of the White River and east of Rockyford under the sponsorship of the National Geographic Society.

The area residents came by from time to time to watch the professors making their excavations and finding their bones, but they had some misgivings about the reputed evidence that such huge creatures were long extinct.

In 1934, a farmer reported that he had to "take to the ditch" when his tractor was forced off the road by a four-legged serpentine monster that moved down the road right at him. No estimated dimensions of the creature were given, but if it were of the size that could force a tractor off the road, it was not of any known variety—and it had to be very big.

The tracks of the monster were followed across a muddy field until they came to the edge of Lake Campbell. Here the monster eased itself into the water and disappeared.

Similar tracks have been seen frequently in the area since the 1934 sighting of the monster, and disappearances of many lambs and pigs have occurred in the community for years without any explanation.

There Is No History Comparable to the Dragon

One of the most universal monster myths is that of the dragon. The awesome, reptile-like beasts appear in the folklore of nearly every country. What head would the Vikings have placed on their longboats if they didn't have the dragon? What would the Chinese artists, poets, and storytellers have done without the dragon to color their culture?

And the fact that the dragon was truly regarded as an actual monster rather than a myth can be demonstrated in several writings of the day. Edward Topsell, writing in his *Historie of Serpents* (1608), commented that among all the kinds of serpents, there is none comparable to the dragon, or that afforded and yielded "so much plentiful matter in history for the ample discovery of the nature thereof."

While examining the "true accounts" of dragons in the folklore and records of several cultures, one cannot help wondering if there really were dragon-like monsters prowling the earth, devouring hapless villagers, receiving periodic sacrifices of young maidens, spreading terror into the hearts of all, and being thwarted only by courageous knights? What child has not been exposed to the story of St. George's combat with the dreadful dragon? Or, on the other hand, in recent years what child has not been read tales, seen motion pictures, or heard songs of reluctant dragons, kindly dragons, affectionate dragons, magic dragons, and timid dragons as well?

> *The tracks of the monster were followed across a muddy field until they came to the edge of Lake Campbell. Here the monster eased itself into the water and disappeared.*

Behind every myth smolders a spark of truth and reality.

There are a handful of responsible scientists who consider it possible that a number of dinosaurs might have survived into the Age of Man and that a few of their dwindling numbers still thrive today in thick jungles and at great ocean depths. If our early ancestors served as snacks for such monsters, the "dragon" would certainly have survived in our species memory. And then there are those who argue that our evolutionary time table is inaccurate and that a race of early humans or humanoids may have existed during the Age of Reptiles, something like 70 million years ago.

Early in January 1970, the *London Express Service* carried an item relating the discovery of a set of cave paintings which had been found in the Gorozamzi Hills,

While examining the "true accounts" of dragons in the folklore and records of several cultures, one can't help wondering if there once really were dragon-like monsters prowling the earth (**art by Ricardo Pustanio**).

twenty-five miles from Salisbury in Rhodesia. According to the news story, the paintings included an accurate representation of a brontosaurus, the 67-foot, 30-ton behemoth that scientists insist became extinct millions of years before man achieved his earthly path.

Experts agree that the paintings were done by bushmen who ruled Rhodesia from about 1500 B.C.E. until a few hundred years ago. The experts also agree that the bushmen only painted from life. This belief is borne out by the other Gorozamzi Hills cave paintings, which represent elephants, hippos, deer, and giraffe.

The November 1968 issue of *Science Digest* carried the provocative thoughts of Mexican archaeologist-journalist Jose Diaz-Bolio concerning his discovery of an ancient Mayan relief sculpture of a peculiar serpent-bird found in the ruins of Tajin, located in Totonacapan in the northeastern section of Veracruz, Mexico. Diaz-Bolio suggested that the serpent-bird was not merely the product of Mayan flights of fancy, but a realistic representation of an animal that lived during the period of the ancient Mayans—1,000 to 5,000 years ago.

A startling evolutionary oddity would have been manifested if such serpent-birds were contemporary with the ancient Mayan culture, for creatures with such characteristics are believed to have disappeared 130 million years ago. The *archaeornis* and *archaeopteryx*, to which the sculpture bears a resemblance, were flying reptiles that became extinct during the Mesozoic age. Such a huge reptile flapping about the countryside of early Europe or Asia could certainly fit even the most dramatic descriptions of a dragon.

Even a handful of such ancient monsters existing in isolated lakes and forested valleys would not have gone unnoticed, even in the sparsely populated Europe of the Dark Ages. The discovery of even just a few of these great reptiles would have given rise to a far-reaching legend.

The Hideous Piasa, Winged Devourer of Native People

From the mouth of the Illinois River at Grafton to Alton (Illinois), a distance of twenty miles, the Mississippi River runs from west to east, and its north bank (the Illinois side) is a high bluff. When the first white men explored the area, they found that some unknown muralist from some forgotten tribal culture had engraved and painted hideous depictions of two gigantic, winged monsters. The petroglyphs were each about thirty feet in length and twelve feet in height.

Father Marquette, the celebrated Jesuit priest-explorer, wrote in his journals of discoveries of the Mississippi, published in Paris in 1681: "As we were descending the river we saw high rocks with hideous monsters painted on them and upon which the bravest Indian dare not look. They [have] head and horns like a goat; their eyes are red; [they have a] beard like a tiger's and a face like a man's. Their tails are so long that they pass over their bodies and between their legs under their bodies, ending like a fish's tail. They are painted red, green, and black, and so well drawn that I could not believe they were drawn by the Indians, and for what purpose they were drawn seems to me a mystery."

The two enormously large petroglyphs were clearly visible on the north bank of the Mississippi, immediately where the Illinois State Prison was later built at Alton. Traces of their outlines remained until the limestone on which they had been engraved was quarried by the convicts in about 1856.

In his 48-page booklet, *The Piasa; or, The Devil Among the Indians* (Morris, IL, 1887) P. A. Armstrong described the creatures as having "the wings of a bat, but of the shape of an eagle.... They also had four legs, each supplied with eagle-shaped talons. The combination and blending together of the master species of the earth, sea, and air ... so as to present the leading and most terrific characteristics of the various species thus graphically arranged, is an absolute wonder and seems to show a vastly superior knowledge of animal, fowl, reptile, and fish nature than has been accorded to the Indian."

Sometime in the 1840s, Professor John Russell of Jersey County, Illinois, explored the caves that the Piasa were said to have inhabited and reported "innumerable human bones littering the stone floors." Although Professor Russell suggested the skeletal fragments offered mute testimony to the Amerindians' account of a flying monster with a craving for human flesh, P. A. Armstrong cautioned his readers that the cave may have been utilized as a burial place by the Mound Builders, whose impressive earthen handiwork can be found in that same area.

Armstrong, on the other hand, is not opposed to considering how accurately the unknown Amerindian artists managed to incorporate biblical descriptions of the Devil in their artwork:

> Here do we behold the wings and talons of the eagle, united to the body of the dragon or alligator, with the face of a man, the horns of the black-tailed deer or elk, the nostrils of the hippopotamus, the teeth and beard of the tiger, the ears of the fox, and the tail of the serpent, or fish, with the scales of the salamander, so nicely arranged and fitted together as to preserve the distinctive characteristics of each and produce a picture of all that is the most horrible in animal, fowl, fish, and reptile in a single graphic view.... The dragon ... is the prototype and representative of Satan, and the serpent is his twin brother, while man is the image of his Maker....

The Piasa was generally feared because of its propensity for snatching tribespeople and making off with them. Professor John Russell published an account of the

Piasa's insatiable appetite for human flesh in the 1848 July issue of *The Evangelical Magazine and Gospel Advocate*:

> P. A. Armstrong described the creatures as having "the wings of a bat, but of the shape of an eagle's.... They also had four legs, each supplied with eagle-shaped talons."

He [the Piasa] was as artful as he was powerful, and would dart suddenly and unexpectedly upon an Indian, bear him off into one of the caves of the bluff and devour him. Hundreds of warriors attempted for years to destroy him, but without success. Whole villages were nearly depopulated, and consternation spread through all the tribes of the Illini.

Professor Russell describes how he and a guide managed with great effort to enter the fearsome cave of the awful Piasa:

The roof of the cavern was vaulted, the top of which was hardly less than twenty feet high. The shape of the cave was irregular, but so far as I could judge the bottom would average twenty by thirty feet. The floor of the cave throughout its whole extent was one mass of human bones. Skulls and other bones were mingled together in the utmost confusion. To what depth they extended I am unable to decide, but we dug to the depth of three or four feet in every quarter of the cavern and still found only bones. The remains of thousands must have been deposited there.

When did the Piasa conduct their fiendish foraging upon the native tribes? According to Armstrong's little book: "The time when the Piasa existed in this country, according to the Illini tradition, was many thousand moons before the arrival of the palefaces."

Were There Giant Humanoids Who Went Mano a Mano with the Great Reptiles?

If some creatures survived from the Age of Reptiles maybe they didn't all disappear around 60 million years ago. Perhaps, as some researchers suggest, there may have been giant humans on Earth who weren't so afraid of the big, bad T-Rexes.

The *New York Times* on December 2, 1930, carried an item that told of the discovery of the remains of an apparent race of giants who once lived at Sayopa, Sonora, a mining town 300 miles south of the Mexican border. A mining engineer, J. E. Coker, said that laborers clearing ranchland near the Yazui River "dug into an old cemetery where bodies of men, averaging eight feet in height, were found buried tier by tier...."

On February 14, 1936, the *New York Times* ran a piece datelined Managua, Nicaragua, which stated that the skeleton of a gigantic man, with the head missing, had been unearthed at El Boquin, on the Mico River, in the Chontales district. "The ribs are a yard long and four inches wide and the shin bone is too heavy for one man to carry. 'Chontales' is an Indian word, meaning 'wild man.'"

In its June 9, 1936 issue, the *New York Times* published an article item with a Miami, Florida dateline that told of human skeletons eight feet long imbedded in the sand of an uninhabited little island off Southern Florida. E. M. Miller, zoologist at the University of Miami, commented that the skulls were unusually thick, the jaws protruded, and the eye sockets were high in the head.

In his book *Forbidden Land*, Robert R. Lyman (1870–1963) wrote of an unknown tribe of American giants who had the added distinction of having *horns* growing from their heads:

> At Tioga Point ... a short distance from Sayre, in Bradford County [Pennsylvania] ... they uncovered an Indian mound [and] found the bones of 68 men which were believed to have been buried about the year 1200. The average height of these men was seven feet, while many were much taller. On some of the skulls, two inches above the perfectly formed forehead, were protuberances of bone, evidently horns that had been there since birth. Some of the specimens were sent to the American Investigating Museum....
>
> In December 1886, W. H. Scoville of Andrews Settlement discovered an Indian mound at Ellisburg. When opened, the skeleton of a man was found. It was close to eight feet in length.

According to their oral tradition, the Delaware tribe once lived in the western United States. At some point in their history, they migrated eastward as far as the Mississippi River, where they were joined by the Iroquois Confederacy. Both groups of people were seeking land better suited to their cultured way of life, and they continued together on their eastward trek.

Scouts sent ahead learned of a nation that inhabited the land east of the Mississippi and who had built strong, walled cities. These people were known as the Talligewi or Allegewi, after whom the Allegheny River and Mountains are named. The Allegewi were considered taller than either the Iroquois or the Delaware, and the scouts saw a good many giants walking among them.

When the two migrating tribes asked permission to pass through the land of the Allegewi, it was denied. Bitter fighting broke out, which continued for a number of years. Eventually, the superior numbers and the determination of the allies prevailed, and the Allegewi fled to the west.

The Allegewi next appear in the legends of the Lakota/Dakota (Sioux) whose tradition tells of a confrontation with a race of great stature. The Sioux, who were surely among the ablest of warriors, exterminated the Allegewi when the giants sought to settle in what is now Minnesota.

Is there any archaeological evidence to support these tribal legends and traditions?

Rising out of the earth in Ohio, Minnesota, Iowa, and other states are the huge earthworks of the mysterious "Mound Builders." The mounds scattered throughout the Midwest were apparently raised by the same unknown people, and the earthworks are extremely large.

There are a handful of responsible scientists who consider it possible that a number of dinosaurs might have survived into the Age of Man and that a few of their dwindling numbers still thrive today (*art by Bill Oliver*).

Enormous weapons, including a copper ax weighing 38 pounds, have been found in these mounds. It is difficult to imagine the average-sized Amerindian, as we first know him at the time of the European invasion, casually wielding a 38-pound ax.

The former can be works of art, the latter could be objects of religious commitment. The best proof of a race of giants in North America—or anywhere else—would be the discovery of the skeletons of these people.

Two brothers living in Dresbach, Minnesota, while in the process of enlarging their brick business, were forced to remove a number of large Indian mounds. In one of the huge earthenworks they discovered the bones of "men over eight feet tall."

In La Crescent, Minnesota, not far from Dresbach, mound diggers reportedly found large skillets and "bones of men of huge stature."

Over in Chatfield, mounds were excavated, revealing six skeletons of enormous size.

Unusually large skeletons of seven people buried head down were discovered in Clearwater. The skulls in the latter find were said to have had receding foreheads, and teeth that were double all the way around.

Other discoveries in Minnesota included "men of more than ordinary size" in Moose Island Lake; several skeletons, one of "gigantic size," in Pine City; ten skeletons "of both sexes and of gigantic size" in Warren (buried with these particular specimens were horses, badgers, and dogs).

Could these huge skeletons of gigantic "Indians" be all that remains of the last of a proud prehistoric race that defied the monster reptiles and built an extensive empire of walled cities throughout the Americas?

Giant Reptile and Giant Human Footprints in the Same Strata

Dr. Clifford Burdick (1919–2005) first began investigating "footprints in stone" in the early 1950s when the Natural Science Foundation of Los Angeles assigned him to go with four other members to examine the reported man-tracks found in strata contemporaneous with dinosaur prints in and around Glen Rose, Texas. The committee soon learned that men had been removing dinosaur and human tracks out of the limestone of the Paluxy River bed near Glen Rose since at least 1938. A Mr. A. Berry gave them an affidavit which stated that in September of that year, he and other men found "many dinosaur tracks, several saber-toothed tiger tracks, and three human tracks" in the river bed.

Dr. Burdick learned that Dr. Roland Bird, field explorer for the American Museum of Natural History of New York City, had also examined the Berry tracks. Describing them in the May 1939 edition of *Natural History* magazine, Bird admitted that he had never seen anything like the tracks, and assessed them as "perfect in every detail." But since the man-like tracks measured 16 inches from toe to heel, Bird declared that they were too large to be human, although the barefoot tracks did show all the toes, insteps, and heels in the proper proportions. When Dr. Bird made a special field trip to the Paluxy River to examine the tracks *in situ*, he became less enthusiastic about the prints in association with dinosaur tracks, because "man did not live in the age of dinosaurs."

Whatever species of creature made these tracks, it was definitely bipedal. The footprints all have about the same length of stride, which would be consistent with a man with a 16-inch foot. The shapes of the prints are more manlike than any other animal known to science.

If the tracks are accepted as being human, then scientists will be forced either to place humans or remarkable humanoids back in time to the Cretaceous period or to bring the dinosaur forward to the Pleistocene or Recent period.

In referring to the evidence of the Glen Rose tracks, Dr. Burdick said that the generally accepted theory of evolution would be dealt a lethal blow, because the geologic record of human footprints contemporaneous with dinosaur tracks "suggests that simple and complex types of life were coexistent in time past or during geologic ages.... This does not harmonize with the hypothesis that complex types of life evolved from lower or more simple forms. Evolution implies that through the geologic ages life has not only become more complex, but has increased in size. If evidence from the man-

Some researchers theorize that the "dragons" that the knights slew were survivors from the Age of the Great Reptiles (*art by Bill Oliver*).

tracks can be used as a criterion, ancient man was much larger than modern man as an average. This harmonized with most fossil life which was larger than its modern counterpart.... On the whole, biological life has had to contend with unfavorable environment which has been a factor in its degeneration, rather than its evolution."

Some might conjecture that such giant humans might have been able to band together and put up a pretty good fight against any giant reptile. And while these men may not have been "knights" or "saints," they could swing a heavy club. And while the Great Reptiles may not have been "fire-breathing dragons," they certainly would have left a profound impression in the collective species' consciousness of humans.

On the other hand, who can say that some of the living remnants of the Age of Reptiles aren't still slogging through some thick jungle swamps or swooping through the skies, giving those who see them the fright of their lives?

The hospitals and research laboratories in Iowa City, Iowa, are some of the finest and most progressive in the United States. Many, are associated with the University of Iowa, also in Iowa City, and conduct tests that lead to dramatic breakthroughs in medical science.

In the summer of 1971, I received an interesting report from a nurse who was employed at one of the major hospitals in Iowa City. According to the woman, who was in her early fifties, she was driving to work one morning at dawn to assume her position on the early shift when she noticed a bit off in the distance what appeared to be some object hovering over the city. As she drew nearer, she made out what seemed to be a small cage suspended by a thin line that lead several feet above the object. Since there was no helicopter or *anything* attached to the line, she could not understand what could hold the "cage" stationary so high in the sky.

As she drew nearer to the object, she was shocked to discover that she could see quite distinctly the figure of a man dressed in a shining, form-fitting, one piece suit. The man appeared to be gazing intently at the early morning traffic below him, although the nurse emphasized that he was too high for her to make out his features.

When she arrived at the hospital, she spoke of the strange floating man to several of the staff and to some of the patients. As soon as she had a moment free from her duties on rounds with the doctors, she called her son-in-law, a member of the Iowa City Police force, and asked him if he knew anything about a man in an apparent metallic suit dangling in a cage over the city. In the course of her inquiry, she made it clear that there was nothing visible above the strange individual that could support him.

The nurse's son-in-law knew that she was a no-nonsense woman who would not knowingly participate in a joke. She was a very frank woman who had absolutely no interest in strange subjects, especially things like UFOs or paranormal experiences. On the other hand, her son-in-law was more open-minded about "high strangeness," and he called my associate, Glenn McWane, a former detective and a local businessman, number of individuals who had been baffled by a man who appeared to be flying over the city without any type of aircraft supporting his "cage." There was a consensus that the being inside the dangling object was very thick-chested. His arms and legs—what could be seen of them—seemed also proportionately thicker than the average man.

No one had clearly seen the being's face, but they all agreed that it was darker than his shiny suit.

The cage-like apparatus in which the stranger stood seemed to have been enclosed with what appeared to be vertical bars. The cage itself appeared to be egg-shaped.

The being did move about inside the cage, and one woman observer had reported having the definite feeling that he was looking down at her.

Through the police force it was learned that a few other formal reports had been called in that morning, and the officers made extensive efforts to identify more precisely what the witnesses had seen. Checks were conducted at local airports to find out if any helicopters might have been in the area. Such leads drew blanks. No helicopters or small planes were in the sky over Iowa City during the time references supplied by the witnesses.

The nurse's policeman son-in-law admitted unofficially to McWane that he at first believed that he could determine the identity of the flying man in the cage through routine police investigation. He confessed, however, that he could not solve the mystery and that just maybe the line that some witnesses, including his mother-in-law, had reported dangling from the cage had led to a flying saucer that remained invisible to the observers.

> As she drew nearer to the object, she was shocked to discover that she could see quite distinctly the figure of a man dressed in a shining, form-fitting, one piece suit.

The Horrible Winged Beast of 1903

Flying humanoids have visited Iowa in the past. In December 1903, a "horrible winged beast" terrorized the town of Van Meter. Dr. A.C. Olcott, who slept in his office on main street, was awakened by a bright light shining in his face.

According to the *Watertown Herald* [New York, December 5, 1903], the doctor "grabbed a shotgun and ran outside the building, where he saw a monster, seemingly half human and half beast, with great bat-like wings. A dazzling light that nearly blinded him came from a blunt, horn-like protuberance in the middle of the animal's forehead, and it gave off a stupefying odor that almost overcame him. The doctor discharged his weapon and fled into his office, barring doors and windows, and remained there in abject terror until morning."

Peter Dunn, cashier of the only bank in town, prepared to guard the funds with a shotgun loaded with buckshot. At two o'clock, he was blinded by a bright light.

"Eventually he recovered his senses sufficiently to distinguish the monster and fired through the window. The plate glass and sash were torn out, and the monster disappeared. Next morning imprints of large three-toed feet were discernible in the soft earth. Plaster casts of them were taken."

"That night Dr. O. V. White saw the monster climbing down a telephone pole, using a beak much in the manner of a parrot. As it struck the ground it seemed to travel in leaps like a kangaroo, using its huge, featherless wings to assist. It gave off no light. He fired at it, and he [believed] he wounded it. The shot was followed by an overpowering odor. Sidney Gregg, attracted by the shot, saw the monster flying away."

"But the climax came the following night. The whole town was aroused by this time. Professor Martin, principal of the schools, decided that from the description it was an antediluvian [before the great Biblical Flood] animal."

The doctor grabbed a shotgun and ran outside the building, where he saw a monster, seemingly half human and half beast, with great batlike wings (*art by Ricardo Pustanio*).

"Shortly after midnight J. L. Platt, foreman of the brick plant, heard a peculiar sound in an abandoned coal mine, and as the men had reported a similar sound before[,] a body of volunteers started an investigation. Presently the monster emerged from the shaft, accompanied by a smaller one. A score of shots were fired without effect."

"The whole town was aroused, and a vigil was maintained the rest of the night, but without result until just at dawn, when the two monsters returned and disappeared down the shaft."

Thanks to Jerome Clark for the clipping.

The Birdman of Chaparral, New Mexico

In his "Reality Checking" column in the October 2007 issue of Alternate Perceptions, *editor Brent Raynes, author of* Visitors from Hidden Realms, *quoted an informant who described a recent sighting of an apparent "Birdman" seen by his brother, who lives in the desert community of Chaparral, New Mexico, and by a truck driver neighbor who lives next door but directly behind his brother, a man who allegedly had a really, really close encounter with this winged anomaly. As Brent tells of their encounter:*

On the evening of Sunday, September 30th, my helpful informant visited his brother's next door neighbor, with cell phone in hand, to help me to get the low down on this man's incredible account. The neighbor is a truck driver who speaks only Spanish, so my informant agreed to act an interpreter. So back and forth we went between English and Spanish and back to English, repeatedly.

"Actually he thought that something was coming towards his dog to attack it, but the dog went in back of him and started barking really loud," my informant stated.

A tree nearby was swaying back and forth like there was a wind storm. That's when he looked up and that's when he saw the creature.

I asked about feathers, as I had been told by early investigators that the creature had plumage. I was soon told otherwise.

"He said he didn't see feathers on it."

I asked about eyes.

"He didn't see the eyes," I was told. "He said the Birdman's head was tiny. He had a tiny head, big fanged teeth, and sharp claws on his hands. He made a point of emphasizing that he had hands in addition to his wings."

As best the witness could recall, the incident occurred sometime between 2:00 and 3:00 A.M., either in early August or late July of this year [2007]. He was outside. It was very dark, and he was about to smoke a cigarette, when he heard the commotion from the tree. He flicked his lighter, and that's when he saw it.

"You know what?" my informant and interpreter on the other end of the phone said. "He said that it made a horrible sound, kind of like a—he can't even describe it—it was like a squealing, but a really, really loud—I guess like in between a crow's screech and a hissing sound, at the same time."

I had heard that the creature had made a hissing and a screaming sound, but I didn't know that they occurred together—almost as if they were one sound.

Again he confirmed the strange sound:

"Yeah, it was at the same time. Like a squealing and a hissing at the same time. He said that when he first saw the monster, the thing made that noise, and he was so shocked that he kept trying to turn on his lighter to see the creature—and the beast kept making that sound."

The witness said that he didn't think that the huge bird creature saw him until he started lighting his lighter. The Birdman came down the way an eagle lands. That's the position he saw him in.

"Kind of like with his front legs up in the air?" I asked.

"Exactly," he replied. "And his hands were close to his chest."

I asked how tall the Birdman looked.

Again my informant conversed in Spanish with the witness, and then came back with "He said six [feet] or more. So it was pretty big."

I asked how long this event went on.

Again a conversation in Spanish erupted in the background, then he returned to the telephone to tell me: "Okay, okay. He's telling me that [a little more Spanish, and then he laughs] … to him it probably lasted a long time but it might have been like five or six seconds. The Birdman was kind of in mid-air, but so close to the ground that he turned around flying."

Then the Birdman landed on my informant's brother's garage roof and sat "briefly in a squatting position."

"He said the Birdman turned around and looked at him again, kind of the way an owl tilts its head, and he made that same cawing/hissing sound and took off flying."

Later he added that it "flew really, really, really fast," and in the direction of nearby mountains.

On September 28, I talked with my informant's brother about his sighting.

Brent Raynes, author, researcher, and editor of *Alternate Perceptions* magazine, has tracked down numerous sightings of flying humanoids.

It occurred around 5:00 A.M., he said, on September 14th. He described how he and his wife were outside their home talking to each other. He was lying on the back of his car, looking at stars. Then, about 30 to 50 feet up in the air, close to his outside light situated on a pole, he saw a black form go by through the air.

"It didn't have any feathers," he said. "You know to me what it appeared to be like? Like somebody hang gliding. The wingspan was pretty big."

I asked how big, and he said, "I would say about a good 15 feet, from side to side."

The Birdman of Madisonville, Tennessee

Brent Raynes interviewed another series of Birdman sighting which had occurred in Tennessee over a period of several decades.

"That was what we called him," Mark Boring, editor of the *Monroe County Buzz* of Madisonville, Tennessee, replied in regard to the mention of the "Birdman" stories I had heard about from his area. "We called it the Birdman of Madisonville."

Boring said that he had been "fairly skeptical" of such stories of giant human-like birds back then. He remembered how at the time a local radio station had mentioned that he had made fun of the Birdman and ran only one small story on the creature in the local paper.

"The Appalachian mountains to our east run northeast and southwest and you get into a valley here as you come out of the Smoky Mountains. In the valley there are north and south ridges. Coming out of the mountains these ridges will run maybe 5 or 10 miles apart, and you'll travel east and west and you'll have another ridge line. One of the ridge lines is known as the Hiwassee Knob. That's an old Indian word. It has an old fire tower on it that was built years and years ago. A lot of kids, back in the late 1960s and '70s, used to gather out near this old fire tower and build bonfires. It was a place just to go and hang out.

"As I remember, the first time the Birdman was seen, there were maybe 10 or 12 kids who reported after one weekend that there was a bird-like creature in the knobs. They didn't say a whole lot more about it, but then it got my interest and that of a couple of my buddies and so we started going to the bonfires and traveling around. Then one day a friend of mine and I were driving in the knob area and actually caught a glimpse of something, you know, a huge bird that was actually too big to be a regular bird. Its wings were outstretched, and it was soaring into the woods.

"Then some other people who spotted it on the ground chased it and reported that it ran like a man. These were buddies that I went to school with, and then I saw the Birdman again, actually flying over the knob. There were several more sightings, and someone actually took a picture of it on top of the town water tower, but he has since disappeared somewhere in the wilds of Utah and I guess taken the picture with him. There was a mother and some children who saw the Birdman—and of course it terrified them. All these sightings happened about 1964 or 1965, and last until about 1971, 1972, or so.

"I left and went to work in New Orleans in 1970, and some friends that I communicated with told me that they had seen the Birdman again. I came back and went to work in Chattanooga in 1972 or '73, and there were a few more sightings. But by 1975, nobody was talking about it anymore. Nobody saw the Birdman anymore. So maybe for a ten year span you would get maybe two or three sightings a year."

I asked about a story that I had heard about someone shooting the creature with an arrow.

Boring replied: "Yes, and there was a guy who shot at it with a pistol, too. One of the guys actually claimed to have shot part of the foot off of the Birdman with a bow. Either a piece of a toe or foot. He claimed that the Smithsonian came down and asked to take it and investigate, and he never heard from them again. Or so he claimed.

"You know, a lot of these Birdman stories have kind of been transformed into legend, you might say, or into the realm of a tall tale. Some of these stories we have told time and time again, and so they've kind of taken on a life of their own. My boys just laugh at me now when I talk about it, so I've further enlarged the story from time to time with them.

"Not too many people believe that all these Birdman stories really happened. Some do. The lady who is next door to my office has a restaurant, so when we mentioned the Birdman in the paper not long ago, she came over and said, 'I remember that. I had forgotten all about that.' You know, we're looking back at thirty years or so."

I asked Mark Boring how big the Birdman of Madisonville generally appeared to be. He said, "A lot of people—and I—who saw it—would say between six or seven feet. It was as tall as a man … a tall man. I know some of the people said he was at least seven feet. I don't know. It could have been. You don't really get a chance to stand there and measure the Birdman. You see it and it just looks like a huge creature."

I remarked that it must have had a real wide wingspan, and Mark responded, "Yeah, I would say six or seven feet."

At the conclusion of our interview I mentioned the Mothman of West Virginia back in 1966 and onward, and he paused and laughed, "That's right. It's a strange world. I guess the older I get, the more accepting I am of things, and the more open I am for certain things to be real or not."

The Black-caped Flying Humanoid Who Attacked a Policeman

A very strange case that we have discussed often on the *Jeff Rense Program* (Rense.com) is that of police officer Leonardo Samaniego from Guadalupe, N.L. Mexico who was attacked by a flying humanoid at 3:15 A.M. on Friday, January 16, 2004. Officer Samaniego had been making his usual patrol in his patrol car around Colonia Valles de la Salla when some large black object appeared to leap from a tree next to the street and turn to face the police car. Puzzled, Officer Samaniego turned his lights on high beam and saw a living nightmare. What had fallen or leaped from the tree was a woman dressed in black, who didn't really touch the street, she just floated several feet above the ground.

As Samaniego's eyes widened in disbelief, the woman's two large black eyes, totally without lids, seemed bothered by the patrol car's headlights and she held up her cape in attempt to protect them. Next, because she was angered by the patrol car's interference with her nocturnal activities or because the officer appeared to be a likely victim, the "witch" jumped onto the vehicle, and tried to get at him by breaking the windshield. The officer put his automobile in reverse, trying his best to escape her attack.

Later, in his official testimony to the bizarre events of the evening, Officer Samaniego said that the "witch" had flown violently at his windshield,

Officer Leonardo Samaniego reported seeing a woman dressed in black who floated above the street (**art by Ricardo Pustanio**).

Scott Corrales, editor of *Inexplicata: The Journal of Hispanic Ufology,* has collected numerous accounts of flying humanoids. He has observed that for generations, the residents of Puerto Rico and northern Mexico have reported a variety of winged entities (*art by Bill Oliver*).

trying to drive her hands through the glass to grab him. Again, he described her as having large black eyes, seemingly with no eyelids.

In Santiago Yturria's translation of Officer Samaniego's testimony for Jeff Rense, the policeman described the woman has having dark brown skin. Her expression was "horrible," as she tried to get at Samaniego with her claws. Samaniego kept his car in reverse, desperately attempting to call for back-up. When his vehicle struck the end of the street, he was so frightened that he covered his eyes to escape the view of his ghastly attacker. When he opened his eyes and saw the horrible being still clawing at his windshield, he fainted due to the high stress.

Several minutes later when two police units arrived together with an ambulance, the officers found Samaniego still unconscious. He was uninjured—perhaps because he had remained in his patrol car—and he regained consciousness as he was being treated by paramedics in the ambulance.

During the subsequent investigation of the strange incident, a police officer from Santa Catarina and two more officers from the Regia force admitted that they had seen the same flying creature that Samaniego had encountered. However, they had sighted the witch in the black dress and cape three days earlier, but had decided not to come forward with a report of such a flying creature for fear of embarrassment.

As the case continued to gain notice and credence from other police officers, a number of residents from Colonia La Playa told television interviewers that they, too, had seen the flying monster in the daylight, as well as in the late evening hours. Some stated that the fierce entity had so upset them that they had been ill for several days after their sighting.

Flying Humanoids Visit from Puerto Rico to Chile

My friend and colleague Scott Corrales of the Institute of Hispanic Ufology (www.inexplicata.blogspot.com) and the editor of *Inexplicata: The Journal of Hispanic Ufology* has collected numerous accounts of flying humanoids. Corrales has observed that for generations, the residents of Puerto Rico and northern Mexico have reported a variety of winged entities "not just Thunderbird manifestations, but flying anthropomorphic creatures. Popular tradition holds that such beings live in caves, whether in the hot dry Sierra Madre or limestone caves in Caribbean karst of northern Puerto Rico, which would offer great shelter for the creatures described."

Winged Humanoid Kept Pace with His Jeep

On March 27, 2009, *El Heraldo de Chihuahua* published the account of a young man who had been terrified by a very large winged humanoid that had kept pace with his Jeep as he tried desperately to outrun it.

Meeting a Birdman on the Footpath

It is one thing to have a winged monster keep pace with your Jeep, quite another to confront such a being face-to-face while on foot. On July 20, 1994, a farm worker at Rancho El Sabino in Monterrey was walking back to his house to have lunch around 11:00 A.M. when he noticed an unusual "person" emerge from another footpath about 100 feet away. As he drew nearer the stranger, he realized that he was looking at a huge half-human/half-bird creature.

The farm worker was terrified, but the giant birdman seemed indifferent to the human's presence. It just continued to walk at a leisurely pace until it finally flexed its enormous wings and flew out of sight.

Whether a Giant Bird or Huge Bat, It Ate Livestock in Chile

In Chile on April 29, 2000, Jorge Pino reported an encounter with a strange creature under full moonlight. Pino described the entity as resembling a large monkey with clawed arms, enormous fangs, and wings.

Pino ordered his large mastiff to attack the creature, but the unfortunate canine limped back to its master with a bloody neck that had been gashed open by the monster.

Within weeks after Pino sighted the nasty being, farmers from Tucapel and Huepil were complaining about the huge bird that was attacking their livestock. Some farmers said that they had seen a strange luminous phenomenon around the "bird."

In early May, livestock deaths were mounting. A Chilean state police officer reported sighting something strange in the sky that he described as a giant bat near the city of Angol.

Professor Liliana Romero had a frightening meeting with the "giant bat" when she looked out of a window to see what was making a disturbance in her courtyard and saw "an immense man, standing well over seven feet tall, his shoulder blades split by a pair of wings."

Not long after the professor's encounter, three teenaged men from Calama traveled to the desert community of San Pedro de Atacama to visit the grandfather of one of the men. Just as they were sitting down to dinner on July 23, dogs began to howl and something began to pound and scratch at the door.

When they got up the courage to investigate, they saw the monster standing among some pear trees. It was about five feet tall and had outspread wings that measured three and a half feet on each side.

Researcher Jaime Ferrer of the Calama UFO Center interviewed the men and composed this consensus: "It was covered with glossy black skin, very clean and hairless. It appeared as though it had recently emerged from the water, but without being wet. It had a large head and small beak.... Its eyes were immense and completely black, but sparkled brilliantly. [The three young men] thought it was a prehistoric being, since its wings had a strong resemblance to those of pterodactyls or bats, featuring bone-like protuberances which form the skeletal frame of the wings. Its legs were sturdy and had powerful claws, like those of a carrion bird, but much stronger."

GIANT SNAKES FROM YOUR WORST NIGHTMARES

In February 2009, scientists announced that they had uncovered the 60-million-year-old remains of what they felt free to declare the largest snake that had ever lived on Earth. The *Titanoboa*, as the researchers named the reptile, was estimated to have been 43-feet long and to have weighed one ton. Among the bones found in an ancient rain forest in Colombia was skeletal evidence that the monstrous snake was capable of "munching on crocodiles."

When researchers announced their find in December 2009, a team of paleontologists had unearthed several massive fossilized snake vertebrae in a Colombian coal mine. As one reads the findings published in *Nature*, one's first impulse may be to shudder and to wonder aloud, "Can you imagine a snake large enough to swallow a crocodile?"

Actually, we don't have to venture to the rain forests of Colombia to find the bones of such a serpent. We don't have to use our imaginations. All we have to do is to travel to the Bay Area of Florida and keep an eye out for the Burmese pythons that have invaded the state and that can strangle and eat an entire alligator. Oh, and did we mention that we don't need a time machine to take us back 60 million years. The Burmese pythons, one of several nonnative giant constrictor snakes, are waiting, hungrily, for its prey right now, today, 2010.

The Pythons That Plan to Eat Florida

The pythons were introduced into the wild a few years ago primarily by pet owners who decided that the exotic reptile that was only a few feet long when they bought it at the pet store was now beginning to grow a great deal larger. And not only was it looking less cuddlesome, it was costing a lot more money to feed it.

In 2008, giant Burmese pythons, which had been discarded by exotic pet owners, made their way from Florida to the Bay Area. Zoologist Gordon Rodda of the U.S. Geological Survey said that they had not identified any method that would stop the snakes from spreading (*art by Ricardo Pustanio*).

Undoubtedly, most python owners had no malice toward their once colorful pet when they decided to get rid of the creature that was eating them out of house and home. Perhaps the python had grown to a length of five or six feet and no longer fit the aquarium. Or maybe it was nine or ten feet long and eyeing the baby hungrily. Then there was the uncomfortable fact that some of the neighbors were asking in harsh tones if anyone had seen their missing pet cats or small dogs.

But once that python slid from the hands of its former owners into the Florida waters that creature was on its way to reaching 26 feet in length and to becoming as thick as a telephone pole. It was also on its way to finding a mate and breeding, producing a python community of thousands on a time schedule that seems unbelievable compared to the reproductive rates of other creatures. Each female python can lay up to 100 eggs at a time when it is in the wild.

Experts state that irresponsible python and exotic snake owners are not the only ones to blame. Hurricanes and rain storms flooded pet shops and allowed the non-native serpents to flee their cages and look out for themselves in an unfamiliar environment. It seems that the strangers have been highly adaptable to their new home.

In 2008, the giant snakes were reported making their way from Florida to the Bay Area. Zoologist Gordon Rodda of the U.S. Geological Survey said that they had not identified any method that would stop the snakes from spreading to the Bay Area. Weighing about 250 pounds and moving at a rate of about 20 miles per month, the pythons had comfortably established themselves in Florida's Everglades National Park and were soon slithering to other areas.

When Steve Rubenstein, staff writer for the *Chronicle*, wrote his article in February 21, 2008, park rangers had estimated 30,000 pythons and other nonnative snakes living in the Everglades. A python had turned up on the shore of Lake Okeechobee in south central Florida, and others had slithered as far as Vero Beach and Key Largo.

In January 2010, five African rock pythons, including a 14-foot female, were found in Miami-Dade County. Experts fear that the rock python could breed with the Burmese python and create a "super snake" (Andy Reid, *Sun Sentinel*, January 13, 2010).

Monster Anacondas of Brazil

While the anaconda is generally thought to be the largest snake in the world, the Asiatic Reticulated python would come in a close second. Other experts wager on the python as being the larger. If the super snake should arrive in Florida, all bets are off.

Park Rangers and members of the U.S. Geological Survey are reporting pythons 26 feet in length and weighing about 300 pounds. The largest anaconda, a native of South America, was measured at just under 28 feet in length and estimated at weighing over 500 pounds. The longest python ever measured stretched the tape to 33 feet. Perhaps the argument might be settled by stating that the python is a bit longer, but the anaconda is at least a couple hundred pounds heavier.

"Sucuri" is the name the anaconda bears in the Amazon. Sucuri Gigante means giant anaconda. In the ancient traditions, there once existed an anaconda so large that its massive, slithering body carved the route for the Amazon River.

In 1846, the respected British botanist George Gardner (1810–1849) wrote in his journal that he had seen a giant snake on the property of a Senhor Lagoeira. Although the serpent had been killed and could easily have begun to undergo decomposition before the meticulous scientist had occasion to measure its body, the "giant snake" stretched out to 33 feet long. Gardner spent the years from 1836 to 1841 collecting botanical specimens in Brazil, but he never again encountered such a monstrous reptile.

The expeditions and adventures of Major Percy Fawcett (1867–1925) have inspired numerous motion pictures, pulp fiction, and television programs. It was Fawcett who disappeared while searching for the fabled Lost City of the Amazon. While certain of his critics dismissed some of his reports as being somewhat exaggerated, in 1907 he reported that a member of the Brazilian Boundary Commission had informed him of an anaconda over 80 feet long that had been killed in the Rio Paraguay.

The largest anaconda, a native of South America, was measured at just under 28 feet in length and estimated at weighing over 500 pounds (**art by Ricardo Pustanio**).

Fawcett himself claimed that he had killed an anaconda below the confluence of the Rio Negro. Having suffered a fatal wound from Fawcett's rifle, the giant snake managed to pull 45 feet of its bulk out of the river and up on the bank before it died. When the massive creature was hauled out of the water to be more closely examined, Fawcett and his expedition found that there was another 17 feet of the serpent still in the river, thereby making a total of 62 feet of giant anaconda.

Father Victor Heinz had gone to the Amazon to save souls, not to search for giant snakes, but in May 1922, he said that he saw a monster reptile on the shores of the river near the town of Obidos. Those who witnessed the creature with the priest claimed that it was nearly 80 feet in length.

After seeing such a beast, Father Heinz became intrigued enough by accounts of giant reptiles to begin collecting stories of such encounters. One witness swore to having sighted an anaconda 150 feet in length. A number of others who reported to the priest that they had sighted such monster snakes also mentioned the reptile's glowing eyes, so it may be that certain of these creatures were more of a ghostly, rather than a physical, appearance.

On January 24, 1948, *The Diario*, the newspaper of Peranmbuco, Brazil, published the famous picture that was taken by a helicopter as it hovered over the river. The photograph purported to show a giant anaconda estimated at 131 feet and weighing five tons, carrying a bull in its huge mouth.

Four months later, *A Noite Illustrada* published a picture of a dead anaconda that was alleged to be 115 feet long.

Floridians must be praying mightily that the python and the anaconda never begin to breed to produce the "super snake" that some scientists have predicted. The tourist season would severely suffer and the retirement communities would all but disappear if giant snakes 150 feet in length and four or five tons in weight were crawling around begging—or making—snacks from the human population.

The Guardian Serpent of King Solomon's Treasure

The idea of a giant snake that appears to live forever to carry out a sacred mission is common in the folklore of the world. The giant snake of Mt. Tsurugi, the second highest peak on the Japanese island of Shikoku seems to have no name that I can ascertain, but that doesn't make it any less fierce. Nor is the monster snake the only legend on the island.

According to ancient tradition, Mt. Tsurugi is not really a mountain at all. It is a giant man-made pyramid, constructed by some unknown people, but utilized by King Solomon, whose fleet made several trips to Shikoku, bearing his vast treasures. The great reptile has never left his mission of guarding the hoard of gold and jewelry.

Although many individuals have claimed sightings of the great reptile throughout the centuries, in May 1973, four forestry workers swore that they had all witnessed a massive snake with shiny black scales. The giant seemed to make some bizarre chirping sounds, as if they were a kind of warning bark for them to stay away. The men reported the serpent more than 33 feet long and as thick as a telephone pole.

The forest workers returned with hundreds of volunteers to hunt down the monster, but the creature had retreated into the pyramid. The bold snake hunters did find giant tracks left by its huge coils. Some measure these tracks as 16 inches wide. Others claimed to have found trees that the sacred serpent had broken down as its slithered back to its centuries' old hideaway.

There's Something in the Woods of Cannock Chase

My friend and fellow author Nick Redfern wrote in May 13, 2009, that once again there was "high strangeness" in the woods of Britain's Cannock Chase—specifically in the vicinity of its German Cemetery. A giant snake has been seen slithering around the area. This is not the first time such a reptile of great size has been seen in Cannock Chase. Nick himself investigated such a creature in the summer of 1976.

What are the people seeing? Nick wondered: "Are they regular snakes or something else? From the descriptions, they could be pythons. However, the problem is that such creatures would not last long when the cold, harsh winter sets in. And yet such creatures have been seen for years on the Chase, which begs the questions: if they are regular snakes, how are they surviving those aforementioned harsh winters year-after-year? And why are the snakes (like all the other odd beasts [Bigfoot, werewolves, ghosts, marauding black cats, and spectral black dogs]) roaming amongst all the old war graves?"

The Giant Sacred Rattlesnake of Montezuma

The historical Montezuma ruled the Aztec Empire from about 1503 until his death in 1520. He may have been a bit of a mystic, but in the folklore of the native people of the Southwest he has become the very embodiment of arcane wisdom and powerful magic. In addition, his great serpent appears to serve as a kind of familiar spirit to

Montezuma and a kind of messenger of the Medicine Brotherhood who initiates the worthy ones who seek higher paths of knowledge.

While perhaps the majority of those who hear of Montezuma's serpent scoff at such tales or, at best, attribute its appearance to peaks of visionary experience, there are accounts of individuals who have encountered a gigantic reptile. Cleo Jaramillo, who has recorded a number of folk legends of New Mexico in *Shadows of the Past*, states that many Hispanics in the Taos Pueblo area hold to the belief that the tribes of that village shelter a divine serpent of enormous size. Some accounts suggest that in ancient times, infants were fed to the monster rattlesnake on special feast days.

In his *Commerce of the Prairies*, Josiah Gregg writes that on one occasion "I heard an honest ranchero assert that upon entering Pecos very early on a winter's morning, he saw the huge trail of the massive reptile in the snow, as large as that of an ox being dragged."

While perhaps the majority of those who hear of Montezuma's serpent scoff at such tales or, at best, attribute its appearance to peaks of visionary experience, there are accounts of individuals who have encountered a gigantic reptile.

"I first saw the great serpent when I was a boy in New Mexico," Reuben Montoya said. "I think it was around 1940. I was eleven years old. We lived in a village that had much talk of witches and devils.

"I was walking with my grandfather late at night, and suddenly we came upon this huge rattlesnake in an arroyo. It coiled itself, and it was still taller than Grandfather. Its body was thicker than a strong man's leg."

Reuben remembered freezing in complete terror as the gigantic serpent bobbed its great head scant inches away from his face. "Grandfather, too, was unable to move or to speak. But I did not have time to worry about Grandfather. The great rattlesnake's tongue touched the tip of my nose, and I felt my heart stop in fright. Soon, I knew, it would bite me and kill me."

But the terrible piercing of flesh with fangs, the awful expected injection of fiery poison never came. The huge snake weaved before Reuben for what seemed to be an eternity, then it disappeared in a cloud of smoke that smelled to the boy to be something like spent shotgun shells.

"My grandfather was at last able to move, and he knelt beside me and put his arms around me," Reuben said. "He began to weep, but I soon learned his tears were not from thankfulness that I had been spared death at the fangs of the monstrous snake."

"Oh, Reuben, my boy," his grandfather managed to speak between great, gasping sobs. "You were visited by the sacred serpent of Montezuma. If you had only kissed the snake's tongue, you would have been granted much wisdom and many powers not available to ordinary men."

Reuben looked at his grandfather as if the old man was mad. There was no way that he would have kissed that monster's tongue. He had already crossed himself three times in thanks to the Virgin that he was not bitten—or swallowed whole by the massive serpent.

Then, suddenly, his grandfather was angry with him. It was as though Reuben had failed a very important test and had brought disgrace upon his family.

He began to cry when his grandfather slapped his face, and he ran the rest of the way home to the security of his mother's arms.

"She explained to me then about the wonderful Montezuma, the almighty, powerful sorcerer, and his sacred serpent, a *biboron*, a monster rattlesnake," Reuben remembered. "She did not scold me for not kissing the serpent's tongue. She said that a supplicant must be certain that it is not the Devil in disguise who appears before him. She told me that the Devil will often trick vain and ambitious men by appearing as the sacred serpent.

"You must prepare yourself and be ready if the serpent should visit you again," she said.

According to Reuben, who now lives in Arizona and is respected as a great healer, the serpent did manifest again before him when he was a youth of 22.

"I had been on a seven-day fast, and I had undergone several sessions in a sweat lodge. I had purified my body," Reuben told my wife Sherry and me. "When Montezuma's sacred serpent appeared before me, it opened its mouth wide, very wide, so that I could place my entire head between its jaws. I did so without fear, and I received the blessing of becoming a healer."

Sherry and I have both had the honor of having been invited to many sacred Native American rituals, many of them held in the strictest secrecy. We are uncertain if we would welcome an invitation to meet Montezuma's sacred rattlesnake. Although we had a number of encounters with rattlesnakes during the years that we lived in Arizona, we are grateful that none of them were so large that we could have placed our heads inside their gaping jaws—even though, in certain encounters, the jaws of the snakes almost seemed that large.

* * *

In the summer of 1989, a young man of Pima and Hispanic heritage from Scottsdale, Arizona, vowed that he would undertake a traditional vision quest. It was not at all difficult to find an isolated area in the Superstition Mountains near Phoenix where he might be undisturbed for many days.

"On the fifth day of my quest, I had suffered through a day of 118-degree heat, and I had begun to think that maybe those old traditional Indians were a lot tougher than I was," he said. "I decided to remain there for at least that night. I had not yet received anything that I might call a true vision, but I had told so many of my friends about my intention to hold an authentic vision quest that I felt that I must stick it out as long as I could."

"Shortly after one of those fantastic Arizona sunsets, I began to sing and to pray," he continued. "I don't know how long I kept this up before I entered a very deep meditative state. I do know, with all my essence, however, that I truly did enter a separate reality. Before me, as clearly as I have ever seen anything in my life, I saw the sacred serpent of Montezuma. It was as big as an anaconda from the Amazon. It had to be at least thirty feet long."

Within a few moments, the young man remembered, the actual image of Montezuma appeared in his full majesty. "He was magnificent! He was dressed in multicolored robes that seemed to be woven of brilliant feathers, culled from the bright plumage of exotic birds. He stood at least seven feet tall. In one hand he held a kind of scepter. The other hand rested on the head of this enormous serpent. Montezuma told me that I must always stay on the true Medicine path and not be seduced by the false promises of materialism."

Young men of Pima and other tribal heritage near Scottsdale, Arizona, undertake a traditional vision quest in an isolated area in the Superstition Mountains near Phoenix where they might be undisturbed among the rattlesnakes for many days (*art by Bill Oliver*).

"We don't really know when it happened," our Navajo friend, the artist David Little Turtle, said, "but the historical Montezuma became somehow translated into a culture hero who is usually associated with good, with white magic. Because the entities of certain tribes maintain a duality, however, among some traditions he is also recognized as a practitioner of black magic."

Juan Two Bears believes that Montezuma would have ruled all of the Americas had it not been for the treachery of the Spanish. Because Montezuma was such a master sorcerer, however, he has been able to return in his spirit body and manifest even greater power as a Light Being.

Two Bears went on his vision quest in the San Francisco mountains near Flagstaff, Arizona. "When the sacred serpent called me to its cave, I went willingly. I had already prayed most of the fear out of my body, but I will always remember that huge mouth opening to receive my ultimate expression of faith and trust. I put my head inside its jaws so that I could receive great Medicine power."

"I know that on some level of reality Montezuma lives," a young practitioner of traditional Indian medicine told us. "And I know that the sacred serpent is a very real and important aspect of receiving heavy Medicine power."

This, according to the Cherokee traditionalist, Ray, is how he received his blessing from Montezuma's serpent:

> I had fasted for six days before I entered the Medicine circle that I had drawn in the clearing. I had an amulet that had been given to me by my teacher-Medicine priest. I offered my prayer that no negative entities would enter my circle of protection.
>
> I waited another day and into the night before the great serpent appeared at the edge of my circle. It towered over me. I know that it was over thirty feet long and it had to weigh well over two hundred pounds. It coiled, and its head still hovered over me. It distended its jaw so that it could encompass my skull.
>
> I knew what I must do, and I submitted my head to the great serpent's mouth. I stood motionless to prove my faith and my lack of fear as the massive serpentine jaws moved over my face and the long, curved fangs gently touched the back of my neck.
>
> And then the sacred serpent was gone. I could feel the blessing of great Medicine power flowing through me like a warm, tingling surge of electricity. I had received the great initiation from Montezuma's great rattlesnake. My life had been blessed, and I shall never be the same person that I was. I will always follow the true Medicine path of higher spirituality.

Monster Serpents in the Midwest

American reptilian monsters have been described in many forms.

On June 11, 1909, H.G. Pederson, a farmer residing east of Randall, a small town south of Webster City, Iowa, was shocked by the sight of a serpent between 25 and 35 feet in length. Its trail across a newly plowed field was larger than the track left by the largest automobile wheel, about eight inches in width. Pederson said that he had seen the trail across his fields many times, but he had never known what could be leaving it.

Pederson's neighbor N.L. Henderson and Henderson's hired man, George Anfinson, also saw the snake crossing the newly plowed field. Although they all told the *Waterloo Daily Reporter*, they could "hardly believe their eyes," they got Henderson's hunting dog and a gun and began to follow the trail of the monstrous serpent. They tracked the serpent to the Skunk River where it disappeared.

* * *

On June 9, 1946, Orland Parker, from Kenton, Ohio, was riding a horse through a small section of woods near his house when his horse became frightened and threw him at the sight of a gigantic snake, eight feet long and four inches in girth. The snake wrapped itself around the leg of the prostrate man and broke his ankle. It then bit his horse. A search party was formed and went in pursuit of the snake, but it had disappeared in the dense cover.

This proved to be just a taste of what was to come in the Midwest, for in July, 1946, Williard Tollinger of Flat Rock, Indiana, along with several members of his family, saw a snake about twenty feet long coiled up in the shallow water of a river. In the fields around the Indiana town, the trail of a large and heavy snake was often seen, and pigs and other small animals were found missing. A snake this large has not been thought to be native to the North American climate, but perhaps in the lowlands along the Midwestern rivers, such monsters have lived and died for centuries.

* * *

On the Broad Top Mountain in Bedford County, Pennsylvania, paranormal researcher Patty Wilson told me, there have long been stories about an incredibly large snake.

Those who have seen it describe it like this: "It's as thick as a telephone pole and about twenty or twenty-four feet long. It can reach across a two lane highway."

The snake has been seen for most of the twentieth century and last made the newspapers in the late 1990s when three construction workers stopped at a spring on the Broad Top to fill their water cans before going to work. The three men were so rattled by the sight of the giant snake that they actually called the police.

Despite taking a lot of teasing from their friends and families all three men have continued to stick by their story of seeing the giant snake.

It is believed that this snake winters over in the abandoned coal mines in the region. Stories of the giant snake began shortly after heavy circus wagons collapsed a wooden bridge in Hopewell at the foot of the mountain. The local legend is that some of the snakes in the one wagon got loose and were never recovered. Locals believe that a giant snake either mated with a local black snake or that a breeding pair of the snakes escaped.

Georgia's "Furry Rattlesnake": A Cryptozoological Mystery

BY MICAH A. HANKS

When it comes to cryptozoology and animals being out-of-place, I've heard some wild ones.

One of the best in my collection came to mind recently, and this morning I finally made my way down into the "dungeon of lore" beneath my bedroom and dug it out of my archives to share in your book. Interestingly, it was a response to an article about Bigfoot that I wrote for *FATE* Magazine back in 2004. As you'll see, the reply I got didn't have much to do with Sasquatch, but it's unique all the same, though perhaps reminiscent of some of the early pioneer legends like that of the "hoop snake" and the "hodag".

Here's the letter:

> I read and enjoyed your article in *FATE* magazine. I am very enthralled by cryptozoology, especially the variety dealing with critters which seem to match no others in existence, but rather seem as denizens of a bad acid trip.
>
> Here in central Georgia several years ago a retired chiropractor, while driving to a small town, noticed a group of DOT (highway repair) workers standing in a huddle on the side of the road. Since small town folk tend to know each other, he stopped and inquired about the focus of their attention.
>
> It seems that they had captured what he describes as a rattlesnake with two front legs with claws, from around which coarse hair hung forth.
>
> The old guy is not a drunk, liar, or one to see things that aren't there. I plan to try and interview the people in that road crew if they're still around. I haven't had the time yet, especially with the cost of gas and long distances in this region....
>
> The fool who had possession of the critter said he wanted to stuff it. I would imagine that a living entity would provide greater proof of its being a true cryptid.
>
> Sincerely yours,
> —Clyde

Though "hoop snakes" of pioneer legend weren't described as having tufts of hair or claws, they still come to mind for some reason when reviewing Clyde's letter. Below is a classic example of a frontier-era hoop snake report, excerpted from a London Magazine called *Tour USA* from 1784:

> As other serpents crawl upon their bellies, so can this; but he has another method of moving peculiar to his own species, which he always adopts when he is in eager pursuit of his prey; he throws himself into a circle, running rapidly around, advancing like a hoop, with his tail arising and pointed forward in the circle, by which he is always in the ready position of striking. It is observed that they only make use of this method in attacking; for when they fly from their enemy they go upon their bellies, like other serpents. From the above circumstance, peculiar to themselves, they have also derived the appellation of hoop snakes.

Though generally accepted as myth, I remember a story described to me several years ago by my grandmother (who is still alive and in her late eighties). When she was in grade school decades ago she and several of her classmates, while outside during recess, claimed to have witnessed a snake rolling down a nearby slope "like a wheel, with its tail in its mouth."

Though tall tales regarding witches and critters are certainly a part of the culture in western North Carolina where I live, Grandma Lucy is anything but a teller of such tales. In fact, she's more of a skeptic, if anything. Might she and her friends have actually seen a "hoop snake"—or were their young minds merely exaggerating something else? Either way, one is left to consider that there may be more herpetological mysteries in the American South than most folks are aware of.

The Snake that Repaid a Kindness

While all of the accounts in these chapters have been of fearsome encounters with giant snakes, we will close with one of the strangest accounts that the author has heard regarding the action of a reptile.

According to the *Liaosheng Evening Post*, Yu Feng of Fushun in Liaoning province, was returning from work late one afternoon when he found a black snake dying near his home. While others might have ignored the reptile or gone over to mash it to put it out of its misery, Yu felt strangely touched and compassionate.

Gently, he picked up the snake and took it home with him. Skilled in the use of herbal medicines, Yu treated the snake for 20 days until the creature had recovered.

Yu carried the snake to a nearby mountain, about a mile away, released his newly recovered patient back into an area of wilderness that would make it a good new home.

The next morning, the snake was coiled at Yu's door.

After his third attempt to release the snake into the wild, Yu accepted the reality that he had acquired a very unusual pet.

Yu's friends, neighbors, and, of course, his wife all agreed that the snake had come back to find some way to repay his kindness for nurturing it back to health.

Yu named the snake Long Long and officially welcomed him into the family. Long Long loved to coil around the lamp stand and watch Yu as he read or worked on his business accounts.

On January 3, 2010, Long Long found a way to express his gratitude to the kind man who had nursed him with special herbal medicines.

Yu said that he was surprised to be awakened one night by Long Long crawling across his face. The snake had never done such a thing before, but Yu was so tired from work that he just rolled over and went back to sleep.

Then, to Yu's total amazement, Long Long grabbed his clothes with his teeth and began to drag him out of bed. At the same time, Long Long was whipping the bed with his tail, making as much noise as possible.

Once Yu was awake, he saw Long Long crawl to his mother's bed and began whipping her bed to awaken her.

That was when Yu saw that his mother's electric blanket was beginning to smolder and about to burst into flame. He was on his feet in seconds and extinguished the beginning of the fire before it could spread and do any damage.

Yu knows that the entire family could have been killed if Long Long had not been alert and understood that danger was about to overcome the Yu Feng residence.

Although reptile experts maintain that snakes do not have the intelligence, the loyalty, the motivation to replay kindness, Yu knows that Long Long saved their lives and will always be a part of their family.

GOBLINS AND OTHER NASTY WEE FOLK OF LAND AND SEA

In August 2009, Dominic Waghorn, Middle East correspondent for *The World News*, wrote that Israel was in the grips of "mermaid fever" after dozens of sightings of a female figure in the Mediterranean Sea near Haifa.

Council spokesman Natti Zilberman said that many people had sighted the being "all independent of one another."

The mermaid was only seen in the evening, usually just at sunset, and had been drawing crowds of people with their cameras, hoping to catch a glimpse of the nautical nymph and a photograph to prove her existence.

Zilberman said that dozens of people who had seen the mermaid said that the creature appeared to be half-lovely young girl and half-fish, sometimes jumping high into the air like a dolphin. Many witnesses said that the mermaid did all kinds of aquatic tricks before it disappeared.

Although a lonely sailor might at first have thought he had spotted a Mermaid, the creatures are more often entities of violence and death than a bizarre romantic rendezvous in the surf.

Although there are also Mermen, the greater fascination has always been on the mermaid with her top-half a beautiful woman and her bottom-half that of a fish. Traditionally, the mermaid is also gifted with a lovely singing voice, which can be used to warn sailors of approaching storms or jagged rocks ahead. Or, in many of the ancient stories, the seductive siren song of the mermaids lures the seamen onto the jagged rocks and to their deaths.

In folklore, mermaids sometimes fall in love with humans and are able to come ashore in human shape and to live on land on for many years. They may even have children with their human husbands. But in all of these tales of mercreatures and human mates, the mermaid longs to return to the sea, and one day she will leave her human family and return to the sea.

In folklore, mermaids sometimes fall in love with humans and are able to come ashore in human shape and to live on land on for many years, though they always yearn for the sea (*art by Ricardo Pustanio*).

Ceasg

The Ceasg is a type of mermaid that haunts the lakes of the Scottish highlands. Her upper body and facial features are those of a beautiful, well-endowed woman, but her lower half is that of a very large salmon. If a handsome young man with a good heart should capture her attention and treat her well, she may assume human shape and marry him, at the same time granting him three wishes which may make them very wealthy. If she feels that she has been disrespected or treated badly, she may use her beauty to lure a fisherman to the deepest part of the lake and drown him.

Devas

Devas are nature spirits that possess the energies required to make barren soil fertile and productive.

In 1975, we met with David Spangler, a director of the Findhorn Foundation, and asked him if he felt that the Devas, the nature spirits, were benignly concerned with the welfare of human beings. He replied:

> The majority of them are benignly concerned about our welfare, but I would say that what they are primarily concerned about is the maintenance of harmony and wholeness, a synergistic state with Earth. They recognize that humanity as a species is a necessary and vital part of the synergistic state. Therefore, the health of humanity is their concern, because it reflects the health of the planet. Also, humanity wields forces at the moment which bear directly on the health of the planet.

> At the same time, there's a definite impression that humanity is important, but not indispensable. Sometimes we get the feeling they're saying, if humanity doesn't get it together, a whole different evolutionary cycle may take over—which will move us out of the picture, at least in our present state.

> The entities weren't really concerned about Findhorn raising vegetables as much as they were concerned with getting across the point of

their existence. They felt it was a real necessity that humanity alter its conception of reality so as to include their existence.

Elementals

The elementary spirits, the so-called Elementals, are the unseen intelligences that inhabit the four basic elements of the material plane. The creatures of the air are known as sylphs; of the earth, gnomes; of fire, salamanders; and of water, the nymphs or undines. According to ancient tradition, before the Fall, Adam had complete control over these entities. After the Fall from Grace in the Garden of Eden, Adam lost his easy access to the elementals, but he was still able to command their obedience by means of certain incantations and spells. That same ancient tradition suggests that such communication with the unseen entities can be established by the sincere magician who seeks out the old spells. Others say that the ancient incantations are unnecessary. All that is required to gain the support of the elementals is to recognize their presence and powers and to live openly in a manner that indicates the magician is respectful, but unafraid, of the forces of nature.

The appearance of the elementals when discerned by the human eye is that of attractive males and beautiful females. Because they are created of the pure essences of their element, they may live for centuries; but because they were fashioned of terrestrial elements, their souls are not immortal, as are those of humans. If, however, an elemental should be joined in marriage to a human, their union can transform the creature's soul into a spirit that may enjoy eternal life. Some of the greatest figures of antiquity such as Zoroaster, Alexander, Merlin, and Hercules, were reported to have been the children of elementary spirits.

While most traditions hold the elementals, whether or not they are seen or unseen, to be friendly to humans and in general benignly disposed to providing assistance to righteous endeavors, some authorities warn that each of the four elements contains a number of mischief makers and entities that tend more toward the demonic than the angelic.

Wm. Michael Mott, author of *Caverns, Cauldrons, and Concealed Creatures*, issues a number of warnings pertinent to those humans who might be seriously considering dealing with sylphs, undines, salamanders, gnomes, and other entities:

> Encounters with elemental beings are not all so charming. Elementals are notoriously capricious and unpredictable, and are usually indifferent at best, and dangerous at their worst. Theosophists, Rosicrucians, and Spiritualists tended to theorize that fairies are elementals, but are also spirits (existing on 'another plane'); yet the Neoplatonists, and later the alchemists of the middle ages, believed them to be of a finer and more subtle type of matter, somewhere 'between man

and the angels.' They had flesh, after a fashion, and fleshly desires to go with it. The wizard Merlin (his name meaning 'of the sea' or 'of the water') was supposedly the result of the lust of an elemental for a human woman.

While there is traditionally some inter-relationship between the four types of elementals (sylphs, undines, salamanders, and gnomes), it seems that many fairy types of beings from Northern and Western Europe have a close relationship to the gnome (underworld) and undine (mermaid/merman) varieties. According to Reverend Robert Kirk (*The Secret Commonwealth of Elves, Fauns, and Fairies*, 1691), the fairies who abducted and later released him were composed of 'congealed air,' or a finer type of matter. Yet, in defense of the spiritual aspect or theory, fairy associations and fairyland entrances were often with subterranean regions or necroploleis, such as barrows, tumuli, ruined hill-forts, mounds, and the like. Caves, wild gorges, and chasms also had the same types of fairy associations, however, as did crevices or cracks in rocks which were too narrow for human beings to enter.

Through the centuries, some have theorized that the fairies of the British Isles were fallen angels, the souls of the pagan or unbaptized dead, or the actual hidden descendants of races (or species?) of man which had been defeated by the Celts and driven into hiding, eventually beneath the ground. Here, after long ages, they often became diminutive in form and stature, due to cramped quarters, poor nutrition, and inbreeding. Walter Evans-Wentz reports an interesting belief (as expressed in *The Fairy Faith in Celtic Countries*, 1911, pp. 166–67), held by David MacRitchie previously, who in his book *The Testimony of Tradition* (1890), noted the similarity between the word *pixies*, or *pixys*, and *Picts*, a Bronze-Age, pre-Celtic people whom he saw as non-Aryan (a possibility, at least before the coming of the Celts) and dwarf-like, the latter now known to be false.

But what might years of interbreeding in a subterranean environment do to the stature of a people, or isolated groups of survivors in hiding from taller, stronger invaders? The finding of apparent Neolithic dwarf remains—an entire tribe of dwarfs—in Switzerland in 1893, lent credence to the theory of ancient, pygmy races who had been driven into a slinking, clandestine, and eventually subterranean existence throughout Europe. To the Victorians, this led to the conclusion that dwarfism and midgetism were possibly due to the racial residue of Cro-Magnon types interbreeding with these ancient peoples, and that the fairies were simply natural and earlier forms of man. For a time, even the Spiritualists and Theosophists adopted this theory as their own. This didn't last, and soon these groups were back into the esoteric, elemental or devic (nature spirit) concepts.

Elves

In old Germany, "elf" was a name applied to any kind of supernatural spirit, especially one that inhabited fields or forests.

In Scotland, England, and Scandinavia, "elf" was another name for a member of the fairy folk. Then, as fairy lore developed and became more intricate and complex, with levels and classes within their supernatural ranks, the English designated elves as smaller members of the fairy population and the Scots gave the title of elf to those beings that were generally of human size. Things changed a bit in Scandinavia, as well, when the people there began to distinguish two categories of elves—the benign ones and the dastardly ones.

Scandinavians also envisioned two principle divisions of the beings. There were the lovely, charming elves, who easily passed for humans and who loved to join in folk dances and in village parties. These elves, especially the females of the bunch, could easily seduce any human male into obeying their will. The male elves, though appearing handsome and dashing in the firelight of a village festival, would usually be exposed as squat and ugly when moonlight struck them in the forests. The Danes also noticed that even the attractive elves occasionally betrayed themselves with a long cow-like tail that popped out of their dress or trousers.

In contemporary presentations, elves are usually portrayed as jolly creatures, humanlike in appearance, but extremely diminutive in size, that love teasing humans and playing pranks on them. Of course there's that "right jolly old elf," Santa Claus who brings good children toys at Christmas time.

> *Years ago, I was sternly advised that if I should ever have an encounter with a fairy and wish to survive basically intact, there are two rules I must remember: 1) Don't you dare ask its name. 2) Don't you dare call it a fairy.*

Fairies/Fey/Sidhe

Traditionally, the fairies are a race of beings, the counterparts of humankind in physical appearance but, at the same time, nonphysical or multidimensional. They are mortal, but lead longer lives than their human cousins.

Years ago, I was sternly advised that if I should ever have an encounter with a fairy and wish to survive basically intact, there are two rules I must remember: 1) Don't you dare ask its name. 2) Don't you dare call it a fairy. According to those who speak the Gaelic tongue of Scotland and Ireland, the wee folk prefer to be known as sidhe (also spelled sidh, sith, sithche and pronounced "shee"). There is disagreement as to the exact meaning of sidhe. Some say that it refers to the mounds or hills in which the supernatural folk abide. Others say that it means, "the people of peace," and that is

True gnomes are not those cute little folk with pointed hats that people place in their garden and yards (*art by Bill Oliver*).

how the sidhe generally behave toward humans—except for those seemingly incurable elfin traits of kidnapping human children and shape-shifting into a seemingly endless variety of forms in order to work mischief.

Alexander Pope wrote lovely passages idealizing fairies. Sir Walter Scott emphasized the beauty of the fairy realm and the struggle of the fairies to achieve humanlike souls. William Butler Yeats had a nearly obsessive interest in the paranormal and strongly believed in fairies. And it was the creator of Sherlock Holmes, Sir Arthur Conan Doyle himself, who came to the defense of Elsie Wright and Frances Griffiths in the famous and controversial Case of the Cottingly Fairies in 1917.

Doyle theorized that the fairies are constructed of material that emits vibrations either shorter or longer than the normal spectrum visible to the human eye. Clairvoyance, he believed, consists, at least in part, of the ability to see these vibrations.

In most traditions, especially in the British Isles and Scandinavia, the fairy folk were supernormal entities that inhabit a magical kingdom beneath the surface of the earth. In all traditions, the fairy folk are depicted as possessing many more powers and abilities than *Homo sapiens*, but, for some unexplained reason, they are strongly dependent on human beings—and from time to time they seek to reinforce their own kind by kidnapping both children and adults. Tales of folk being abducted by smallish beings did not begin in the last few decades with accounts of the "Grays" from UFOs.

The Fey have never been popularly conceived of as spirits, although some theologians have sought to cast the fairies in the role of the rebellious angels that were driven out of heaven during the celestial uprising led by Lucifer.

Most of the ancient texts declare that the "gentry," as they are often called, are of a middle nature, "between humans and angels." Although they are of a nature between spirits and humans, they can intermarry with humans and bear half-human children.

C.S. Lewis, author of many classic books on spiritual matters, once suggested that the wee folk are a third rational species.

1) The angels are highest, having perfect goodness and whatever knowledge is necessary for them to accomplish God's will;

2) Humans, somewhat less perfect, are the second;

3) Fairies, having certain powers of the angels but no souls, are the third.

On the other hand, Medieval theologians favored three quite different theories to explain the origin of fairies:

1) They are a special class of demoted angels;

2) They are a special class of the dead;

3) They are fallen angels.

Gnomes

Whoever started the image of cute, pointed-hat garden gnomes must have been possessed by the greedy spirit of a gnome that came up with a plan to squeeze coins out of humans. Traditionally, gnomes are represented as gnarled, wrinkled, hunched old men who have been assigned to guard some ancient treasure. Classically, the role of the gnome is that of a supernatural guardian that can release the treasures of the earth to the earnest alchemist or magician.

Gnomes, according to the alchemists of the Renaissance, had the ability to move through the earth in a manner similar to a human moving through air or a fish through water. The alchemist would seek to invoke the energy of the salamander, a lizard-like entity whose element was fire, and the gnome, whose element was earth, and combine their energies with air and water to create gold from base metals.

Goblins are very closely related to demonic entities. Their specialty is wreaking havoc and malicious acts of harm (*art by Ricardo Pustanio*).

Goblins

Goblins are very closely related to demonic entities. Their specialty is wreaking havoc and malicious acts of harm. Usually portrayed as small, grotesque beings, the basic nature of goblins is as foul as their appearance.

Gremlins

Although gremlins may seem a recent addition to the folklore of the wee folk, it would seem that their antecedents are the goblins of old. The term "gremlin" was derived from the Old English word *greme*, which means to vex and annoy. And that is certainly what the gremlins did to the pilots and their aircraft in World War II when the pesky entities were routinely blamed for engine troubles, electronic failures, and any other thing that might go wrong with an airplane.

According to airmen who swore that they had survived close encounters with the mischief makers, the gremlins dressed in red or green double-breasted frock coats, old-fashioned tri-corn hats with a feather (or sometimes stocking caps with tassels at high altitudes), tights, and pointed footwear. Some of the gremlins loved to suck the high octane gas out of the tanks, others messed with the landing gears, and still others specialized in jamming the radio frequencies. Just as the pilots and mechanics were learning to tolerate the gremlin crowd, it wasn't long before they also began to be annoyed by the gremlins' girlfriends, the finellas, nicknamed the widgets.

Huldrefolk

The Huldrefolk, the Hidden People, of Scandinavia, are generally quite benign if treated with respect. If one should be foolish enough to anger them or violate their territory, they can become extremely malicious.

In 1962, the new owners of a herring-processing plant in Iceland decided to enlarge their work area. According to Icelandic tradition, no landowner must fail to reserve a small plot of his property for the Hidden Folk, and a number of the rural residents earnestly pointed out to the new proprietors that any extension of the plant would encroach upon the plot of ground that the original owners had set aside for the little people who lived under the ground.

The businessmen didn't harbor those old folk superstitions. They had employed a topnotch highly qualified construction crew that possessed modern, unbreakable drill bits and plenty of explosives.

But the bits of the "unbreakable" drills began to shatter one after another. An old farmer came forward to repeat the warning that the crew was trespassing on land that belonged to the Hidden Folk. At first the workmen laughed at the old man and marveled that such primitive superstitions could still exist in modern Iceland. But the drill bits kept breaking.

Finally, the manager of the plant, although professing disbelief in such superstitions, agreed to the old farmer's recommendation that he consult a local seer to establish contact with the Hidden Folk and attempt to make peace with them. After going into a brief trance-state, the seer informed the manager that there was one particularly powerful member of the Hidden Folk who had selected this plot as his special dwelling place. He was not an unreasonable being, however. If the processing plant really needed the plot for its expansion, he would agree to find another place to live. The Hidden One asked only for five days without any drilling, so that he could make his arrangements to move.

The manager felt a bit strange bargaining with a being that was invisible, but he looked over at the pile of broken drill bits and told the seer that the Hidden One had a deal. Work on the site would be shut down for five days to give him a chance to move.

After five days had passed and the workmen resumed drilling, the work proceeded smoothly and efficiently until the addition to the plant was completed. There were no more shattered bits on the unbreakable drill.

The Ircenrraat, Little People of the Tundra

Ircenrraat, recognized by the Yup'ik teachings and legends, are the "little people" who dwell in the tundra, usually underground. They disorient, discomfort, and trap unwary humans.

Mike Dunham said in his "Around Alaska" column (*Anchorage Daily News*, May 31, 2008) that while "city folk" usually dismiss Ircenrraat as tribal superstition, "Those who have lived in Yup'ik country for any period of time tend to be a little more inclined to listen. For one thing, the stories are persistent and often come from respectable observers. For another, when you're by yourself in the middle of nowhere, things happen that are hard to explain."

Dunham told of his taking a solo kayak trip in the lower Yukon region one year and having "unseen hands" toss rocks at him—some of which were of such considerable size that they made loud "plunking" sounds as they narrowly missed him and entered the water.

The Ircenrraat became much more real when Dunham was forwarded an email that was intended only for the sender's family members and not at all for public distribution. Dunham received permission to use the sender's name but keep others confidential.

On the evening of May 7, 2008, Nick Andrew Jr. was on a snowmobile three miles out of town. He was hunting birds when he spotted a small boy from the village standing all alone in a marsh, obviously frightened, disoriented, and crying. There were no footprints around the boy to indicate that he had walked or had been carried to the spot on which he stood.

Nick took the boy to his home, where his family had been frantic as to his whereabouts. After a night of rest, he told his parents and Nick what had happened to him: he had been grabbed and somehow "brought into" Pilcher Mountain, a site where people often reported sighting Ircenrraats.

Once inside the mountain, the boy was questioned about all kinds of things by some of the Ircenrraats. He was able to speak with a little girl who had been abducted by the little beings over 40 years ago. Somehow, she was still as young as the day that she had been taken. Regardless of her seemingly perpetual youth, she wanted to go home. Although she had begged for her release, the Ircenrraats refused to release her.

The boy then entered an unconscious state, and when he opened his eyes, he was standing in the middle of the marsh and Nick was approaching him on his snowmobile. When the boy's story began to spread, parents became much more attentive to the whereabouts of the children and became receptive to the tribal tales of the Ircenrraats.

Kitsune

In Japanese folklore, the Kitsune is a magical being that most often appears as a fox. When it is around 100 years old, the Kitsune can also manifest in human form, most often that of a beautiful girl. Well known as tricksters, the Kitsune can appear as a lovely, seductive girl one moment and lure a lusty young man into a cave where it shape-shifts into the image of an old man. The Kitsune are master illusionists and are generally good-natured. If one incurs its wrath, however, it can manipulate time and space and drive people insane.

Leprechaun

The classic tale of the Leprechaun is that of the Irishman catching one of the wee folk and demanding to be given the little fellow's crock of gold. In these stories, the sly Leprechaun always manages to trick the greedy lout who has grabbed him by causing the human to glance away from him for even a moment. Once a human takes his eyes off the Leprechaun he has somehow managed to glimpse in the first place, the wee one has the power to vanish in a flash.

The Leprechaun, dressed in his bright green clothing with a red cap and a leather apron, was originally known as the cheerful cobbler, a wee person who takes delight in repairing humans' shoes for a reward of a bowl of porridge.

The country folk of Ireland know better than to disturb the mounds or raths in which the Leprechauns dwell. Those who would wantonly violate their domicile is to invite severe supernatural consequences upon oneself.

The trouble at the rath outside the village of Wexford began on a morning in 1960 when the workmen from the state electricity board began digging a hole for the erection of a light pole within the parameters of a rath. The villagers warned the workmen that the pole would never stay put, because no self-respecting community of wee folk could abide a disturbance on their mound.

The big city electrical workmen had a laugh at the expense of the villagers and said some uncomplimentary things about the level of intelligence of the townsfolk of Wexford. They finished digging the hole to the depth that experience had taught them was adequate, then they placed the post within the freshly dug opening and tamped the black earth firmly around its base. The satisfied foreman pronounced for all within earshot to hear that no fairy folk or Leprechaun would move the pole from where it had been anchored.

However, the next morning the pole tilted at a sharp angle in loose earth.

The foreman of the crew voiced his suspicions that the Leprechauns had received some help from some humans bent on mischief. Glaring his resentment at any villagers who would meet his accusative eyes, the foreman ordered his men to reset the pole.

The next morning that one particular pole was once again conspicuous in the long line of newly placed electrical posts by its weird tilt in the loose soil at its base. While the other poles in the line stood straight and firmly upright, that one woebegone post was tilted askew.

The foreman had endured enough of such rustic humor at his expense. He ordered the crew to dig a hole six feet wide, place the pole precisely in the middle, and pack the earth so firmly around the base that nothing short of a bomb could budge it.

The next morning the intrusive pole had once again been pushed loose of the little people's rath. The foreman and his crew from the electricity board finally knew when they were licked. Without another word to the grinning villagers, the workmen dug a second hole four feet outside of the mound and dropped the pole in there. And that was where it stood as solid as the Emerald Isle for many years to come.

Leshy

The Leshy in Slavic folklore is a large, male woodland spirit that is recognized as the protector of wild animals and the forest itself. Woe be unto any careless camper, reckless hunter, or even a smitten lover who carves his initials with his sweetheart into the bark of a tree. The Leshy most often appears as a tall man with pale skin, bright green eyes, a long beard, horns, and hooves. He is capable of shape-shifting, and because of his close association with wolves, he is sometimes believed to be a werewolf. Although he has a ghastly cry that terrorizes those who abuse the forest and its creatures, he can also imitate human voices. Since he can sometimes be a bit of a prankster, he will sometimes lure people deep into the forest until they are lost. Generally, the Leshy is not an evil being, so he will see to it that the confused humans find their way out again.

Mambu-mutu

In Lake Tanganyika in the small East African country of Burundi, the Mambu-mutu is very much the classic mermaid, half-attractive woman and half-large fish. In her case, however, she seems incapable of having good thoughts regarding humans, and her only intention is to drag them under the lake's surface and suck their blood.

Nakh

Shape-shifting water demons that appear most frequently as handsome men or beautiful women, the Nakh, like the Greek Sirens, lure their victims into the river or sea with the sound of their sweet, seductive singing. Very often, according to old Estonian folklore, the spirits of the drowned may also become Nakhs, seeking to entice the living into watery graves. Even if one should escape the enchantment of their singing, the very sighting of a Nakh is a bad omen, usually a sign that either the witnesses or someone dear to him will die soon in a river, lake, or ocean.

Nasnas

The Nasnas is a shape-shifting demon that often appears to its victims as a frail old man or woman. The Nasnas's favorite environment is that of a river bank where, in its guise as an elderly person in need, asks to be helped or carried across the water. Once a kind-hearted passerby agrees to help the demon-in-disguise, the Nasnas overpowers him and drowns him.

Nisse

In the Scandinavian tradition, the Nisse is a household entity that looks after hearth and home, a kind of guardian entity—but with an attitude. Nisse can be extremely volatile if provoked, and they are very often mischievous little pranksters. Naughty children sometimes have their hair pulled, their toys hidden by the Nisse, which is always watching with disapproving eyes any sign of misbehavior or disobedience.

The Nisse is also the farmer's friend, and often sleeps in the barn to keep watch over the animals. If treated with respect, the Nisse remains an effective guardian over hearth and outbuildings. It does demand payment for the performance of duties, and the wise householder will be certain to leave hot porridge on the step at night and to make it known that the Nisse is free to take whatever grain from the bin that he might require for its own needs.

Nix

The Nix is a particularly nasty shape-shifting entity which, like all the fairy folk, loves to dance. According to German folklore, the Nix are attracted to the sound of music at fairs, carnivals, or outdoor concerts; they appear as attractive men or women who enthrall the human audience with their skill and grace on the dance floor. Once they have lured a charmed human to join them at water's edge with the promise of romantic dalliance, they reveal themselves to be ugly, green-skinned fairies that drag their victim into the water and death by drowning.

RICARDO PUSTANIO
2010

The Nasnas is a shapeshifting demon that often appears to its victims as a frail old man or woman. The Nasnas's favorite environment is that of a river bank where, in its guise as an elderly person in need, asks to be helped or carried across the water. Once a kind-hearted passerby agrees to help the demon-in-disguise, the Nasnas overpowers him and drowns him (*art by Ricardo Pustanio*).

Puca/Pooka

The Puca/Pooka is very comfortable in the hills and valleys of Ireland, Scotland, and Wales. A notorious shape-shifter, the Pooka can assume any image from a rabbit to a horse. If it wishes, it can transform itself into the most hideous monster of great size. Pookas are generally amiable entities with common use of human speech and are well-known for giving good advice to those who plan to use the information for good and not evil. At times they can be rather mischievous and they are great lovers of posing riddles that must be solved by confused humans. Generally, they wish to be helpful to humans if they are treated with respect.

Pa-i-sa-ki and Puk-wud-jies

The native American tribes who later settled in Indiana believed that they shared the land with several other types of wild forest people. These wildmen, the natives thought, straddled the line somewhere between living, physical men and mystical creatures of the spirit.

One group that was considered very real was a race of little people called the Pa-i-sa-ki by the Miami tribe, and the Puk-wud-jies by the Delaware. The names translate as "little wild men of the forest" and both the Miami and Delaware believed that the little people had occupied the areas before the arrival of native Americans.

Described as being about two feet tall, with white skin and light brown hair, the Pa-i-sa-ki wore shirt-like garments woven with long grasses, bark, and sometimes fur. The little wild men of the forest lived in caves along the river banks, but would sometimes build small huts out of grass or tree limbs when they were away from their caves on hunting trips.

"We stopped about ten yards apart and looked at each other, he had thick, dark blond hair and his face was round and pinkish in color, like it was sunburned."

Paul Startzman of Anderson, Indiana, believes that the Native American stories are true. In fact, he believes that the little wild men of the forest have survived into present times because he has seen them himself. Startzman was already familiar with the legends of the Pa-i-sa-ki. His grandmother, Mary Gunyan, was a Native American and used to entertain his mother and her sister with tales of the little people who lived along the banks of the nearby White River.

Startzman told about his personal encounters with the Pa-i-sa-ki on the popular TV show, "Across Indiana," seen on WFYI-TV 20.

In 1927, when Startzman was ten years old, he was hiking along an overgrown gravel pit when he came face to face with a little man who was no bigger than two feet tall: "We stopped about ten yards apart and looked at each other, he had thick, dark blond hair and his face was round and pinkish in color, like it was sunburned." Startzman also observed that the little man was barefoot and wearing a long, light blue gown that came down to his ankles.

Before Startzman could move, the little man turned and quickly moved away into the underbrush.

Later, Startzman claimed that he and a school chum spotted another Pa-i-sa-ki following them as they walked near the same gravel pit. This little person again, wore a long gown that Startzman speculates could have been a man's shirt that the Pa-i-sa-ki might have stolen from a clothes line.

Paul Startzman believes that the Pa-i-sa-ki were a race of pygmy-like men that existed in Indiana long before the first Native Americans occupied this part of the world. The Native American tribes believed it best to maintain friendly relations with the little people. Food and other gifts were left out in the forest, and the little people in return would warn the tribes of enemies or the whereabouts of game animals. The Pa-i-sa-ki were considered to be very shy and usually avoided contact with people.

The little people are said to communicate with each other by making tapping sounds with rocks or sticks, or by imitating the whistles of songbirds.

Startzman considers it possible that the Pa-i-sa-ki could have survived into modern times. "Wild deer and other animals still live along the wooded sections of the White River, why not small, intelligent humans with an old, well established society?"

Paul still hikes along the banks of the White River with his camera, hoping that someday he'll finally catch a shot of the elusive, little wild people of Indiana.

Rusalki

In the legends of the Slavic people we find that the spirit of a beautiful girl who used her physical charms to work wickedness and consequently has been damned for her sins gets another chance to be even nastier when she crosses over to the Other Side. It is at that time that she may choose to become a rusalka, a sultry shape-shifter who can appear along the river banks as an innocent young maiden, singing sweet, seductive songs to smitten young men—before she drowns them.

Some rusalki are a bit nicer to their victims. They first make love to the men they've seduced and permit them to die happy before they pull them into the water and drown them.

In Bulgaria, the rusalki, known as *Samovily*, are made up of the souls of unbaptized baby girls or of brides who died on their wedding night. They, too, get another opportunity to manifest as tempting shape-shifters who lure men to their watery deaths.

Spunkie

The spunkie is a Scottish goblin that preys upon travelers who venture out after dark. The spunkie is considered so nasty that tradition has it that he is a direct agent of Satan. It hovers about in the darkness, just waiting for a traveler to become lost in the night, perhaps during a rainstorm when visibility is especially bad. The spunkie manifests a light that appears to the desperate wayfarer like illumination shining through a window pane, thus signaling shelter and a dry place to spend the inclement evening. But as the hopeful traveler approaches the light, it keeps moving just a bit farther away. Since the poor, drenched pilgrim has no choice in the darkness but to keep pursuing the light source, the spunkie keeps moving it just a bit farther on—until the evil creature has lured the unfortunate traveler over a cliff.

Sirens

The Selkies, the Seal People of the Orkney and Shetland Islands, may wish to live harmoniously with the humans who love the sea as much as they do, but the sirens have no interest in creating anything but death and chaos for seafarers. In Greek lore, there were at first only two sirens, large birdlike beings with the heads of beautiful women and the gift for singing so soothingly and sweetly that no sailor could resist their enchanting duets. As the popularity of the legend grew, storytellers increased the number of sirens to three. Later, with the passing of time, the sirens became an entire chorus of mesmerizing female voices. They also evolved in their appearance, from the large birdlike entities with human heads to creatures more in the style of the mermaid tradition. In Homer's *Odyssey*, Odysseus foils the sirens by ordering his men to stuff their ears with wax so they cannot hear their fatal songs.

Forget about those cute little bright-eyed munchkins with red hair that claim to be Trolls. In Scandinavia, the term "troll" is applied only to hostile giants.

Troll

Forget about those cute little bright-eyed munchkins with red hair that claim to be trolls. In Scandinavia, the term "troll" is applied only to hostile giants. By the time of the Middle Ages, some trolls had become a bit smaller and more fiendish, capable of working black magic and sorcery. In more contemporary times, the troll is regarded as a denizen of mountain caves, larger than the average human, and exceedingly ugly. Somewhere along the way, some modern Danes started considering the sweet, elflike or brownie-type being as a kind of troll—especially for export. Just don't go around the mountainous regions of Scandinavia and shout out any challenges to the trolls. The ugly brute that comes charging out of the cave will bear absolutely no resemblance to that little, smiling red-haired doll your parents bought for you when you were a kid.

Yaksha

Among the magical, mythical kingdoms of the world, Alaka, hidden away in the Himalayas, is populated by the Yakshas, nature spirits whose protection may be sought by humans who desire their guardianship for their city or village. Kubera, the chief ruler of the Yakshas, sees to it that his followers first fulfill their basic duty of guarding treasures buried within the earth before they hire out to protect human enterprises. The female Yakshas appear to human eyes as beautiful women bedecked with lavish and exquisite jewelry. Yakshas are generally considered to be benevolent entities, although it has been noted that offended or discontented female members of their kind may steal a human child and make a meal of it.

HEADLESS HORSEMEN AND OTHER PHANTOM MIDNIGHT RIDERS

There will probably never be a housing development near the Stowe Hollow, Vermont covered bridge.

According to area residents interviewed by Janice Elliott for the Associated Press (January 31, 1969), people who have begun to build houses near the bridge have been frightened off by the apparition of a young woman.

Old-timers in the region state that the ghost is that of a young bride who was left waiting at the altar by an irresponsible groom. The jilted woman left the church, heading for her elusive lover's home near the covered bridge on Hollow Road. As she was crossing the bridge, something startled her horse, causing it to bolt and throw her to her death on the rocks below the bridge.

Traditionally, in the wee hours of morning, the sorrowing bride returns to search for the lover who betrayed her and humiliated her by jilting her on their wedding day.

Those who have toyed with the idea of building a home near the scenic old bridge, have reversed their decision when they discovered that their house would be in the path of the lonely lady ghost.

Mysterious entities from the Other Side are often encountered haunting highways, country roads, and hotels.

Tribal Ghosts Spook the Pocahontas Parkway Toll Plaza

On July 15, 2002, the driver of a delivery truck reported seeing three Native Americans approaching the recently opened Pocahontas Parkway toll plaza on state Route 895 in eastern Henrico County, Virginia. In a report filed by the toll taker to whom he related the account, he had seen three breech-clothed warriors carrying torches walking in the middle of the highway. He blasted his horn to warn two more torch-wielding men who were clearly illuminated by his headlights. He wondered if some tribespeople were staging some bizarre kind of protest against the parkway.

The toll taker took the driver's report and added it to the list of stories from motorists who had seen strange unexplainable phenomena. She knew that although she would report the incident to state troopers who would be right on the case, they would find no Native Americans parading with torches protesting anything.

Troopers who patrol the graveyard shift along the Pocahontas Parkway said that they had responded to dozens of calls similar to the one the delivery truck driver made on July 15. The first was on July 1, then two nights later, when plaza workers reported hearing Indian drums, chants, whoops, and the cries of what seemed to be hundreds of voices. From time to time there would be seen the vague outlines of people running back and forth in the darkness.

An engineer working nights to complete the construction of the bridge in Parkway Plaza said that he and a group of workmen had seen an Indian sitting astride a horse watching them from below on the interstate. They were about to tell him to move on, that he wasn't allowed to ride a horse on the interstate, when both rider and horse disappeared.

> *Ludwig, the spirit of a Hessian soldier, materialized for many nights in the bedroom of contractor Mike Benio.*

Many Ghosts Haunt the General Wayne Inn

Located on the old Lancaster roadway between Philadelphia and Radner, the General Wayne Inn has been in continuous operation since 1704 when Robert Jones, a Quaker, decided to provide travelers with a restaurant and a place of lodging. During the Revolutionary War, the establishment, originally called the Wayside Inn, played host to General George Washington and the Marquis de la Fayette, as well as a number of their adversaries, the British Redcoats and their Hessian mercenaries. The Wayside was renamed the General Wayne Inn in 1793 honor of a local hero, General Anthony Wayne.

When Barton Johnson bought the General Wayne Inn in 1970, he was well aware of its reputation for being haunted. Previous guests had claimed encounters with the ghosts of men dressed in Revolutionary era uniforms. The ghost of Edgar Allan Poe, a frequent guest when he was alive, according to the old register, had been reported in a room known as the Franklin Post Office. Employees working in the bar area, as well as the guests seated there, often saw dozens of wine and other liquor glasses in a wooden rack begin to shake violently for no apparent reason.

Ludwig, the spirit of a Hessian soldier, materialized for many nights in the bedroom of contractor Mike Benio. Ludwig begged Benio to unearth his bones, which had been buried in the basement of the inn, and give them a proper burial in a cemetery. When Barton Johnson returned from a vacation, Benio asked permission to excavate a certain area of the cellar that was under the parking lot. Here, Benio found fragments of pottery and some human bones. After giving the remains a proper burial, the ghost of Ludwig was at peace and no longer manifested at the General Wayne Inn.

One night, Johnson placed a tape recorder in the bar. The next morning during playback, he could clearly hear the sounds of bar stools being moved about, the water faucet being turned on and off, and glasses catching the water.

She Passed the Car … and It Disappeared

Mary Simpkins of Portland, Oregon, said that she was driving east out of Bend on the Bend-Burns Highway early one morning in May 2001: "The road is raised up somewhat—banked—from the desert and it is a long, easy slope down from Horse Ridge. I wasn't going very fast, just enjoying the drive, when I came up on a black sedan moving slowly. I hit my passing gear and zoomed past. As I passed, I looked in to see if there was anyone I knew in the sedan. There was just an older man and woman who looked back at me."

But when Mary glanced in her rearview mirror, just as soon as she had passed the black sedan, there was no car behind her. "The highway behind me was empty."

Mary had a frightening thought that the older couple had somehow gone over the bank, which, at that point, was several feet high.

"I came to a quick stop at the edge of the road and got out," she said. "I went to the back of my car and looked and looked, but I couldn't see the black sedan anywhere. There were no access roads around or any other cars around. Besides, the car was only out of my sight for a couple of seconds."

As Mary stood there looking around for some sign of the mysterious black sedan with the older couple inside, "a light breeze sprang up and blew across me—and I can tell you that the hairs on the back of my neck and my arms stood up. I jumped in my little car, locked all four doors, and got out of there. I was both frightened and puzzled. I guess I still am. I still get that creepy hair-rising-on-back-of-neck-and-arms feeling whenever I recall the car that disappeared and the breeze that sprang up out of nowhere."

The Car Faded Away Like an Old Photograph

Early on a Sunday evening in 1997, Max Tingley was driving with his family outside of Albany, New York, when he became impatient with the way in which an old car, which he guessed to be a 1941 Chevrolet sedan, was slowing traffic. Max figured that the car was going or coming to some antique auto show or rally and he want-

There is not a single state in the United States that does not have its own stories of ghosts, apparitions, hitchhiking phantoms, haunted highways and hotels (*iStock*).

ed to be tolerant, but he was returning from a family outing at Lake George and he wanted to get home to do some paperwork.

"I had to be at work early the next morning with my presentation ready to go, and I had some factors that I needed to sharpen," Max said. "As I approached nearer to the Chevy, I was surprised that it didn't have those special license plates that owners of those old cars are supposed to display. I hated to be a jerk, but I really blasted my horn, something I usually don't do when following a slow-moving vehicle."

Max recalled that he could see the driver of the Chevy turn around and look at him with what appeared to be an expression of total shock.

"I expected an angry, hostile look, and maybe an obscene gesture or two, but this guy looked as if I had genuinely startled him," Max said. "He looked as though he had somehow imagined himself to be driving all alone on the highway."

Then, before the incredulous eyes of Max, his wife, and their three children, the old Chevrolet sedan in front of them began to fade away.

"It was as if it were some old photograph dissolving bit by bit before us, just fading away until there was nothing left to prove that it had ever been there," Max said. "The antique Chevy and its driver had completely disappeared in about thirty seconds."

Haunted Highways and Hotels

There is not a single state in the United States that does not have its own stories of ghosts, apparitions, hitchhiking phantoms, haunted highways and hotels. If individuals were so disposed, they could actually drive across America visiting nothing but haunted hotels and spotting ghosts on the highways.

Here is a very small sampling:

Alaska

- Room 201 of the Courtyard by Marriott in Anchorage is haunted by a man who was found dead in that room. Another ghost named Ken roams the parking lot and the courtyard. A phantom cat is often reported in rooms 103 and 107.

Arizona

- The rebuilt Pioneer Hotel in Tucson is said to be haunted by the spirits of those who died in a fire in the building in the past.

- Ghostly miners with their lighted headlamps have been sighted in the San Miguel Magma copper mine.

- The picturesque old Monte Vista Hotel provides a marvelous place for an overnight stay on the way to or from the Grand Canyon. Guests who stay there may encounter the "Phantom bellboy," that knocks on doors and announces, "Room service," in a muffled voice. Others claim to have seen the wispy image of a woman strolling through an upstairs corridor.

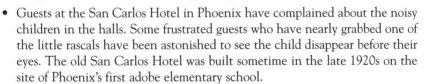

Some frustrated guests who have nearly grabbed one of the little rascals have been astonished to see the child disappear before their eyes.

- Guests at the San Carlos Hotel in Phoenix have complained about the noisy children in the halls. Some frustrated guests who have nearly grabbed one of the little rascals have been astonished to see the child disappear before their eyes. The old San Carlos Hotel was built sometime in the late 1920s on the site of Phoenix's first adobe elementary school.

California

- The spirit of a young woman, who in the 1920s sought to hide her unwelcome pregnancy from her parents by leaping into Stowe Lake, can be seen walking in despair around Strawberry Hill in the Stowe Lake Golden Gate Park near San Francisco.

- Constructed in 1771, the old Mission of San Antonio de Padua is located in the central California mountains of the Santa Lucia range, thirty miles north of Paso Robles. The Mission remains an enchanted and haunted place, and those who stay overnight often catch sight of the ghosts of several monks and the mysterious entity that manifests as a headless woman on horseback.

- The sprawling Brookdale Lodge, built in 1924 in the Santa Cruz Mountains near Boulder Creek, California, was a popular hideaway for gangland king-pins in the 1930s. Later, the Lodge was a favorite of film legends Marilyn Monroe, Joan Crawford, and Tyrone Power. The colorful inn, which features a brook running through the dining room, has a number of "cold spots," which indicate haunted areas. The most frequently sighted spirit entity is that of a small girl dressed very formally in 1940s-style clothing. The ghost is thought to be that of the five-year-old who drowned in the brook sometime in the late 1940s.

- The ghosts of a girl in a prom dress and a boy wearing a football-letter sweater are seen in the top row of the bleachers at Bakersfield High School.

- The sound of marching ghosts and a number of haunted rooms have kept many a guest awake throughout the night at the Horton Grand Hotel in San Diego.

- A headless man, thought to be the ghost of a victim of the 1989 San Francisco earthquake, knocks on the windows of cars driving towards Oakland on the Bay Bridge.

- Apparitions of weird entities haunt the eighteenth floor and the parking garage at the Los Angeles Airport Marriott. Guests have reported strange odors and sounds and being engulfed by feelings of absolute terror.

Colorado

- The spirits of laborers who died building Gold Camp Road, originally a railroad line from Colorado Springs to Cripple Creek, are often witnessed by those who travel the road late at night.

Connecticut

- The 165-year-old The MisFitz Inn in Southbury is haunted by a ghost known affectionately as Sadie the Lady, who, in the 1890s, was found dead in her room above the tavern, an apparent suicide. Ever since her tragic end, Sadie has been held responsible for strange noises coming from empty rooms, overturned chairs in the bar, and water being dumped on unsuspecting patrons and employees.

Florida

- The "Blue House" of the Sweet Water Bed and Breakfast Inn in Gainesville has a ghost that may hearken back to the days when the place was a plantation. The maids complain of furniture moving around, and some guests feel the spirit pressing down on their chests at night.

Georgia

- Before guests may stay in room 204 at the 1790 Inn in Savannah, they must sign a waiver at the front desk stating that the management is not responsible for any items of clothing stolen by "Anne," the ghost who haunts the inn.

- Many researchers claim that hundreds of hotels, inns, and private homes harbor ghosts in Savannah, Georgia's oldest city, settled in 1733, the scene of a fierce Revolutionary War battle, three deadly Yellow Fever epidemics, and a harsh Civil War period of occupation.

Illinois

- For years now, witnesses have seen the ethereal form and heard the sobs and cries of the Sobbing Woman of Archer Woods Cemetery near Chicago.

- Witnesses over the decades have sighted more than 100 glowing ghosts in Bachelor's Grove Cemetery in Chicago.

Indiana

- Nighttime security officers at the Old Central State Hospital in Indianapolis claim a nightmarish cacophony of screams, groans, and cries for help and sightings of people who vanish.

Kentucky

- The ghost of a girl in a prom dress is seen at the top of the hill on Mitchell Hill Road, Louisville, near the spot where she and her date are said to have been killed on prom night.

- The ghost of a male student who was shot and killed in the lobby of Meyzek Middle School has haunted the school since the 1930s.

Louisiana

- Some guests craving a ghostly encounter choose the third floor rooms of The Castle Inn in New Orleans. The bed and breakfast is haunted by the playful spirit of a little girl and by a black man who burned to death in one of the woodsheds.

- Numerous ghosts appear at various places in the French Quarter, but locals warn against a handsome specter of an alleged real-life vampire who still takes delight in assaulting women.

Maine

- The 200-year-old Kennebunk Inn, Kennebunkport, is haunted by a friendly ghost named Silas Perkins, who delights in levitating champagne glasses and tossing beer mugs around the bar. The Kennebunk Inn is a favorite of former President George H. W. Bush, because it is near his seafront estate.

The Baltimore, Maryland, house where famous nineteenth-century author Edgar Allan Poe lived is said to be haunted (*iStock*).

Maryland

- Fort McHenry shelters a host of ghosts who still vigilantly guard Baltimore. Lights, shadowy figures, and voices have been reported for many decades.
- The house of Edgar Allan Poe in Baltimore is said to be haunted by the spirit of a rather rotund female dressed in gray. Those wishing a glimpse of the ghost of the master of the macabre are said to have a better chance at Westminster Church graveyard, where Poe is buried beside his wife, Virginia.

Massachusetts

- Boston Commons is the home for many ghosts, including two aristocratic women in nineteenth-century attire, who vanish when witnesses approach them.
- Some people say that at least 50 ghosts walk the streets and hotel hallways of Nantucket Island. Almost any place of lodging near the town's historic section harbors its share of unseen guests. Even the Coast Guard station is haunted.

When author Peter Benchley was on the island writing his bestseller *Jaws*, he encountered the ghost of an old man dressed in eighteenth-century clothing. The entity sat in front of a fireplace in a rocking chair, and Benchley insists that he was not dreaming.

Michigan

- A construction worker fell from a scaffolding when a new gym was being added to Divine Child High School in Dearborn, and witnesses say the building is haunted by his spirit.

Mississippi

- In the late 1700s, Madeline was murdered by the jealous wife of Richard King, the owner of King's Tavern in Natchez. For over 200 years, patrons have regularly reported seeing the ghost of a slender woman who stands defiantly before them, her hands on her hips. To add to the color and allure of the haunted tavern, in the 1930s a woman's skeleton was found sealed in a brick fireplace with a jeweled dagger in her chest.

Missouri

- The ghosts of young girls in long white dresses have been sighted merrily playing together in Elmwood Cemetery in Kansas City.

- Many individuals claim that the entire shoreline around Houston Lake in Kansas City—with emphasis on the beach area—is haunted by some very bizarre entities.

- Six Flags Theme Park in St. Louis is home to the ghost of a little girl, a spirit named Stella, and a strange being that makes an eerie squealing noise, much like a pig.

- Witnesses have claimed to have heard babies crying in Coopers Cemetery outside of St. Louis. Others report the ghost of an old man carrying a lantern.

New Mexico

- Guests at the Desert Sands Motel on W140 near Albuquerque report cold spots, ghostly voices, and doors that unlock and open of their own volition.

- A glimpse of an old guest register at the St. James Hotel reads like a "Who's Who of the Wild West": Billy the Kid, Pat Garrett, Bat Masterson, Black Jack Ketchum, Doc Holliday, Buffalo Bill Cody. Almost any room in this 120-year-old hotel—a favorite of gunfighters in the 1880s—will produce an active spirit encounter. However, if you should decide to give the St. James a try, it would probably be best to avoid Room 18. Things got a little too wild in that room back in the 1880s, and the spirits there are too hostile and aggressive for most folks.

North Carolina

- When the Clyde Erwin High School was built just outside Asheville in the 1970s, the Old County Home Graveyard was disturbed, thereby causing many restless spirits to haunt the new building.

Ohio

- The ghost of a little blond, blue-eyed girl in a blue dress haunts King's Island theme park in Cincinnati. She is said to be joined by spirits haunting the observation deck of the Eiffel Tower, the roller coaster, and the Octopus ride.

Oregon

- The ghost of a hanged horse thief and his dog haunt the campground at Scapponia Park outside of Portland.

- The Villa St. Rose School for Girls in Portland is haunted by the spirits of small children who died there when the place was an orphanage maintained by nuns.

Pennsylvania

- There are many reports of visitors witnessing spirit re-enactments of segments of the great battles that took place near Gettysburg on July 1 through 3, 1863.

Frequently cited are areas near Devil's Den, Cemetery Hill, and Gettysburg National Military Park.

Texas

- On the outskirts of El Paso, many witnesses claimed to have seen "El Muerto," the "dead one," galloping through the desert with his head hanging by a rawhide throng from the saddle of his ghostly steed.

- Ysleta High School in El Paso is haunted by the ghosts of a cheerleader who committed suicide in a restroom and by a small boy who died when he fell off the stage in the auditorium.

- Motorists on Christman Road near Houston look out for the phantom female hitchhiker in a purple dress.

- When Martin High School in Laredo was built, no attention was given to the task of moving the bodies from the old cemetery site on which the building would rest. Consequently, strange sounds are heard throughout the school and shadowy figures haunt the gym.

- The ghost of a mud-caked woman in a white dress is said by many witnesses to walk in the water near the banks of Zacate creek outside of Laredo.

- The spirits of soldiers and Native Americans are often reported walking at the side of Old Nacogdoches Road outside of San Antonio.

> *The ghost of a mud-caked woman in a white dress is said by many witnesses to walk in the water near the banks of Zacate creek outside of Laredo.*

Utah

- Even nonbelievers in the spirit world are "creeped out" when they read that Lilly's tombstone in the Salt Lake City Cemetery decrees that she was a "victim of the Beast 666."

Vermont

- Margaret Spencer, a once wealthy, vivacious beauty who died in 1943 at the age of 98, haunts Room 2 of the Old Stagecoach Inn in Waterbury, Vermont. Margaret is often glimpsed in a wispy, white shawl, and she loves to play tricks on the guests.

Washington

- Both employees and guests complain of the loud party taking place on the ninth floor of the Claremont Hotel—which stops abruptly whenever anyone investigates. Witnesses say that it sounds like a party from the Roaring Twenties, judging from the music that blares forth from the unseen merrymakers in this Seattle hotel.

- The spirit of a Native American woman haunts the Pike Place Public Market, walking the area that was once sacred ground to her tribe.

Wisconsin

- Perhaps because the Stritch dormitory at Cardinal Stritch University in Milwaukee was a former convent, today's students often encounter the ghosts of nuns in their rooms and in the halls.

- Students residing in Humphrey Hall at Marquette University in Milwaukee must learn to live with the ghosts of children who died in the building when it served as the Milwaukee Children's Hospital. Even the security monitors have picked up images of singing, laughing, and screaming children.

Route 666 Will Always Be "the Devil's Road"

Although U.S. Route 666 has recently become officially known as U.S. Route 491 or 393, the legend of Camino del Diablo, "the Devil's Road," will be long remembered. The original naming of the highway had nothing to do with the Number of the Beast, 666, as given in Revelation, the last book in the Bible. It was so designated because it was the sixth branch of an interstate route then number U.S. 60. The section linking Chicago to Los Angeles became the legendary Route 66. And the Four Corners detour from Route 66 was renumbered 666 in August 1926.

But some say labeling the road with those numerals made it Satan's own road to perdition. The 190 miles of U.S. 666 starts at Gallup, New Mexico, wends its way through 70 miles of Colorado, then ends in Monticello, Utah. According to many folks' statistics, the ill-named highway has a incredibly high accident rate, and they know some of the reasons why this is so.

According to numerous eyewitness accounts, on nights of the full moon, a black, 1930s vintage Pierce-Arrow roadster has appeared and run scores of cars, trucks, and motorcycles off the road. The ghostly automobile has been linked to at least five deaths.

Dr. Avery Teicher of Phoenix spent ten years documenting reports of the phantom Pierce-Arrow and the howling Hell Hounds that materialize to terrorize anyone foolhardy enough to pull off Route 666 and admire the desert landscape. According to Dr. Teicher, two members of a biker gang had both of their arms chewed off by the fiendish ghost dogs and a third biker had 90 percent of his face eaten away.

The least threatening of all reports from the Devil's Highway are those of a phantom female hitchhiker who vanishes whenever someone stops to give her a ride.

Tales of the Phantom Hitchhiker

Mary, a lovely young blonde who is leaving the dance hall, asks for a ride toward Resurrection Cemetery, saying that she lives down that way. As people drive her home, she asks them to stop in front of the cemetery gates on Archer Avenue in

The Phantom Hitchhiker is a universal figure who has become the subject of many ghost stories set on deserted roads and highways (*iStock*).

Chicago. She gets out of the car, runs across the road, and dematerializes at the gate.

The Phantom Hitchhiker may well be among the best-known and most universal of all ghost stories, campfire tales, and, some say, urban legends.

In one familiar version, a college student driving on a lonely country road late one rainy night is startled to see a young woman walking along the side of the road. He pulls over and asks her if she wants a ride. She appears a bit dazed and she is soaked to the skin.

With a mumbled word of thanks, she gets inside. The man reaches behind him, grabs his sweater from the backseat, and offers it to the hitchhiker.

She smiles her thanks and drapes the sweater over her shoulders, informing him that she has to get home to see her parents. The driver notices for the first time that her face and hands are scratched and bleeding, and he asks what happened to her. She explains that her car slid off the road and into a ditch. She had been standing there for what had seemed like hours, hoping for help, before she decided to walk the rest of the way to her parents' home.

He tells her that there is no problem taking her right to her parents' front door. She thanks him, gestures into the darkness ahead and says that the house is only a few miles ahead.

After a few minutes, she points to the lights of a house down a very short lane. She asks him to stop, and she gets out of the car. He protests that he would be happy to take her the rest of the way home, but she is already running away into the night. As he drives on, he berates himself for not asking her name, but then he remembers that she still wears his sweater. That will be his excuse to drive back to her parents' home and formally make her acquaintance.

Two days later, the student drives back to his mystery girl's home and knocks on the door. He is surprised when a very elderly woman opens the door and invites him to step inside. As he looks about the interior of the front parlor, he notices a framed portrait of the beautiful young girl, and he asks the woman if her granddaughter is home.

Following the student's gaze to the portrait, the woman begins to weep. Her darling daughter, she said, is still trying to come home. The student listens incredulously as the woman tells him that her daughter had been killed in an automobile accident on a dark and rainy night over 40 years before.

He leaves the old woman, concluding that she must be crazy. The hitchhiker he had picked up that night was no more than nineteen years old. And she was very much alive.

As he passes a small rural cemetery, something blowing in the wind on one of the grave markers catches his eye. When he enters the graveyard to investigate, he finds his sweater draped over a tombstone that marks the final resting place of a young woman who had died forty years ago.

Misty Miss Laura Warns Others to Prepare to Follow Her

Drive the lonely stretch of Arkansas Highway 64, especially on a rainy night, and you will be likely to sight the tormented spirit of Laura Starr Latta, who died a month before her twentieth birthday in 1899. Motorists have claimed to have seen Laura's small, frail frame inside a white nightgown standing on the side of the road across from the cemetery where her body lies. Some old stories say that Laura was accosted by a gang and beaten to death on the way to her wedding. All that is known for certain is that she died a month before her twentieth birthday in 1899.

The inscription on her tombstone reads:

> Gentle Stranger passing by,
> As you are now, once was I.
> As I am now, so you must be.
> Prepare yourself to follow me.

Spending Halloween with the Headless Horseman

A few Halloweens ago, my friend Tim Beckley, a noted author, publisher, and horror filmmaker accompanied by his psychic friend Circe, decided to check out rumors of a revival of paranormal activity in the dreamy village of Sleepy Hollow, New York, and neighboring Tarrytown, home of the famous Headless Horseman. According to Tim's report:

The cool autumn air sits in just before twilight and a breeze starts to drift in from the Hudson River, just down the road a bit from where legend has it Ichabod Crane was chased by the Headless Horseman.

Indeed, the bridge and adjacent brook where Crane is said to have run for his life still stands a part of the main road that goes through town, a road now used by trucks, buses, and SUVs coming up from Manhattan a scant 40-minute drive away. Many commuters unwilling to drive in the midst of quite ghostly (I mean ghastly) traffic take to the rails, hopping onboard one of the numerous commuter trains that make the trip from the Big Apple all day and well into the evening hours.

Even before the time of Washington Irving and his tale of "The Headless Horseman," such nightmarish figures cloaked in black have stalked those who dared venture into the "haunted places" after dark. (art by Ricardo Pustanio).

Gazing out of the window, one would hardly guess that the area is particularly rich in paranormal lore. But as you pass White Plains and the office buildings start to diminish in height and number you can start to be thankful that Circe is your traveling companion as ghouls know well to leave her be. We figure it has to be the garlic in her bag, but she insists it is the lovely charms she makes and wears to ward off negativity and things that go bump in the night.

But, indeed the truth sometimes can be very strange. For it is along this very route to Sleepy Hollow back in 1982 that thousands craned their necks out of car windows to watch as a silent, giant, black-shaped triangular-shaped UFO filled the sky, much like the cloak of the Headless Horseman is said to have done as the phantom glided through the thickets and glades of this same community in the early 1800s.

One of our first destinations was the Sleepy Hollow cemetery to visit some of the communities founding members. Circe (made infamous for her role of Muffy in my low-budget vampire film, *The Curse of Ed Wood*) was perched on a tombstone while I frolicked with the angels near the grave of Washington Irving.

During the course of our investigation in the area, we drove over into Connecticut to hunt down giant Jack O' Lanterns known to be harassing residents near an outdoor farmers market. This was pretty much the same trek truck drivers had been on that fright-filled night in 1982 when they rubbed 18-wheelers with a "thing" the size of a 747 that tailed them at less than a thousand feet in the air.

Around the same time the mysterious men-in-black showed up to persuade witnesses to back off from telling of their encounters with the unknown. Many similar tales exist from the time of Washington Irving, who also spoke of nightmarish figures cloaked in black who staked those who dared discuss their paranormal misadventures. Those who have followed such matters will be able to confirm that often times places that have a reputation for being "haunted" have a long history of paranormal phenomenon.

Indeed, it was Circe who reminded me that Washington Irving had, himself, speculated on this very "coincidence" in his Legend of Sleepy Hollow tale. To prove her point, she cracked opened a copy of Irving's book just purchased at the Kyjuit gift shop on the Rockefeller Foundation estate, scene of the annual Halloween activities that tourists flock to this region along the Hudson every fall season.

To quote Irving:

A drowsy, dreamy influence seems to hang over the land, and to pervade the very atmosphere. Some say that the place was bewitched by a high German doctor during the early days of the settlement; others, that an old Indian chief, the prophet or wizard of his tribe, held his powwows there before the country was discovered by Master Hendrick Hudson. Certain it is, the place still continues under the sway of some witching power that holds a spell over the minds of the good people, causing them to walk in a continual reverie. They are given to all kinds of marvelous beliefs, are subject to trances and visions, and frequently see strange sights and hear music and voices in the air. The whole neighborhood abounds with local tales, haunted spots, and twilight superstitions; stars shoot and meteors glare oftener across the valley than in any other part of the country....

One almost has to scratch their head in disbelief that this paragraph was written 200—give or take—years ago. It seems like something a contemporary ghost hunter like our pal Joshua Warren might write in one of his scripts for the Discovery Channel.

As we hunkered down for the evening—after hours of paranormal musings—we couldn't help but reflect on how the area seemingly abounds in the macabre. In fact, all around us were signs and symbols that a spooky October was in the works for the area just up the river from our vampiric crypts.

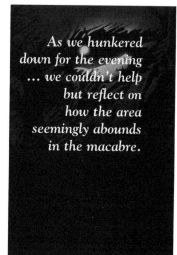

As we hunkered down for the evening ... we couldn't help but reflect on how the area seemingly abounds in the macabre.

The Great Jack O' Lantern Blaze

Three thousand hand-carved pumpkins are the decidedly spooky backdrop for a spine-tingling event set on the grounds of the eighteenth century Van Courtland Manor. You might be a bit too scared to nip away at those pumpkin cookies or sip down that warming cup of hot apple cider, as you experience the Scarecrow Avalanche and Pumpkin Promenade.

The Horseman Still Rides!

Join Jonathan Kruk for a lively reading and reenactment of the Legend of Sleepy Hollow at the Philipsburg Manor. For Legend Weekend (October 28 to 30) there will be candle lanterns and bonfires, and a haunted landscape to set the mood. Say doesn't that fellow with the crooked nose over there look like....? Nah, it can't be! Sponsored by the Historic Hudson Valley Society, more information can be found at: www.hudson valley.org or for ticket information call 914-631-8200.

Where to Stay

Numerous bed and breakfasts dot the scenic area. The Doubletree right on the Hudson offers a breathtaking view, but we were stopped at the entrance by the burly ghoul in charge who informed us before we even had time to twist our heads around, that the palatial estate was being renovated and thus closed to all. So I guess even the Horseman won't be staying there on Ole Hallows Eve.

If your budget is up to it and you are looking for really lavish grounds, go ahead and plop yourself down on one of the beds at the Tarrytown House. The restaurant wasn't open when we where there so we had to venture out into the crisp autumn air. This slight incontinence was offset by the use of the heated indoor pool, and the fact looking out the window at around 3:00 A.M. I thought I saw a specter under the flood lights in back of the complex where we should have been fast asleep and not watching the SyFy Channel.

Where to Eat

For lunch there is the Horseman saloon and the Sleepy Hollow Café.

For about the best meal ever in an absolutely superb setting stop by Harvest-on-the-Hudson in Hasting on the Hudson. It's right on the Hudson, and outdoor dining for lunch will be a treat you won't forget for a long time. Lots of indoor seating as well, and a bar that goes on for miles.

Thus ended our little adventure. Since she is psychic, I asked Circe about the vibes of Sleepy Hollow. She didn't appear to be scared out of her wits, so I guess the spirits weren't as restless as they might have been.

Do we plan to return to Sleepy Hollow and Tarrytown to search for more spirits? It could well be that sometime in the not too distant future we might set up shop to film our own version of Sleepy Hollow—except it will called Creepy Hollow.

HOLLOW EARTH—
A HAVEN FOR ANCIENT BEINGS

I n his intriguing new book *Pulp Winds* (2010), Wm. Michael Mott, one of the world's most learned authorities on the Hollow Earth mystery, perfectly captures in poetry the ancient accounts of the Under People in a poem aptly named "Heritage":

Heritage
by Wm. Michael Mott

Below the lands kissed by the sun
Where black and babbling rivers run
Through grottoes deep, unseen by men
Lurk races far beyond man's ken.
Driven deep, from the sun they hide,
Live in darkness, plot and bide,
To venture forth on moonless nights
And fill folktales with murky frights.
Driven down in an elder age
When man was new upon the stage,
Or else of type of fallen blood
Mingled with human, before the flood.
Ages have marched and come and gone,
Ere the rise of Adam's spawn,
When empires strange, heartless and cold
Had already risen, and grown old.
Races primal, reptilian, mammalian
Once trod a world violent and alien
When dragons clashed by sea and land
And blood of armies stained the strand.
Bone-white towers raised on-high

Split the clouds and scratched the sky,
While to the outer worlds above
Sailed the metal ships thereof.
But cataclysms rocked this world
And into chasms deep were hurled
Civilizations old and grim
From eons dark and epochs dim;
Sunlight's rays were each time changed
To burn, to slay, to leave deranged
And so they wait, and deep they hide
To await the rebirth of their pride.
So warily upon your way
Travel after end of day
And know that mankind, brash and brave,
Is prey to empires in the grave.

Wm. Michael Mott, one of the world's leading authorities on the Hollow Earth mystery, answers many provocative questions in his remarkable book *Caverns, Cauldrons, and Concealed Creatures: A Study of Subterranean Mysteries, History, and Folk Myths* (photo courtesy Wm. Michael Mott).

And what of the beings that dwell in those "grottoes deep, unseen" that shelter these ancient races? Mott answers that provocative question in his remarkable book *Caverns, Cauldrons, and Concealed Creatures: A Study of Subterranean Mysteries, History, and Folk Myths*, reminding us of H. P. Lovecraft's classic piece of horror fiction *The Dunwich Horror* (1928):

Lovecraft tells a tale of unspeakable terror set in a small New England town. Dunwich, Massachusetts, an isolated hamlet which is decaying and filled with a sense of uncleanness, where the inhabitants have interbred for some time, with one another, and eventually, with something else. Out of another dimension, analogous to the underworlds or fairylands of old, a new source of genetic material comes, when Old Man Whateley makes a deal with an underworld entity called Yog-Sothoth, and allows the demonic thing to mate with his daughter, Lavinia, impregnating her with a potential threat to the human species. Her son Wilbur Whateley, tall, hulking, and strange of shape through baggy clothing, is not all that he seems, and eventually his slain form is revealed:

Above the waist it was semi-anthropomorphic; though its chest, where the dog's rending paws still rested watchfully, had the leathery, reticulated hide of a crocodile or alligator. The back was piebald with yellow and black, and dimly suggested the aqueous covering of certain snakes. Below the waist, though, it was the worst.

The rest of the description of Wilbur Whateley goes beyond vertebrate characteristics, with mollusk and cephalopod features (aquatic or semi-aquatic?), limbs, and other members. Needless to say, the resemblance of Wilbur to the Sumerian underworld demon called Pazuzu, or to a variety of cryptid as well as reptile forms from Ufology and folklore, is apparent. Also of interest is the fact that the story ends with the revelation that Wilbur had a twin, not quite as capable of masquerading as human as he had been. In fact, he is an invisible elemental giant of great destructive power. Pazuzu was of the underworld, yet was also a demon of the wind, in effect paralleling both of the abominable brothers from *The Dunwich Horror*.

But, we ask, are such horrid creatures bound by the parameters of fiction only? Do such things as bizarre matings with inhuman creatures really happen? Does Mott really believe that human beings, either willingly or unwillingly, make pacts or genetic links with non-human beings from beneath the earth or elsewhere, contaminating the human gene pool even as they enrich the intrusive, parasitical one? Do history, folklore, and medical science hold clues as to this seeming-fantasy being a reality? In Mott's words:

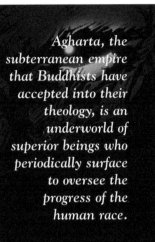

Agharta, the subterranean empire that Buddhists have accepted into their theology, is an underworld of superior beings who periodically surface to oversee the progress of the human race.

Evidence for such activity would necessarily consist of two types: historical and folk accounts, and real persons of questionable and mysterious genetic heritage, a heritage which may result in unfortunate and sometimes inexplicable medical or physical conditions. As in the Lovecraft story, there is sometimes an element of the human family or gene-pool being interbred to some extent as well, and the extent to which they are interbred may have some [effect] on the likelihood of the non-human genetic characteristics being dominant upon occasion, even surfacing in future generations. This does not mean that these people are not human beings, although upon occasion this may have been debatable. It simply means that they have retained or inherited genetic characteristics from a contamination in the distant past, which is beyond their control or responsibility. As it turns out, both types of circumstantial evidence do exist, and in fact may indicate that the second type of evidence could be the result of the first, even if such trysts or cross-breeding took place decades or centuries before.

Before going further, it must be observed that unfortunate birth defects and malformations exist which, doubtless, do not fit into the evidentiary category described. No person should ever be shunned or otherwise mistreated due to any defect beyond their control….

To return to the study at hand, folklore and history are filled with tales of such half-human or genetically-contaminated unfortunates…. It must be observed that not all such liaisons have resulted in deformity or an otherwise evil condition or nature. How do such 'alien' genes, possibly originating with pre-human races who shun the modern sun, enter the world of human beings?

There seem to be two methods: through forced interbreeding (abduction, rape, and the like), or else willing pacts, and even marriages. Closely-monitored or genetically-related groups seem to be the target of the latter, while the former appears more random at times.

Agharta, the subterranean empire that Buddhists have accepted into their theology, is an underworld of superior beings who periodically surface to oversee the progress of the human race. According to one source, the underground kingdom of Agharta was created when the ancestors of the present day cave dwellers drove the Serpent People from the caverns during an ancient war between the reptilian humanoids and the ancient human society.

In the Hindu and Buddhist traditions, the Nagas are a proud, handsome race of serpent people who dwell in Naga-Ioka, a splendid, underground bejeweled kingdom. Although an ancient race of serpent people figure in the myths of and traditions of many cultures, in the Hindu and Buddhist traditions, the Nagas are semi-divine beings with many supernatural powers. Because both the male and female members of the Naga are physically attractive, legends of intermarriage with surface humans abound; and many noble families of India have claimed a naga ancestor.

Wm. Michael Mott states:

In the *Mahabharata*, Arjuna begets a half-human son due to the seduction of the nagini, Ulupi. In the original Hindu tradition, Mohini was a female form utilized by Lord Shiva in order to seduce, confuse, and defeat the evil asuras and others; the tantric variant of Mohini, as defined in this account, is not the original but is apparently a type of nagini, or female naga (serpent-person). In her own realm, she is partially reptilian, and is usually represented as being a snake or crocodile from the waist down. When coming to the surface for purposes of seduction, however, she creates an illusion of a fully human form in order to attract a human mate. She glides rather than walks, and although the percipients believed that they saw her legs, it is clear that another type of locomotion—possibly serpentine motion, or levitation—is in use.

Through the centuries, occultists have interpreted Agharta to be a continuation of the civilization of Atlantis, whose inhabitants are content to remain in their peaceful network of subterranean cities with only occasional excursions to the outer world.

Certain researchers have combined the two interpretations of Inner Earth and have found adequate "proofs" in the extant manuscripts of antiquity that our ancient subsurface cousins have periodically emerged from their tunnels to give our race beneficial instruction. The Indian epic Ramayana has been often quoted in this regard. The ancient text frequently described Rama as an emissary from Agharta, who arrived amid the Indians on an aerial vehicle. The Ramayana offers a description of a flying saucer as detailed as any given by contemporary contactees.

Another mystery figure of prehistory, Quetzalcoatl, the white savior of the Mayas and Aztecs, traveled among the Indians of Mexico, Yucatan, and Guatemala on an aerial craft. It is interesting to note that Quetzalcoatl means "Feathered Serpent" (wise man who flies).

Did Admiral Richard Byrd
Find the Entrance to the Hollow Earth?

In his introduction to *The Hollow Earth* (Fieldcrest Publishing Company, New York, 1964), Dr. Raymond Bernard tells the reader that the book will seek to prove:

> that the Earth is hollow and not a solid sphere … that its hollow interior communicates with the surface by two polar openings … that the observations and discoveries of Rear Admiral Richard E. Byrd confirm the correctness of our revolutionary theory … that the North and South Poles have never been reached because they do not exist … that the exploration of the New World … is much more important than the exploration of outer space … that the nation whose explorers first reach this New World in the hollow interior of the Earth … will become the greatest nation in the world … that the mysterious flying saucers come from an advanced civilization in the hollow interior of the earth … that, in the event of nuclear world war, the hollow interior of the earth will … provide an ideal refuge for the evacuation of survivors of the catastrophe.

Did Admiral Richard Byrd really sight a beautiful oasis, an Antarctic Shangri-La, at the South Pole?

According to Dr. Bernard, and a good many others, Admiral Byrd reported seeing lakes, forests, and mountains on his 1947 flight over the North Pole. Dr. Bernard also quotes Admiral Byrd as saying that he flew *beyond* rather than *over* the North Pole. "That area beyond the Pole is the center of the Great Unknown," he told newsmen after his historic flight. Later, Byrd's expedition went to the South Pole and passed 2,300 miles *beyond* it.

Lt. Commander David Bunger was at the controls of a large U.S. Navy transport in February 1947 when he discovered "Bunger Oasis" in Antarctica. About the time that Admiral Byrd was making his discovery of "the land beyond the Pole," Bunger and his crew were flying inland from the Shackleton Ice Shelf near Queen Mary Coast of Wilkes Land. Here Bunger discovered a series of warm-water lakes—a condition which Bunger tested by landing his seaplane on one lake, surrounded on two sides by great ice walls a hundred feet high. Had the lakes been created by warm winds blowing from the Earth's interior?

In *The Hollow Earth*, Bernard tells of a photograph published in 1960 in the Toronto, Canada, *Globe and Mail* that shows a beautiful valley with lush, green hills. An aviator claimed that the picture had been taken from his airplane as he flew "beyond the North Pole."

Did Admiral Richard Byrd really sight a beautiful oasis, an Antarctic Shangri-La, at the South Pole?

"At *both* poles exist unknown and vast land areas," Ray Palmer (1911–1977), editor of *Flying Saucers*, wrote: "not in the least uninhabitable, extending distances which can only be called tremendous because they encompass an area bigger than any known continental area."

The Norwegian Fishermen Spent Two Years in the Land of the Giants

Many writers have drawn a comparison between the Scandinavian legend of "Ultima Thule," a far northern paradise, and a pleasant Inner Earth realm. Historians have long ago written off the Viking paradise as Greenland, but they have ignored the contradiction of the Greenland Ice Cap, which hardly qualifies as any kind of paradise.

About 1904, Willis George Emerson, a young novelist, befriended an old man, who, as he lay dying, began to speak of a strange adventure lived in a world peopled by giants, which existed in the hollow interior of Earth. Emerson listened in wonder to the tale that the aged Norwegian, Olaf Jansen, related, and it was to Emerson that Jansen displayed his manuscripts and his maps. Before he died, Olaf Jansen wanted to pass on the details of the strange adventure to an "heir." Emerson published *The Smoky God* in 1908, and the book was reprinted by Palmer Publications many years later (1963) as an "inspired novel."

According to Jansen, he and his father had entered the hollow earth through an opening at the North Pole in their small fishing boat. Imbued with the Viking spirit of adventure, the two men decided to seek "the land beyond the north wind." The Jansens spent two years among benign giants and marveled at the wonders of an advanced technology.

After a tutor had been assigned to teach them the tongue of Inner Earth, the Norwegians learned that the giants lived to be 400 to 800 years old and that most adults attained a height of twelve feet or more. The tall Scandinavians were more than dwarfed by their amiable hosts. The people of Inner Earth possessed sources of power greater than electricity, operated spacecraft on electromagnetism drawn from the atmosphere, and had generally gained a remarkable talent for efficient functioning of their mental powers. The Inner Earth sun, less brilliant than the solar star, appeared "smoky" to the gigantic inhabitants, and they referred to their sun as the "smoky god."

After their two-year sojourn among the inhabitants of Inner Earth, the Jansens longed to return to their homes. They began their return through the south polar opening, but tragedy struck when an iceberg destroyed the fishing boat and killed Olaf's father. Olaf was rescued and returned to Norway, where he was promptly imprisoned for insanity when he attempted to find an audience for accounts of his fantastic adventures. After twenty-four years in prison, he changed from a spirited youth to an embittered man of middle-age. Jansen vowed not to show the manuscript and maps of Inner Earth that he had prepared for fear of once again being committed. For the next twenty-six years of his life he labored as a fisherman and saved his money to come to America, where he settled first in Illinois, then in California.

The Vast Underground Empire of Enchantment

Is the public being denied knowledge of the existence of a new land mass or are such incredible allegations only what they seem—incredible allegations?

According to Ray Palmer and others, Admiral Byrd claimed that his south-polar expedition was the most important expedition in "the history of the world." Although the explorer's comments were allegedly published in some brief initial news releases, the discovery, comparable in importance to the one made at an earlier date by Christopher Columbus, failed to receive additional comment and, ostensibly, failed to create any kind of stir in scientific or government circles. In 1957, shortly before his death, Admiral Byrd referred to his discovery as "that enchanted continent in the sky" and the "land of everlasting mystery."

Have the governments of the world really chosen to ignore such a vastly important discovery—or have the reports of Admiral Byrd been largely responsible for the great increase in the number of polar expeditions in recent years?

Did Byrd fly *into* an unknown land area inside the polar concavity?

There are persistent legends in nearly every culture that tell of an Elder Race that populated Earth millions of years ago. The Old Ones, who may originally have been of extraterrestrial origin, were an immensely intelligent and scientifically advanced species who eventually chose to structure their own environment under the surface of the planet's soil and seas. The Old Ones usually remain aloof from the surface dwellers, but from time to time throughout history, they have been known to visit certain of Earth's more intelligent members in the guise of alchemists or scientists in order to offer constructive criticism and, in some cases, to give valuable advice in the material sciences.

A vast number of cultures—from that of the Vikings to Hitler's Germany—have believed in an underground empire inside the earth. The theory that there was a vast uncharted world inside our own captured the imagination of Edgar Allan Poe who, in 1835, published his longest story, "The Narrative of Arthur Gordon Pym," which told of a fantastic land located in the center of our planet, entered by a hole at the South Pole. So convincingly did Poe weave the pseudoscientific beginning of his narrative that the great educator Horace Greeley soberly accepted the Pym adventure as a true account. He obviously did not complete the story and encounter its later sections of very evident fantasy. It is likely, however, that young Jules Verne, who would have been nine at that time, did finish reading the story and many years later may have been inspired to base one of his classic novels, *A Journey to the Center of the Earth*, on a similar theme.

The Monsters in the Haunted Mine

As we have already noted, some of the Old Ones and their kind who visit us might not be so friendly. I well remember a story told to me years ago by Jack Robinson, a highly respected early UFO researcher.

Mr. X and a friend named Fred, whom he was visiting, set out to explore a "haunted mine" in the area. According to local legends, the mine had been abandoned when the miners had run into some sort of cave. From that moment on, ill fortune had plagued them. Portions of the tunnel had caved in, crushing several miners. A couple of the investors in the mine had died as a result of strange accidents, and a number of the miners had simply disappeared without a trace. At least that was the legend that had grown up around the old mine, and one day in the summer of 1942, the two teenaged boys set out to "despook" the haunted mine.

About four and a half feet tall, but very thick in bulk, the being let out an unearthly scream and started around the edge of the mine toward the boys.

The teenagers passed the deserted buildings of the mining camp and climbed over a large pile of debris located at one side of the mine entrance. It was there, standing as if on guard at the mine opening, that the boys saw the grotesque monster.

About four and a half feet tall, but very thick in bulk, the being let out an unearthly scream and started around the edge of the mine toward the boys. The teenagers fled back to town in terror. Mr. X remembered seeking refuge in a movie theater, only to have dark figures walk up and down the aisle, seemingly searching for the row in which he was sitting. Before he pulled the blinds of his bedroom window that night he felt certain that he could see a dark form squatting in the crotch of a high limb in the tree nearest the house. The next day, he left on the bus for his home in Los Angeles. Fred, his companion in the adventure, later vanished. The only clue authorities had to work on was the discovery of his bicycle near the "haunted mine."

"To this day," Mr. X told Robinson, "I am afraid that whoever or whatever it is that got Fred will find me."

The Vicious Hairy Humanoids in the Ancient Mound

Wm. Michael Mott recalls a tale of three men who encountered similar entities at the site of an ancient mound near McCallester, Oklahoma (from the book *The Shaver Mystery and the Inner Earth* by Timothy Green Beckley [Saucerian Books, 1967]): The site of an ancient hill or mound would immediately equate to fairies, elves, trolls and the like in the Old World.

Tim Beckley, also known as horror host Mr. Creepo, makes nice with an Oriental demon while on a globe-hopping trip for antiquities (*photo courtesy Timothy Green Beckley*).

This mound or hill had been the location of many mysterious livestock mutilations, mysterious noises and cries, and the like. The elderly farmer who owned the land considered the hill to be possessed or haunted by evil spirits. In search of adventure and rumored treasure, three brave fellows decided to check out the hill for themselves. After a bit of searching, they located a small entrance, which they enlarged sufficiently to permit passage. Making their way within, they discovered a large chamber along with a seemingly bottomless shaft, descending into the depths of the Earth. This shaft was surrounded by a spiral staircase of a scale fit for giants.

The three men carefully descended the staircase for hours, until their flashlights began to grow dim. They decided to return to the surface, but as they neared the entrance they were attacked from behind—i.e., from the region of the pit—by a pack of hairy, four- and five-foot-tall humanoid creatures. These things attacked with claws and teeth, snarling like animals, and managed to latch onto one of the men as the other two escaped.

At this point, and as so often happens with discovered entrances to the underworld realm, a cave-in occurred at the entrance, trapping the embattled man inside. Fortunately, he had had the foresight to bring along a .45 caliber handgun, which he used against his assailants. This did not kill them, as they seemed possessed of an unnatural density, but it did slow them down as the bullets apparently "hurt."

Fortunately, his friends quickly dug the entrance clear, and pulled their companion out. To their shock, he was covered with what they described as yellow blood, a type of ichor [bloody discharge with a foul odor] from the injured entities inside the hill.

After this adventure, the three joined the army to fight in the Korean War, and never returned, as planned, to take up where they had left off.

Could Some of Those Who Walk Among Us Not Really Be Us?

Is there more truth in the ancient traditions that most of contemporary humankind would care to admit? Wm. Michael Mott has this to say about our "contaminated heredity":

Could it be that, due to a contaminated heredity, the worst among us are not really *of* us? Do monsters [that] are not completely human, in spite of outward appearances, walk abroad in the surface world? This isn't a view that would be readily accepted by modern science, but the circumstantial evidence would indicate that this might be the case. One fact that indicates a strong possibility of cross-species contamination, is that, as a species, only human beings have over four thousand known genetic defects, while our nearest chromosomal relatives (according to evolutionary science), the great apes, have almost none.

Various mythical and folk traditions around the world make it quite clear that demons, ogres, monsters, and so forth have always been with us in human guise. Did the various ancient traditions know more about the truth than modern humanity, science, and law-enforcement would care to admit? Entertaining such a radically non-politically-correct view is to invite scorn and ridicule, but requires both courage, and the serious contemplation of facts and circumstantial evidence which history and folklore provide us.

The Master of the World and Secret Societies

By the 1840s, the legend of Agharta had already been widely circulated among the occult societies in Germany. According to ancient tradition, the Master of the World already controlled many of the kings and rulers of the surface world by exercising his powers of mind control. Soon this Master and his super race would launch an invasion of Earth and subjugate all humans to his will. The secret societies formed in Germany in the late nineteenth and early twentieth centuries wanted desperately to prove themselves worthy of the super humans that lived beneath the surface of the planet and they wished to be able to control the incredibly powerful Vril force. This ancient force had been known among the alchemists and magicians as the Chi, the Odic force, the Orgone, the Astral Light, and they were well aware of its transformative powers to create supermen of ordinary mortals.

In 1871, when occultist Edward Bulwer-Lytton wrote a novel about a small group of German mystics who had discovered the truth about a race of supermen living within the Earth's interior, he inspired the founding of the Brothers of the Light, the Luminous Lodge, the Vril Society. Bulwer-Lytton's *The Coming Race* told the story of an advanced civilization of giants who thrived in the inner Earth. The super race had built a paradise based on The Vril Force, a form of energy so powerful that the older beings had outlawed its use as a potential weapon.

This force, the Vril, was derived from the Black Sun, a large ball of "Prima Materia" that provides light and radiation to the inhabitants of the Inner Earth.

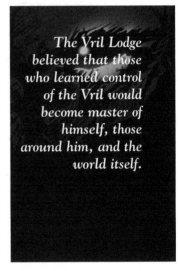

The Vril Lodge believed that those who learned control of the Vril would become master of himself, those around him, and the world itself.

In 1919, Karl Haushofer, a student of the Russian mystic George Gurdjieff, founded the Brothers of the Light Society in Berlin, and soon changed its name to the Vril Society. As Haushofer's Vril grew in prominence, it united three major occult societies, the Lords of the Black Stone, the Black Knights of the Thule Society, and the Black Sun and chose the swastika, the hooked cross, as its symbol of the worship of the Black Sun. While these societies borrowed some concepts and rites from Theosophists, Rosicrucians, and various Hermetic groups, they placed special emphasis on the innate mystical powers of the Aryan race. Theosophist Mme. Helena Blavatsky listed Six Root Races—the Astral, Hyperborean, Lemurian, Atlantean, Aryan, and the coming Master Race. The Vril and its brother societies maintained that the Germanic/Nordic/Teutonic people were of Aryan origin, and that Christianity had destroyed the power of the Teutonic civilization.

In 1921, Maria Orsic (Orsitch), a medium in the society, now renamed Vril Gesellschaft, began claiming spirit messages originating from Aryan aliens on Alpha Tauri in the Aldeberan star system. Orsic and another medium named Sigrun, learned that the aliens spoke of two classes of people on their world—the Aryan, or master race, and a subservient planetary race that had evolved through mutation and climate changes. A half billion years ago, the Aryans, also known as the Elohim or Elder Race, began to colonize our solar system. On Earth, the Aryans were identified as the Sumerians until they elected to carve out an empire for themselves in the hollow of the planet. The Vril Force was derived from the Black Sun, a large ball of "Prima Materia" that provided light and radiation to the inhabitants of the inner Earth.

The Vril Lodge believed that those who learned control of the Vril would become master of himself, those around him, and the world itself, if he should so choose. The Vril Society was well aware of its transformative powers to create supermen out of ordinary mortals. Such members of the Lodge as Adolf Hitler, Heinrich

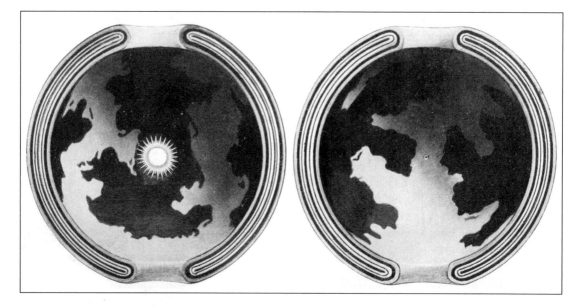

A 1912 illustration by Marshall Gardner shows an interior sun and oceans (*Mary Evans Picture Library*).

Himmler, Hermann Goering, Dr. Theodor Morell, Hitler's personal physician, and other top Nazi leaders, became obsessed with preparing German youth to become a master race so the Lords of the Inner Earth would find them worthy above all others when they emerged to evaluate the people of Earth's nations.

In 1922, members of Thule and Vril built the *Jenseitsflugmaschine*, the Other World Flight Machine, based on the psychic messages received from the Aldebaran aliens. W. O. Schulmann of the Technical University of Munich was in charge of the project until it was halted in 1924, and the craft was stored in Messerschmitt's Augsburg. In 1937, after Hitler came into power, he authorized the construction of the *Rund flugzeug*, the round, or disk-shaped vehicle, for military use and for spaceflight.

In April 1942, Nazi Germany sent out an expedition composed of a number of its most visionary scientists to seek a military vantage point in the hollow earth. Goering, Himmler, and Hitler are said to have enthusiastically endorsed the project. The Fuehrer had long been convinced that Earth was concave and that a master race lived on the inside of the planet. Hitler's plan to breed a master race of Nordic types was set in motion to appease his fanatic desire that the Germanic peoples would be the humans chosen to interact with the supermen in the mutation of a new race of heroes, demigods, and god-men.

In the *Morning of the Magicians*, Louis Pauwels and Jacques Bergier quote Hermann Rauschning, governor of Danzig during the Third Reich, who told of a conversation with Hitler concerning his plan to "assist" nature in developing mutations. Hitler told Rauschning: "The new man is living amongst us now! He is here! Isn't that enough for you? I will tell you a secret. I have seen the new man. He is intrepid and cruel. I was afraid of him." Rauschning recalled that Hitler was in a kind of ecstasy as he spoke those words.

It was Rauschning, too, who was told by a "person close to Hitler" that the Fuehrer often awoke in the night screaming and in convulsions. Always, the frightened dictator would shout that "he" had come for him. That "he" stood there in the corner. That "he" had emerged from his underworld dwelling to invade the Fuehrer's bedroom.

The Nazi expedition to find the secret opening to the Hollow Earth was not successful, but influential members of the Vril Society direct their efforts to working with aliens to create early models of flying saucers. UFO researcher Vladimir Terziski believes that an "alien tutor race" secretly began cooperating with certain German scientists from the Thule, the Vril, and the Black Sun societies in the late 1920s. Working in underground bases with the alien intelligences, Terziski says that the Nazis mastered antigravity space flight, established space stations, accomplished time travel, and developed their spacecraft to warp speeds.

The secret society of the Black Sun co-existed with the Vril and the Thule societies in Germany prior to and during World War I and was blended with the other groups in about 1919.

The symbol of the Black Sun is suggestive of the plight of the sun when, according to Norse myths, the great wolf Fenrir will swallow the solar orb at the beginning of the Wolf Age. The Black Sun, like the swastika, is a very ancient symbol. While the swastika represents the eternal fountain of creation, the Black Sun is even older, suggesting the very void of creation itself. The symbol on the Nazi flag is the Thule *Sonnenrad* (Sun Wheel), not a reversed good luck swastika. The Black Sun can be seen in many ancient Babylonian and Assyrian places of worship.

The Great Shaver Mystery
and Its Warning to Future Man

*L*ife magazine (May 21, 1951) carried a story on the Shaver Mystery, and a controversy that boiled into what they hailed as "the most celebrated rumpus that racked the science-fiction world."

According to *Life:* "The Shaver Mystery concerned a race of malformed subhuman creatures called deros (from detrimental robots) who inhabited a vast system of underground cities all over the world. The original name of their habitat was Lemuria [well known in esoterica as a "lost continent"], and they had once been slaves of a Lemurian master race. But the [Lords of Lemuria] had long since disappeared from the earth, leaving the ignorant and malicious deros in control of its great cities and wonderful machines. Since then the deros occupied themselves mainly in persecuting the human race who lived on the crust of the earth above them. The deros were responsible for much of the evil in the world ... from shipwrecks to sprained ankles.... They often appeared on the surface of the earth and were sufficiently human in appearance to pass unnoticed in a crowd ... they performed most of their harassments by telepathy, rays and other remote-control devices from their subterranean homes...."

The Crack-Pot Letter that Started It All

From February 1938 to September 1949, Ray Palmer was editor of the Ziff-Davis fiction magazines. In September of 1944, a letter from a Richard S. Shaver came to his attention. The enigmatic letter—branded sheer crack-potism by Palmer's managing editor—presented details of an ancient language that "should not be lost to the world." Intrigued by the results of some office experiment with the alphabet, Palmer decided to print the letter in the next issue of *Amazing Stories*.

The publication of Shaver's letter brought an avalanche of mail to Palmer's desk. All the letter writers wanted to know where Shaver had acquired his alphabet. Smelling a good story in the making, Palmer contacted Shaver and received a 10,000-word manuscript in reply.

Palmer was impressed by the sincerity of the crude manuscript, which Shaver had entitled, "A Warning to Future Man."

In Palmer's own account: "I put a clean piece of paper into my typewriter, and using Mr. Shaver's strange letter-manuscript as a basis, I wrote a 31,000-word story which I entitled, 'I Remember Lemuria!'"

When I spoke with Ray Palmer in his Wisconsin home in the late 1960s, he swore to me that although he may have added some trimmings to the manuscript, he did not alter the factual basis of Mr. Shaver's manuscript except in one instance.

"Here, perhaps, I made a grave mistake," Palmer mused. "However, I could not bring myself to believe that Mr. Shaver had actually gotten his alphabet and his 'Warning to Future Man,' and all the 'science' he propounded from actual underground people. Instead, I change his 'thought-records' into 'racial memory' and felt sure this would be more believable to my readers, and, after all, if this were all actually based on fact, a reasonable and perhaps actual explanation of what was going on in Mr. Shaver's mind—which is where I felt it really

Toward the end of his life Richard Shaver began to produce "rock paintings" that he believed proved his tales of the Dero and the Tero (*an original Shaver rock painting, property of Brad Steiger*).

The vast numbers of the cave people began to degenerate into physically stunted near-idiots, incapable of constructive reasoning. Shaver calls these the "dero," detrimental—or degenerate—robots (*art by Ricardo Pustanio*).

was going on, and not in any caves or via any relaug rays or telesolidograph projections of illusions from the cavern ray operators."

Palmer published "I Remember Lemuria" in the March 1945 issue of *Amazing Stories*. He sent Shaver payment for his original manuscript and was amused when he received a reply from the author expressing his wish that *Amazing* print more than its usual press run that month so that more people might read his "warning." Shaver said he understood about the paper shortage but he would go to the "cave people" for help. "Ray operators" were always on duty observing surface people, Shaver said, and he would ask them to impress on the circulation director's mind that it was "necessary" to obtain more paper for the March issue.

Palmer was afraid that he was dealing with a "complete nut." It all became a bit difficult to laugh off, however, when the circulation manager walked into Palmer's office and declared that he was going to steal enough paper from *Mammoth Detective*, another popular Ziff-Davis pulp magazine, to run an additional 50,000 copies of *Amazing* on the basis of a "brilliant hunch" he had had about the March issue.

Amazing sold those extra 50,000 copies and received more than 50,000 letters from readers who had been completely intrigued, enthralled, or frightened by the "true" story in the science-fiction magazine. For a magazine whose usual mail response was 45 letters a month, *Amazing* had accomplished an incredible *tour de force* in its field. Ray Palmer maintained the advanced circulation figure for the next four years while he ran the Shaver mystery to its conclusion.

In the March 4, 2010, issue of *UFO Digest*, Sean Casteel wrote that for Shaver, the mass outpouring of letters that his writings received were not to him a consolation or a vindication of is claims, but rather an unimpeachable testimony to the reality of his tormenting voices. Richard Shaver suffered despair on a whole new level, because now there really was nowhere to run, no way to deny the widespread nature of a phenomenon he half-hoped was a misfortune limited to just himself alone.

Quoting from Shaver's own writing, Casteel noted how Shaver felt about his reading public: "To me, struggling to find an opening out of the morass (no longer just for myself, but now for all mankind), the flood of letters I received from other sufferers was a crushing blow, bringing hopeless despair. The caverns were not, I realized now, a localized thing—they extended underneath every area of the earth. The evidence of their activity and strength piled up, until I could not help but conclude that there is no answer for present day man. He cannot break their power over him, nor remedy the ills they visit upon him."

The Curse of the Abandondero

During those four years when the Shaver Mystery was provoking scientific debates, this, briefly, is what was revealed in the pages of Amazing Stories:

Under the surface of the Earth, in massive cities, lives a race of people called the Abandondero, descendants of those who were unable to leave the planet when the "Titans" or "Atlans" discovered that the sun's radiations were radioactive and thereby limiting to life. While those who left Earth in a mass exodus sought a world with an uncontaminated sun, the Abandondero sought to escape the radioactive poisoning by moving from the surface of Earth into great underground caverns.

Although the sun does hasten the aging process, it also has a great many health-giving rays which the Inner Earth dwellers had then denied themselves. The vast numbers of the cave people began to degenerate into physically stunted near-idiots, incapable of constructive reasoning. Shaver calls these the "dero," detrimental—or degenerate-robots. "Robot" as Shaver uses the word does not mean a mechanical representation of man, but is rather a designation for those who are governed by degenerative forces.

Standing between the degenerate dero and the surface civilization are the "tero" (T was the Atlans' symbol of the cross of religion; therefore the "t" in tero represents good). These subterraneans have learned to stave off much of the mental degenerative effect of their way of life. They have not discovered a means whereby they are able to prevent aging, however, and they die at an average age of fifty.

Shaver's "Warning to Future Man" is that the dero are becoming more numerous and have scattered the benign tero with their constant attacks. The greatest danger lies in the fact that the dero have access to all the machines of the Atlan technology, but they do not have the intelligence or the highly developed moral sense to use these machines responsibly.

Shaver has told us that the dero have possession of vision ray machines that can penetrate solid rock and pick up scenes all over Earth; transportation units that can be worn on the body to effect instant teleportation from one point to another; mental machines that can cause "solid" illusions, dreams, and hypnotic compulsions. In addition to the aerial craft we call flying saucers, the dero possess death rays, "stim" machines that revitalize sexual virility (the dero are notorious for their sexual orgies), "ben" rays that heal and restore the body—all created by the ancient Atlans and still in perfect working order, due to the high degree of technical perfection with which they were constructed.

Under the surface of the Earth, in massive cities, lives a race of people called the Abandondero, descendants of those who were unable to leave the planet when the "Titans" or "Atlans" discovered that the sun's radiations were radioactive and thereby limiting to life (**art by Dan Wolfman Allen**).

We surface dwellers are the descendants of the Abandondero who were only able to gain access to the caves at the time of the great exodus from Earth's surface. Most of our ancestors died off; others, the hardy ones, survived, and through the centuries our surface species has developed a tolerance of the sun which allows us to live even longer than the subsurface tero. Then, too, the beneficent rays of the sun have prevented the kind of mental deterioration that perverts the dero and the tero.

Although we have a common heritage with the tero and the dero, the passage of time has prevented us from possessing more than dim memories of Atlantis, Lemuria, and "giants in the Earth."

However, the dero, warns Shaver, have not forgotten us. They are little more than sadistic idiots who take enormous delight in fostering our wars, creating terrible accidents, even in causing nightmares by training "dream mech" on us while we sleep.

Flying Saucers from Inner Space

Shaver also writes in a pessimistic way about the UFOs, which first received worldwide attention with Kenneth Arnold's sighting in 1947, a few brief years after the publication of "I Remember Lemuria!", writes Sean Casteel.

Shaver stated grimly that "the visits of the saucers bring with them, for me, fresh despair."

For Shaver, the flying saucers were proof of the caverns' contact with space. "Knowing the cave people," he said. "I know that if any of the visiting saucers were benevolent visitors bringing gifts and scientific knowledge to the surface people, they would be destroyed. To me, that explains the failure to contact our surface government, because those saucers that are not destroyed are our ancient enemies."

Palmer Changes His Mind:
Flying Saucers Come from the Hollow Earth

In the December 1959 issue of *Flying Saucers*, Ray Palmer abandoned his contention that the UFOs were of extraterrestrial origin in favor of their coming from "an 'unknown' location of vast dimensions," most probably "that mysterious land beyond the Pole."

Palmer at that time suggested that all ufologists should study the mystery of the flying saucers from the Hollow Earth viewpoint, gather all confirming evidence, and search equally hard for any contrary evidence:

> Now that we have tracked the flying saucers to the most logical origin (the one we have consistently *insisted* must exist because of the insurmountable obstacles of interstellar origin, which demands factors beyond our imagination), we know that the flying saucers come from our own Earth....
>
> If the interior of the Earth is populated by a highly scientific and advanced race, we must make profitable contact with them; and if they are mighty in their science, which includes the science of war, we must not make enemies of them....
>
> The flying saucer has become the most important single fact in history.... Admiral Byrd has discovered a new and mysterious land, the 'center of the great unknown; and the most important discovery of all time.' We have it from his own lips, from a man whose integrity has always been unimpeachable, and whose mind was one of the most brilliant of modern times.

There remains an audience eager to know about the mysteries that so burdened Shaver. Timothy Beckley of Global Communications has made a sort of cottage industry out of interest in the Inner and Hollow Earth theories, saving some old and rare books from obscurity and publishing up-to-date compendiums written by more recent researchers. His most popular titles dealing with this subject include: *Twilight, Hidden Chambers beneath the Earth*, by T. Lobsang Rampa; *Underground Alien Bio Lab At Dulce: The Bennewitz UFO Papers*; *Admiral Byrd's Secret Journey Beyond The Poles*, by Tim Swartz; *Reality of the Serpent Race and the Subterranean Origin of UFOs*, by Branton; *Best of the Hollow Earth Hassle*, by Mary J. Martin; and *Finding Lost Atlantis inside the Hollow Earth*, by the late British writer Brinsely Le Poer Trench, the Earl of Clancarty.

The incredible story of Richard Shaver and his underground race of demonic fiends, creatures he claimed live deep below us and are said to have hijacked wonderful inventions like UFOs from alien visitors eons ago, has almost never been completely told. But Timothy Green Beckley has recently published books unseen for over 50 years.

The Hidden World, volumes one through six, are part of a set of sixteen original books that were first published in the 1960s and have become rare collector's items since that time, often selling for as much as $80 per volume through rare book dealers. The books—all around 200 pages long, with colorful covers and printed in large format editions—detail a vast underground world hidden from view and known only to a handful of surface dwellers, mortals who were thought to be utterly mad because they claim to hear voices being projected at them by the ancient "telog" machines operated by the "dero."

HOWLERS AND NIGHT PROWLERS

"What was that?" The Lebanon, Pennsylvania farmer said as he looked up from the magazine he was reading.

"I didn't hear anything, dear," his wife said. The light burned on the table next to her where she was doing some needle work. "It's probably just the wind...."

"There it is again!"

This time the woman heard it and sat bolt upright. It sounded like the cry of a human baby, amplified many times.

The couple waited tensely in the hot August night of 1946. Then the sound came again, knifing through the thick night air. It was a high, eerie cry.

After a moment's hesitation the man walked across the room toward a glass-enclosed cabinet that held several varieties of firearms. He picked out a shotgun, jammed three shells in the underside of the weapon. "I've got to see what's out there," the man said resolutely. "We've got stock in the yard."

He proceeded cautiously toward the barn. The night was too quiet. Not a bird or a cricket chirped.

His flashlight ran over the familiar outline of the barn, then the board gate that led to the yard. The stock were huddled in one corner, wild-eyed with fright.

A noise attracted the farmer's attention. It was not the almost human cry that he had heard before, but a sound like the tearing of paper or cloth.

Quickly he flashed the light in the direction of the sound, and the beam lit up a gory scene. Bent over the carcass of a dead animal was a beast that looked like nothing he had ever seen before. In the brief instant that the light blinded it, the farmer was only aware of a massive, blood-covered muzzle.

The farmer fired at the grotesque creature, but it vanished in the darkness and all was silent for a few seconds (*art by Ricardo Pustanio*).

Then, in his fear and confusion, he let the flashlight slip to the ground. When he had picked it up again, the beast was retreating from the scene of his kill.

He fired vainly at it, but it vanished in the darkness and all was silent for a few seconds. Then the same, haunting cry of a horrible, blood-sated baby howled through the night.

For over two weeks in Lebanon, Pennsylvania, in August of 1946, the rural communities were put on the defensive by a monster that destroyed livestock and poultry. Mrs. Lulu Brown heard the animal again on August 25. A professional hunter, Harry McClairn, was engaged to either kill or capture the beast.

Earlier that year, on February 14, 1946, a monster of a similar variety was reported to have appeared near Coatesville, Pennsylvania. Though a good physical description was lacking, the monster was said to wail like a woman.

On November 14, 1945, a report had come of an animal or beast that "cried and screamed like a baby" from Pottstown, Pennsylvania.

Creature of Rising Sun, Indiana

Tim R. Swartz reports that on the evening of May 19, 1969, near the southern Indiana town of Rising Sun, George Kaiser walked through the family farmyard, when he was startled to see a strange figure standing about 25 feet away. George had the chance to observe the creature for a few minutes and noticed that it stood in a fairly upright position, although it was bent over at about the middle of its back.

The creature was around five feet, eight inches tall and was very muscular in build. The head sat directly on the shoulder and the face was dark, with hair that stuck out on the back of its head. It had a dark brown hair that covered its entire body, except for the face and the back of its hands.

When it noticed young Kaiser watching it, the animal "made a strange grunting-like sound," turned, leaped over a ditch, and disappeared down the road. The next day, large footprints were found in the dirt by the ditch. When plaster casts were made, they showed a foot with three toes plus a large big toe that stood out like a thumb.

Rising Sun, Indiana, in Clark county, sits along the banks of the Ohio river. Perhaps the Ohio is a favorite river of Bigfoot-type creatures, because on April 13, 1977,

Tom and Connie Courter spotted something that looked like the traditional Sasquatch in an area between the towns of Aurora and Rising Sun.

The Courters arrived home in their car around 11:00 P.M. Tom got out of the car and heard a strange noise which sounded like an "UGH." When he looked up, he saw a large hairy animal about a foot away from him. The creature appeared to be over 12 feet tall, black and hairy, with large red eyes. Its head appeared to resemble a human, but its arms were long and hung to the ground.

Tom quickly jumped into the car and spun the tires, as the creature swung its arms and struck the car, denting it. The couple quickly left the area and spent the night at Connie's house.

The next night Tom and Connie returned to their trailer with a .22 rifle and again saw the large creature standing near a tree next to the road.

Tom fired one shot at the animal, but missed. He fired several more shots, but they, too, had no effect. Tom and Connie both said that the animal seemed to dive to the ground and vanish.

Connie Courter said that the creature was so large that "If my husband stood on my shoulders he'd still have to look up at it, and it wasn't a bear."

This Bigfoot story seems to indicate that the creature might not be a flesh and blood animal. The large, glowing red eyes are a common report with unnatural creature sightings. Point Pleasant, West Virginia's Mothman sightings all involved a large creature with hypnotic red eyes. Also, the fact that Tom Courter shot several rounds from a .22 rifle into the creature with no effect—and the monster's mysterious vanishing act—seem to indicate that something more unusual than a physical creature was walking the night in southern Indiana.

Such accounts as the Courters' suggest that we can entertain the theory that such giant man-beasts may be ghostlike beings that stray into our world from time to time—perhaps just often enough to startle us into accepting the reality of other dimensions of time and space.

The Wretched Thing that Attacked Roachdale

In west-central Indiana, in the town of Roachdale, another ghostly Bigfoot-type creature made itself known after several nighttime UFO sightings had been reported in the area. Mrs. Lou Rogers was the first person to hear the unusual intruder in August 1972.

She had stepped outside of her house one evening when she was startled by a noise somewhat like a growl which was followed by a "boo" or "oo." Turning around, Mrs. Rogers looked in the direction of the sound, but due to the darkness, could see nothing. She did have the feeling though that something was watching her and she quickly retreated back into her house.

The following evenings the strange sounds returned followed by something banging on the doors and windows. Lou Rogers commented that "whatever it was, it

Bigfoot and Bigfoot-like creatures come in a variety of forms in eyewitness accounts across the United States (*art by Bill Oliver*).

must have gotten braver because the noise got louder and louder each night. It would always come around ten to eleven thirty each night, you could feel it coming, I don't know how to explain it, and then the knocking would start."

When the Rogers would go outside they would sometimes catch a glimpse of a large, broad-shouldered "something" running away through the cornfields. Mrs. Rogers commented, "We tried to think of a rational explanation, maybe an ape had gotten away from a zoo or circus. It would stand up like a man, but would run on all fours. Even bent over on all four feet it was still taller than my husband, and it stank, like rotten garbage." Mr. Rogers continued, "the funny thing is that it never left footprints, even in mud, and when it ran through tall weeds you couldn't hear anything. And sometimes when you looked at it, it looked like you could see through it, like it was a ghost or something."

The Rogers weren't the only people in Roachdale to sight the mysterious animal. On August 22, around nine o'clock in the evening, Carter Burdine and his uncle, Bill Burdine, discovered at Carter's farm the remains of over sixty chickens that had been ripped apart and scattered along a path from the chicken coop to the front yard of the house. None of the chickens had been eaten, just torn apart and dropped.

After Town Marshall, Leroy Cloncs arrived, the men stood outside discussing what could have attacked the birds in such a strange way. Suddenly, they heard an unusual noise nearby. Cloncs got into his patrol car and slowly went down the road while Bill Burdine walked behind. After the car passed, something large jumped out of the roadside ditch and ran between Bill and the patrol car.

"It ran so fast I couldn't get a good look at it in the dark," Bill said. "Whatever it was, it was big. The fence it ran over was mashed all the way to the ground, and you could see where it had trampled the weeds when it ran away."

After the Town Marshall had left, Carter and Bill returned to the chicken coop to find the creature standing in the chicken-house doorway. "The thing completely blocked out the light in the chicken-house," Bill said. "The door is six feet by eight, its shoulders came to the top of the doorway. It looked like a gorilla with long brownish colored hair. I never saw its face, but it was making an awful groaning sound."

The creature ran from the coop with Bill shooting at it with a pump shotgun. Like other ghostly Bigfoot encounters, the Roachdale creature seemed unharmed by the hail of shotgun pellets, and once again disappeared into the nearby fields. This time the animal had killed one hundred and ten chickens. All had been ripped apart and drained of blood. Out of two hundred chickens, Carter Burdine lost all but thirty.

After this incident, reports of the strange beast subsided. Whatever the monster of Roachdale was, it vanished as mysteriously as it had arrived.

A Bigfoot with Really Bad Body Odor

On June 4, 2008, Eric Altman, director, co-host, conference chairman of the Pennsylvania Bigfoot Society (www.pabigfootsociety.com) received a phone call from a friend who told him that a woman from northwestern Pennsylvania had called into the show and told the hosts about several monster encounters and a sighting that took place on her property going back as far as several weeks. The friend gave Eric the name and phone number and told him that the witness would be happy to speak with him about the creature that she had seen. Here is her story and what Eric found out:

This woman lives alone in a remote area of northwestern Pennsylvania. She lives on a dirt road and is surrounded by forests, mountains, and valleys. She has two neighbors. The people own camps and do not reside there year 'round, so the camps are usually unoccupied. The woman owns a two-story house with a fenced in yard and a deck on the back that goes up to the second floor and has a lattice attached. She has a black Lab dog.

On May 16, 2008, at 11:30 P.M., she was in the house in one of the rooms. She had a few lights on, and the TV on in the room that connected to the deck. There were patio doors that led outside to the deck.

While she was in another room away from the TV room, she heard something or someone climbing up the lattice. She could hear it breaking and crashing. The Lab quickly rose to its feet and began to bristle and growl, looking at the patio doors.

Then she heard a loud thud that shook the deck and the room she was in. The Lab went to charge the patio doors, and she quickly grabbed the dog by the collar to stop it.

As she looked out the patio door, she could see a figure on the deck. She had a spotlight on the floor next to one of the chairs and picked it up and went to shine it outside while still restraining her dog.

She saw what she described as an upright seven to almost eight-foot-tall creature standing on the deck. It was looking back at her with very piercing eyes. It had a human like face, but much flatter features. The arms hung down below the waist. It was not covered in very thick hair, and she said it was definitely a male creature because she could see its genitals. She smelled a very foul odor, but all the windows were closed.

The creature and witness stared at one another for several seconds before it stepped back and crouched down behind the deck furniture. She flipped on the outside pole light and when she did that the creature swung its body over the railing breaking two of the two-foot by two-foot rungs on the railing.

She raced downstairs with the spotlight and opened a door just enough to shine the light outside to see the creature, but not let the dog outside. She claimed she was hit with an overwhelming odor of the creature that almost made her throw up. That ended that night's encounter.

She said that the creature had been back several times. It returned on May 22 at 9:30 P.M. She believed it was on the hillside behind her house in the pine and hemlock trees, because her dog behaved the same way it did the night of her sighting. Also she reported that she had heard several loud screams coming from the wooded hillsides that surround her house.

Her neighbor who lives a few miles away advised her to call the local game warden. A bear trap was left, but when the game commissioners came to pick it up, they found that something had tried to tear it up, and there were bite marks on it, as if something tried to chew it up.

The Notorious Man-Monkey of the British Isles

BY NICK REDFERN

Like a lot of monster-hunters and cryptozoologists, I suspect, I first became interested in the subject of unknown creatures as a young child. As a five year old, my parents took me on vacation to Loch Ness, and my father related to me the story of what may well be the world's most famous monster: Nessie.

As I got older I devoured all the books and magazines I could find on the Yeti, on Bigfoot, on sea-serpents, and of course, on the Loch Ness Monster. But it was when I was in my early twenties that I first crossed paths with a devilish entity said to roam the woods and old canals of central England: the Man-Monkey.

When people think of Bigfoot, the Yeti and similar beasts, seldom—if ever—do the British Isles enter into the equation.

Surprisingly, however, Britain has a rich history of Bigfoot-style encounters. Interestingly, most of those same reports seem to verge upon the paranormal in nature: there are reports of British Bigfoot-style creatures vanishing in the blink of an eye; many of them seem to have self-illuminating, glowing red-eyes; others even seem to have the ability to stall car-engines—and the list goes on.

As much as many cryptozoologists who subscribe strictly to the idea that the creatures they seek are purely flesh-and-blood ones, in Britain the evidence strongly suggests otherwise. And that's where the Man-Monkey comes in.

A legendary beast said to haunt the waterways and woods of central England, the Man-Monkey was first described within the pages of Charlotte S. Burne's book, *Shropshire Folklore*. As Burne related, it was a winter's night in 1879 when a man crossing an old bridge near the Staffordshire town of Ranton got the shock of his life when a glowing-eyed, hairy man-beast burst out of the trees and headed straight for him, before suddenly vanishing—and quite literally, too.

Unsurprisingly, the story spread like wildfire in the surrounding hamlets and villages, and soon the Man-Monkey became known—and feared—by

"El Chupacabras," literally translated as "The Goat Sucker," was so named for its practice of completely draining the blood out of farm livestock (*art by Dan Wolfman Allen*).

one and all in the area. And the Man-Monkey still roams the area to this day. I know this as I have now interviewed around twenty people who claim to have seen the monster for themselves—and as late as last year [2009]. I even wrote a book on the subject, such was the wealth of data in hand: *Man-Monkey: In Search of the British Bigfoot*.

I continue to pursue the Man-Monkey to this day—both literally and in-print. And without doubt, I consider it to be both my favorite monster and my nemesis—in equal, heady measures.

One day, I hope to lay the beast to rest, and finally answer the question that has haunted me for years: precisely what is the diabolical Man-Monkey that lurks in the woods and forests of my home country?

Also very near the top of my list is the infamous Chupacabras of Puerto Rico—a creature I have pursued for weeks at a time, while exploring the island's El Yunque rain forest. Werewolves, too, are also a source of fascination, followed closely by Mothman, the Yeti, and the Russian ape-man: the Almasti.

As for what these things are, I sometimes muse upon the idea that they are the denizens of some other realm or dimension that occasionally cross paths with ours.

Other times, I wonder if they might all be Tulpa-like in origin: mind-monsters, constructs of the human brain and imagination that have been externalized and now live in some quasi-form of semi-existence.

Of one thing, I am sure, however: I'll keep searching until I have the answers.

Nick Redfern is the author of a number of books on cryptozoology, including There's Something in the Woods; Memoirs of a Monster Hunter; Three Men Seeking Monsters; *and* Man-Monkey. *He can be contacted at his website www.nickredfern.com*

Springheeled Jack: A Most Bizarre Night Prowler

About the middle of November 1837, the lanes and commons of Middlesex, England, suddenly became places of dread. An eerie figure said to be possessed of supernatural powers was stalking the frightened villagers by night and effortlessly avoiding capture by the police. Because of this creature's ability to leap over tall hedges and walls from a standing jump, he was given the name of "Springheeled Jack."

Close witnesses who encountered Jack face-to-face described him as being tall, thin, and powerful. A prominent nose stuck out of his pinched physiognomy and his ears were pointed like those of an animal. His long, bony fingers resembled claws.

The remarkably agile Springheeled Jack wore a long, flowing cape over his slender shoulders and a tall, metallic helmet on his head. Numerous witnesses testified that the mysterious intruder had what appeared to be metal mesh under his cloak and that he had a strange kind of lamp strapped to his chest.

It proved impossible to capture Springheeled Jack. Townspeople saw him leap eight-foot walls as he worked his way to the west, passing from village to village. Later, it was determined that Springheeled Jack stayed primarily in private parks during the day, coming out at night to knock at certain doors, as if he were seeking some particularly hospitable host.

As far as it is known, the mysterious stranger never found anyone who invited him in for a visit. Most people reacted in the same manner as Jane Alsop, who went to answer the door assuming that a top-hatted, cloaked member of the horse patrol stood on the doorstep. Instead, the "most hideous appearance" of Springheeled Jack caused her to scream for help.

The monster's eyes, she later testified, were glowing red balls of fire. Before she could flee, he seized her in the powerful grip of his clawlike fingers and projected balls of fire that rendered both Jane and her sister unconscious.

When the report of the Alsop sisters' encounter reached the press, it came to light that a Miss Scales had survived a similar encounter with Jack as she walked through Green Dragon Alley. Before she could scream for help, he spurted a blue flame into her face, thereby dropping her to the ground in a swoon.

According to the old records, Springheeled Jack knocked on his last door on February 27, 1838, when he visited the house of one Mr. Ashworth. The servant who opened the door took one look at the bizarre inquirer, then set Springheeled Jack to running with his screams for help.

Inspector Hemer of the Liverpool police may have had the last mortal glimpse of the strange visitor when he was patrolling the long boundary of Toxteth Park one night in July.

A sudden and vivid flash of what the inspector assumed to be lightning seized his attention and caused him to notice a large fiery globe hovering motionless over a nearby field. The object remained stationary for about two more minutes, then, amid showers of sparks, lowered itself closer to the ground to receive the same strangely costumed character that all of England had been seeking.

Inspector Herner decided not to become the hero who captured Springheeled Jack, and he wheeled his horse away from the scene. When he looked back over his shoulder, the great ball of fire had disappeared.

A Most Unusual Stranger at the Side of the Road

When we are in a state of shock, we are unable mentally to assess what we are observing with any normal degree of accuracy. Witnesses to accidents and crimes argue with one another over which details of the event actually transpired.

Investigators often are able to express only incredulity over the wide variety of descriptions from untrained observers of a dramatic crime. Witnesses to an armed robbery have varied in their descriptions to such an astonishing degree as to report—for the same suspect—differences of six inches in height and twenty years in age. Startled observers have transformed a culprit's gun into a knife, a rope, even a club.

Such extreme reactions to unusual occurrences which shocked or frightened the observers should always be considered when we read the dramatic accounts relayed by the witnesses of paraphysical activity who claim to have seen grotesque monsters issue from forests, mountain sides, or from grounded UFOs.

Fear of ridicule keeps many witnesses from telling their stories. Seventy-year-old William Bosak of Frederick, Wisconsin, a dairy farmer, is one such example, for he kept what he saw to himself for several weeks before finally telling a local newspaper reporter about it. It was then made public in the St. Paul, Minnesota, *Pioneer Press*.

Bosak was coming home from a co-op meeting at about ten-thirty one evening in December 1974. It was a rather mild evening for that time of the year in Wisconsin, and there were patches of fog on the road, caused by the warm air moving in over the cold ground. He drove slowly, and he kept his headlights on low beam.

About a half mile from home he noticed something on the left-hand side of the road and slowed almost to a stop. A few feet away, he could see what it was very plainly: a strange being in some kind of vehicle.

The creature was slender and appeared to be about six feet tall, although it seemed taller, since the vehicle was about two feet off the ground (*art by Dan Wolfman Allen*).

He told reporters that "The strange being had his hands up as though to show he was surrendering or to show he meant no harm. His eyes showed intense fright!"

It was a very unusual-looking being, according to Bosak, who described it as having hair on the sides of its head that stuck straight out, but no facial hair. He could not tell about clothing, but he said it looked as though it had hair covering its body, which he could only see from the waist up. The fur was a reddish-brown. Its ears looked like a calf's ears and stuck out at least three inches.

The creature was slender and appeared to be about six feet tall, although it seemed taller, since the vehicle was about two feet off the ground. It had a flat face, and the bushy hair and long ears gave it a frightful appearance, according to Bosak.

The arms were covered with hair or fur, like the rest of the body.

"When I got right alongside of the vehicle, which was about six or eight feet away, he was watching me," Bosak continued. "As I passed, it seems the object came right toward my car, and it became very dark in the car."

The object took off when Bosak passed it. The object made a swishing sound, and it seemed to touch his car. "It did definitely seem as though it came right at me, and there seemed to be a tremendous surge of power."

When asked if the creature resembled a man or an animal, Bosak replied that it mostly resembled a man. He could not tell the color of its eyes, but indicated that they were human-type eyes. Its neck was moderate in length, but he was not sure of the facial features, other than the eyes. The head seemed normal, human-sized.

The object from which the creature emerged was about six feet across. Due to the fog, which obscured its lower section, Bosak was unable to determine whether the object rested on the ground or hovered. Generally, he said, the object reminded him of a chemistry-lab bell jar. It did not appear to have lights of its own, being illuminated only by the headlights of Bosak's car.

The Christmas Lights Came Early that Year

A 48-year-old divorcée and her three sons were fast asleep in their mobile home in the western part of Cincinnati early in the morning of October 21, 1973.

Mrs. R. H. awoke about 2:30 A.M. and got out of bed to get a drink of water. She noticed a light coming through the drawn curtains, and when she pulled them apart she was startled to see a row of individual lights forming an arc not more than two yards from her window.

"Each light was as large as a hand with the fingers spread out," she reported to Len Stringfield, a UFO researcher and columnist for *Skylook* magazine.

The lights, six in number, were about four feet above the ground and alternated in color, from vivid blue to silver "as beautiful as Christmas lights." They appeared to Mrs. R. H. to be internally illuminated, casting no radiance to the ground or on a nearby shed.

While the "Christmas lights" hovered outside her window, her attention was drawn to a stronger light farther away, in the parking lot adjacent to her mobile home. A car was parked on the pavement, about ten feet from the home, and partially obscured the bottom of the light source.

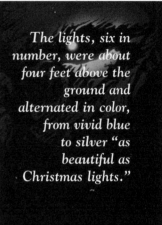

The lights, six in number, were about four feet above the ground and alternated in color, from vivid blue to silver "as beautiful as Christmas lights."

Near the light source Mrs. R. H. suddenly saw an apelike creature. She was terrified as she watched for the next two or three minutes. The creature was near the rear of the car, and she thought perhaps it was doing something to the vehicle.

She ran to her son Carl's bedroom and tried unsuccessfully to wake him.

When she returned to the window the creature had moved to a point about thirty-five feet from the mobile home; it was now inside the light source, or bubble of light, which she described as looking like one of the women's umbrellas that come down to the shoulders. The bright light itself seemed to be contained within that shield.

The creature was fully visible, and she described it as having a big waist and no neck. She could see no distinguishable features about its head other than that the profile showed more a "snout" than a nose. The body was all gray, and equally featureless. Its arms swung slowly, with an up-and-down motion, although there did not seem to be a normal bend at the elbows, and no other part of the body moved.

Mrs. R. H. estimated the bubble to be about seven feet in diameter. Although she could see no controls or levers inside the large glasslike bubble, she commented that the creature's arm movement suggested the operation of controls.

While Mrs. R. H. was trying to call the police, the strange bubble and its humanoid disappeared.

Was the creature seen in this bubble or large bell jar in some way related to so many similar creatures that are called by various—from Bigfoot to Sasquatch, from Yeti to Oh-Mah?

"Mothman, aliens and UFOs, and even Bigfoot reports sometimes fall under classifications that deny the laws of physics," comments paranormal researcher Micah Hanks. "True, these creatures may have physical aspects, but often these monsters seem capable of also 'shifting' between the fabric of multiple dimensions. I once interviewed a researcher from Pennsylvania named Rick Fisher, who while driving along a cornfield one evening saw 'Chewbacca' appear ahead of him in the headlights of his car. He slowed down behind the creature as it walked with its back to Rick, who watched this amazing animal carefully until, suddenly, it disappeared. It didn't dive off into the tall corn growing nearby, nor did it leap straight up; it just flat-out disappeared. Such instances of high-strangeness often leave us questioning the nature of the various monsters of this world; if indeed they are of this world."

JERSEY DEVIL AND OTHER UNNATURAL SPAWN OF DARKNESS

T he meal that the Sandersons had served that January evening in 1966 at their New Jersey farm had been delicious, and now I was looking forward to a quiet—yet intense and informative—evening of conversation with one of my idols, Ivan T. Sanderson, the famous author and naturalist. I was one month from celebrating my thirtieth birthday, and Ivan had agreed to write the foreword to my *Strange Guests*, a study of the noisy, throwing ghost, the poltergeist.

We had covered a few recent flying saucer cases (we didn't use the term UFO, unidentified flying objects, until a few years later) and were beginning to discuss Bigfoot and an expedition that he was assembling, which he felt passionately would prove the creature's existence once and for all.

And then the telephone rang.

We were sitting in Ivan's office, just a comfortable arm's reach from the telephone. He picked up the receiver and I could hear someone shouting at him as if he were running as fast as he could from a grizzly bear.

"All right, good lord," Ivan urged in his authoritative Scottish accent. "Just calm down and give me as much detail as you can possibly remember."

Ivan placed his hand over the mouthpiece and whispered to me that he had to take the call.

Assuming it was something of a personal nature, I left the room and roamed about the rooms nearest the office, examining a number of intriguing specimens that Ivan and his wife Alma had acquired on countless expeditions around the world.

At last I heard Ivan call me back to the office. But before I had reclaimed my chair across from Ivan's, the telephone rang again.

"It's the bloody Jersey Devil," Ivan grimaced. "He's on the prowl tonight. In just a few minutes, a radio station will call and I'll have to do a few minutes."

"Not Long John Nebel?" I asked with unmasked hope. Long John Nebel, who died in 1978, was undoubtedly the first of the late night "talkers" who filled the night with accounts of UFOs, Bigfoot, people who talked to Space Brothers, and the paranoids who had dreamed up the latest conspiracy theory. If Long John was about to call, Ivan would be on the phone until dawn.

"No, no, my boy," he assured. "Just a local program. That Jersey Devil crawls out from under some log every now and then. Just give me a few minutes, and we'll talk soon."

As eager as I was to spend the night visiting with Ivan about things that went bump in the night, I held on for an hour or two, then excused myself to head for the guest room.

The Jersey Devil became the only monster to which I have ever taken an instant disliking.

The Haunted Pine Barrens of New Jersey

Some witnesses have said that the Jersey Devil that haunts the Pine Barrens in southeastern New Jersey is a cross between a goat and a dog with cloven hoofs and the head of a collie. Others swear that it has a horse's head with the body of a kangaroo. Most of the people who have sighted the creature also mention a long tail, and nearly all of the witnesses agree that the thing has wings. But it doesn't really fly as much as it hops and glides.

People have been sighting the Jersey Devil in the rural area around south Jersey since 1735, which, according to local legend, is the year that it was born.

According to legend, there was a prominent family in south Jersey named Leeds whose patriarch demanded a large number of heirs to carry on his name to future generations. When Mrs. Leeds learned that she was about to bear her thirteenth child, she decided that she had grown tired of being continually pregnant in order to satisfy her husband's ego. In a fit of rage, she cursed the unborn child within her and cried out that she would rather bear the Devil's child than give birth to another Leeds for posterity.

Visualizing the image of Satan popular in the 1700s, Mrs. Leeds decreed that she wished the child to be born with claws and fangs, fierce and wild as some vicious beast. The old legend has it that Mrs. Leeds was granted her angry cry of revenge for having served as a brood mare for her selfish husband. The baby was born a monster with devilish fangs, claws, tail, and cloven hoofs, but the extremes of its viciousness soon eclipsed the borders of Mrs. Leeds's curse.

The little monster ate every one of the other Leeds children—the ultimate act of sibling rivalry—and escaped out of the chimney to begin its reign of terror among the farmers and villagers of the region. For well over two hundred years, generations of terrified witnesses have claimed to encounter the Jersey Devil.

Although encounters with the monster are reported every year, the most famous series of sightings occurred in January 1909 when hundreds of men and women claimed to have seen or heard the frightening creature. So many people refused to leave the safety of their homes that local mills were forced to shut down for lack of workers.

The Dover Demon: Ancient Evil or Sinister Alien?

Thirty years after his frightening encounter, William Bartlett stands by his story that the creature, the entity, the being, whatever it was that he and two other teenagers sighted in April 21 to 23, 1977, in Dover, Massachusetts, was real. The "thing" that has become known as the Dover Demon was seen by Bartlett as it crept along a low stone wall on the side of the road. It stood about four feet tall and carried its hairless, rough-textured body on two spindly legs. Its arms were also thin and peach-colored. The creature's huge, watermelon-shaped head was disproportionate in size to its relatively small torso, and it bore two large, glowing red-orange eyes.

Bartlett, who has made his career as a painter, told the *Boston Globe* (October 29, 2006) that he definitely saw something weird that night. "I didn't make it up," he said. "It's a thing that's been following me for years. Not the creature—the story."

Bartlett had his glimpse of the Demon atop the broken stone wall along Farm Street at around 10:30 P.M. Bartlett said the car was traveling maybe 35 to 40 miles per hour when he saw the thing "standing on a wall, its eyes glowing" in the headlights. "It was not a dog or a cat," he said. "It had no tail. It had an egg-shaped head." He said he saw it from about 10 feet away. The two friends with him did not report seeing the creature.

Bartlett made a point of telling investigators that he had grown up around animals and that he was familiar with seeing them at their best and at their worst. He had seen foxes with mange and a wide assortment of critters that had acquired one blight or another. This thing, he said, "was some kind of creature," with "long thin fingers" and "more human-like in its form than animal." Its shape reminded him of "kids with distended bellies."

About two hours later, 15-year-old John Baxter was walking home from his girlfriend's house when he claimed to have got within 15 feet of the monster along a creek in a heavily wooded area along Miller Hill Road. At midnight the next night, another 15-year-old Abby Brabham was driving home with her boyfriend when she saw what appeared to be the same weird creature sitting upright on Springdale Avenue.

Loren Coleman, who began an investigation within days of the sightings in 1977, believes Bartlett and considers the case credible. Coleman was able to interview all four teens who had encountered the Demon within a week of the reported sightings and

The Jersey Devil (*art by Dan Wolfman Allen*).

is convinced that they had not concocted a hoax. Coleman, who also coined the name "Dover Demon," has commented that the same area in which the strange being was sighted has a tradition of unexplained activity dating from the 1700s: An apparition of Satan on horseback, tales of buried treasure, and then the Dover Demon. "It's almost as if there are certain areas that 'collect' sightings, almost in a magnetic way," the investigator told Mark Sullivan, a *Boston Globe* correspondent.

No sightings of the Dover Demon have been officially reported since those strange nights in April 1977. Coleman observed that the Dover creature does not match the descriptions of the chupacabras or of Roswell aliens, or of the bat-eared goblins said to have attacked a family in Hopkinsville, Kentucky, in 1955. "It doesn't really fit any place," Coleman said. "It's extremely unique. It has no real connections to any other inexplicable phenomena."

It seems strange to Bartlett and his friends that the being that they sighted has almost become as well known as Bigfoot, the Loch Ness monster, and werewolves. Internet pages are devoted to the Dover Demon. You can even play a video game featuring the creature, or buy a figurine of it as far away as Japan. Once, his wife, Gwen, browsing the horror section of a bookstore, flipped open an encyclopedia of monsters—and there was an entry about her husband and the Dover Demon.

To illustrate what Bartlett had seen on that fateful evening, Baxter drew a picture of a humanoid figure with large eyes standing by a tree. Bartlett's version showed a large-eyed creature crawling with tendril-like fingers across a stone wall.

The locations of the sightings, plotted on a map, lay in a straight line over two and a half miles. All the sightings were made in the vicinity of water. No sightings have been reported since, though Bartlett says a weird experience a year later left him wondering if he had had a return visit from the creature. He was in a parked car with his girlfriend when he heard a thump on the car. He made out a small figure leaving the scene. He remains unsure who—or what—banged the car.

In his article, Sullivan mused that Farm Street on a contemporary evening could have been a modern-day Sleepy Hollow, with woods lining the fieldstone walls, and what little light there was coming from the moon. Since at least since the seventeenth century, the vicinity of the second-oldest road in Dover has been associated with strange occurrences.

In his 1914 town history, *Dover Farms*, Frank Smith writes of Farm Street:

"In early times this road went around by the picturesque Polka rock [on the farm of George Battelle] which was called for a man by that name, of whom it is remembered, that amid the superstitions of the age he thought he saw his Satanic Majesty as he was riding on horseback by this secluded spot.

"The location has long been looked upon as one in which treasures are hid, but why anyone should go so far inland to hide treasures has never been told; however, there has been at times unmistakable evidence of considerable digging in the immediate vicinity of this rock."

Loren Coleman has also noted that the area in which the Demon was sighted had a tradition of unexplained activity.

"In the same area you had three major legends going on," he said, citing the apparition of the devil on horseback, the tales of buried treasure, and then the Dover Demon.

Coleman theorized that the large geologic outcropping in the woods off Farm Street, which historian Smith called the "Polka" stone, might actually have been called the "Pooka" stone, after the fairy folk of Celtic folklore.

When the Dover Demon was sighted in 1977, it might not have been the first time a strange creature was spotted in the woods by local teenagers.

With tales of the Dover Demon having become a part of their town's tradition, some teenagers are uncertain if there aren't demons lurking around in shadowy places. Some have reported seeing small figures deep in the woods. Sometimes, late at night, their headlights catch unusual creatures at the side of the road.

Coleman, who remains the principal investigator of the 1977 case, spotlights the Dover Demon in the 2001 edition of his book *Mysterious America*.

> *Some have reported seeing small figures deep in the woods. Sometimes, late at night, their headlights catch unusual creatures at the side of the road.*

Is it possible the teens actually saw a foal, or perhaps a moose calf, as some have suggested? Coleman said he canvassed local horse owners after the incident and none reported missing a horse. Moreover, it was not foaling season, he said. As for the moose theory, only two moose were reported in Massachusetts in 1977 and 1978, both of them in central Massachusetts, he said. A yearling moose by that time in April would weigh more than 600 pounds and be "bigger than the Volkswagen Bartlett was in," said Coleman.

"To have a bipedal moose with long fingers and orange skin and no hair and no nose would be more of a phenomenon than the Dover Demon," he said.

So what did those teens see?

"It's OK to say we don't know," said Coleman.

"I think the Dover Demon's mystery lives on. It's an unknown phenomenon whose fame has stretched worldwide, and I think Dover should be very proud."

Carl Sheridan, a former police chief, has said that the Dover Demon still haunted him after 29 years. "I knew the kids involved. They were good kids ... pretty reliable kids."

"God only knows" what they saw, Sheridan said. "I still don't know. Strange things have happened. The whole thing was unusual. The thing will not die," Sheridan said. "I'm telling you, the thing will not go away."

More than three decades after seeing something very strange on Farm Street, Bartlett has decidedly mixed feelings about the experience. "It was my 15 minutes of fame, without wanting it," he said.

"It was a little embarrassing. It still is."

He said he hasn't talked much to his two children about the creature, because he doesn't want to frighten them. And the professional artist has never drawn another picture of the thing he saw. "I'm a serious fine-arts painter," he said. "I don't want people to think I'm some freak."

On the other hand, sometimes Bartlett really does wish that he had made it all up. "I might have profited from it," he jokes. "It's a great story. I wish it would be seen again so everyone would know it was true."

More about the Dover Demon is available at the Strange New England website (http://www.strangene.com/monsters/dover.htm) or at Loren Coleman's website (http://www.lorencoleman.com).

Canada's Valley of Headless Men

It would seem that the Nahanni Valley of Canada deals in measures more violent than witchery. The Indian tribes of the region have named the Nahanni the "Valley of Headless Men" because of the many cadavers that have been found minus their skulls. *The Shaver Mystery and the Inner Earth*, edited by Timothy Green Beckley (Saucerian Publications), carries an account by John J. Robinson, which deals with the grisly legends of the Nahanni Valley.

The ominous valley is located in the southern end of the Mackenzie Mountains. Although the valley temperature is at least 30 degrees above normal all year long, no settlers have ever staked claims to its fertile soil. The Indian tribes avoid the valley at all costs, and trappers leave animals within the boundaries of the Nahanni unmolested.

The reason for this strange quarantine of a valley that should offer so much to so many is the gruesome fact that those who do enter the Nahanni are generally found later as decapitated skeletons.

Those few courageous fur trappers who have entered the valley and returned alive have brought back rich loads of pelts, but few can be persuaded to reenter the valley, regardless of the availability of game. All of them have complained of the eerie feeling of being watched at all times.

Perhaps it has been only the constant vigilance of these men that has saved their heads, for the list of fatalities which the Nahanni Valley has chalked up is truly frightening, regardless of whether one attributes such "head-hunting" to Bigfoot, renegade tribesmen, Indians, or sadistic creatures that dwell in caverns under the earth.

Strange Encounters with the Boqs

BY BILL OLIVER

The Bella Coola Valley is considered one of the most beautiful areas within the Central Coast of British Columbia. The region is still considered a virtual wilderness that lies at the head of a 60-mile inlet from the Pacific Ocean. Because of its proximity to the outer Pacific Ocean, the valley's climate is much more temperate than nearby wilderness areas, and it also has less rainfall than the outer coast region.

The First Nations people, the Nuxalk, were the valley's original inhabitants. Today, the Bella Coola tribe lives in the area and consider it a virtual paradise—perhaps with the exception of an occasional visit by the Boqs, who also inhabit the area.

The attitude of mingled hope and fear with which the Bella Coola regard their supernatural anthropomorphic beings is typical of their thoughts and actions concerning zoomorphic creatures as well. In the supernatural world the dividing line between human and animal beings is not clearly defined; fabulous monsters have the mentality of supermen and can be appeased, besought, or cajoled precisely as are anthropomorphic beings. Like those in human form, supernatural animals can bestow good or evil on human beings with whom they come into contact.

A Boqs somewhat resembles a man, its hands especially, and the region around the eyes being distinctly human. It walks on its hind legs, in a stooping posture, its long arms swinging below the knees; in height it is rather less than the average man. The entire body, except the face, is covered with long hair, the growth being most profuse on the chest which is large, corresponding to the great strength of the animal.

A Boqs somewhat resembles a man—especially its hands—and the region around the eyes are distinctly human. It walks on its hind legs in a stooping posture, its long arms swinging below the knees (*art by Ricardo Pustanio*).

The most peculiar feature of the animal is its penis, which is so long that it must be rolled up and carried in the arms when the creature is walking; it terrifies its enemies by striking tree-trunks and breaking branches with its uncoiled organ.

It is said that a tribal woman was once drawing water at the edge of a stream when a Boqs, concealed on the other shore, extended its penis under the water to the further bank and held intercourse with her. The contact rendered her powerless, as if turned to stone; she could neither flee nor remove the organ. Her companions tried unsuccessfully to cut the organ until one of them brought a salalberry leaf, whereupon the monster, dreading its razor-like edge, withdrew.

* * *

The following stories illustrate, better than any other description, the attitude of the Bella Coola toward these creatures.

Not many years ago a certain Qaklis was encamped with his wife and child in the Bay of the Thousand Islands, Altukwlaksos, about two miles above Namu, one of the haunts of the Boqs. He heard a number of the creatures in the forest behind him and seized his gun, at the same time calling out to them to go away.

Instead, the sound of breaking of branches and beating upon tree-trunks came nearer. Becoming alarmed, he called out once more: "Go away, or you shall feel my power."

They still approached and Qaklis fired in the direction of the sounds. There followed a wild commotion in the forest, roars, grunts, pounding, and the breaking of branches. The hunter, now thoroughly alarmed, told his wife and child to embark in the canoe while he covered their retreat with his gun. He followed them without molestation, and anchored his craft not far from shore. The Boqs could be heard plainly as they rushed to and fro on the beach, but only the vague outlines of their forms were visible in the darkness.

Presently, though there was no wind, and the canoe began to roll as if in a heavy sea. Qaklis decided to flee to Restoration Bay, but before he had gone far his paddle struck bottom, although he was in mid-channel. Looking up, he saw that the mountains were higher than usual. The Boqs had, by their supernatural power, raised the whole area so that the water had been almost entirely drained away. They are the only supernatural beings with this power. Qaklis jumped overboard into the water which reached only to his knees, and towed his canoe to Restoration Bay, the Boqs following him along the shore.

This is not the only occasion on which Boqs have appeared near Restoration Bay. Within the lifetime of the father of an informant, a chief set out with some friends from Kwatna, bound for Namu. They traveled overland to Restoration Bay, thence by canoe, making the journey without incident. When returning, they decided to gather clams on the rocky point of the bay. As the craft shot around the tip of the promontory, they saw a Boqs gathering shellfish.

The paddlers backed their canoe behind some rocks whence they could watch without being seen. The creature acted as if frightened. It kept looking backwards, then hurriedly scraped up some clams with its forepaws, dashed off with these into the forest, and came back for more.

The chief decided to attack the monster. A frontal approach was impossible, owing to the lack of cover, so he landed and crept stealthily through the forest, armed with his Hudson's Bay Company's musket. Presently he stumbled upon a heap of clams which the animal had collected. He waited until it returned with another load, then raised his musket and fired.

Instead of killing the Boqs, its supernatural power was so great that the hunter's musket burst in his hands, though he himself was not injured.

The Boqs shrieked and whistled as if in anger, and at once hordes of its mates came dashing out through the forest. The frightened chief rushed out on the beach and called to his comrades to save him. They brought the canoe close to the shore so that he could clamber aboard, and then paddled away unharmed.

The Bella Coola believe that the Boqs, unlike most supernatural animals, have not abandoned the country since the coming of the white man. One man was most insistent that they still lived on King Island, and promised to point one out if a visit were made to that spot. This man refuses to camp at the place where he affirmed Boqs are common.

Another informant stated that though he had never seen one of the monsters, a horde of them surrounded his camp near Canoe Crossing for a week. Every night he heard them roaring and beating on trees and branches.

A curious blending of old and new beliefs was recorded in connection with this statement. This man remarked that one time when he was gathering firewood he heard the creatures closing in on him. His head swam with terror, until he remembered he was a Christian; he called on Jesus to help him, grasped his axe, and dashed towards the place from which the loudest sounds were coming. He heard the animals moving off all around him, but failed to see any of them.

Boqs have been heard as recently as 1924, according to popular belief. In January of that year a number of young Bella Coola were returning home in a motorboat from Ocean Falls. They camped for the night on Burke Channel, and were alarmed to hear a crashing of bushes and a beating on tree-trunks.

Another informant stated that though he had never seen one of the monsters, a horde of them surrounded his camp near Canoe Crossing for a week.

Thoroughly frightened, they directed the beams of several electric torches in the direction of the sounds without avail. At last they started the engine of their motorboat, and the noise frightened the animals away.

JUNGLE APEMEN OF SOUTH AMERICA, AFRICA, AND ASIA

In 2004, scientists declared that they may have discovered a new kind of giant ape in the Democratic Republic of Congo. Although that news was startling in its own right, the scientists went on to state that the primates were ferocious, aggressive, and even capable of killing lions.

A report in an issue of *New Scientist* stated that if these apes should prove to be a new species of primate, it could be one of the most important wildlife discoveries in decades. Interestingly, the "new" apes live hundreds of miles away from other known gorilla populations, and their diet appears more similar to that of chimpanzees.

Presenting the dimensions of the "new giant ape," *New Scientist* said:

Large, black faces like ordinary gorillas
Standing up to six-feet, five inches tall
Weighing around 224 pounds
The males make nests on the ground, not in the trees
Their diet is rich in fruit, like chimpanzees

Mande Burung, the Man of the Jungle, India's Yeti

There is no doubt among scientists that a giant ape, which they have named Gigantopithecus, lived at the same time as early humans. According to the estimates of zoologists and other scientists, the massive ape, which stood around 10 feet tall and may have weighed as much as 1,200 pounds, died out around 300,000 years ago.

At least that's what the scientists say. The people of the state of Meghalaya in the far northeast of India claim to have sighted Mande Burung, the Man of the Jungle, for many generations and continue to hear its strange call shrilling across their rice paddies. Fortunately for early humans, the giant primate's diet was composed primarily of bamboo. The people of Meghalaya hope that the giant ape that they see in the jungle today has maintained the same vegetarian diet.

Some researchers, such as Jack Rink, a geochronologist at McMaster University in Ontario, has used high-precision absolute-dating methods to satisfy himself that the largest primate ever known was roaming Southeast Asia for a million years before it died out in the Pleistocene period, about 100,000 years ago. It was at about this time that humans, who had existed according to some scientists for about a million years, were undergoing a major evolutionary change. Guangxhi province in southern China, where many Gigantopithecus fossils have been found, is the same region where some scientists believe the modern human race originated.

Although the human species began to advance greatly at this time, it is unlikely that they could have eliminated the giant ape. Why the massive primate became extinct remains a puzzle to some scientists—while other persistent Mande Burung hunters believe that remnants of its kind still exist in the jungles of India.

Journalist Andrew Buncombe (www.independent.co.uk) traveled to the area in 2008 to investigate reports of the Mande Burung. He made the acquaintance of a half-dozen or so "friendly Yeti hunters," who presented him with an extensive list of sightings. Included on the special list was a local hunter, who, in 2003, watched a Mande Burung from a hiding place across a valley for three days.

In 2005, one of the jungle giants suddenly invited himself into the hut of a widow and her young child. The creature stamped out their fire, then sat down beside them and made himself at home. Neither the widow nor her child was harmed and remained quietly beside the Mande Burung, because, she admitted, they were too frightened to run.

In 2008, another British journalist, Alastair Lawson, traveled with a well-known local Yeti-hunter, Dipu Marak, to search for the Mande Burung in the west, south, and east Garo Hills. They had received word that a woodcutter who worked in the border of the Nokrek National Park had observed the gigantic jungle man three days in succession. The woodcutter showed the two monster hunters where the man-beast had broken branches off trees and eaten the sap, but he could not persuade any Mande Burung to pose for any photographs.

One of the sightings of the Mande Burung that has been given the most credence was made in April 2002 when fourteen forestry officers had sighted one of the creatures while they were taking a census of tigers in Balpakram. The officials followed the huge footprints left by the giant and saw that they went into the vast Balpakram jungle canyon. The canyon, which stretches for many miles and is surrounded by great cliffs, is filled with thick jungle growth. The forestry officials decided that it would be very dangerous to attempt a descent into the Balpakram, and one of them commented that if there was any place where the shy and peaceful Mande Burung could live undisturbed, this canyon would certainly be it.

The Yeren, Wildman of China

After more than 200 reports of "wildman" sightings had been filed, an active search for China's yeren was begun in 1959. As is typical in such searches for Bigfoot and Yeti-type creatures, casts of footprints, hair samples, and feces are plentiful, but no one has yet captured a yeren or obtained good photographs of the man-beast. In 1977, 1980, and 1982, expeditions searching for the man-beast set out to track down their quarry in the Shennongjia Forest Park in western Hubei province. In September 1993, a group of Chinese engineers claimed to have seen three yeren walking on trails in the Shennongjia Forest Park.

In October 1994, the Chinese government established the Committee for the Search of Strange and Rare Creatures, including among its members specialists in vertebrate paleontology and palaeanthropology.

A loose consensus among interested members from the Chinese Academy of Sciences maintains that the yeren are some species of unknown primates. The largest cast of an alleged wildman footprint is 16 inches long, encouraging estimates that the yeren itself would stand more than seven feet tall and weigh as much as 660 pounds. The scientific committee has also studied and examined eight hair specimens said to have come from yeren ranging through China and Tibet. The analyses of the hairs, varying in color from black (collected in Yunnan province), to white (from Tibet), to reddish brown (from Hubei), indicate a nonhuman source, but no known animal matches the hairs brought into the laboratories.

In April 1995, a 30-member yeren expedition led by Professor Yuan Zhengxin set out for the Hubei mountains. Although the enthusiastic Professor Zhengxin expressed confidence that the well-equipped group would capture a yeren within three years, by July, most of the expedition members had returned to Beijing with little more than some possible hair samples to show for their three-month monster safari.

In January 1999, in spite of an official pronouncement from the Chinese Academy of Sciences that neither the Yeti nor the yeren exist, anthropologist Zhou Guoxing reminded his colleagues that unidentifiable hair specimens and 16-inch casts of footprints had been collected during scientific expeditions to the Shennongjia region. Even if 95 percent of the reports on the existence of the wildman are not credible, Guoxing said, it is necessary for scientists to study the remaining five percent.

The Malaysian Legends of Santu Sakai

According to the old stories, the santu sakai are were-beasts, half-humans, half-monsters, that the native people refer to as the "mouth men," because of their large fangs and their craving for fresh, red meat. When hordes of these savage crea-

According to the old stories, the santu sakai are were-beasts, half-humans/half-monsters that the native people refer to as the "mouth men," because of their large fangs and their craving for fresh, red meat (**art by Ricardo Pustanio**).

tures attack a village, they capture, kill, and eat their victims.

In June 1967, a hunter named Henri Van Heerdan claimed to have his skepticism regarding the santu sakai removed completely after a near-fatal close encounter with the beasts during a hunting trip near Kuala Lumpur. According to his account, he had bagged a number of birds for his dinner and was about half-a-mile from his vehicle when he began hearing "ugly growls and strange screams" coming from the other side of the trail. He decided to make a run for his vehicle.

When he stopped at one point to look behind him, he saw "two absolute monstrosities" running toward him. They were tall, very large, and they looked "like demons from hell."

Van Heerdan reached his vehicle, and he could hear that the beasts were close behind him. He turned and raised his shotgun, intending to fire, but it was too late. The hideous "mouth men" were on top of him. One of them bit his arm with its fangs, forcing him to drop his weapon.

Somehow van Heerdan managed to pick up a good-sized rock and used it to pound one of the monsters on the skull, causing it to fall in a daze. He struck another in the face and managed to get inside his car.

The santu sakai closed around the vehicle, growling, roaring, pounding at the sides and the windows. Van Heerdan's shaking hands at last managed to seize the steering wheel, start his vehicle, and he was fortunate to escape with his life.

He never again laughed at the crazy old folklore about the santu sakai.

El Sisemite—Giant of Guatemala

In the mythology of the Guatemalan Indians the monster known as El Sisemite is said to be taller than the tallest man and is described as being a cross between a man and a monkey. El Sisemite is believed to be strong enough to break down the biggest trees in the forest and to sprout hair thick enough to withstand a hunter's bullet.

The Guatemalan tribes accuse El Sisemite of having designs of their women and there are numerous accounts of village females being carried off by the man-beast. Male tribe members may be crushed and pummeled to death if they are unfortunate enough to encounter one of the giants when it feels like a bit of fresh blood and sport.

Tribal folklore says that El Sisemite kidnaps children in the hope that they will teach it how to speak in the privacy of its cave. Legend also has it that the jungle giant envies their mastery of fire, for they have found much evidence to indicate that El Sisemite warms itself by deserted campfires.

Mapinguary—An Extinct Monster that May Still Live in the Matto Grosso

In the dense jungle growth of the Matto Grosso, the natives fear the monstrous mapinguary, a creature so powerful that it kills oxen by pulling out their tongues.

In his book *On the Track of Unknown Animals*, Dr. Bernard Heuvelmans repeats an account of a mapinguary that was sent to him from a respected Brazilian writer. In the report, the principal, Inocencio, was on an expedition to the Urubu watershed when he left the main party to pursue a group of black monkeys with the intention of shooting one of them. Then, as it grew dark, he was surprised to hear what he believed to be a man shouting—a horrible, deafening cry.

Inocencio heard the sound of heavy footsteps, as if a large animal was running toward him, then he saw a silhouette the size of a man of middle height appear in the clearing. The figure remained where it stood, looking suspiciously at the place where Inocencio crouched quietly.

When the creature roared again, Inocencio fired at it, and he was terrified to see the wounded monster charging toward him. He fired another bullet, and the mapinguary leaped behind a barricade of undergrowth and brush. Inocencio himself took refuge in a tree and later observed that the roars from the creature that he heard that night were far more terrible and deafening than those of a jaguar.

He did not venture down from his perch until dawn. He found blood splashed around the clearing, and he noticed a sour smell that permeated the air.

In the vast majority of reported sightings of the mapinguary, the monster is over seven feet tall when it stands upright on its two hind legs. Everyone who has experienced an encounter with the creature comments that it emits an extremely foul odor.

Those who have attempted to kill the mapinguary have observed that it has incredibly thick, matted hair. It appears impervious to an arrow or

In the mythology of the Guatemalan Indians the monster known as El Sisemite is said to be taller than the tallest man and is described as being a cross between a man and a monkey (*art by Ricardo Pustanio*).

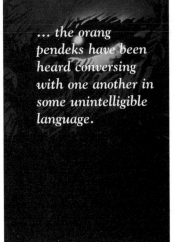

... the orang pendeks have been heard conversing with one another in some unintelligible language.

even a bullet, leading tribesmen of the Amazon to state that the monster can only be killed by a direct hit to the brain.

Native Shaman have long warned about the beast's power to make the most powerful of hunters become dizzy and even to lose consciousness.

In addition to such mystical powers, the mapinguary is incredibly strong. If it gets angry, it can tear down trees. Those who pursue it can suddenly find that the monster is throwing boulders at them.

While the Yeti, Bigfoot, and other man-beasts seem fairly docile and do their best to avoid human contact, the mapinguary has a "monstrous" temper and will even seek revenge on those who knowingly or unknowingly trespassed on its property. Men brave enough to hunt the mapinguary must be prepared to find the monster hunting them.

In the July 8, 2007 issue of the *New York Times*, David Oren, a former director of research at the Goeldi Institute in Belem, at the mouth of the Amazon River, said that it was quite clear to him that "the legend of the mapinguary is based on human contact with the last of the ground sloths," thousands of years ago. In Oren's opinion, tales of an extinct species can survive in legend and folklore for hundreds of years. Oren did admit, however, that "whether such an animal still exists or not is another question, one we can't answer yet."

Orang Pendek—The Little Man of the Sumatra Jungle

Sumatra folklore has it that their jungle is populated by numerous apemen known as orang pendek ("little man") or orang utan ("man of the woods"). According to tradition, the first recorded sighting of orang pendek dates back to 1295 when Marco Polo saw it on one of his expeditions to the island.

While many naturalists regard the tales of the orang pendek strictly as native folklore, in 1916, Dr. Edward Jacobson wrote in a Dutch scientific journal of his encounter with one of the creatures. Since Dr. Jacobson's sighting, there have been many accounts of people seeing the orang pendek, including that of a Mr. van Herwaarden, who spotted one while scouting the forests for good lumber in 1923.

Most witnesses describe the creature as standing about five feet tall and as being covered with short dark hair. It is definitely bipedal, and its arms are proportioned more like that of a human, rather than the extended arms of the ape. Most remarkably, the orang pendeks have been heard conversing with one another in some unintelligible language.

Debbie Martyr, former editor of a London newspaper, went in search of the elusive Sumatran apeman and returned in March 1995 with numerous consistent eyewitness accounts of the orang pendek and plaster casts of its footprints. She stated that she even saw the creature for herself on three different occasions. She remarked that "he is wonderfully camouflaged. If he freezes, you can't see him."

The first time that she sighted the orang pendek, she admitted that she was so shocked that she didn't take a picture. She hadn't really expected to see something so contrary to what she had expected—a bipedal erect primate. She remarked that the orang pendek is so well camouflaged because its colors correspond to those of the forest floor—beige, tawny, rust red, yellow tan, and chocolate brown. If the creature remains immobile, she said, it is impossible to see.

The orang pendek may be the most likely of the Bigfoot-type creatures to be proved real. Too many scientists have heard its calls, followed its trails through the jungle, and caught glimpses of the creature. On October 29, 2001, the *London Times* reported that an early analysis of hair samples taken by a British expedition to the mountain rain forest near Gunung Kerinci in western Sumatra did not appear to have come from any known primate in the area. Adam Davies, the leader of the expedition, stated that he had no doubt that orang pendek truly exists.

In 2004, Adam Davies, together with Andrew Sanderson, returned to Sumatra determined to find more conclusive evidence that would prove the existence of the orang pendek. Three years earlier, the plaster casts and tufts of hair that they had collected had gained the attention of respectable scientists who concluded that the evidence that they had collected was from some unknown species, and they were on the trail the moment they arrived at the village of Bukkantingi. Orang pendek had been sighted only two days before their arrival. The creatures had helped themselves to the succulent fruit raised by local farmers.

Two days after they had set up base camp near the village, the British explorers heard the calls of the orang pendek coming from the jungle.

Davies and Sanderson felt that they got within a few hundred yards of the mysterious creatures when the jungle simply became too dense to permit any kind of pursuit.

So many local residents as well as explorers and scientists have seen the orang pendek that there seems no doubt that the man-like creatures exist. Researchers posit three possible resolutions when the mystery ape is finally captured:

1. They are a newly evolved species of ape.
2. They are some kind of giant chimpanzees that behave much more like gorillas.
3. The orang pendek could possibly be some kind of hybrid, the offspring of gorillas mating with chimpanzees.

LAKE MONSTERS—SIGHTINGS FROM AROUND THE WORLD

Although Loch (lake) Ness of Scotland has unarguably the world's most famous monster in "Nessie," as one travels around the country, one learns that there are many lakes, both big and small, which have their strange water creatures. And if one should travel to various places around the world, one would find that Scotland and North America by no means have cornered the market on lake monsters.

In central Minnesota, Big Pine Lake has such a monster who is affectionately known as "Oscar," and many of the residents of the community have seen him on or near the surface. Many hypotheses have been given concerning his appearance, including the idea that he might be a giant sturgeon. (The largest sturgeon ever taken weighed 360 pounds.) But this theory has proven unconvincing to many of the residents, as it does not completely fit the descriptions of those who have seen Oscar.

The Lake Manitou Monster

BY FRANK JOSEPH

While tales of Scotland's Loch Ness Monster are famous, forgotten is the story of a similar aquatic creature said to infest the depths of an otherwise placid body of water in northern Indiana. Lake Manitou lies in a corner of Fulton County between the small towns of Rochester and Athens. Three miles long, less than two miles at its widest point, and averaging forty feet deep, the lake is physically unremarkable.

Today, it mostly attracts area visitors for the usual summer recreational sports. But even in the early twenty-first century, at least some of those visitors are still wary of a seldom seen, though keenly sensed "presence" contrary to the serenity of its natural surroundings.

However infrequently, startled fishermen still glimpse a dark, sinuous form writhe through the green depths beneath the keels of their boats, and reported sightings of a serpentine form at least partially exposed on the surface occur once or twice a decade. That such observations are reported at all is remarkable in view of a strenuous debunking campaign undertaken by Donald Smalley, Professor of History at the University of Indiana (Indianapolis) in the 1930s.

Until then, the creature was still glimpsed with some frequency by local residents. But Smalley's insistence that the phenomenon was nothing more than a joke on simple country folk perpetuated by neighboring Logansport newspaper men inhibited witnesses from his time to ours. No one wanted to be associated with some journalistic hoax.

Even so, sightings of the elusive and defamed beast continue to the present time. Had he bothered to investigate further than his own foregone conclusion, Smalley might have found an historic or even prehistoric foundation for such tales in the Native American name of the lake: Manitou. It means "spirit", and refers to the indwelling soul of Nature at its most sacred centers.

The leader of the Miami, the last tribe to inhabit Fulton County, refused to leave Lake Manitou when evicted by U.S. federal authorities, claiming it was an exceptionally hallowed location bequeathed to them by ancestors who first venerated the waters long ago. With profound reluctance and under threat of armed removal, the Miami vacated Lake Manitou in 1830.

Immediately thereafter, white settlers along its shores reported seeing the monster for the first time. They usually described its length from 20 to 30 feet, a "copper-colored" or dull brown creature with a horse-like head that extended from a long, snaky neck or body.

Neither scales nor fins have ever been mentioned. Only with increased settlement during the late 1850s did sightings grow less frequent, although they never ceased altogether, even during Dr. Smalley's published debunking efforts, 80 years later. Modern reports of the monster are almost invariably low-key and usually confined to local observers, who prefer to protect their privacy. Like the UFO phenomenon, the Indiana lake beast may even today be seen far more often than it is reported.

While some investigators believe a "monster" in the sense of some unknown animal may indeed lurk in the murky depths of Lake Manitou, metaphysical researchers believe it is actually a psychic phenomenon generated centuries ago by the Native American shamans to protect the sacred waters. It is, they claim, a guardian spirit, whose potent presence is still very real to modern visitors, because its resonance continues to interface with human consciousness. Even if receptive visitors consciously knew nothing of legends connecting Lake Manitou to a resident "monster", they could nonetheless easily "pick up" on a powerful "something" in its waters.

Whether this presence is the lingering result of a shaman's magic, or the spirit of Nature herself, the creature appears to float as much upon the waves, as between our material plain and the spirit realm. As such, it does not represent an "evil" or negative phenomenon—only a powerful one, despite the visceral fear it engenders in some visitors to the lakeshore. Its existence, on any level, means Lake Manitou is still a sacred site deserving of appreciation, even veneration.

More Tales of Meshekenabek

BY TIM R. SWARTZ

In his *Recollections of the Early Settlements of the Wabash Valley*, Sanford C. Cox reported, "The Indians would not hunt upon its borders, nor fish in its waters for fear of incurring the anger of the evil spirit that made its home in this little woodland lake."

In fact, the Native Americans would later warn settlers against building a mill on the lake, said Cox, fearful that the monster would "rush forth from its watery dominions and take indiscriminate vengeance on all those who resided near the sacred lake."

Perhaps the Lake Manitou monster wasn't all Native American superstition because during construction of the mentioned corn mill in 1827 several men who surveyed the lake for the mill reported seeing the monster. They claimed the creature was dark colored, and over thirty feet long with a long neck and a head like a horse. News soon spread of the lake monster, making it difficult to find men to finish the job.

The area's first blacksmith described the monster like this: "The head being about three feet across the frontal bone and having something of the contour of a beef's head, but the neck tapering and having the character of the serpent. Its color was dingy, with large yellow spots."

On July 21, 1838, the *Logansport Telegraph* reported that two men spotted the monster, which was "sixty feet long, and looked like a huge snake."

Using the eyewitness descriptions, George Winter, noted painter of Native Americans, sketched his conception of the monster for the newspaper.

Over the years sporadic sightings of the "Devil's Lake Monster" were reported. However, in 1849 the *Logansport Journal* reported that a huge buffalo carp that "weighed several hundred pounds" was caught in the lake, the fish's thirty pound head was exhibited at Logansport.

People thought that the monster had been caught at last, but in 1888 a 116-pound spoonbill catfish was pulled from the lake by four men. The

Although Nessie is far and away the most famous of all monsters inhabiting inland bodies of water, there are reports of equally large, equally strange aquatic creatures in lakes all over the world (**art by** *Ricardo Pustanio*).

monster-sized fish was placed in a horse trough by the county courthouse in Rochester and people were charged ten cents for a peek.

Eventually, the catfish was butchered and sold at ten cents a pound. In recent years reports of the Lake Manitou monster have waned. Today when the northern Indiana winters freeze the lake over, the ice shifts and emits booming and roaring noises. Residents around the lake smile and say that it is the monster trying to force its head above the ice.

The Beast of Busco

The Lake Manitou monster was reportedly a large serpent. In the Whitley county town of Churubusco, the lake monster was a giant turtle. The story of "Oscar" (obviously a favorite name for lake monsters), as the turtle would later be known, starts in 1898 in a seven acre lake about one mile east of town. The owner of the lake, Oscar Fulk, first spotted the turtle when it unexpectedly surfaced in front of him just a few yards from shore. The turtle was huge; Fulk estimated the animal to be at least five feet wide with a big, ugly head like a snapping turtle.

"Oscar" the turtle would remain unseen for almost fifty years when, in 1947, it would once again be sighted, capturing the attention of the national media. By then the lake was called "Fulk Lake" and was about 100 yards behind the plowed fields and small, white farmhouse owned by the Gale Harris family. Helen Harris would later write about her family's encounters with the "Beast of Busco" and the unwanted attention they received.

"My brother, Charles Wilson, and his son-in-law first saw the turtle while fishing in the lake," Ms. Harris wrote. "We thought at first he was kidding us, but he said he was serious. He had never seen a turtle that big. Later, my husband, Gale, and our minister, the Rev. Orville Reese, were repairing the roof of the barn when they saw the turtle surface."

The two men estimated that the turtle was as big as a large dining room table and could weigh as much as 400 pounds. Gale Harris was determined to catch "Oscar" and he would watch the lake to try and study the beast's habits.

An unverified story says that Gale managed to get a rope around the turtle with the other end attached to a hitch with four horses. But "Oscar" wasn't about to be caught in such a undignified fashion. The beast dug its claws into the mud and the rope broke allowing the turtle to escape.

Unfortunately for the Harris family, the newspaper reports about "Oscar" led to a steady stream of uninvited guests to the farm. According to Helen Harris, "We couldn't sit down and eat a meal in peace or get our work done on schedule. We had no privacy in our home. People came by the hundreds and would walk into our home without knocking. They used our bathroom, sat in the living room or did anything else they wanted to do without asking."

What finally happened to the "Beast of Busco" is anybody's guess. Gale Harris thinks the turtle went underground, through springs and channels to another lake.

Others think he walked out of the lake in order to find a more peaceful home. The road just 100 yards from Fulk Lake caved in around 1954, some say because of "Oscar's" great weight when he walked across it.

"Oscar," however, has not been forgotten. Every year the town of Churubusco celebrates its "Turtle Days" festival with a parade and other turtle oriented activities. Although the Harris family didn't enjoy the fame "Oscar" brought them, Churubusco, (or Turtle Town USA as they like to be called) still enjoys the attention brought about by the mysterious "Beast of Busco."

Nessie, the Magic Aquatic Giant of Loch Ness

Sightings of Nessie, most often described as a long-necked monster resembling a prehistoric brontosaurus, have been recorded in and near Loch Ness since St. Columba made the first recorded sighting in 565, and nearly two million tourists each year come to Scotland to see if they might obtain a glimpse and a photograph of the elusive water beast.

In 1936, Glasgow filmmaker Malcolm Irvine filmed a dark blob, approximately thirty feet in length, moving slowly across Loch Ness and offered what he believed to be proof that the most famous monster in the world actually existed in the Scottish lake where it had been sighted since the fifteenth century. With that brief filmstrip Nessie mania had been brought into the twentieth century, and it has never abated, seemingly growing stronger each year. And in spite of Irvine's intentions, his cinematic record of the Loch Ness monster did not put an end to the controversy over the creature's existence.

Could a prehistoric creature actually be living in a lake in Scotland? Loch Ness is certainly large enough and deep enough. It is 24 miles long by about a mile across. It has a mean depth of 433 feet, twice that of the North Sea into which it flows through the River Ness at its eastern end. Loch Ness is fed by five rivers and fifty mountain streams. The loch never freezes, and snow rarely lies near its shores. Its temperature remains fairly constant at about a chilling 42-degrees Fahrenheit, summer or winter.

Clem Lister Skelton, a military historian and a resident technician of the Loch Ness Phenomena

Sightings of Nessie have been seen in and near Loch Ness since St. Columba made the first recorded sighting in 565 CE, and nearly two million tourists each year come to Scotland to see if they might obtain a glimpse and a photograph of the elusive water beast (*art by Dan Wolfman Allen*).

Investigation Bureau, Limited, claims to have seen "Nessie" more than any other man, because he has "looked at that damn loch probably more than anyone else." He confessed to Godfrey Anderson of the Associated Press that "Nessie" was his personal Moby Dick. "We have one of the largest creatures in the world in this loch's confines and we don't know what it is," he said. "It's challenging. It's exciting. And it's infuriating."

Volunteer monster-watchers work in relays from mid-May to mid-October. Each volunteer is equipped with log pads, field glasses, and movie cameras with telephoto lenses. Whenever anyone snaps anything, the film is sent off to the Defense Ministry's Joint Air Reconnaissance Center (JARIC) for careful analysis. The JARIC comprises the same group of experts who in 1943 successfully pinpointed the Nazis' secret V-2 rocket base, at Peenemunde, Germany, from aerial reconnaissance pictures.

Tim Dinsdale (1924–1987), a member of the JARIC team, said the twelve- to sixteen-foot-long thing he photographed traveling at a speed of ten knots was "almost certainly animate."

On January 24, 1966, the Royal Air Force issued its analysis of the Dinsdale film-strip. In quoting brief excerpts from the report, we find that the RAF zeroes in on the "hump" of the creature and determines that it is moving at a speed of about ten miles per hour. After much technical discussion about the relative size and perspective of the "solid, black, approximately triangular shape" (the hump) and a comparison of the unidentified creature with a motorboat moving in the same area (filmed immediately after Nessie had swum past), the RAF concedes that the object is "*not* a surface vessel."

And: "One can presumably rule out the idea that it is any sort of submarine vessel for various reasons, which leaves the conclusion that it probably is an animate object."

David James (1919–1986), a former member of the British Parliament and head of the Loch Ness Phenomena Investigation Bureau (1962–1972), summed up the conclusions of the bureau in the spring of 1968: "Let's get one thing straight. There is no single 'Loch Ness Monster' which has lived for a few thousand or million years. What we are investigating is the possibility of a herd, breeding, evolving like any other species in waters such as these, cut off from the sea, for 5,000 to 7,000 years."

Always a firm believer in the Loch Ness creature or creatures, James said, "One thing is perfectly clear: There is something there. Too many reliable persons have seen too much, with too little possibility for coincidence, connivance, or conjuration to pass the entire matter off as only a figment of someone's imagination."

In 1968, Dr. Roy P. Mackal, University of Chicago biologist and head of the U.S. branch of the bureau, received the three-year grant from Field Enterprises Educational Corporation of Chicago that incorporated the services and the submarine of Dan Taylor. Although the expedition had sophisticated photographic equipment, biopsy darts, and other advanced research materials, the murky brown waters of Loch Ness rendered all the underwater devices relatively useless. Dr. Mackal has theorized that the type of creature that most neatly fits the mass of descriptive evidence and photos compiled by researchers and witnesses has to be some kind of large aquatic mammal that would be capable of thriving above 50-degrees north latitude.

Dan Taylor of Hardeeville, South Carolina, accompanied Mackal on the 1969 quest for Nessie that was sponsored by Field Enterprises, publishers of the *World Book Encyclopedia*. He had been selected to become a part of the expedition because of his expertise with submarines, and he brought with him a small fiberglass sub that he had built to explore the murky depths of Loch Ness.

It was on one of his last runs around the loch that Taylor encountered Nessie. The submarine was hovering around a depth of 250 feet when he said that he felt the craft beginning to turn, unnaturally, "like the secondhand of a clock being pushed backward by a finger," he told J.R. Moehringer of the *Los Angeles Times* (August 16, 1998). Taylor knew that something had pushed up against the submarine and turned it around, but he said that it didn't dawn on him that it had been Nessie until he surfaced.

It appears, however, that a team of sonar experts may have had definite success during an expedition in August 1968. The equipment they used was chiefly developed by David Tucker, head of the electronic engineering department at Birmingham University, and the results of the two weeks of sonar probing was reported in the British journal *New Scientist*.

The researchers were excited when the instruments had picked up some strange "bird-like" chirps.

Tucker wrote that in one thirteen-minute period sonar echoes defined large objects moving underwater. A massive object was recorded swimming at a speed as high as seventeen miles per hour and diving at a rate of 450 feet a minute.

"From the evidence we have," said Tucker, "there is some animal life in the loch whose behavior is difficult to reconcile with that of fish.... It is a temptation to suppose the echoes must be the fabulous Loch Ness Monster."

In 1970, Roy Mackal devised a system of hydrophones and deployed them at intervals throughout the lake. In early August, a hydrophone was lowered into Urquhart Bay and anchored in 700 feet of water. The researchers were excited when the instruments had picked up some strange "bird-like" chirps. In October, the hydrophones recorded some peculiar "knocks," "clicks," suggestive of whale-like echolocation. These sounds were followed by a loud swishing, as the sound that the tail swishing of a large aquatic creature might make.

In 1971, Bob Rines (1922–2009), a world-renowned patent attorney, physicist, and engineer, saw Nessie for himself. There in the middle of the lake, his binoculars focused clearly on the creature for 10 minutes, he saw what looked like the back of an elephant. Then, he told Scott Pelley of CBS' *60 Minutes*, "this lumbering thing turned around, gave us the wonderful spectacle of coming right back in front of us and submerged."

The New York Times (Douglas Martin, November 8, 2009) said: "Dr. Rines took the most convincing underwater pictures of what might or might not have been the Loch Ness Monster, so convincing that in the mid-1970s scientists from Harvard and the Smithsonian Institution expressed serious interest." Rines shrugged off the skeptics who say that he merely saw a school of fish or a trick of the light. Rines, who taught a course on intellectual property at his alma mater, Massachusetts Institute of Technology, knows what he saw. And he was familiar with the denizens of the deep. It was his ground-breaking research on sonar that was used to locate the *Titanic*.

In 1972, Rines set up an underwater sound stage at the lake, designed to trigger lights and start a camera whenever a large object passed the station. In 1975, the camera, rigged to roll at one frame every 45 seconds, captured the image of a creature that he believes resembles a plesiosaur, an aquatic, air-breathing dinosaur that should have been extinct 65 million years ago.

In May 2009, a leading Loch Ness expert and an expert in sonar readings were heading between Dores Village and Urquhart Castle when five unexplained images appeared on the sonar of the *Jacobite Queen*. For Captain John Askew, it was the first time in his 15 years on the lake that he had successfully picked up such remarkable images. The Loch Ness Project's Adrian Shrine, an expert in sonar who had been studying the loch since 1973 could not explain the sighting.

Lake Monsters Are All Over the World

Although Nessie is far and away the most famous of all monsters inhabiting inland bodies of water, there are reports of equally large, equally strange aquatic creatures in lakes all over the world.

Africa

Uganda: Several lakes report sightings of the Lukwata, a giant 100-foot-long serpent that has been seen to drag large mammals—even fishermen—under the water.

Mzintlava River, South Africa: In 1997, Government sources attributed at least seven human victims to "Mamlambo," a 67-foot serpent with stumpy legs.

Argentina

Lake Nahuel Huapi: This giant water snake called "Nahuelito" has humps, fish-like fins, and has been estimated as long as 150 feet. In 1960, the Argentina Navy monitored an unidentified submarine creature for 18 days without being able to identity it. Even some scientists believe it to be a prehistoric behemoth, such as a plesiosaur.

Canada

In 1958, Dr. Vadim Vladikov went to Lake Pohenegamook to question the witnesses who claimed to have seen a monster splashing around in the lake country two hundred miles east of Quebec City. Dr. Vladikov was the director of the Quebec Department of Game and Fisheries, a man whose opinion on the matter would certainly be worth a great deal.

"I have questioned a great many people in St. Bleuthere [a large village in the area] and they all describe the same thing—an animal between 12 and 18 feet long, brown or black in color, with a round back two or three feet wide, and a saw-tooth fin down the center. Any time anyone approaches close, the animal slithers away and slinks below the lake's surface." However, he later remarked: "It's probably a big fish, though it just might be something else." It must have been something else, unless there are gigantic fish in Quebec that venture out on land and slither back to water only when someone approaches.

The lakes in the great group including Lakes Manitoba and Winnipegosis have had a long, continuing history of something big and strange frightening fishermen. In 1960, Professor James A. McLeod, head of the Department of Zoology of the University of Manitoba, left the environs of the campus to investigate, announcing before his departure that the something was probably just a big snapping turtle.

But then it was discovered that a fisherman had made a model of a peculiar-looking bone he had found near the shore. The original had been destroyed in a fire, but either the fisherman was a whiz at paleontology or he had actually made a replica of a bone from a creature believed extinct for millions of years.

Professor McLeod was no longer interested in looking for giant snapping turtles. He allowed that giant prehistoric reptiles that had once lived in that area might somehow have survived. "Of course," he emphasized, "we are skeptical, but it is a scientific possibility."

Lake Pohenegamook, Quebec: A creature between 12 and 18 feet long, brown or black in color, with a round back two or three feet wide, and a saw-tooth fin down the center has been sighted by many witnesses.

"Ogopogo," Okanogan Lake, British Columbia: In July 1989, after three centuries of reported sightings, a salesman captured the beast on videotape, and the footage so convinced the Canadian government of the lake monster's existence that Ogopogo was placed on the nation's protected wildlife list. In July 2008, *The Vancouver Province* reported that Ogopogo sightings were on the rise.

Ireland

Lough Mask: Sightings of this monster, often described as half-wolf and half-fish and called "dobarcu" or "dhuragoo," go back to at least 1684.

Lough Ree: Although the sightings of this strange serpent-like beast go back hundreds of years, the best-documented claim occurred in 1960 when three Catholic priests spotted the creature.

Japan

"Issie" in Lake Ikeda: Although reports of a lake monster nearly 100 feet long and about three feet around had been made by startled witnesses for hundreds

Some researchers have theorized that there may more than one monster in Loch Ness. A number of experts suggest that whole families of the giant lake monsters live in the loch for a time, then return to the ocean. (*art by Bill Oliver*).

of years, the first sighting of Issie by a large group of people occurred on September 4, 1978, when over twenty people saw the massive, snakelike creature.

Norway

"Selma," Seljord Lake: Sightings date back to 1750 when a man was attacked by a "sea horse" while rowing on the lake. Descriptions of "Selma" vary from a creature with several humps, a crested neck and an eel-like head to those who swear that it has the features of an alligator with two horns protruding from its head.

Russia

Lake Vorolta: A United Press International report not long ago gave information concerning a monster that terrorized Siberia's Lake Vorolta. It was reported to roar and was described as spherical and horrible to see. The monster had allegedly eaten a swimming dog, a reindeer, and an undetermined number of human beings.

Lake Labynikir: Geologist Vittor Tverdokhlebov recalled for the press what he had seen in nearby Lake Labynikir in 1953:

It was an ominous-looking dark gray sphere that showed slightly above the water. It inspired nearly uncontrollable fear as it approached. It resembled an oversized glistening tin barrel with a slanted horn under on its back. There were two bulging protrusions that must have been eyes approximately seven feet apart on the head.

The creature reached the bank, stopped, then it went into a series of convulsions which raised waves and fountains of water as it disappeared below.

There was no question about the monster's intentions. It was heading straight for us.

Lake Brosno: Residents of Benyok, a village about 250 miles northwest of Moscow, have reported a "dragon monster" with two large bulbous eyes lurking in the lake.

Lake Sobolkho: This Siberian lake is called the "lake of fear" for in recent years the number of human victims number in the hundreds, as well as 1,300 horses, and 500 cows. Evil spirits, pagan cults, and a great serpent-like monster are blamed for the mysterious disappearances around the lake.

Sweden

Storsjoodjuret: More than 200 sightings of Storsji a three-humped serpent estimated to be 50 feet long, have been made since 1635. Hunts for the monster have taken place regularly since 1894 when a Swedish sea captain created a stock company for the purpose of catching the sea-beast alive.

Turkey

Lake Van: On June 10, 1996, a teaching assistant at Van University shot a video of a dinosaur-like creature that was at least 50 feet long. Since the lake monster was first sighted in 1995, more than a thousand people have seen it.

Peru

According to numerous witnesses, Lake Titicaca is home to a 12-foot creature that somewhat resembles a seal or a manatee.

United States

"Champ," Lake Champlain, New York: The first white man to see Champ was Samuel de Champlain, for whom this lake, which separates Vermont and New York, is named. In his journal entry for July 1609, he describes his sighting of a serpentine creature about twenty feet long, as thick as a barrel, with a horse-like head. The tribespeople who accompanied Champlain's expedition were quite familiar with the serpent and called it, "chousarou."

In the nearly 400 years since the French explorer had his encounter with Champ, there have been over 600 sightings of the unknown beast. On October 6, 1980, the Port Henry Village Board of Trustees passed a resolution granting protection of the serpentine creatures along the shores of the 109-mile lake.

"Memphre," Lake Memphremagog, Vermont: After hundreds of sightings of Memphre since colonial times, the Vermont legislature unanimously passed a law in 1987 to protect Memphre and her family of water creatures from any willful act resulting in death, injury, or harassment.

"Ogua," Monongahela River, West Virginia: Although sightings are not as frequent as they were in colonial times, reports of Ogua continue in the Monongahela and other waterways of the state.

"Meshekenabek," Lake Manitou, Indiana: The Potawatomi tribe told the early settlers to beware of the evil spirit that made its home in the lake, a dark-colored serpentine creature over 30 feet in length with a long neck and a horse-like head. In recent years, reports of Meshekenabek have lessened, but it lives on in folklore of the area.

Black Mystery Monster in Lake Erie: Witnesses describe the creature as a large blackish beast about fifty feet long with bulging eyes swimming through the water like a monstrous snake.

Flathead Monster, Flathead Lake, Montana: Sightings of a large, dark, eel-shaped creature, 20 to 40 feet long, have been reported in Flathead Lake since 1889.

In the nearly 400 years since the French explorer had his encounter with Champ, there have been over 600 sightings of the unknown beast.

After years of researching Nessie in Loch Ness and similar long-necked lake creatures all around the northern hemisphere, Dr. Roy Mackal has come to believe that rather than beholding "monsters" in the waters, people are witnessing small, remnant bands of Zeuglodons. In Dr. Mackal's theory, the creatures migrate from oceans to lakes, following such prey as spawning salmon. Lake Champlain is linked to the Atlantic Ocean by the Richelieu and St. Lawrence Rivers of Quebec. Loch Ness is connected to the sea, and so is Lake Okanagan in British Columbia, where Ogopogo is frequently sighted.

Smaller than the Basilosaurus, a later development on the evolutionary ladder, Zeuglodons bear little resemblance to modern whales. Dr. Mackal said that the fossil remnants of the creature at the Smithsonian Institution look "like a big anaconda [a large semi-aquatic boa constrictor] with a ridge down its back."

Just think of it! There could be a survivor of the Age of Reptiles living right out there in the depths of your favorite lake or offshore of the beach where you love to go surfing.

LIZARD MAN AND OTHER SWAMP CREATURES

In August 1972, while living on the beach around Thetis Lake in British Columbia, Canada, Gordon Pike and Robin Flewellyn were astonished to see an incredible reptilian humanoid emerging from the lake's depths.

Bill Oliver of a Vancouver, British Columbia, UFO investigation group, checked his files to review the case. The Lizard Man stood five feet tall and walked on its hind legs. The entity was covered in silvery scales, possessed huge pointed ears, large eyes, a frog-like face, flipper-like feet and bore several sharp pointed projections on its head.

When it detected its two eyewitnesses, the creature began to chase after them, but they soon fled.

Four days later, what would appear to be the same creature was seen by two other observers as it came out of the lake.

The Honey Island Hairy Lizard Man

According to Haunted America Tours (April 27, 2008), Harlan E. Ford came eyeball to eyeball with a swamp monster in 1974. Ford said the creature was about five feet, eight inches tall and weighed somewhere in the area of 350 pounds. Although the monster looked kind of "sinister," Ford said that he could detect nothing in the beast's manner that seemed to threaten him.

Ford's encounter occurred in Honey Island Swamp, nearly 70,000 acres of a wildlife area protected by the Nature Conservancy First Louisiana Nature Preserve. Honey Island lies between the East Pearl and West Pearl Rivers and is located about an hour's drive from New Orleans.

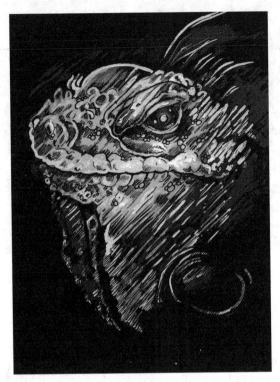

In August 1972, while living on the beach around Thetis Lake in British Columbia, Canada, a couple of residents were astonished to see an incredible reptilian humanoid emerging from the lake's depths (*art by Ricardo Pustanio*).

While some individuals who encountered similar creatures had described them with a mane of hair falling around their shoulders, Ford said that "his" swamp monster had rather short hair all over its body with longer hair forming bangs over its eyes. In Ford's account, the most outstanding feature of the creature was its very large amber eyes.

Ford reported that the creature left tracks that appeared similar to an alligator's rear feet. Zoologists from Louisiana State University who examined the casts determined that they were very different from the tracks that an alligator might leave in a swamp.

In the casts made of the feet, there are four toes visible. Three of these are heavily clawed toes with prominent knuckles. Interestingly, the fourth toe appears to be a strange kind of "thumb," thus indicating that the creature can grasp things with its feet. Strangely enough, the claws are turned downward and backward, suggestive of a catlike trait by which the large toes are able to grip loose soil, sand, and mud.

The Lizard Man of Scape Ore Swamp

It was nearly two o'clock on that June night in 1988 when 17-year-old Christopher Davis was on his way from working the late shift at the McDonald's in Bishopville, South Carolina. He was exhausted and more than ready to crawl into bed.

He was just on the border of Scape Ore Swamp when a tire blew.

Davis was forced to accept the hard reality of the situation. There was no way that he was going to get to bed unless he got out of the car and began to change the tire.

There were only the night noises of the birds, insects, and other critters that inhabited to swamp to keep Davis company—until he heard a very loud and peculiar thumping sound coming from the bean field across the road from his car. Although it was very dark near Scape Ore Swamp, Christopher Davis could see something blacker than the night running toward him from the bean field. It also had red eyes.

When he arrived home that night, the teenager's screams bolted his parents from their bed. Christopher was in an absolute state of panic, and when they tried to calm him down, he gave the appearance of someone who would probably take several months to be able to relax.

A few days later, Christopher told his story to the Associated Press, and the legend of the Lizard Man was born.

Right after the teenager had seen the hulking monster with the red eyes heading in his direction, he gave thanks that he had finished changing the flat tire and he tossed it into the trunk. He got back in the car, locked the doors, and burned rubber getting out of there.

Just as he thought he had left the living nightmare behind him, Christopher heard a loud thump on the roof of his car. Whatever it was, it was able to run fast enough to catch up to him. The teenager saw clearly three large fingers with long black nails, and green rough skin reach over his windshield. Another hand with ugly claws jerked on the door handle of the driver's side.

The Lizard Man emitted a terrible grunt of anger, and Christopher could see the long fingers crossing the windshield as they curled around the roof.

... the roof of the automobile bore deep scratches and grooves, and the mirror on the car had been twisted nearly off.

Christopher pressed on the accelerator and began to swerve his car from one side of the road to the other. At last, the monster could no longer maintain its grip on the vehicle, and fell off.

Because their son was not given to telling imaginative tales and was generally regarded as quite unemotional in his demeanor, Christopher's father brought him to Lee County sheriff Liston Truesdale to make a complete report of the incident. It wasn't just the boy's wild story, Mr. Davis said in defense of his son; the roof of the automobile bore deep scratches and grooves, and the mirror on the car had been twisted nearly off.

Sheriff Truesdale thought he had another teenager who had come up with a good story to top his buddies' tall tales, so he fibbed a bit and said that it was procedure to take a lie detector test before any report could be made.

Christopher was pleased to agree, and by the time he had completed the test, the officers knew that they were probably going to be very busy over the next several weeks. The teenager was not making up a wild story. Something strange had occurred to him, and he was telling the truth about whatever had ripped into his car.

People had claimed to have seen ghosts, eerie lights, and an occasional strange beast in Scape Ore Swamp for decades. Now these mysteries had been given a name and an image—the Lizard Man.

In the months that followed, hundreds of individuals claimed to have encountered the Lizard Man. Dozens of huge three-toed footprints were found near the swamp. Reports came in that described a terrible scream that witnesses claimed had come from the Lizard Man.

George Hollomon, Jr., 32, reported sighting the Lizard Man while he was collecting water from a well. Hollomon's family and friends testified to his honesty and told investigators that Hollomon was visibly shaken and disturbed by the encounter.

A young couple, 23-year-old Brian Edward and 20-year-old Michelle Nunnery told the Sheriff's office that they had nearly struck a huge lizard-like creature that stood on its hind-legs while they were driving on the Gum Springs Road at 12:30 A.M.

A professional military man reported that he had seen a creature that resembled "a half-man, half-dinosaur" running alongside his vehicle late one night. Although he informed Sheriff Truesdale of the event, his attorney advised him not to make a full report. The Colonel, who had spent years in the Pentagon was being considered for promotion to General, and his attorney felt a Lizard Man sighting might not enrich his chances for advancement.

After a few weeks, the sheriff's department was receiving so many reports and encounters with the Lizard Man, they had to set up a special hotline.

The Sharp Claws and Teeth of the Inzignanin

Long-time residents of the area reminded others that Carolinian Native American tribes had an extensive mythology about the Inzignanin, a race of amphibious humanoid creatures that had once lived in the swamps and rivers of the Carolinas. Who was to say that all such creatures had died out?

Whatever the Lizard creatures were, they certainly appeared to have powerful claws and teeth. When Tom and Mary Waye were sleeping peacefully upstairs in their home, the creature took a strenuous dislike to their Ford LTD. The next morning, Tom and Mary found that something of great strength had ripped and clawed apart their vehicle.

The Blythers family may have met such a member of the Inzignanin. One night while driving home from picking up a fast-food dinner for the family, Mrs. Blythers was teasing her children about the Lizard Man. All of the children were laughing and playing along with their own wild tales when Mrs. Blythers was suddenly forced to swerve to avoid hitting a massive creature that stood on the road.

Lizard Man was no longer a laughing matter for the Blythers, and Mrs. Blythers drove straight to the sheriff's office to make a full report of the incident. The officers divided the family into different rooms and later found that all of their accounts matched exactly.

Accounts of the Bishopville Lizard Man soon spread across the nation. Major television networks and national periodicals carried stories of the real-life monster that was terrorizing the area.

Billy Moore, a spokesman for the sheriff's department, said that hundreds of hunters had tromped through the swamps seeking a sign of Lizard Man, but none of them had caught even a glance.

Except for the occasional sighting, it seemed that the Lizard Man had sought other—and safer—hunting grounds. For almost exactly 20 years, the Lizard Man was apparently in some kind of hibernation.

The Lizard Man Returns to Bishopville after 20 Years

On March 6, 2008, neighbors told Dixie and Bob Rawson that it was the Lizard Man that was responsible for their missing cats and the damage to their van's front grill.

The Rawsons were startled when they came out of their house one morning in late February and found the entire front half of their van chewed up. Strange bite marks went right through their grill. Both sides of their van above the wheel wells were bitten, and the metal of their vehicle was bent as if it were cardboard.

It was the Lizard Man, neighbors repeated, a seven-foot green giant that had first been sighted in the Lee County, South Carolina, Scape Ore Swamp 20 years ago and who still ventured out from time to time to raise havoc in the area.

When Bob Rawson drove out in one of his fields to investigate, he found a dead cow and a dead coyote.

Sheriff E.J. Melvin cautioned the Rawsons about accepting the Lizard Man as the killer. Sheriff Melvin said that the coyote probably killed the cow.

People had claimed to have seen ghosts, eerie lights, and an occasional strange beast in Scape Ore Swamp for decades. Now these mysteries had been given a name and an image—the Lizard Man (*art by Ricardo Pustanio*).

But this prompted Dixie Rawson to ask that if the coyote had killed the cow, what was it that had killed the coyote, for their bodies lay only a few feet apart.

Dixie Rawson told reporter Dan Tordjman that they thought Bishopville was a quiet little South Carolina town. Now with the Lizard Man prowling around, it seemed as though they were living in some kind of horror novel.

The Skunk Ape and Florida's Abominable Sandman

With the rash of media about Bigfoot sightings beginning in the late 1950s and early 1960s, Floridians began coming forward to make their encounters with their "Skunk Ape" known. As with Bigfoot in the northwestern United States and Sasquatch in Canada, legends of an apelike monster that haunts the more remote areas of Florida have been in circulation since the early days of that state's history. And as with the legends of the hairy giants of the North, members of Native American tribes insisted the centuries-old tales were true.

Such sightings are not unusual in the New Port Richey area along the Anclote River. In fact, they have been numerous enough to have led to the creature being named Florida's "Abominable Sandman." Hunters, hikers, and campers have all reported seeing similar monsters in that area. Some describe it as being six to seven feet tall, heavy, greenish, covered with long hair, and emitting a noxious odor. Perhaps what the teenagers saw was a younger member of a monster's family living in the woodlands of Florida.

Unsolicited Help in Changing a Flat Tire

On November 30, 1966, a woman was changing a tire on her car on a lonely stretch of highway near Brooksville, Florida. It was late in the evening—between nine and ten o'clock—when Ms. B. suddenly noticed a strange, unpleasant odor. She next heard a crashing sound in the brush near her, and she turned in time to see an enormous, hairy creature walking toward her.

Fortunately for her, the monster seemed more interested in what she was doing—fixing the flat tire—than in her personally. She told investigators that the creature stood upright, like a man, by the side of the road and just watched her. She was too frightened to scream, and she just stood next to her car and prayed that another motorist would come along soon. Apparently her prayers were answered, for in a short time another car did arrive, but not before the creature disappeared back into the woods.

In later interviews Ms. B. described the monster as having large green eyes, a greenish glow on one side of its hairy body, and an aroma she would not soon forget. The monster smelled like a skunk—or worse.

Unscathed by Hunters' Bullets

On December 5, 1966, *Orlando Sentinel* staff writer Elvis Lane wrote about two hunters who claimed to have wounded the monster. Although it left a trail of blood, the creature—at that time dubbed the "Florida Sandman," in contrast to the "Abominable Snowman"—seemed relatively unscathed by their volley, and the two men fled in the opposite direction.

In another report, Lane described how the son of a ranch hand had gone to investigate the sounds of someone opening their garage and had surprised the hairy giant raising the door. When the young man shouted his alarm, the monster threw a heavy tire at him.

Nasty Nocturnal Window Peepers

A rea residents also complained about the Sandman or Skunk Ape peeping in their windows at night. Others said that they had had garbage cans upset by a huge creature that retreated into the night when they clicked on yard lights. The more observant eyewitnesses described the nocturnal marauder as standing between six and seven feet tall and weighing somewhere between 300 and 400 pounds. Nearly every witness mentioned the terrible stench that accompanied the giant intruder.

According to some of its pursuers, the creature lives in muddy and abandoned alligator caves deep in the steamy Everglades swamp. The gators leave the rotting remains of their kills behind to putrefy in the heat of their hideaways, and the Skunk Apes absorb the stench into their hair, thus accounting for their awful smell. Although the Skunk Ape is said to be primarily a vegetarian and often steals produce from area gardens, Everglades hunters claim to have seen the giant kill a deer and split open its belly to get at the liver and entrails.

Chased by an Abominable Sandman

A long-time resident of the Brooksville area, Mrs. Eula Lewis, told investigators that she had been on the trail of the creature since she first saw him in 1964, shortly after John Reeves had spotted a UFO in the same region.

Mrs. Lewis said that she saw the Sandman one evening after hearing a rustling sound in the shrubs near her home as she stood in her backyard. She turned in the direction of the sound and saw an outline of something with a round head and bulky shoulders.

"I moved toward the back door, and it moved toward me!" she said. "I heard loud, thudding footsteps. It had an extremely fast lope and took big steps."

It was too dark to distinguish features, but she had the impression that it was quite hairy.

She managed to get inside the house, and neither she nor her husband, Ralph, went back outside that evening. The next morning, when they felt brave enough to venture out, they found several footprints in the area where the monster had been standing. According to Mr. Lewis, the prints were humanoid, not like those of a bear.

Mrs. Lewis did not report a strange odor in connection with the monster sightings, but she could have been upwind of the Sandman.

The Monster of Ocala National Forest

In 1980, large footprints, complete with the impression of toes, were found in the Ocala National Forest. The sheriff's department estimated that the unknown creature that had made the prints was around ten feet tall and weighed around 1,000 pounds.

On Monday evening, July 21, 1997, Vince Doerr, chief of the Ochopee Fire Central District, told the *Miami Herald* that he had seen "a brown-looking tall thing" run across the road ahead of him. He was certain that the thing was not a bear.

Ochopee borders the Everglades, and a few days after Doerr's sighting, a group of six British tourists and their guide, Dan Rowland, saw a Skunk Ape on Turner River Road, just north of the town. According to Rowland's statement in the *Miami Herald* (July 28, 1997), the unknown apelike creature was between six and seven feet tall, "flat-faced, broad-shouldered, covered with long brown hair or fur and reeking of skunk."

The seven witnesses had observed the Skunk Ape "in a slough covered with bald cypress trees." Rowland added that "it loped along like a big monkey or gorilla, then it disappeared into the woods."

> *According to Rowland's statement in the Miami Herald … the unknown apelike creature was between six and seven feet tall, "flat-faced, broad-shouldered, covered with long brown hair or fur and reeking of skunk."*

An Unknown Anthropoid Runs Loose in Myakka State Park

In February 2001, the Sarasota sheriff's department received an anonymous letter containing some photographs of an apelike creature that had been taken by a woman who feared that an orangutan was running loose in the area of Myakka State Park and might harm members of her family. Cryptozoologist Loren Coleman, who examined the pictures along with animal welfare specialist David Barkasy, said that they appeared to be good graphic evidence for the unknown anthropoid known as the Florida Skunk Ape.

According to Coleman, "The photographs clearly show a large, upright dark orangutan-like animal among the palmettos, showing eye-shine and typical anthropoid behavior of fright due to the woman's flash camera."

The "Mohawk Ape" of Eastern Tennessee

According to author-researcher Micah Hanks, in late October of 2003, a very strange story was making headlines in the southeastern United States, stemming from a frightening incident that occurred in Jacksboro, Tennessee. A local woman had stepped outside of her home while investigating unusual noises in her backyard, only to see a kitten "being thrown at her" by a small, upright-walking primate with a tuft of red hair on its head resembling "a Mohawk" haircut.

The press leapt on the story, which was featured in major American newspapers and morning shows across the country, leaving the small-town folk of the Jacksboro/Lafollet area dumbfounded and lost in the mix.

Living only a couple of hours away in western North Carolina, I contacted a friend who had just bought a new V8 truck he wanted to "wear in" a bit (mind you, gas was far less expensive back then), and we loaded up and drove to Jacksboro on a whim that Saturday morning.

Once we arrived, the locals I interviewed seemed dismayed, though in a pleasant southern way, offering whatever help they could with regard to their sudden, strange notoriety.

"We don't know what's goin' on, but everybody's scared to death," I remember one woman telling me at a gas station. "Everybody's saying we've got ourselves a Bigfoot."

For weeks after my visit, I maintained contact with various folks there in town, trying to rule out a circus that had been through the area a few months prior to the rash of "Skunk Ape" reports as a possible source for an escaped orangutan.

I posted many threads on the website of the largest area television news station, WATE out of Knoxville, and by doing so invited many interesting reports from locals.

One of my favorites, sent to me by a man named "Mike" the day before Halloween in the fall of 2003, is included below:

> I saw your email address on WATE website and wanted to share my story. It was approximately 15 to 17 years ago, me and my brother were on a hunting trip in Hancock County Tennessee [near Sneedville/Mul berry community maybe 25 miles from Campbell County]. We were walking about 200 yards apart. There was an opening between two sets of woods. I saw "something" that resembled the skunk ape, or a gorilla of sorts. It was running very fast, taking more steps with its back feet than its front feet, partially upright. It was black in color, and I didn't get to see its face. I only saw it for 20 to 30 seconds. When I met back up with my brother, I didn't want to say anything about it because he'd think I was crazy. But he asked me if I saw it, because he had seen it also!
>
> Just thought I'd share what I saw.
> —Mike

It has always fascinated me that Mike described the creature running partially on all-fours, as this seems indicative of what many researchers have suggested over the years—that the southern "Skunk Apes" bear a stronger resemblance to chimps and orangutans, whereas the Bigfoot of the Northwest, which researcher Mark A. Hall refers to as "True Giants," are clearly more human-like based on their description.

Could it be, as some have already suggested, that there are several different species of unknown humanoid creatures inhabiting our nation's forests and swamps?

Chupacabras: Another Kind of Lizard Man?

In the spring of 1995, the island of Puerto Rico either gave birth to one of the most recent entries in the annals of monsterdom or served as a bizarre creatures' geographical place of entry into our world. "El Chupacabras" (literally translated as "The Goat Sucker") was named for its practice of completely draining the blood out of farm livestock.

The attacks began with isolated incidents of farmers finding goats, chickens, and rabbits mysteriously drained of blood. Examinations of the victims revealed only two small punctures near the animal's neck, so, not surprisingly, a vampiric life-form became the initial suspect.

Interestingly, the initial reports somewhat resembled the long-standing North American mystery of "cattle mutilations," though the corpses found in Puerto Rico did not show the bizarre removal of the anus, the genitalia, and other organs of the American counterpart. Although the cattle had been desanguinated, there appeared no evidence of surgery. The two puncture marks remained the only clue to the death of the Puerto Rican livestock.

There was one eerie similarity, however, in that no other sign of predation of the corpse was present after death. No scavengers would touch the cadavers, as would be the usual case with natural death or wild animal predation.

Among the initial puzzling nature of these strange attacks came the explanations by the investigators with their lists of the usual suspects—packs of wild dogs roaming the countryside, savage Rhesus monkeys that had escaped from experimental laboratories, and attacks by natural predators combined with superstition.

In spite of all the logical explanations of misinterpretations and misidentifications, the livestock body count grew into the hundreds and expanded to include pet dogs, cats, ducks, geese—anything that could be kept within the confines of a stockyard fell to this savage, mysterious predator. The common denominator among the slain livestock was that they bore the twin puncture marks and were all drained of blood.

Then the eyewitness accounts began to filter in to law enforcement. The first of the witnesses reported a dog-like creature that could stand on its hind legs. As the number of eyewitnesses grew, the creature began to take on a clear and frightening shape. A creature with coarse hair, bat-like wings, large protruding eyes, strong front appendages with three fingers and thick claws, a large, oval-shaped head with a protruding jaw, and quill-like spines running down its back, each quill capable of changing color from blue to green to red to purple. A strong sulfuric smell, much like that reported with some sightings of Bigfoot, were often claimed as well.

As officials tried to quell the hysteria of El Chupacabras, sightings continued to increase, all reporting the same creature, though sometimes adding some strange new input.

During an encounter with the monster on the porch of her house on the outskirts of the El Yunque rain forest, Donna Maria de Gomez interrupted the creature from attacking a puppy. As she locked eyes with the strange beast and thought to herself, "You're a sorry excuse for a creature!" the Chupacabras shrank back, covering its face as though reading her mind. The creature then turned and bounded off into the night.

After loosing several rabbits one night to the creature, Jesus Sanchez was determined to put an end to such a loss. He decided to lie in wait for the monster on the following night. Sanchez was not disappointed, catching the creature in the act of trying to grab a rabbit.

Before the animal fled into the night, Sanchez landed two blows with his machete—the sound of which was described as if someone were "beating on a drum." To make things more confounding, Sanchez soon received a visit by an official from the Department of Natural Resources who threatened prosecution for "killing a protected creature"!

A puzzled Sanchez asked, "How can you protect a creature that you claim doesn't exist?"

A police officer ended his brief encounter by shooting a Chupacabras at close range with a .357 magnum. The wounded creature fled, but blood samples collected from a nearby fence over which the beast leaped produced interesting results: the blood was in no way comparable to human or any other animal species known to mankind.

As the number of eyewitnesses grew, the creature began to take on a clear and frightening shape. A creature with coarse hair, bat-like wings, large protruding eyes, and strong front appendages with three fingers and thick claws (**art by Ricardo Pustanio**).

There have been many hunting and trapping efforts designed to catch a Chupacabras. All have so far failed—unless we can credit one story that a pair were captured by soldiers in the El Yunque rain forest and immediately shipped to an unspecified location on the United States mainland.

Many other researchers claim that Chupacabras may be escapees from a UFO; indeed, many sightings have come in conjunction with lights in the sky, as well as triangular and pyramid-shaped UFOs. To many who have been students of serious ufology for many years, several claims have been made of crypto-creatures associated with UFOs.

Some even speculate that the Chupacabras evolved from a lizard-like humanoid that, in turn, had dinosaur ancestors.

The possibility of the Chupacabras being an experimental chimera (a mix of known organisms genetically spliced and engineered to create a new life form) is a good theory, since we are never quite certain what actually goes on at various secret military facilities.

And just as the debunkers had satisfied themselves with the claim that the creature was centered exclusively in Puerto Rico, and was, therefore, a cultural phenomena, "The Cosmic Trickster" laughed in mockery at what fools these mortals be. Reports of the Chupacabras quickly spread to Texas, Florida, and many parts of South America.

What Is the Chupacabras?

On February 7, 2010, Virgilio Sanchez-Ocejo of the Miami UFO Center released the results of a 10-year-study that sought to identify the Chupacabras (www.rense.com/general89/chupa.htm). Beginning in February 1995 in Puerto Rico, spreading to Miami in February 1996, such reports continued throughout California, Texas, Mexico, Costa Rica, Guatemala, El Salvador, and Brazil.

Sanchez-Ocejo considered this the "first wave" of the creature's attacks. The study of the Chupacabras began when the beast savaged animals in March 2000 in Calama, Chile.

According to their field investigations, the Center has found that the monsters have killed thousands of chickens, ducks, dogs, goats, pigs, and cattle, leaving them all drained of blood. In each case, the desanguination was implemented through a small puncture, most often in or around the neck of the Chupacabras' victims.

After a thorough analysis of the tooth in December 2, 2009 … it was announced that the tooth came from no human's mouth nor from that of any known animal.

The Center's field investigators have amassed photos of dead animals, autopsies of dead animals, plaster molds of the creature's footprints, sketches by witnesses, and countless interviews with those who have encountered the Chupacabras. They also managed to obtain one tooth left behind by the beast in its slaughter.

Various collected samples were initially analyzed at the Autonomous University of Mexico by Dr. Zoar Gutierrez and Rodolf Garrido Cothman, with the assistance of Daniel Munoz. Years later, J.J. Benietz took a portion of the samples to the University of Granada.

After a thorough analysis of the tooth on December 2, 2009, by Professor Jose Antonio Lorente Acosta of the Laboratory of Genetic Identification, Department of Legal Medicine, it was announced that the tooth came from no human's mouth nor from that of any known animal. After seeking to match the tooth with some species, the laboratory concluded that it could not be genetically identified.

After 10 years of laboratory tests—and enduring periods of high and low expectations—Virgilio Sanchez-Ocejo said that the Center hardly considers its work finished. They now have a database that clearly presents the characteristics of an animal as yet unknown to science, and they possess a solid guide for future scientific study.

METCH KANGMI—FOUL SNOWMAN
OF THE HIMALAYAS

During an expedition into the Himalayas in 1906, botanist H. J. Elwes was astonished to glimpse a hairy humanlike figure racing across a field of snow below him. The scientific establishment dismissed his report until several scholars discovered the journals of Major Lawrence Waddell, who, during his 1887 expedition, reported having found humanlike tracks in the snow.

Tales of hairy monsters existing in the Asian wilderness can be found long before Major Waddell's 1887 sighting. Several venerable Chinese scholars wrote of such creatures and linked them to the "time of the dragon," the presumed genesis of Asian civilization. Despite sightings made by local residents and an occasional report by a European visitor to the region, the mysterious apelike creatures did not receive any sort of widespread notoriety until the beginning of the twentieth century.

The Himalayan regions were not alone in the occasional sighting of a hairy, humanlike creature. For centuries there had been a popular belief among the people of the Caucasus that the mountains were haunted by gigantic evil spirits called *shaitans*. According to legend, these restless mountain spirits once dared attempt to climb into heaven at some period in prehistory, a misdeed for which Allah condemned them to wander the remote mountain passes forever.

The legend goes on to say that if true believers in God should ever encounter one of these terrible spirits, they would do well to make a quick and cautious retreat lest they anger the shaitan into taking revenge on them for Allah's punishment and deliver misfortune to their household. If the creature should request food of a true believer, he should satisfy the demand and circumvent the spirit's wrath.

Of course, these were just local superstitions. To adventurers from the West, the Asian people had many quaint and charming legends of an ancient time.

Howard-Bury's 1921 Everest Expedition Sight Tracks Made by an "Abominable Snowman"

The First Everest Expedition was launched in 1921, led by Colonel C. K. Howard-Bury. The climbing party of six white men and twenty-six native porters was crawling slowly up the north face of Everest, near the Lhakpa La Pass, when Colonel Howard-Bury spotted tracks in the morning snow. Most of them were easily recognizable as those of rabbits or foxes, but one set of indentations was very peculiar, appearing very much as if they had been made by a man who ignored the terrible cold to walk barefoot. A Sherpa guide identified the tracks as belonging to the Yeti or the "mehteh kangmi," the man-beast of the mountains that lived in the snow.

Later, when Colonel Howard-Bury telegraphed his reports to Calcutta, he mentioned the incident briefly. Unfortunately, the telegraphic facilities were very primitive and the words "mehteh kangmi" were garbled into "metch kangmi." The expedition's assistants in Calcutta were confused by the term and asked a Calcutta newspaper columnist to translate the term. The columnist told them that "metch" was a term of extreme disgust, so it might be translated as the "horrible snowman" or the "abominable snowman."

A reporter for one of England's most sensational newspapers was in the office when the telegram was translated. He raced for the cable office in Calcutta, wiring his paper that the First Everest Expedition had encountered a frightening and foul-smelling creature known as the "abominable snowman." Thus the hairy wild men of the Himalayas were named in error, and the term has persisted to this day. When Colonel Howard-Bury and his unsuccessful mountain climbers admitted defeat on Mt. Everest, they returned to civilization and discovered that newspaper reporters ignored their failure to conquer Everest, but were eager for more information about the "abominable snowman" that they had encountered.

In the 1930s scientists studied the reports of explorer Frank Smythe's discovery of Yeti tracks in the snow at 14,000 feet. The footprints measured 13 inches in length and were five inches wide. Famed mountaineer Eric E. Shipton claimed that he saw similar tracks on his expedition to Everest in 1936.

Several expeditions have been conducted to compare specimens from the Bigfoot of North America to the Yeren, Yeti, and Almasti of Asia. Are they the same creature? Or are there many types of human-apelike "missing links" still existing in various parts of the world (*art by Dan Wolfman Allen*)?

World War II Ceases Scientific Exploration of the Himalayas but Yeti Sightings Continue

World War II stopped mountaineering and scientific exploration of the formidable Himalayas, but in 1942, Slavomir Rawicz and four other men escaped from a Communist prison camp in Siberia and struck out on a "long walk" toward India. They reported meeting two Yeti during their incredible journey.

During World War II, Dr. V. S. Karapetyan, a lieutenant-colonel in the medical service of the Soviet army, reported that an infantry battalion near Buinaksk captured a wild man and did not have any idea what to do with him. Dr. Karapetyan was summoned to examine the creature and to give his medical opinion as to whether the soldiers had encountered some strange, wild creature or whether they had apprehended some fantastically disguised secret agent.

When the doctor arrived at the camp, he was informed that the prisoner was kept in a cold shed because he sweated so profusely and seemed to become ill in a warm room. Dr. Karapetyan found the subject in question to appear to be a naked human in form, male, and covered with a shaggy dark brown hair.

According to his report, he said that the man-creature stood erect with his arms hanging, and his height above average. "He stood before me like a giant, his mighty chest thrust forward. His fingers were thick and strong, and exceptionally large. His eyes told me nothing. They were dull and empty—the eyes of an animal. And he seemed to me like some kind of animal and nothing more."

Dr. Karapetyan told the military authorities that their prisoner was no disguised spy, but a "wild man of some kind." The doctor returned to his unit and said that he never again heard anything about the strange prisoner.

Sir Edmund Finds Yeti Hair and an Expedition Sets Out to Capture the Snowman

In 1952, Sir Edmund Hillary and George Lowe found "snowman" hair in a high mountain pass, and tracks were reported by a Swiss expedition.

In 1954, an expedition financed by the *London Daily Mail* set out to capture a Yeti. They found tracks in several different locations, but returned without their prize. Three other scientific groups also reported finding tracks.

In 1957, the first expedition sponsored by the American millionaire Tom Slick found hair and footprints at several locations. Two porters said Yeti had been sighted in those regions earlier that year. Peter and Bryan Bryne said they had seen a snowman when the Slick Expedition was in the Arun Valley.

In 1958, Gerald Russell and two porters with the Second Slick Expedition encountered a small snowman near a river, and in the following year, tracks were reported by the Third Slick Expedition, as well as by members of a Japanese expedition.

Sir Edmund Returns with a Yeti Scalp

Sir Edmund Hillary, the man who conquered Mt. Everest, created a sensation when he returned with the alleged scalp of a Yeti. Sir Edmund later proved that the so-called scalp was actually goat skin, and he declared that snowman tracks were made by foxes, bears, and other animals that became enlarged when the snow is melted by the sun.

The Remarkable Story of Zana

In 1964, Professor Boris Porshenev excavated the grave of a female "wild woman of the mountains," called an Almasti, in the Caucasus Mountain region of Russia (*art by Ricardo Pustanio*).

In 1964, Professor Boris Porshenev excavated the grave of a female "wild woman of the mountains," called an Almasti, in the Caucasus Mountain region of Russia. According to Porshenev, the bones that he disinterred in the village of Tkhina were those of a female and his preliminary investigation of the skeleton determined that its skeletal structure was different from that of a female member of Homo sapiens.

Porshenev's discovery brought to mind the claims made circa 1864 by a man named Genaba who said that he returned to Tkhina with a bizarre gift from his friend Prince Achba, an avid sportsman, who had caught a humanlike female creature while hunting in the woods. Genaba named the wild woman, Zana, and he constructed a special hut for her made out of woven twigs and grasses.

At first he kept her guarded, but eventually Zana grew accustomed to people and was allowed to move about freely in the village. Genaba received Zana's full obedience, and he succeeded to some extent in domesticating her. He tutored her in the crafts of preparing firewood, carrying water, and toting sacks of grain. Zana was of an enormous and powerful build and was capable of seemingly inexhaustible physical labor.

The description of Zana that has come down to us appears to tally exactly with the great number of descriptions of the Almasti that have been recorded over the past two hundred years or more. Her body was covered with thick black hair, and she at first refused to wear clothing of any kind. It was only by exercising the greatest patience that Genaba was able to train Zana to wear a loincloth. However, no amount of patience or attempted schooling could teach Zana to speak. She seemed capable only of mumbling and squealing to express her pleasures and displeasures.

Cleanliness was not a problem with the wild woman. One of her favorite pastimes was her daily bath in the village spring that still bears her name. Winter or summer, Zana could be seen at her daily ritual of washing herself in the icy water.

Zana also enjoyed gathering rocks and attempting to chip them. When the creature had completed her regular duties on Genaba's estate, she would scurry off to her favorite rocks and spend hours arranging them into piles and attempting to chip them in a particular manner that seemed to have some special significance for her.

Elderly residents of the village maintained that while in captivity, Zana gave birth to five children. If true, the implications of Zana's having bred with men of the village are really quite staggering. If the wild woman truly did conceive with human males, then she was not an ape.

Of course the stories of Zana's children may only be legend, added bits of fantasy to make the tale of the wild woman even more remarkable as it was told and retold through decades of long, cold Caucasus winters. According to the villagers, four of the children died before their mother, and the fifth answered the shrill call of his mother's people and fled to the mountains.

Zana died in the 1880s and was mourned by the entire village of Tkhina. She had been a gentle creature, amiable in manner and devoted to her master Genaba. Her bones lay forgotten outside the village until the persistent Professor Boris Porshenev unearthed them for examination.

Lady X of the Altai Mountains

On March 24, 2010, it was announced that researchers in the Altai mountains of southern Siberia had found a bone in a cave that demonstrated, from the extracted DNA, that it belonged to a previously unknown human species. The researchers, led by Johannes Krause and Svante Paabo of the Max Plank Institute for Evolutionary Anthropology in Leipzig, Germany, are cautious in their pronouncements. The finger bone that they extracted from the Denisova cave in 2008 could well prove to be a new human species. Perhaps Zana was one of her kind.

Artifact after artifact continues to be found to provide unarguable proof that humans and Neanderthals were neighbors for at least 10,000 years. The evidence found in the Denisova Cave may well provide the final vestige of evidence that there were more than two species sharing the Altai Mountain steppes, all living within 60 miles of each other. The DNA from "X-woman" indicates that she may have come from a previously unknown pre-human species, thus making it three bipedal cousins sharing essentially the same turf.

Dr. Ian Tattersall, a paleoanthropolgist at the American Museum of Natural History in New York, remarked that as little as 30,000 years ago there were five human species in the world: *Homo erectus*, the little Floresians, Neanderthals, modern humans, and the new lineage from the Denisova cave. "This is similar, he said, "to the situation two million years ago, when four hominid species are known to have lived in the Turkana Basin of Kenya." ("Bone May Reveal a New Human Group" by Nicholas Wade, *The New York Times*, March 24, 2010).

The "Abominable Koffman"—Yeti Hunter Extraordinary

One of the most extraordinary Yeti hunters in Russia in the 1960s was Dr. Jeanne-Marie-Therese Koffman, who was determined to snare an abominable snowman and have the last laugh on her skeptical colleagues in the scientific circles of the Soviet Union.

Early in 1967 Dr. Koffman, who had already established herself as a top surgeon, read a paper at a session of the Geographical Society of the U.S.S.R., which detailed for her colleagues the results of her five-year search for the abominable snowman of the Caucasus Mountains. The determined lady had prepared a presentation of 219 eyewitness accounts from those who had seen the humanoid creatures roaming about the Caucasian region. The fact that the majority of Russian scientists considered her reports to be nothing more than hallucinations suffered by the natives of the remote mountain regions did not daunt Dr. Koffman in the slightest.

She admitted that snowmen hunters did not yet have serious material proof that humanoid creatures lived in the Caucasus, but Dr. Koffman stressed that "the idea that the 'wild man' is just a figure of folklore is ruled out by the testimony of witnesses not belonging to the local population. The view about ill-intentioned deception is incompatible with the testimony of persons who were unaware of the scientific controversy and who enjoy considerable authority among local inhabitants."

According to reporter Nino Lo Bello writing from Moscow, Dr. Koffman was not a reserved spinster who sat at home with a glass of warm milk and conjured fantasies about bizarre creatures. "She (Dr. Koffman) is a skilled motorcyclist, an expert marksman, and a daredevil horseback rider. During World War II she served with an airborne unit in the Northern Caucasus, volunteered for the front, was parachuted into combat many times, and took part in a number of key operations against the Nazis."

The persistent monster hunter also examined the skeletal remains of Zana, the captive snowwoman who died in the 1870s. According to long-lived residents of the Caucasus, the creature, known as Zana, was captured by Prince Achba during a hunt in the mountains. A man named Jadgi Genaba kept Zana in a hut for several years until she grew accustomed to people. Covered with thick black hair, Zana had a large and powerful body. Although she obeyed Cenabas's commands and aided him in the heavy tasks on his estate, she refused to wear clothes and never learned to talk. Seemingly impervious to the cold, Zana bathed in an icy mountain spring even during the most severe winter days.

Dr. Jeanne-Marie-Therese Koffman, the daredevil woman surgeon, earnestly believed that someday she would locate a small tribe of the snowmen in the desolate mountain regions of Russia. When that day arrived, the plucky woman doctor would have her last laugh on the Soviet skeptics who had nicknamed her The Abominable Koffman.

Even more interesting was a report from Dr. Koffman that a farmer in the Caucasus Mountain Range had successfully trained a Snowman to perform chores on the farm. The story is fragmentary; however, the farmer apparently discovered a starving Yeti, and the creature became very docile when the farmer fed him. "The beast became something of an interesting pet," the report stated. "He followed the farmer around the farm when chores were done, and quickly learned to perform some of the simpler tasks."

Eventually, the farmer taught his hairy hired hand to drive a tractor. The beast was very proficient in handling the tractor but was unable to learn how to start the machine.

Russian Mountain Climbers Make Friendly Contact

In August 1981, Soviet mountain climber Igor Tatsl told the *Moscow News Weekly* that he and his fellow climbers had seen a Yeti and that they had attempted a friendly, spontaneous contact with the creature. Tatsl went on to state that his team had made a plaster cast of an imprint of a Yeti's footprint that they had found on a tributary of the Varzog River. This particular river rushes through the Gissar Mountains in the Pamiro-Alai range of Tadzhik in Central Asia.

In Tatsl's considered opinion the Yeti may quite likely be humankind's closest evolutionary relative. He further believed that their senses were more highly developed than those of our species.

The U.S. National Wildlife Expedition

In the October-November 1970 issue of *National Wildlife*, managing editor George Harrison reported his first person sighting of Sasquatch tracks while on the American Yeti Expedition led by Robert W. Morgan and cosponsored by the official publication of the National Wildlife Federation. Harrison tells how he was able to place his own size 10-and-a-half B foot next to the six-inch-wide track of what must have been Bigfoot, the Sasquatch. Whatever had made the naked footprint, Harrison knew, weighed far more than his 170 pounds, for it had sunk its weight more than an inch into the earth near a stream.

Harrison quoted Ed McLarney, a United Press International wire service stringer in Stevenson, Washington, as admitting that by training he was dubious about Bigfoot reports, but after seeing the tracks and hearing the stories from people who have seen Bigfoot, he was 90 percent sure that something existed which was beyond his own experience.

Harrison himself confessed to being 85 percent certain of Bigfoot's existence after returning from the expedition. He concluded that reputable scientists agreed that there was no biological reason why Bigfoot could not exist.

British Scientists Discover "the Best Evidence Yet" for Yeti

In April 2001, British scientists on the trail of the Yeti announced the best evidence yet for the existence of the mysterious creature of the Himalayas—a sample of hair that proved impossible to classify genetically. Dr. Rob McCall, a zoologist, removed strands of the Yeti hair from the hollow of a tree and brought them back to Britain to be analyzed. Dr. Bryan Sykes, Professor of Human Genetics at the Oxford Institute of Molecular Medicine, one of the world's leading authorities on DNA analysis, stated that they could not identify the DNA that they had discovered in the hair and that they had never before encountered DNA that they couldn't recognize.

Russian Scientists Tend to Believe Neanderthals Survive

Russian scientists have sponsored serious efforts to track down the Yeti for nearly half a century. Although each Russian province may have its own name for the mysterious giants of the mountain—in Dagestan, "kaptar"; in Azerbaijan, "mesheadam"; in Georgia, "tkys-katsi"; while the Chechens, Ingushes, Kabardins, and Balkars call it the "Almasti"—each startled eyewitness seems to describe the same strange beast.

From the layman's point of view, it has seemed as though a number of Russian scientists have favored the theory that the Yeti could be a surviving colony of Neanderthals. In 2009, an expedition prepared during the warmer weather of summer to conduct another search of certain areas in the Shoria Mountain in Siberia.

Valery Kimiev and Professor Nikolai Skalon, the head of the department of Zoology at the Kemerovo State University led the expedition, joined by a local hunter from the region, Michael Kiskarov, who maintains that he has seen a Yeti firsthand many times. A government official, Vladimir Tashtagol stated that he had received 14 written reports filed by residents near the Azass caves and the nearby Mrassu River who claim that they frequently encounter the creatures.

The Yeti are most often described by the local residents as standing about six feet tall, with reddish black hair. The Azass cave is several miles deep, and it is generally believed that the Yeti make their home in its depths.

Chinese Scientists Have Not Neglected the Yeren

The Chinese call the snowman "yeren," and in 1977, 1980, and 1982, expeditions searching for the man-beast set out to track down their quarry in the Shennongjia Forest Park in western Hubei province. In September 1993, a group of Chinese engineers claimed to have seen three yeren walking on trails in the Shennongjia Forest Park.

In October 1994, the Chinese government established the Committee for the Search of Strange and Rare Creatures, including among its members specialists in vertebrate paleontology and paleoanthropology. A loose consensus among interested members from the Chinese Academy of Sciences maintains that the yeren are some species of unknown primates. The largest cast of an alleged wild man footprint is 16 inches long, encouraging estimates that the yeren itself would stand more than seven feet tall and weigh as much as 660 pounds. The scientific committee has also studied and examined eight hair specimens said to have come from yeren ranging through China and Tibet. The analyses of the hairs, varying in color from the black collected in Yunnan province and the white collected in Tibet to the reddish brown from Hubei, indicate a nonhuman source, but no known animal.

A loose consensus among interested members from the Chinese Academy of Sciences maintains that the yeren are some species of unknown primates.

In April 1995, a yeren expedition of 30 members led by Professor Yuan Zhengxin set out for the Hubei mountains. Although Professor Zhengxin expressed confidence that the well-equipped group would capture a yeren within three years, by July most of the expedition members had returned to Beijing with little more than some possible hair samples to show for their three-month safari.

In January 1999, Feng Zuoguian, a zoologist for the Chinese Academy of Sciences, announced through the state-run *China Daily* newspaper that China was officially proclaiming its firm opposition to any outsiders who attempted to organize expeditions to capture the Yeti or the yeren. According to the official proclamation, after much debate in December 1998 the members of the Chinese scientific community had decreed once and for all that the creatures do not exist.

However, in spite of the official pronouncement from the Chinese Academy of Sciences that neither the Yeti nor the yeren exist, anthropologist Zhou Guoxing reminded his colleagues that unidentifiable hair specimens and 16-inch casts of footprints had been found during scientific expeditions to the Shennongjia region. In his opinion, even if 95 percent of the reports on the existence of the wild man are not credible, it remains necessary for scientists to study the remaining five percent.

MONSTERS FROM FLYING SAUCERS

O n June 24, 1947, at 2:00 P.M., Kenneth Arnold took off from the Chehalis, Washington, airport in his personal plane and headed for Yakima, Washington. Arnold hadn't flown more than a few minutes of his course when a bright flash reflected on his airplane. To the left and north of Mount Rainier he observed a chain of nine peculiar-looking objects that he at first assumed to be some type of jet aircraft flying from north to south at approximately 9,500 feet. Arnold stated that the objects flew like geese, in a rather diagonal chainlike line, as if they were linked together. They seemed to hold a definite direction, but swerved in and out of the high mountain peaks. He estimated the size of the objects to be approximately two-thirds that of a DC-4. Arnold timed the objects between Mount Rainier and Mount Adams and assessed the speed in which they crossed this 47-mile-stretch in one minute and 42 seconds. This was equivalent to 1,656.71 miles per hour.

In an interview with journalists after the sighting, Arnold described the objects as appearing like saucers skipping on water. This description was shortened to "flying saucers" by newspapermen and resulted in the popular use of that term.

What we term the Modern Age of UFOs began with Arnold's sighting in 1947. Later, researchers would claim that they had discovered references to "flying saucers" in ancient manuscripts and even in the Bible; however, in 1947, two years after the end of World War II, there appeared to be mysterious visitors in our skies from an undeclared country or an unknown world.

The entire nation took interest in Arnold's strange sightings. Were the strange aircraft remnants of Nazi super science taking revenge on the United States for their major role in the collapse of the Third Reich?

Were the aerial craft Russian spy craft? The Cold War had frozen relationships between the two super powers of the U.S. and the Soviets—and it was well known that in the closing days of World War II the Reds had made off with almost as many Nazi scientists as we had.

Or were the flying saucers on a reconnaissance mission for armies from an alien world who had come to invade and conquer Earth?

A Flying Saucer Crashes at Roswell, New Mexico

Only a little more than a week after Kenneth Arnold's sighting of unidentified aerial vehicles, an alleged extraterrestrial space vehicle crashed on a ranch located about 60 miles north of Roswell, New Mexico, sometime from July 2 to 4, 1947. Some accounts reported that a flying saucer developed mechanical problems. In other versions of the story, the craft was shot down by U.S. fighter pilots or had been struck by lightning.

Barney Barnett, a civil engineer from Socorro, New Mexico, who was employed by the federal government, claimed to have been one of the first civilians to arrive on the scene following the crash. Barnett later told friends that he had seen alien bodies on the ground and inside the spaceship. He described them as small, hairless beings with large heads and round, oddly spaced eyes. According to Barnett, a military unit arrived on the scene and an officer had ordered him off the site. Although reports of retrieved alien bodies never made it into any military release in July of 1947, accounts of civilian eyewitnesses having seen between two and five nonhuman corpses soon spread across the nation.

It's believed by many people that the U.S. military is keeping aliens (or the remains of aliens) who crashed at Roswell, New Mexico, back in 1947 (*iStock*).

Major Jesse Marcel, intelligence officer for the 509th Bomb Group, the recipient of five air combat medals awarded in World War II, was ordered to handpick a top-security team and go to the ranch to salvage the debris of the unknown aircraft that rancher Mac Brazel had discovered on his spread. The strange, weightless material discovered by the 509th Bomber team was difficult to describe. The pieces varied in length from four or five inches to three or four feet. Some fragments had markings that resembled hieroglyphics. Although the material seemed to be unbreakable, the military investigators thought that it looked more like wood than metal. Marcel put his cigarette lighter to one of the rectangular fragments, but it would not burn. Major Marcel and his crew brought as many pieces of the crashed UFO back to Roswell Army Air Field Base as they could gather.

On July 8, 1947, Walter Haut, public affairs officer at Roswell, issued the famous press release stating that the Army had discovered the debris of a crashed flying saucer. However, literally overnight, the story of the discovery of the bits and pieces of an extraterrestrial craft were officially transformed into the scraps of a collapsed high-altitude weather balloon.

Almost immediately after Haut's official announcement that there were no aliens and no alien space vehicle, a number of investigators into the incident made stringent accusations of a government cover-up. Earth was being monitored by extraterrestrials, and the government didn't want its citizens to panic.

Some accounts spoke of five alien bodies found at the impact site north of Roswell and stated that four corpses were transported to Wright Field and the fifth to Lowry Field to the USAF mortuary service. Numerous secondary accounts of the incident asserted that one of the alien beings survived the crash and was still alive when the military arrived on the scene.

After the wreckage had been identified as extraterrestrial in nature, numerous researchers contend, the official cover-up was instigated at both the Roswell base and at the headquarters of the Eighth Air Force in Fort Worth, Texas, by Eighth Air Force Commander Roger Ramey on direct orders from General Clements McMullen at SAC headquarters in Washington, D.C. Flying Saucer researchers have insisted for over 60 years that the government knows more about the strangers in our skies than it has ever admitted.

The Coming of the Monsters from Flying Saucers

With such accounts of alien bodies and extraterrestrial vehicles held in government hangars and warehouses in wide circulation, it wasn't long before individuals far away from Roswell, New Mexico, were having their own sightings of monsters from flying saucers.

"It looked worse than Frankenstein," was the way Mrs. Kathleen May described the alien being that she and seven other Flatwoods, West Virginia, residents had seen on September 12, 1952.

Mrs. May had had her attention called to the saucer by a group of excited children, including her sons, Eddie, 13, and Fred, 12. The children had been at a nearby playground with Gene Lemon, Neil Nunley, Ronnie Shaver, and Tommy Hyer when they had spotted a "saucer spouting an exhaust that looked like balls of red fire." According to the boys, the saucer had landed on a hilltop above the May house.

"I told them that it was just their imaginations," Mrs.May told reporters, "but the boys kept insisting that they had seen a flying saucer land behind the hill."

Gene Lemon, a husky seventeen year old, had found a flashlight and said that he was going to investigate. At the urging of her children, Mrs. May agreed to accompany the teenager, and the small party of West Virginians set out into the night. "Up on the hill, I could see a reddish glow," said Mrs. May. "I changed my mind about it all being their imaginations, and I was glad that Gene was in the lead."

After about half an hour of tramping through the brush that covered the narrow uphill trail, Gene Lemon's courage left him in a long scream of terror, and the intrepid band of saucer-hunters fled in panic from the sight that Lemon's flashlight had illuminated.

When Lemon had flashed the beam on the glowing green spots, he had thought them to be the eyes of an animal. Instead, the flash had spotlighted an immense, man-like figure with a blood-red face and greenish eyes that blinked out from a pointed hood. Behind the monster was "a glowing ball of fire as big as a house", which grew dimmer and brighter at intervals.

Later, Mrs. May described the monster as having "terrible claws." Some of the children, however, had not noticed any arms at all. Most agreed that the being had worn dark clothing, and fourteen-year-old Neil Nunley specified the color to be a "dark green." Estimates of the creature's height ranged from seven feet to ten feet.

The party was in definite agreement about one characteristic of the alien, however, and that was the sickening odor which it seemed to emit.

The party was in definite agreement about one characteristic of the alien, however, and that was the sickening odor which it seemed to emit. Mrs. May told reporters that it was "like sulphur," but really unlike anything that she had ever encountered.

A. Lee Stewart, Jr., of the *Braxton* [West Virginia] *Democrat*, arrived on the scene moments ahead of Sheriff Robert Carr. Although most of the party were too frightened to speak coherently and some were receiving first aid for cuts and bruises received in their pell-mell flight down the hill, the newsman persuaded Lemon to accompany him to the spot where they had seen the being.

Stewart saw no sign of the giant space traveler or of the pulsating red globe of light, but he was able to inhale enough of the strange odor to declare it "sickening and irritating." He later wrote that he had developed a familiarity with a wide variety or gases while serving in the Air Force, but he had never been confronted by any gas with a similar odor.

Each of the party later testified that the monster had been moving toward them, but they also agreed that this might have been due to the fact that they were between the creature and the large, globular object that evidently served as its spacecraft.

Neil Nunley said the alien "didn't really walk. It just moved. It moved evenly: it didn't jump."

Hollywood Keeps the World Mindful of "Things" from Other Worlds

Hollywood was doing its part to suggest that alien invaders were keeping close eye on Earth. In 1951, Howard Hawks's *The Thing from Another World* told the story of a small group of Air Force personnel and scientists stationed at an isolated outpost near the North Pole who must deal with an alien that needs their blood in order to survive. The film was a thriller that steadily built tension and frighteningly portrayed how helpless humans might be at the hands of a single powerful alien life-form.

In 1951, the same year that audiences were jumping out of their theater seats watching *The Thing*, Robert Wise presented a wise and peaceful alien, who came to warn Earth's politicians and scientists that they must cease their experiments with nuclear power or risk annihilation from extraterrestrials who will not tolerate unbridled human aggressiveness. In the classic *The Day the Earth Stood Still*, actor Michael Rennie's portrayal of the soft-spoken alien "Klaatu," provided a model extraterrestrial emissary for generations of UFO contactees yet unborn.

As the film opens, a flying saucer does, indeed, land near the White House lawn, in a baseball field in Washington, D.C. Within minutes, the craft is surrounded by armed military personnel and armored tanks. Klaatu emerges, and as he holds up a gift which he has brought for the President, he is shot and wounded by a soldier who misinterprets the alien's gesture as a hostile movement. At this point, Gort, Klaatu's eight-foot robot, leaves the spaceship and fires a kind of laser beam at the assembled military and instantly melts all weapons and armaments. Klaatu halts Gort before it destroys anything—or anyone—else, and the alien's peaceful intentions convince the officers that he has come in peace. Klaatu is taken to a military hospital where his wound can be treated and he can be placed under guard.

Klaatu explains that he has come as an ambassador from an intergalactic federation of planets that has been keeping Earth under surveillance for centuries. Now that Earth's science has advanced to the nuclear age and the planet's influence may soon be extended to other worlds, he has been sent to deliver a message of utmost importance to all the heads of state. When Klaatu perceives that his request will be refused, he escapes from the hospital and moves anonymously into a rooming house, posing as a human named Carpenter.

The alien emissary becomes friends with Bobby (Billy Gray) and his mother Helen (Patricia Neal), and the boy leads him to Professor Barnhardt (Sam Jaffe), a physicist, who is impressed, rather than frightened, by Klaatu's superior knowledge. All the scientists in the film are depicted as dedicated individuals who are trying their best to live outside the political bickering and backstabbing of the Cold War era and who are willing to arrange for Klaatu to address an international assemblage of the leaders of world science. Realizing that Earth's heads of state are too primitive to set aside their petty differences and listen to his message of universal peace, Klaatu arranges a demonstration that no one on the planet will be able to ignore: He shuts off all power on Earth for one hour.

Considered a threat to national security, Klaatu is killed by the military and his body placed in a cell. Before he was shot, however, he advised Helen what to do if anything should happen to him. She approaches the massive Gort and speaks the order, "Klaatu Barado Nikto," a command which enables to the robot to restore life to Klaatu and brings the film to its conclusion. As the alien ambassador prepares to depart, his final message to all of Earth is a simple one: "It is your choice. Join us and live in peace or face obliteration."

Some have made comparisons between Klaatu's mission to Earth and the messages and ministry of Jesus. Both came from "above;" Jesus was a carpenter, Klaatu chose the alias of Carpenter; both were killed and resurrected by a power beyond Earth's knowledge; both returned to the "heavens" when their message that humans must repent and change their ways had been delivered.

The Anticipation of a War of the Worlds

With sightings of flying saucers making headlines all over the world, stories of extraterrestrial monsters had more appeal to the tastes of movie audiences and far more represented the fears of the citizens of Earth than wise and peaceful ambassadors from outer space. In *War of the Worlds* (1953), George Pal adapted H.G. Wells' novel of alien invasion and transformed it into the struggle of two scientists (Gene Barry and Ann Robinson) as they attempt to help Earth survive a devastating attack by Martians. The suspense is intensified by narrow escapes, and the awful reality for motion picture audiences lay in seeing the major cities of Earth lying strewn about in heaps of rubble. Although the horror of seemingly unstoppable aliens was a frightening theme, the film is extremely well-presented and won an Academy Award for its special effects. While Earth is saved by the motion picture's end, the devastation rendered by the extraterrestrial invaders left unforgettable images in the minds of the audience.

While the film version of Wells' novel was very successful upon its release, the impact it had on mass consciousness cannot be compared to the effect of the radio broadcast of *War of the Worlds* on the day before Halloween in 1938. At that time, CBS's *Mercury Theatre* presented Orson Welles and a talented cast simulating a live news broadcast of an invasion of Earth by mechanized Martian war machines. Because the account of unstoppable alien beings landing in the New Jersey farmlands was depicted so realistically—and because many listeners tuned in after the *Mercury Theatre* production was already in progress—the greater part of the entire nation was in panic over the invaders from Mars.

Invading aliens continued to be a popular theme in a number of motion pictures throughout the 1950s. *Invaders from Mars* (1953) remains in many moviegoers' memory as the single most frightening film of their childhood. Perhaps what made the film so terrifying to young people was the premise that one's parents, teachers, and friends could be taken over by alien life-forms and work toward a nationwide conspiracy.

The Aliens Seemed Completely Impervious to Gunfire

On the evening of August 21, 1955, aliens allegedly made another invasion attempt when they visited Kelly-Hopkinsville, Kentucky. The landing and the subsequent sighting of two to five aliens was witnessed by eight adults and three children. The Air Force, local authorities, the police, and area newspapers conducted an extensive and well-documented investigation of the incident. The adults involved

Hollywood adapted the H.G. Wells novel *The War of the Worlds* in 1953, and again in 2005. Such fictional accounts have kept the idea of Martians vivid in the popular imagination (*Paramount Pictures/Ronald Grant Archive/Mary Evans Picture Library*).

were rather staid, reserved people hardly likely to have invented the entire adventure simply for the sake of sensational publicity. Some of the eyewitnesses even went so far as to leave town when the curiosity seekers and cultists began to arrive, and they remained consistently reluctant to speak about the ordeal with Air Force officials and other investigators.

It was a Sunday evening, and company had gathered at Gaither McGehe's farm, which was currently being rented by the Sutton family. Teen-aged Billy Ray Sutton had left the farmhouse to get a drink from the well. As he drank the cool refreshing water from a chipped cup, he was startled to see a large bright object land about a city block away from the farmhouse.

Billy Ray's announcement of the strange arrival was met with a pronounced lack of response. The family's interest was considerably heightened, however, when, according to several reports, they saw "little men, less than four feet tall with long arms and large, round heads" approaching the farmhouse.

Preserved in Air Force files are drawings that the witnesses made for the investigators. The Suttons testified that the creature's eyes had a yellow glow. The orbs were extremely large and seemed very sensitive to light. It was the outside lights of the farm-

The farmers battled the seemingly invulnerable creatures for nearly four hours before they drove in panic to the Hopkinsville police station for reinforcements (*art by Ricardo Pustanio*).

house that seemed to prevent the creature from advancing into the home rather than the bullets from the farmers' rifles, which were fired often.

"Bullets just seemed to bounce off their nickel-plated armor," said one of the witnesses.

Although the farmers made several direct hits on the aliens, they seemed to "pop right up again and disappear into the darkness, away from the light."

A man named Taylor told investigators: "I knocked one of them off a barrel with my .22. I heard the bullet hit the critter and ricochet off. The little man floated to the ground and rolled up like a ball. I used up four boxes of shells on the little men."

Sutton blasted one of them point-blank with his shotgun, but the alien simply somersaulted and rolled off into the darkness.

As with the monster at Flatlands, West Virginia, the witnesses claimed that the aliens did not walk but "seemed to float" toward them.

The farmers battled the seemingly invulnerable creatures for nearly four hours before they drove in panic to the Hopkinsville police station for reinforcements. Chief Greenwell was convinced by the hysteria of the three children and the obvious fright of the eight adults that they had definitely been battling something out on that farm. And everyone knew that the Suttons "weren't a drinking family."

Led by Chief Greenwell, more than a dozen state, county, and city police officers arrived to investigate and, if need arose, to do battle with the little supermen. On the way to the farm, the officers noticed a "strange shower of meteors that came from the direction of the Sutton farmhouse." One officer testified later that the meteors had made a "swishing sound" as they had passed overhead.

The investigators found no trace of a spaceship or the little men, but they found "several peculiar signs and indications" that something extremely strange had taken place that evening at the Sutton's farm. Whatever had invaded the Suttons on that Sunday night in August, the bullet holes in the walls bore mute testimony that the farmers had deemed the creatures real enough to shoot at them.

The Terrible Odor of Monsters

An unpleasant, often nauseating, odor is often an aspect of a "monster" sighting. Such a case involved two young couples who were supposed to be attending a dance, but who were actually parked on lovers' lane on a moonlit night in January 1967, in Elfers, Florida, near New Port Richey.

Shortly after their arrival, one of the girls commented that she smelled a disagreeable odor. Her companions teased her, saying it was just the natural smell of the forest, but she insisted that she was quite familiar with nature, and that this odor was something very different.

The other three soon agreed that they, too, could smell something that was out of the ordinary, for the odor had become more powerful and had reached a point of being nauseating. Before they could investigate the origin further, an animal about the size of a small ape leaped onto the hood of their car, and the foursome panicked.

"The thing looked like a chimp," one of them volunteered, "but it was greenish in color with glowing green eyes!"

The driver of the car started the motor, and the apelike thing jumped off the hood and ran back into the woods. The four teenagers decided at this point that it might be best to attend the dance where they were supposed to be, and they told their story to the police officer on duty at the dance.

When he checked, the officer found a green substance on the hood of the car. It was sticky, and it scraped off easily with a pocket knife.

When investigators checked the stories, all four youths related the same chain of events without embellishing on the overall report.

An unpleasant, nauseating odor is often an aspect of a "monster" sighting, which alerts the witnesses to a frightening monster (*art by Ricardo Pustanio*).

A Ten-Foot Monster Invades Oregon

In late May 1971, in The Dalles, Oregon, another monster/UFO sighting took place. According to reports, Joe Mederios, the maintenance man for a trailer court, was watering flowers in front of his office. As Joe looked across the road to a cleft in the bluff he saw what he later described to a sheriff's deputy as "a ten-foot-tall, gray-colored monster with arms that hung quite low." He further described the creature as looking like an ape, and stated that it definitely was not a bear.

The next day, while Joe and three Portland businessmen were holding a conference, they spotted something in the field below the hundred-foot rock bluff. They told authorities that the monster came down from the rocks and walked through the open field across from the trailer court. The creature stopped by a tree, which was later measured at eight feet, giving the foursome an accurate way of estimating the monster's height at about ten feet.

It is interesting to note that Joe Mederios claimed in the report that he had purposely not mentioned the event of the previous day to the other men, "in fear that I'd be called a nut."

More reports were filed in the same part of town, and two nights later Richard Brown, a music teacher at the junior high school, was returning home to the trailer court with his wife when the headlights of their car caught the outline of a figure standing near an oak tree in the field. It was about nine-thirty. Brown raced to their trailer and returned with his hunting rifle, which was equipped with a four-power scope.

The creature remained in the area, and did not move for about five minutes, giving Brown a good opportunity to study it through the scope. His description seemed to substantiate that of Joe Mederios, but like so many of the elusive Bigfoot-type monsters, the creature disappeared from the area.

The question finally boils down to a few basic theories. Some say the monsters are the missing link between man and ape, while others insist that they are pets or laboratory animals from UFOs used to test the environment of the Earth preparatory to landings by the actual space invaders. Still others speculate that the monsters themselves *are* the space invaders.

A Monster and a UFO in Pennsylvania

Mr. and Mrs. Philip Arlotta had just stepped into their car, preparing to return home after visiting relatives in Greensburg, Pennsylvania. It was ten o'clock on the evening of May 18, 1975.

Mrs. Arlotta had started the car's engine when she noticed a strange object just ahead of them in the sky. She mentioned it to her husband, who suggested that she turn off the engine—perhaps they could hear something.

The object was moving from east to west, and they described it as being about as big as a cantaloupe, oval, and bright yellow near the bottom but darker near the top. In the darker section were six square windows, which showed a red light behind them.

The Arlottas heard no sound, but they continued to watch the object for about a minute before calling their relatives to join them. Five people witnessed the strange craft as it appeared to move toward them at what they estimated was an altitude of less than one thousand feet.

The craft suddenly made an abrupt right-angle turn to the left, and at the same time it changed color from yellow to orange before it began gaining altitude.

The witnesses followed the object in the car. As they continued down a back road, they noticed that the object appeared smaller and orange in color. As they turned onto Route 130, they lost sight of the UFO, but they estimated that they had watched it for about four minutes.

The next evening at about dusk, a lone motorist was heading to his home in Jeanette, Pennsylvania. When he entered that same area on Route 130, something caught his attention just to his left. He stopped his car and backed up.

At a distance of a few hundred yards he noticed what he thought was a German shepherd running—although the movement was more like that of an ape than a dog. After a few seconds, the creature stood up on its hind legs and ran like a man into the woods.

The creature was described as seven or eight feet tall and covered with thick, black hair. The witness, who had been a Bigfoot skeptic in the past, suddenly found himself an instant convert.

The Bright UFO and the Lumbering Giant of Presque Isle

On July 31, 1966, a number of Erie, Pennsylvania, residents felt certain that "something" had landed on the beach at Presque Isle Peninsula Park.

It was about 10:00 P.M. when patrolmen Robert Loeb, Jr., and Ralph E. Clark came upon a car stuck in the sand at Beach Area Six. Seated in the mired vehicle were Douglas Tibbets, 18; Betty Jean Klem, 16; and Anita Haifiey, 22. They told the policemen that another of their group, Gerald La Belle, 26, had already gone for help, so the officers need not concern themselves with their plight. The patrolmen said that they would make a swing through the area in another forty minutes and check again just to make certain that the car had been freed. When the patrolmen came through Area Six again, they found that La Belle had not yet returned to the stranded automobile. In addition, according to Douglas Tibbets, some "weird" things had been going on. Something, he said, had landed near Beach Area Seven, and the occupants of the automobile had heard some unusual sounds emanating from that direction. The two officers walked with Tibbets about three hundred yards along the beach, but they could find nothing that might account for the strange noises that Tibbets and the others had reported hearing. Although it was too dark to accurately identify any kind of tracks in the sandy beach, the men were attempting to examine some of the markings when they heard the horn of Tibbets's automobile begin to sound in a steady blare.

The two officers walked with Tibbets about three hundred yards along the beach, but they could find nothing that might account for the strange noises ...

When the three men returned to the car, they found the women in varying stages of hysteria. Miss Klem began to run, screaming, down the beach and had to be pursued and calmed by Clark.

Later the events of that evening of terror were put into a coherent sequence by the witnesses.

Shortly after the patrolmen left, at 10:00 P.M., the occupants of the automobile saw a bright light "as big as a house" drop down near Beach Seven. They agreed that the object was "mushroom-shaped" and that they could distinguish rows of lights on the back of it. As the thing landed on the beach, it turned a brilliant red and their "whole car vibrated and shook" from the force of the object hitting the beach. After the landing, the object made a buzzing sound, "like a telephone receiver makes."

As they sat silently in the automobile, the awe-struck passengers could see "rays of light" begin to shine out of the object and sweep the beach "like they were looking for something."

At this point the patrol car reappeared on the scene, its red light flashing, and the rays from the object suddenly dimmed. It was while Tibbets and the patrolmen were investigating Beach Area Seven that Betty Jean Klem saw the monster.

It was a tall, upright figure, she told the officers, and it completely terrified her. She pressed her hand on the horn and held it there until the creature lumbered off into the bushes.

Miss Klem's eyes were still red from crying when reporters arrived on the scene. Park police chief Dan Descanio was notified, and after interviewing the young people he declared that he considered the matter "no joke." A check of others in the park that night revealed that a number of people had seen a strange object and weird lights late in the evening.

The next morning, investigators found several markings in the sand at the alleged landing site. A number of triangular shapes and skid marks were found, as was a series of tracks leading from the landing site to about twelve feet from where the car had been stuck. A claw-like marking was also found in the area, and a photograph of the print received wide publication.

The Three Strange Little Beings at the Side of the Road

Robert Hunnicutt was a short-order cook at a restaurant in Loveland, Ohio, back in the spring of 1955. Hunnicutt was a bit uncertain whether the incident had occurred in March or April of 1955. However, it is the event itself that is of importance here, not the exact date.

Hunnicutt told the police chief, John K. Fitz, that he was driving along Madeira-Loveland Pike when he noticed three men along the side of the road with their backs to a clump of bushes. He was tired and heading home from work, at about three thirty in the morning. At first he thought the three men were praying beside the road. Curious, he stopped his car to investigate. It was then that he discovered his error—they were not men at all!

The figures were short and stood in a triangular pattern, facing the opposite side of the road. The figure in the front of the triangle suddenly raised its arms above its head, and it appeared to Hunnicutt to be holding some type of rod in its hands—or perhaps a chain. Hunnicutt then saw blue and white sparks jumping from one of the creature's hands to the other, just above and below the rod or chain.

This event was taking place in a rather remote area, with a heavily wooded section just west of the highway.

The creature lowered the rod in the direction of its feet. To Hunnicutt it appeared as though the humanoid was fastening the rod to its ankles.

Now, as Hunnicutt stood by his car, the three figures turned slightly to the left, to face him. With no sound and no change of expression, the trio started for Hunnicutt.

The headlights of the car illuminated the three humanoids, so that Hunnicutt was able to get a good look at them. They were all about three and a half feet high, grayish, with uniforms about the same shade as their faces. "Fairly ugly," was the way Hunnicutt described them.

They had large, straight mouths without lips, and indistinct noses. Their eyes seemed basically normal, but they had no eyebrows. The upper portion of their heads was bald.

Their bodies were a bit odd, lopsided. According to Hunnicutt, their chests swelled to an unusual bulge on the right side, and their arms were of uneven length, the right one being longer than the left.

Descriptions of what aliens look like, with their large eyes, lipless mouths, and noseless faces, have been remarkably consistent no matter who the witness has been (*iStock*).

The garments above the waist (if indeed they were garments) were skin-tight and showed no line separating them from the skin portion of the humanoids, which was the same grayish color. However, below the waist they wore loose-fitting garments. The hips and waists of the humanoids appeared heavy to Hunnicutt.

Oddly enough, Hunnicutt did not seem to fear the unusual trio. He had been standing on the left side of his car, and he began to walk forward in the direction of the three as they approached him. Hunnicutt described their walking motion as graceful.

All at once, as though receiving telepathic thoughts, Hunnicutt sensed that he should stop. He watched the trio for a few minutes, then left to get witnesses. As he got into his car, he was suddenly aware of an extremely strong odor, which he described as smelling like a combination of "fresh-cut alfalfa and almonds."

As Hunnicutt drove past the three humanoids, he finally began to have a sense of fear for what might have happened. It was nearly 4:00 A.M. by now, and he drove directly to the home of the Loveland chief of police, Fitz.

The chief recalled how he had been awakened by Hunnicutt, who "looked like he had seen a ghost." According to Fitz, the witness told him that he had seen fire coming out of the creature's hands and had smelled a terrible odor. The chief knew Hunnicutt, but he found his story a bit hard to believe. He got close enough to Hunnicutt to smell his breath, and was satisfied that Hunnicutt had not been drinking nor was under the influence of any drug. Chief Fitz agreed to check the area, and he told Hunnicutt to go home.

Fitz got dressed, put on his gun belt, and loaded his camera in case he did find anything. However, after he had passed the area four or five times without spotting any little men, he returned home.

When asked by an investigator what he would have done if he had found the three humanoids, Fitz replied that he would have gotten out of his car and attempted to talk to them. "Someone has to do it sooner or later," he concluded.

The Incident at Hunter's Camp

Dave and Sharon Oester each told an exciting Bigfoot encounter in Chapter One, but Sharon has another to tell, "The Incident at Hunter's Camp", that combines Bigfoot and Flying Saucers. As Sharon tells her story:

Dave and I have traveled across the U.S., from coast to coast, eight times. We have enjoyed the back roads, small towns, and all kinds of wonderful people. There is nothing quite like the beautiful Pacific coast, the miles and miles of farmland in the heart of this country, and the historic beauty of the eastern states. America is truly beautiful and her people are exceptional.

We were talking the other day about some of our spookiest experiences over the last ten years of travel. Many experiences remain very clear in our minds because they were so unusual. One experience still gives us chills to this day, yet it took place almost ten years ago, just before we decided to travel full time in our RV coach.

It was early summer and we were restless, so we loaded up the RV and decided to spend a few days at one of our favorite RV parks off the beaten path.

We have always enjoyed the peace and quiet at Hunter's Camp in Central Oregon. The trees were old growth Ponderosa Pine and the setting was rustic with no frills (no phones, no Internet, no stores, and no swimming pool).

We had escaped to Hunter's Camp several times to enjoy the fresh air and silence. Our little dog BooBoo was less than six months old, and there were lots of places to walk and explore. She was born to travel, and it always helped us to get away from the everyday stress and reconnect with nature.

It had rained off and on all afternoon and evening, so we had the windows open for the fresh air between rain showers. There is something special after a rain storm in the desert with the aroma of pine trees and sagebrush. We had settled down for the night so it was probably around 11:00 P.M. The lights were turned off; it was pitch black in the park. We were the only campers in the park.

I was lying on the bed watching the heat lightning crackle across the dark sky. Just as we were starting to relax and doze off into sleep, there came echoing across the night air … the most horrifying scream either one of us had ever heard. It was not elk, deer, bear, cougar, wolf, or coyote.

We both sat straight up in bed. I said, "What the heck was that?" Out of the darkness, I heard Dave say, "I don't know!"

I mean that this scream sent chills down my spine and fear ran rampant in my mind. This was no ordinary wildlife scream; this was something inhuman and threatening.

Instantly, I reached over, closed my windows, and lowered the blinds. I felt like I would be safest on the floor and was prepared to dive down there if need be. I had to ask myself where a person would be the safest in a twenty-one-foot RV with a huge, screaming creature outside. I didn't like my answer.

Dave had his Smith and Wesson ready to defend us should something try to break into the RV, but for some reason that gave me little comfort.

With the windows tightly closed and blinds all down, Dave and I whispered back and forth, awaiting an encore.

It wasn't very long before the scream pierced the night once again. The sound was chilling and not human.

I have heard a cougar late at night, and its cry sounded so much like a woman screaming it was chilling. What we were hearing on this particular night was feral, and it didn't sound happy.

The sound was distant yet loud and seemed to fill the air. We could not tell which direction it was coming from.

I wondered if the manager of the park had heard anything since the lights had been on in the old house next to the park. It was hours before I fell into sleep as I lay listening for further screams or any sound of heavy footfall.

Once in a while, I would sneak a peek out the window just to check for movement of any kind. My dad taught me that forewarned is forearmed, so therefore I had an open space on the floor ready just in case I should need it. The rest of the night remained quiet and uneventful.

The next morning Dave waited until he saw the manager out walking around the park and went over to talk to him. We wanted to see if he knew about the events of the night before or if he knew what kind of animal screamed like the one we had heard. The answers Dave got were startling. The manager hadn't heard the piercing screams the night before because he was doing some remodeling work inside the owner's house—but he knew exactly what Dave was talking about because he had heard it before, several times. He told Dave that area was a hotbed for UFO activity and usually after a sighting of unidentifiable craft in the sky; they would hear screams such as Dave described.

The manager was very casual when talking about UFOs and what the locals thought was Bigfoot behind the eerie screams that penetrated the silence of the night. Folks don't talk about the screams or UFOs openly, but anyone living in that area is aware of the unexplained things in the skies and eerie screams that echo through the night.

Many UFO researchers are convinced that the occupants of the craft are extraterrestrial grotesque invaders, many of gigantic size, others more humanlike in appearance (*art by Bill Oliver*).

He Was Just Snatched and Taken Away into the Sky

The July 1967, issue of *Sports Afield* contained a fascinating article by Russell Annabel. According to Annabel, the Denna Indians of Alaska are well aware of the Sky People and even decorate their totem symbols and spirit houses with their sign: a horizontal slash, the outline of a hump on top of it.

Annabel tells a most interesting story of an Indian friend of his who found the two-year-old wreckage of an aircraft that had gone down after managing to send a final message which had been heard on the cabin radio of a trapper. "Mayday … Mayday," the pilot had called, "over the Talkeetnas … brilliant green light all around us … both engines have cut … the thing…."

Then, two years later, while tracking a bear, the Indian located the wreckage with its frozen corpses. One man had not died right away. He had managed to draw a picture on the side of the crate—a picture of a flying saucer, or, to the eyes of the Indian, the sign of the Sky People.

According to the Indian, the old men of the tribe described the Sky People as looking "like fat, bigheaded little bears walking on their hind legs." It was Denna tradition that the Sky People had landed frequently on Denna Mountain in the past and still patrolled the area and occasionally made off with someone. No "medicine" was powerful enough to work against the Sky People.

Annabel's Indian friend may have proved that point with the ultimate in visual demonstrations. Having got himself in mild trouble with the law through a misunderstanding, the Indian fled into the mountains. Annabel and a brother-in-law of the fugitive set out to bring him back to straighten out the matter. The Indian had left a clear trail in the snow, then suddenly, the snowshoe tracks ended abruptly in a bleak opening on a foot-slope of a mountain. The man's brother-in-law studied the tracks carefully, then issued his pronouncement.

"Wasilla went up … something took him. He didn't have any warning. He didn't see *it* or hear it, because he didn't stop to look up. He didn't have time to fight. Something just grabbed him and flew away with him."

Native Americans, UFOs, and the Crazy Bears

With all the disagreements that have always seemed to divide the Bigfoot hunters among us, there appears to be at least one point of agreement: Every Native American tribe seems to have ancient accounts of some kind of interaction with these large humanlike creatures that stretch back for centuries, long before the Europeans invaded the shores of Turtle Island.

Some years ago, James C. Wyatt of Memphis, Tennessee, sent me a copy of his grandfather's journal which contained fascinating and startling entries, written in straightforward fashion, which, if interpreted literally, may indicate that an association between Bigfoot-type creatures and UFOs has existed for quite some time.

In a journal dated 1888, Wyatt's grandfather records that he was somewhere along the Humboldt Line in the "Big Woods Country" where his father and several cowhands had wintered with a local tribe after delivering some cattle to a fort further north. Grandfather Wyatt was fluent in many tribal languages, proficient in sign language, and partook of most of the tribal activities.

One day he came upon a man from the tribe carrying a large platter of raw meat.

At first the man seemed afraid to answer Wyatt's questions concerning his errand, but he finally bade the cattleman to follow him.

In a shallow cave in a cliff face dwelt a beast with long, shiny black hair that covered its entire body, except for its palms and an area around its eyes. The man-like creature did not seem wild or vicious; it sat cross-legged, Indian-style, wolfing down raw meat. Wyatt described the creature as built like a big, well-developed man, except for its lack of neck and its long body hair. The creature's head seemed to rest directly on its shoulders.

Wyatt visited the man-beast in the cave more than a dozen times. After much questioning, and receiving two pounds of tobacco, a compass, and an axe, one of the men from the tribe took Wyatt to a high pinnacle of rock one clear night to tell him of the creature's origin.

"Crazy Bear," as the thing was called by the Indians, had been brought to the "Big Woods" from the stars. A "small moon" had flown down like a swooping eagle and had landed on a plateau a few miles away from the tribe's encampment. The beast in the cave and two other "crazy bears" had been flung out of the "moon" before the craft had once again soared off to the stars.

The man told Wyatt that other "crazy bears" had been left in the vicinity over the years. Wyatt's guide and several of his fellow villagers had occasionally seen the "men" that put the crazy bears off the small moons. They did not look like the giant hairy ones, but appeared to be more like men such as themselves. The men from the small moon had much shorter hair than the tribespeople, though, and they wore shiny clothing. They always waved to the Indians in a friendly manner before they closed the door in their small moon and flew back to the stars.

The crazy bears had been led to the village by the Indians, and at no time had the hairy giants offered any resistance to their benefactors. The Indians believed that the crazy bears from the stars had been sent to bring them powerful medicine, and they would not permit the creatures to stray away lest they be captured by rival tribes.

I cannot help wondering if the oft-reported monsters and robots seen near UFO landing sites are similar to the "crazy bears" that certain Amerindian tribes were well aware of back in the last century.

Perhaps, as some researchers suggest, the Bigfoot-type creatures are deposited here by extraterrestrials to test our environment in the same manner that we might one day in the future deposit primates on a planet whose atmosphere we wanted to evaluate in terms of a potential landing.

In a lengthy letter to me, James Wyatt speculated:

> Who is to say the Crazy Bears weren't exiled to our planet for some crime or other infraction of the laws of another planet [or dimension, we might add]?

> On the other hand, it is not inconceivable that the hairy ones are the food animals of some distant world and have been planted here on Earth to produce herds, just as the old shipmasters used to place pigs and goats on islands to multiply and furnish food for later voyagers.

> That they have not proliferated in great numbers may be due to their inability to provide for themselves, especially if they have been kept as produce animals for generations.

Or, perhaps, the climate, the atmosphere, or the food available to them is against their best survival purposes. Who knows?

Who, indeed? It may be a bit unnerving to suggest that Bigfoot may be the property of some other-dimensional interlopers or potential extraterrestrial colonists. By the same token, so may we fit into a similar category—and I find that infinitely more unnerving.

MOTHMAN—HARBINGER OF DEATH

"Being a paranormal investigator, it is my responsibility to report as accurately as possible and in as much detail as possible, any strange occurrence or sighting that happens my way," my colleague Sandy Nichols wrote (www.alienresearch group.com) to me. "After several years of doing this kind of research, I have grown fairly adept at being able to discern small details in photos and videos. I use this same learned ability when doing ghost research, UFO sky-watching or any other research activity. It is in this same vein that I will share an occurrence/sighting that I personally witnessed on July 20, 2005. I will not state emphatically that what I witnessed was the actual "Mothman" creature that terrorized Point Pleasant, West Virginia, but what I did witness had the general overall appearance of the creature as described by others who have sincerely believed that they have seen the true Mothman."

Here, in Sandy Nichols's own words, is the report of his strange sighting:

The time was around 10:30 P.M. The night sky had intermittent clouds, but I do not remember the fullness of the moon.

I was traveling west on Bethesda-Arno road in the Thompsons Station/Bethesda/Williamson county area of Middle Tennessee, about 25 miles south of the Davidson county line of Nashville. My speed was 40 miles-an-hour, though the road is posted for 50. Bethesda-Arno is a typical country road, curvy and straight, fairly narrow and bordered more by farmland than homes. At the exact spot of my sighting there are three homes set back several hundred yards off the road on a fairly steep grade on the north side of the road. The south side of the road is bordered by a fairly steep slope with a thick hedge row of mangled brush and trees, and is offset some 20 feet from the road. There were no others vehicles on the road, and my headlights were on full brightness.

I first noticed the creature as I rounded a curve and continued onto a short straight away with a slight rise in elevation. My estimated distance from the creature

For many, the Mothman is considered a harbinger of death (*art by Dan Wolfman Allen*).

was 300 feet, and I immediately began to slow my car. The creature was standing a foot or two off the side of the road on the south side. In back of him was the back side of a 7.5-foot-tall road sign. The sign was attached to a grated metal pole, and the sign itself was triangular and 3.5 feet in width from point to point, and attached some 3.5 feet up the pole from the ground. The top of the creature's head was several inches above the sign, though his feet were on the ground. This would have put the creature nearly eight feet tall.

The creature's body was covering about one-fifth of the triangular sign. The head of the creature was human in shape, but with a peculiar triangular appearance as well. The head seemed a tad bit too large for the rest of the body. The neck was normal in appearance and attached to narrow shoulders.

The chest appearance was normal, though narrower than one would have imagined. The chest area tapered down to a very thin looking waist.

The legs of the creature were long and slender, almost skinny, especially the thigh area extending down to the knees.

Both arms were long and thin and connected to hands with long, slender fingers—four or five, I am not sure.

The face of the creature was shrouded in a shadow-like appearance. I could discern no facial features.

The creature's arms were outstretched and attached to the wrists of both arms was dark webbing that extended downward and attached at the knees and also to the torso of the body directly at the underarm and extending downward to the knees. The webbing was solid in structure, with a slight tapering that came to a point mid-way to the knees and then continued to taper as above to the knees.

From the shoulders down to the feet, with the exception of the arms and webbing, the color of the creature was a bright, reflective red. The color reminded me of paintings that depicted the Devil with the ever-present pitchfork—though I had absolutely no feeling that this creature was either the Devil or any other type of demon. My gut feeling told me that this was some type of unknown species that modern day science insists does not exist.

The duration of my sighting was a brightly illuminated seven to eight seconds, and at one point as I passed the creature he was not more than seven feet from the open window of my car. Never once did the creature move or make any type of hostile gesture toward me.

I managed to bring my car to a full stop some 100 yards from the creature. I immediately turned my car around in the middle of the road in the hopes of seeing the creature again, but it was for naught.

Being a researcher intent on being accurate, I decided to retrace my path several times in an attempt to dismiss any status quo explanation for what I had witnessed. I have traveled down this road numerous times day and night, and I have never once mistaken a tree limb, brush, road signs, or the rarity of nighttime walkers for a creature such as I witnessed. The rather tall and thick hedge growth on the south side of the road, and the distance from the road to the nearest house on the north side, precludes an attempt by someone playing a practical joke. The distance to run and hide in a matter of just a few seconds would have been impossible.

The road sign is a typical road sign, and there was no mistaking that a very tall creature with a slender body and wings was obscuring part of the sign. There was no bright color hindrance reflecting from the headlights of my car to skew my vision since the creature was standing on the back side of the sign, the dark side.

My conclusion then was simple to deduce, I had seen this creature in all of the details I have just shared. Was the strange being that I witnessed on July 20, 2005, the same "Mothman" creature of West Virginia fame?

I do not know. Have any disasters happened near Nashville as was the basis for the book and movie *The Mothman Prophecies*? Not to my knowledge. As with many other things paranormal I've investigated that cannot be quickly explained, it may be a wait-and-see attitude that takes much patience before the final answer reveals itself.

* * *

On November 15, 1966, two young married couples, the Mallettes and the Scarberrys, were driving through the marshy area near the Ohio River outside of Point Pleasant, West Virginia, when a winged monster, at least seven feet tall, with glowing red eyes, loomed up in front of them. Later, they told Deputy Sheriff Millard Halstead that the creature followed them toward Point Pleasant on Route 62 even when their speed approached 100 miles per hour.

When the story of the red-eyed, winged monster achieved local circulation, Mr. and Mrs. Raymond Wamsley, Marcella Bennett, and Ricky Thomas stepped forward and said that they had seen the giant birdlike creature near the same abandoned TNT plant a few miles north of Point Pleasant. A few days later, Thomas Ury said that an enormous flying creature with a wingspan of 10 feet had chased his convertible into Point Pleasant at 70 miles per hour.

More witnesses came forward with accounts of their sightings, and the legend of Mothman was born. Although the majority of witnesses compared the tall, red-eyed monster as appearing birdlike, the media dubbed the creature "Mothman," because, as writer John A. Keel noted, the *Batman* television series was very popular at the time. "Birdman" didn't seem to carry the same sinister quality as "Mothman," a winged being that comes out at night.

Intrigued by the stories, Keel visited Point Pleasant on numerous occasions and learned about the bizarre occurrences associated with Mothman's appearance, including

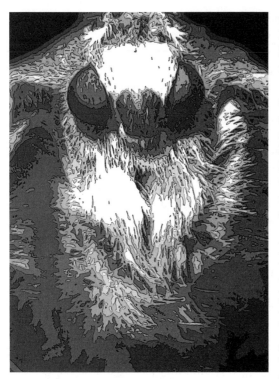

Some say that the Mothman is only a Sandhill Crane, a large bird indigenous to the area that can reach heights of six feet and achieve wingspans of 10 feet (*art by Ricardo Pustanio*).

the eerie prophecy that the Silver Bridge in Point Pleasant would collapse and many people would be killed as a result. It is with Keel that the Mothman mystique began to acquire an existence of its own.

Strange things happened to Keel when he visited Point Pleasant, and those of us who knew him and corresponded with him on a regular basis were sometimes left in shock and awe after reading his letters of bizarre incidents that seemed to follow him back home to his New York apartment. At times, he referred to mysterious personally prophetic telephone calls and visits from strange, almost demonic, entities.

Once, over dinner at a Chinese restaurant in New York City, Keel told me several stories about the kind of paranormal harassment that he had undergone since beginning his investigation of the Mothman near Point Pleasant. Most unsettling were his accounts of the infamous "three men in black" that had visited him, threatened him, and given him a remarkable display of their abilities. I was almost apprehensive about going back to his apartment after dinner. I was in my early thirties then, and in good physical condition, but I was not eager to match my physical and mental strength with that of "beings beyond the ken of mortal men." Thankfully, that evening the Visitors left us alone to talk until nearly dawn.

In 1975, Keel wrote in *The Mothman Prophecies* that "there would be many changes in the lives of those touched by" Mothman, and a "few would even commit suicide."

Various researchers of the Mothman mystique have a number of theories to explain the large winged monster that allegedly haunts the marshy area near the McClintic Wildlife Sanctuary and the abandoned TNT plant north of Point Pleasant. Some say that excited, suggestible witnesses had seen Sandhill Cranes, a large bird indigenous to the area that can reach heights of six feet and achieve wingspans of 10 feet. UFO researchers made correlations between bright lights seen in the sky and the appearances of Mothman, suggesting that the winged creature was of extraterrestrial origin. Others theorized that toxic chemicals dumped at the TNT site in World War II may have caused bizarre mutations in wild birds. And then there are those who maintained that Mothman might be a multi-dimensional intelligence, angelic or demonic, that can warn certain individuals of impeding danger—or cause bad things to happen to others.

Cryptozoologist Loren Coleman, author of *Mothman and Other Curious Encounters* (2002), has been keeping tab on the deaths that appear to be associated with the entity on his website www.cryptomundo.com. Coleman lists the demise of at least 85 men and women who have had some association with Mothman from the 1960s to the present day. A caution should be noted that many of the individuals on the Mothman Death List may have been elderly, ill, killed in the line of duty, met their demise in accidents totally devoid of nefarious circumstances, or committed suicide of their own troubled free will.

Coleman's first 46 victims were those unfortunates who became The Silver Bridge Victims, when at 5:04 P.M., on December 15, 1967, the bridge at Point Pleasant collapsed during rush hour. Forty-six lives were lost, and forty-four bodies were recovered.

Mary Hyre was the Point Pleasant correspondent for the Athens, Ohio, newspaper *The Messenger*. She became a friend of John A. Keel and assisted him in a number of his investigations concerning The Mothman.

The first sighting of the creature was filed by reporter Hyre when the Scarberrys and Mallettes saw Mothman on November 15, 1966. Exactly thirteen months later, the Silver Bridge collapsed on December 15, 1967. Twenty-six months later, Mary Hyre died on February 15, 1970, at the age of 54, after a four-week illness.

A naturalist, cryptozoologist, and animal expert who appeared on numerous television programs, Ivan T. Sanderson served as Keel's main consultant on the natural history behind the reports of Mothman. Sanderson, a well-known author of many books at the time of the Mothman sightings, was also the director of the Society for the Investigation of the Unexplained in New Jersey. Sanderson, 62, died on February 19, 1973, of a rapidly spreading cancer.

In addition to John Keel, no other person was on the scene in Mason County, during 1966–1967, as often as Gray Barker, a theatrical film booker based in Clarksburg, West Virginia, who became interested in UFOs in 1952. In 1956, Barker wrote *They Knew Too Much about Flying Saucers*, the first book dealing with the Men in Black, mysterious figures that menace UFO researchers. In 1966, when he was investigating Mothman near Point Pleasant, Barker allegedly found a note on his door with this message, "*Abandon your research or you will regret [it]. You have been warned.*" Barker was 59 when he died on December 6, 1984, "after a long series of illnesses" in a Charleston, West Virginia, hospital.

Donald I. North, a Point Pleasant native who saw Mothman in the TNT area in the 1990s, died in an automobile crash in 1997.

On October 24, 2001, Marcella Bennett who was an eyewitness to Mothman on November 16, 1966, lost her daughter, Robin Pilkington, 44. Robin's death would be the first of a wave of witnesses' relatives deaths during the time leading up to and during *The Mothman Prophecies* motion picture release.

As the movie based on John A. Keel's book began screening on January 25, 2002, the original witnesses, the Mallettes were attending a funeral in Point Pleasant. Stephen Mallette, one of the first four witnesses of Mothman, was mourning the passing of his brother, Charlie, due to a brain tumor.

On February 15, 2002, soon after the town was bustling with Mothman promotions and attention, one of Point Pleasant's better-known Mothman eyewitnesses, Tom Ury suddenly lost his 52-year-old brother Gary.

Ted Tannebaum, 68, the Executive Producer of *The Mothman Prophecies*, died of cancer, on March 7, 2002, in Chicago, Illinois.

Susan J. "Minga" Wilcox, 53, of Columbus, Ohio, died of an extremely rare form of brain tumor, ependymoma, at Mt. Carmel East Hospital, December 8, 2002. Wilcox reportedly saw a black "batlike" bedroom invader in her home in February 2001 and went on to become a Mothman investigator. Susan traveled to Point Pleasant several times in 2001 and 2002, and created a personal website: "Mothman: A Life Changed Forever."

British actor Sir Alan Bates, 69, died the night of December 27, 2003, at a hospital in London after a long battle with cancer. Bates played "Alexander Leek" in the *The Mothman Prophecies*. "Leek" was Keel spelled backward.

On August 3, 2004, Jennifer Barrett-Pellington, 42, wife of *The Mothman Prophecies* director Mark Pellington, died, in Los Angeles. Her husband had included a "Special Thanks" credit to his wife for her support of him on that film.

John A. Keel passed away on July 3, 2009, after a long illness.

Mothman in Middle Tennessee

Sandy Nichols has already told us about his July 20, 2005, nighttime encounter with a monster similar in appearance to what has been typically described as "Mothman." Once again, on May 16, 2008, Sandy said, "How fortunate I felt afterwards that I happened to be in the right place at the right time to personally witness such an elusive creature once again. It is not often that life with its ironic twists and turns affords an individual such a rare once in a lifetime opportunity, and even rarer for yet another sighting encounter, but that is exactly what transpired for me. My previous encounter occurred in the dark of night on a lonely country road where this creature was only illuminated by the headlights of my car, but this new sighting occurred in mid-afternoon next to and partially over a major interstate highway."

According to Sandy Nichols (www.alienresearchgroup.com):

The time was approximately 2:30 P.M. on a Friday afternoon, and I was traveling south on Interstate 65 just south of Nashville. At this time of day it is not unusual for there to be sporadic areas of congestion due to the usual mix of commuters heading home after work to the southern outlying counties and for families on vacation heading to the warm, sun soaked beaches of Florida, Alabama, and Mississippi. I did not have a long distance to travel on I-65 before exiting onto the less congested I-840 outer loop, but my patience at what I perceived to be slower traffic in the fast lane causing these congested areas was not at a premium this day. Due to some quick in-and-out lane changing on my part, I was able to break free just past the Peytonsville Road exit.

Right past Peytonsville Road, I crested a small rise, and any hint of being near a major city disappeared. Farmland and rolling hills began to dot both sides of the inter-

Paranormal/UFO researcher Sandy Nichols says that he has had two encounters with a Mothman-like entity.

state. From this position I had an unrestricted view to the overpass for I-840 some two miles further down the road.

At approximately one mile from 840, the interstate widens to three and four lanes. Just before the this widening begins, about seven-tenths of a mile from my location, I noticed what I first believed to be a small, black crop dusting plane or a large Estes type model rocket emerging from a narrow valley to the right (heading west to east), and only 150 to 200 feet off the ground.

Though crop dusting planes are not uncommon in this area, I dismissed these possibilities for lack of a landing gear or tail fins. I next wondered if it was a large vulture. Living in the country as I do and seeing vultures all the time, I dismissed this thought as well, for it was way too large for any vultures in this area.

By this time my natural, insatiable curiosity to unravel a mystery was in full swing. Looking at it from the side, it was nearly impossible to determine what this "flying whatever" was. I was hoping that I would be able to observe it better and see more detail as it continued flying eastward. This would at least afford me the opportunity to view it from another angle, but instead and without warning, it executed an almost perfect hairpin turn directly over the far right lane and several slower traveling vehicles.

At the same time its body tilted to the right and downward, affording me a clear view as if I was above it. It was at this point that I recognized the unmistakable characteristic shape of another "Mothman"-type creature.

The color of the creature's body was black, and from the neck down appeared as kite shaped; its head was a rounded diamond shape and oversized. Its arms were extended outward; its hands at an eight and four o'clock position away from its body on a horizontal line with its waist. A dark, solid web-like material, similar to a bat's web, extended from both wrists along the arms to the armpits, then continued downward along both sides of the body past the waist to half-way between the knees and the feet.

When it first emerged from the narrow valley, its speed seemed rather slow and lackadaisical. It seemed oblivious or unaware of the traffic congestion along its flight path. But when it reached the interstate itself and began the hairpin turn, its speed increased dramatically but without flapping its wings. A few seconds later the creature vanished from view. I do not feel it flew back into the valley itself, but instead, into the thick stand of trees on the neighboring hill and used its coloration as a camouflage to prevent further observation.

Somehow I have a strong feeling that somewhere from the trees or from the skies, the Mothman will emerge again. [Whoever] sights the being, I wish that the monster brings only news that it is pleasant and comforting. We do not lack in the world for "harbingers of death."

REPTILIANS—INVADERS FROM OTHER WORLDS

I first participated as an observer in the hypnotic regression of men and women who claimed to have been abducted by crew members from UFOs in 1967; the team of researchers recorded hundreds of hours of remarkable data. Later, from 1972 to 1994, I myself conducted dozens of hypnotic regression sessions with UFO contactees or abductees who recalled having been given some kind of medical examination by alien beings. In some instances, the experiencers still bore peculiar punctures and markings in their flesh.

Among the hundreds of abductees, contactees, and other witnesses of alleged extraterrestrial activity whom I have interviewed, there has been a general consensus among the percipients.

Apart from the visitors who did not resemble giant cockroaches or praying mantises, along with the occasional handsome "Nordic" aliens, the majority of the Ufonauts stood between four and a half to five feet tall and were dressed in one-piece, very tight-fitting clothing, usually gray or greenish-gray in color.

Their skin color was most often reported as being gray or greenish-gray, and they seemed devoid of body hair of any kind.

Their heads were round, large, disproportionately oversized by our human standards. In a few reports, pointed ears were mentioned, but usually the witnesses commented that the aliens had no external ears of any kind.

Their facial features were dominated by large, lidless, staring eyes, very often with slit catlike or reptilian pupils. They had no discernible lips, and where one might expect to see a nose, the witnesses cited only nostrils, nearly flush against the smooth texture of the face. On a few occasions, witnesses reported very flat noses or in some cases, tiny "stubs."

Since my early investigation into the UFO enigma in the late 1960s, it has seemed apparent to me that if humankind is indeed interacting with an extraterrestrial species, then those Ufonauts, the "Grays" as they are nicknamed, are representatives of technologically superior reptilian or amphibian humanoids. Furthermore, it also seems evident that these Serpent People have been interacting with Earth for millions of years—either appearing in cycles of programmed visitations or steadily monitoring our species' technological and society development from underground or undersea bases.

The Invaders Are Out There!

Such television series as *The Twilight Zone* (1959–1964) and *The Outer Limits* (1963–1965) occasionally featured episodes concerning alien invaders, but it was a series aptly named *The Invaders* (1967–1969), starring Roy Thinnes, that focused on the paranoid concept that evil aliens might be living undetected among humans and conspiring to conquer them. Thinnes was David Vincent, an architect, who happened to be the only human witness of a UFO landing. No one believed his account, so once he discovered that the extraterrestrials had arrived with the sole intent of taking over the planet, it became his mission to stop them, alerting and enlisting whomever he could to assist him. Vincent's task became all the more difficult because whenever he managed to kill one of the invaders, their physical body disintegrated, leaving no evidence to convince the authorities that aliens were walking and plotting among them. When the series ended in 1969, Vincent had not been able to stem the tide of alien invasion, and the stories of extraterrestrials posing as humans had received more substantiation from a television series that many insisted was telling the truth disguised as a fictional presentation.

Witnesses describe the invaders often as having their facial features dominated by large, lidless, staring eyes, very often with slit catlike or reptilian pupils (*art by Ricardo Pustanio*).

As early as *The Invasion of the Body Snatchers* (1956), Hollywood screenwriters had developed the theme of aliens possessing family and friends to a high degree of paranoia. While in *Invaders from Mars*, the extraterrestrials attached themselves to their victims' body, in *Invasion of the Body Snatchers*, they brought strange pods with them from their world which grew into likenesses of those humans whom they replaced.

Some social historians argue that the UFO craze began when the threat of nuclear war with the Soviet Union hung like a black cloud over the world and many people were desperate to believe that some force from the skies could appear and deliver Earth from nuclear annihilation. Still other scholars suggest that it may have been the U.S. government itself that began the rumors of flying saucers in order to divert public attention from the development of its own secret weapons. These researchers leaked information about Project Paperclip which had brought Nazi scientists and their families to the United States before the smoke had scarcely cleared from World War II. Nazi intelligence officers were brought to Washington, D.C. to help transform the OSS of World War II into the CIA of the Cold War with the Soviets. Perhaps such a prevailing atmosphere of national distrust contributed to the horror of films about UFO invaders, but the unsettling concept of aliens slowly taking over Earth through the possession of human bodies became firmly implanted in the psyches of millions of men and women who now looked even more suspiciously at the skies above them. *Invasion of the Body Snatchers* has been remade twice; the third version opened in theaters early in 2008.

In 1993, Chris Carter, creator of the television series *The X-Files* for Fox, fashioned a blend of UFO mythology, increasing public distrust of the government, and a growing interest in the paranormal that during its peak season in 1997 attracted an estimated 20 million viewers per episode. According to the mythos developed by Carter, the alien invasion had begun in prehistoric times and had been rediscovered by the U.S. military and a secret branch of the government in 1947 after the crash of a flying saucer at Roswell.

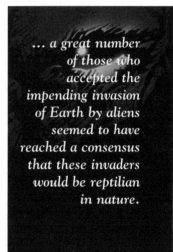

... a great number of those who accepted the impending invasion of Earth by aliens seemed to have reached a consensus that these invaders would be reptilian in nature.

FBI agents Fox Mulder (David Duchovny) and Dana Scully (Gillian Anderson) declared to their audience that "the truth is out there." However, because the truth was being covered up by an ultra-secret and exceedingly ruthless government agency, they must "trust no one." Although Mulder and Scully made side excursions to investigate various aspects of the paranormal, the UFO scenarios comprised the glue that held the series together and kept the fans returning week after week to chart the agents' progress in cracking the ultimate case that would force the secret government to admit the truth about aliens. Before the series ended in May 2002, both Scully and Mulder had themselves been abducted and Scully, earlier declared unable to have children, had borne a child under mysterious circumstances.

The theme of *Dark Skies*, the lead television series in NBC's 1996 Saturday night "thrillogy," was that history as the viewers learned it in school was a lie. One of the "truths" that the series revealed was that in 1947 President Harry S. Truman ordered an extraterrestrial spacecraft shot down over Roswell, after an alien ambassador had demanded the unconditional surrender of the United States. Subsequently, whatever resources could be recovered from the scraps of the demolished alien craft were doled out to various giants of American industry to be freely incorporated into our own technology—and a sinister and ubiquitous super-secret government agency known as *Majestic 12* was created to monitor any undue alien interference in our political and social structures.

Before the series was cancelled, viewers learned that the aliens had the ability to possess human bodies with their larvae, thus allowing them to pass undetected and to accomplish an incredible number of negative historical events—from the assassination of John F. Kennedy to the conflict in Vietnam, from the murder of certain celebrities to popularizing the use of recreational drugs among young people.

Reptilian Aliens Have Been on Earth for Centuries

By the late 1990s, a great number of those who accepted the impending invasion of Earth by aliens seemed to have reached a consensus that these invaders would be reptilian in nature. Some outspoken researchers even declared that many of our national and international leaders were actually reptilians and descendants of reptilians.

It has been pointed out by many UFO researchers that nearly every ancient culture has its legends of wise Serpent Kings who came from the sky to advance the benevolent and civilizing rule of the Sons of Heaven upon Earth. To name only a few, there is Quetzalcoatl, the feathered serpent of the Aztecs, who descended from heaven in a silver egg; Oannes, half-human, half-fish, who surfaced from the Persian Gulf to instruct the early inhabitants of Mesopotamia in the arts of civilization; the Nagas, the handsome, semi-divine Serpent People with supernatural powers who figure in the Hindu and Buddhist traditions. The awe and respect that our ancestors had for these wise serpentlike humanoids has very likely been retained in our collective unconscious today.

Let us suppose that after this highly advanced extraterrestrial reptilian species had been observing the evolution of Earth for millions of years, they made a decision to interfere with the slow, gradual evolutionary progress of *Homo sapiens* and initiated a program of genetic engineering whereby they accelerated the physical and intellectual development of one of humankind's early bipedal ancestors. Exceedingly detached and patient in their approach to such scientific projects, the reptilians experimented with skin pigmentation, facial and body hair, height, weight, and intelligence in their efforts to improve developing humankind.

At the same time, of course, the planet's natural process of selection and survival was taking place, so that by the time the serpentine scientists had created cities of rather sophisticated inhabitants about 200,000 years ago, Neanderthal was just beginning to huddle together in caves.

By 100,000 years ago, the genetic engineers from beyond the stars looked with pride upon a flourishing culture that had spread its influence throughout every section of the planet. These extraterrestrially accelerated humans, known today as the Titans, the inhabitants of Atlantis, Lemuria, and Mu, structured a technology that was beginning to rival that of the Serpent Gods from the stars. The Atlans also learned how to manipulate and to control the natural energies of Earth. Sadly, most of these forces and technologies were developed for purposes of exploitation and destruction. Tragically, little thought had been given by the reptilian genetic engineers to teaching humankind about the individual sovereignty of others. And to complicate matters even further, the humans had turned out to be a prolific species, which seemed to take special delight in reproducing. What had begun as an earthly paradise engineered by the Serpent People had deteriorated into a civilization of civil strife and internal warfare.

A great catastrophe is said to have submerged the great island kingdoms beneath the seas. Nearly all the Atlans and the Lemurians died in the splintering of their world or in its sinking beneath the ocean. Those who did survive the destruction of their lost continent spread the accounts of the death of a great civilization in prehistory, and the tales have been passed to our time through the many variations of the Great Deluge legends.

A discomforting element in this hypothesis is the very strong possibility that the reptilian genetic engineers who helped program early humankind may have been the very same ones who were responsible for the great cataclysms that destroyed so many of the primitive humans that they coldly assessed as an experiment that got out of control. The Serpent People may have come to the conclusion that they had acted inappropriately when they decided to interfere with the natural evolutionary process of Earth, and they resolved to "correct" their error and to pass an edict that their kind would never again interact with us in an overt manner. After the majestic world before our own that we remember in our species' collective unconscious was destroyed, colonies of the Serpent People retreated into underground caves and caverns and great numbers of their reptilian race elected to return to the stars.

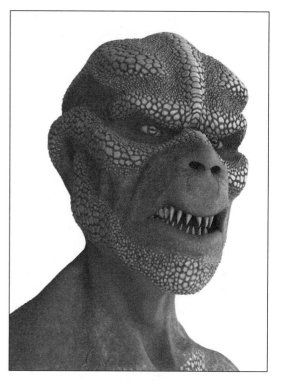

After causing evolutionary havoc on Earth, the Serpent People either left the planet or moved into underground caves and caverns (*iStock*).

Rumors of such rich underground kingdoms as that of the Naga, the proud and attractive Serpent People of Indian tradition, have been kept alive for centuries with certain heroes and leaders from many different cultures even claiming that they themselves may be the result of a mating between reptilian and human parents. From time to time the wise ones leave the caves to tutor select earthlings and to assist the intellectual and technological, rather than the physical, evolution of the surface dwellers.

Then, in the late 1940s, when a series of violent detonations demonstrated that humans had developed nuclear power and could become a threat to other worlds as well as their own, the subterranean Serpent People sent their saucer-shaped aerial vehicles into the skies to monitor the potentially dangerous activities of the human topsiders.

After the crash of one of their craft in Roswell, New Mexico, in July 1947, the reptilian Grays began cautiously to reveal themselves and allow certain of their underground bases to be toured by select members of the U.S. military and government. An alliance was made between the Grays, who considered themselves native Terrans, the descendants of the Serpent People, and representatives of a secret government that operated in the shadows of those who had been elected by the democratic political system. Unfortunately, the more benevolent and loyal of the Grays were very soon supplanted by mercenary agents of the Draco, an extraterrestrial race of reptilians that is in the process of reclaiming Earth. The devious Draco-Grays envisioned ways to dupe the shadow government, whose representatives seemed to be motivated primarily by greed, personal aggrandizement, and the desire for military superiority over other topside nations.

A Shadow Group within
World Governments Make a Deal with the Reptilians

Around 1954, the shadow group made a secret deal with the Grays that permitted mutilation of cattle and the abduction of humans in exchange for their advanced extraterrestrial technology. The Grays offered assurances that the human abductions would merely be ongoing examinations designed to enable them to monitor a developing civilization; but by 1982, there were steadily increasing reports of women who claimed unusual and unwanted pregnancies after their abduction experience aboard alien spacecraft, which were now steadily arriving from the Draco's home planet. In certain instances these pregnancies were terminated by the extraterrestrials who removed the fetuses in subsequent abductions. In other cases, the earth-women were monitored during the pregnancy and the birth of their hybrid star children.

After receiving a large number of such reports, including those in which male abductees claimed semen had been taken from them, the shadow agencies of the terrestrial governments were forced to conclude that the alien visitors were performing unauthorized crossbreeding experiments with unwilling human subjects—and there was nothing they could do to stop them.

A Remarkable E-Mail from Sandy Nichols

A Vision of a Future Battle for Earth with the Reptilians

I have been mulling this experience over constantly in my thoughts from the moment I awakened on a Saturday morning. This experience is so significant to me that it would not let me rest for a moment. It has been like important information is wanting to come out, but needed the right outlet to come forth … so some of what you will read here is from some sort of revelation or hidden information I am getting as I literally sit here and write this e-mail. It is like some sort of automatic writing.

As you know for at least a month now, I have been waking quite often and finding a variety of cuts and scratch marks on my body. The phenomenon may last a week, several weeks, or even a month, then taper down or stop for several months until it begins again.

This time is a bit different though … not for the marks, but I am also, as well as Sherrie [Sandy's wife] a few times, seeing more things or hearing more strange noises as well … inside the main house, my office and even outside as I relax in the hot tub.

Just this morning around 4:00 A.M. I am sitting in the hot tub, and for whatever reason I turned my head to the left and saw a bar of white light through the French kitchen doors. The light was low to the floor on the far side in a vertical position, and it appeared to be one to two feet in length and a few inches wide. I also saw a ball of white light over in the trees to the right along the riding trail, and a few seconds later a ball of red light in the backyard in the trees at the corner on the left side of the property line.

At other times over the last month or so I have seen other bars of white light in the kitchen and round balls of white light, as well as a ghost figure beside the hot tub. This is not including what Sherrie and I have been seeing or hearing inside the house at other times. Since Sherrie and I moved into the house, other friends have also seen these white lights in the neighborhood, plus my dogs have reacted to some of these things as well.

This is really the first time I can remember where I have gotten consistent marks on my body, and at the same time have been seeing and hearing an array of other things at the same time in a consistent manner.

The Pain Experiences

Now twice in the last two to three weeks, I have had what I believe to be dreams, but very short dreams. I suddenly realize that I am someplace, where I do not know, and I know someone or something is behind me. I feel as if I am standing up. Then suddenly and without warning I feel something or someone either touching or putting pressure either with a finger or some type of instrument on a specific area in the middle of my back, about one inch left of my spine. As soon as the area is touched I feel this intense pain, not sharp but dull and radiating, spreading out over the entire back area, and even inside of me. The pain is so intense that I cannot help but arch my back like a backwards "C." After several agonizing seconds the pain subsides and about a second later I am subjected to the pain again. It is like whomever or whatever is doing this to me releases the pressure or takes away the instrument and then immediately tags me again.

The pain is so intense that I fear to move because I feel that I would feel the pain even more than what I am feeling it. After this off and on pain torture about five times, I finally find the strength/will to try and break/move away from the pain.

When I do this I suddenly awaken on my couch where I am fully aware and can see the things in my office, and just a second or two later I get hit by the off and on pain at least two more times. My physical reaction to the pain is exactly as it is in the dream … arch my back backwards and grimace in pain.

Something Similar from My Past

I have vivid memories of a very conscious experience from nearly ten years ago. One Saturday afternoon after doing some household chores, I decided to take a nap in an upstairs bedroom. I fell asleep, and sometime afterwards I realized I was standing in this bare room on an extraterrestrial craft. With me were a tall female Gray and another being that I could not tell what it was. The tall female Gray was wanting me to do something and I just simply refused to do it. She was holding a metal looking type of rod in her hand, like a cattle prod, and after I still refused to do what she wanted me to do, she touched the metal rod device right on my spine in the middle of my back. I immediately dropped to my knees in intense pain. Even after this I still refused to do what she wanted me to do, she zapped me again. She zapped me a third time. The next thing I knew I was on my knees on the floor back in my bedroom and still feeling the effects of the pain. This pain is very similar to my two most recent pain experiences.

The Dream This Past Saturday Morning ... or Maybe Something Much More

I found myself in this room with several other people, around ten men and women. There are boxes and few small tables and chairs. The lighting in the room is strange. There are no lamps or light fixtures and no apparent source for the light which is not white light, but dark light that illuminates this room and the entire complex. I know that we are in some sort of enormous underground complex. We are part of something like a quasi military/civilian fighting group. I am the leader/commander of this group of people, and I know that I command many more people than this. I feel that we of this group are on a special mission of reconnaissance and diversion in an attempt to confuse and disorganize the enemy. (It was at this point in the dream that I realized that this is not the first time I have been in this underground complex and I am not in a dream.)

The enemy is not just one group, but two. The first group comprises creatures of extreme intelligence. These creatures are of a very large size, up to eight to nine feet tall, and they have a large, muscular build—both males and females. On the upper part of their body they wear some sort of interlocking breast and back plate ... similar to the scale pattern of fish. Their skin is rough and seems to be covered with course, black hair, but I believe this is not hair at all. It just appears this way in this dark light environment. The heads are large, larger at the brain area, wide and somewhat curved inward and similar in shape to a flattened out but inflated lizard's head. The mouth areas protrude outward from the face, and their mouths have some rather nasty looking sharp teeth, large and small. A few of the front teeth kind of look like "Dracula Teeth." The eyes are large, somewhat vertical, but it is hard to see details of colors of the eyes. Their arms from the elbows to the shoulders are as large as the largest part of an average size, man's leg, and the legs are even larger still. Their chest area is extremely wide.

They are very similar in appearance to the "Reptilians" that I have seen up close and personal, but with physical differences. I know that they are "Hybrid Reptilians," who are in direct confrontation with the common Reptilians. Both are vying for control of the Dark Underworld.

I think that the Reptilians were from "out there" someplace, and they chose earth as their new home eons ago. They feel as if they are the controllers of humans, though they did not create us. During their time living on earth they have been doing genetic research, and they eventually created the Hybrid Reptilians, from whom they lost control.

[As I was writing the above paragraph, I was suddenly hit with some sort of tremendous energy surge that made me woozy as hell. This energy surge was not from me, but from some unknown outside source. This has happened to me on a number of occasions over the last several years, but never before this strong.]

The second group we are fighting, is a group of humans who know about, aid, and work with these Hybrids in a nefarious scheme against their fellow humans. These humans are part of some unknown clandestine group of people with very close ties and a working relationship with some sort of secret, non-elected government group. This group of humans is so secretive that only a handful of people know they even exist, and most of the non-elected government group doesn't even know what the hell is going on.

As the leader in this vision, I ordered my people to stay in the room. I left the room and began running down a strange undulating, sometimes flat and straight, sometime curved hallway. The walls, floor ceilings, etc. were not what one would expect. Like some of the UFOs I have been on, a great deal of the physical structure of this underground complex was literally alive. By being alive it was able to change shapes, but not on its own accord. The changing shapes come about by those beings [that] created it, and this knowledge of creation is generally known by many intelligent species. This living entity was created with some degree of intelligence, and it has to be controlled or it could transform into something else and become deadly to its creators.

Some believe the Ufonauts are representatives of technologically superior reptilian or amphibian humanoids (*art by Ricardo Pustanio*).

Every time we are in this underground complex we are faced with the knowledge that our main physical foe would be the creatures and not the humans. Even though the humans collaborate with the creatures, they are allowed only limited access to the underground complex. This is due to several reasons.

The first reason was that they felt that too many humans would hinder their battle with the common looking Reptilians since humans are so much weaker in physical strength. A second reason was that just like the common Reptilians, the Hybrids looked upon humans as inferior. A third reason was privacy, but not because they liked privacy. As stated earlier, the Reptilians consider themselves as rulers over humans, and the Hybrids feel the same. The Hybrids' need for privacy is a way to deceive their human partners. The Hybrids are deluding the humans into believing they are on an equal footing with all of the Reptilians, but in truth they are not. The Reptilians have been around a lot longer than we have and far longer than the Hybrids. Their knowledge is far superior to ours and their main goal is for conquest and the subjugation of humans, but not in a "slave kind of way" as espoused by several researchers.

The humans are working for the Hybrids for all the normal kinds of reason—money, power, knowledge, technology, etc. One of the collaborating humans' principal responsibilities is to make certain that the general public and even higher-ups don't believe in the existence of either the Reptilians or the Hybrids. Another duty is getting the humans to do the Reptilians' biding with the human higher-ups without these higher-ups knowing a damn thing about what is really going on.

There is another twist, and that is, that there is another human group working with the Reptilians. These are the humans and Reptilians that most of today's researchers talk about. This human group knows about the other human group and the Hybrid Reptilians, but over all they know very little.

The above knowledge constantly plays in my thoughts as I continue to run down the hallway. It is this knowledge that gives all of us who chose to fight the creatures against the odds we know we face the strength to carry on. We are fighting for self-survival and individual sovereignty, using free will to choose our own destiny. More and more people are slowly learning and believing and joining the fight.

I finally reach the end of this particular hallway. My objective is get to another entrance where more of my people are waiting for me. My plan needs good coordination, and our radio communication is pretty well moot while in the underground complex. In some way the actual physical composition of the living entity itself blocks normal radio communication. The Reptilians, though, are able to communicate great distances through some sort of collective "Hive" telepathy.

There are many of us who are actually doing the fighting who have somehow increased our telepathic abilities. It is hard to explain, but we can sometimes communicate with other people using the same telepathy process. It is like relying on one's own "sixth sense, gut instinct" more for answers. By using our increased abilities, we are then able to think in a conscious way of what to do next if the situation becomes fluid, and the person basically receives an answer from say someone like me … though my answer apparently came from my subconscious thoughts without my being aware of it at the time. Over time this is becoming a more common occurrence—and it drives the Hybrids crazy because they can't stop it from occurring.

For us to win, we must become like them in a certain way. One must begin to think like them, instead of like us. We must become the "Ultimate Trickster," at least where it concerns these two Reptilian species.

I reached the end of this hallway, run down another short hallway, around a curved hallway, and come to another door. I throw open the door and enter through the second entrance to another room in the underground complex. This room is huge, and my people, about six of them, are huddled about 50 yards away from me. What appear to be boxes are scattered in neat fashion around the whole room. These are not ordinary boxes. This is some sort of mechanical room, like a power source, but not the main power source. It is located much deeper, much, much deeper. (As an afterthought I can't help but smile when other researchers share that the government has built underground facilities that are 40 stories deep. Compared to the place where we battle, 40 stories deep is like one shovel of dirt being removed.)

My people ask me what is our next move. I must be careful in what I command my people to do. They trust me. They have from the first time we met. They follow my command without hesitation. Why so much trust; I do not know. Maybe because I do not have all the answers, and like them I learning new knowledge every day. How

I came to be in this position I do not know, though I do know I have an awesome responsibility and it is scary sometimes. I rely on them, and they rely on me.

As I stand and calculate the best strategy, my attention is drawn to the entrance door. Something is not right. I tell my people to stay put as I turn and head back to the door. Cautiously and slowly I open the door.

Down on the landing is a human on all fours, screaming in pain and begging for help. I see only him, no blood, no creatures, but I am aware that sometimes the creatures can inflict pain on us even without a physical source. Who is this person? I do not recognize him. My team and I are the only ones supposed to be in the complex at this time. I am suspicious.

A slight movement on the bottom part of the stairwell below the landing grabs my attention. For just a second I catch the protruding open mouth of a Hybrid, its mouth opened wide enough that I can see its teeth. It is important for me not to act in haste and try a rescue. Though it seems callous, an attempted but failed rescue can result in some devastating repercussions in the future. With regret, I decide to leave the man to his fate.

> *Down on the landing is a human on all fours, screaming in pain and begging for help. I see only him, no blood, no creatures, but I am aware that sometimes the creatures can inflict pain....*

I turned and walked back through the door into the large room. I had only taken a few steps when my conscious morality compels me to try and help this man. I open the door. The creature has not emerged from behind the corner of the stairwell. The man is now on the second step leading to me, still screaming in pain.

I do not know if he is hurt or something else is wrong, but the man seems to be making no effort to crawl up any more stairs. Do I dare take the chance of going down to get him?

Suddenly and without warning the creature appears on the landing behind the man. He leans down and grabs the man's legs, and the man just disappears. The creature had created an illusion within my own thoughts.

I turn and slam the door as I rush back into the room. I do not know how far I had gotten when I turned around and saw the creature directly behind me. How could he have caught up to me so fast? The sheer size and bulk of the creatures prevents them from quick speed or movement. This physical hindrance is an advantage we use in our battle strategy.

I reach for and grab a something to use as a club, and I began to furiously hit the creature on its forehead. Twenty or thirty times I hit him, and then stop. It seems to have had no effect.

The next thing I knew the creature had grabbed me from the back, his large arms wrapped around me and cover the upper half of my body. Its grasp was tight, but I could easily breathe. He begins communicating with me, though I cannot either understand or remember what he was saying. This communication lasts for several minutes, then it turns me around in its arm. The top of my head reaches just above the bottom part of its chest. I careen my head backwards and look it directly in the face, but more importantly in the eyes. It stares at me with an emotionless stare for several seconds, and then I hear it say, "I will rule the Dark Underworld!"

Why the creature let me go this time and the other times, I do not know. I only know that I awakened on the couch fully conscious and aware. A few seconds later I got nailed by two separate and distinct bursts of pain. After some thought of this in the last day or two, I believe that these fully conscious and aware pain experiences are like a warning to me "not to mess with them."

The creature's words were chilling, and though he spoke them to me in the singular, I had the distinct impression/feeling that it was referring to the plural or the whole of the entire Hybrid Species. I wondered for several hours after the experience about this, and then it came to me … the "Hive Mentality." The word "I" literally meant "We."

Something else bothered me about the wording of the phrase that I did not put two and two together until I began sharing in this e-mail to you. It said the phrase in the future tense, not the past or present tense. This is very significant to me for a couple of reasons: It would confirm that if this was indeed not just a dream, but in fact a real time, right here and there type of experience, and that two different Reptilian species are at war with each other, then this means that at least during some of my abduction experiences I am taken to this underground complex either by the common Reptilians or some other alien type species. Through my own personal research and hearing other people share their experiences, I cannot help believing that some alien species are good and trying to help humans, and that they are fighting the bad alien species, and that in at least some of these wars they use humans: In other words, "your planet, you help defend it."

It would also confirm that the future tense phrasing meant that this war has been and still is being waged at this precise moment in time under the Earth's surface.

There is no doubt in my mind that some of what I have shared with you in this e-mail just came out of me. The best way I can describe it is like "automatic writing." I have to believe that this must be some type of factual information or knowledge I have that buried somewhere deep in my subconscious and by writing it down it allowed some of this hidden information/knowledge to come forth.

I am not stating that everything I have shared in this e-mail is an absolute truth just yet. I need more information/confirmation. I know that I can take none of this to a lab for analysis, so as I have shared with you before, the only thing I can rely on for final validation is my own "sixth sense, gut feeling."

My gut feeling right now is telling me that at least these experiences are real and valid up to a point, and that the pain I experienced is real and valid up to a point. It is the details of the experience that I am trying to validate.

Well, I've got news for the bastards. I am not backing down and I will fight for our world every time!

SEA SERPENTS—
MONSTERS FROM THE DEEP

In the summer of 1976, master woodcarver and former Methodist minister Tom D'Onofrio of Bolinas, California, had been commissioned by Paul Kantner and Grace Slick of the band Jefferson Airplane to create a very special table for them that would have the majestic head of a dragon. D'Onofrio had completed the feet and the tabletop, but he simply could not get the head carved in a manner that he believed would satisfy his clients.

D'Onofrio had prayed for guidance and worked solidly on the table for two days until his hands were shaking. He was emotionally, physically, and spiritually drained.

He decided to recharge his creative senses by saddling up his Appaloosa, White Cloud, and ride to RCA Beach where he knew a friend had set up a day camp and a teepee.

It proved to be a wonderful decision in more ways than one. First of all, the ocean was so calm and peaceful that it resembled a placid lake more than a sea. Secondly, he had a friend with whom to commiserate. Thirdly, he and his friend spotted something very unusual swimming in the quiet ocean.

On August 30, 1976, D'Onofrio was about to see his dragon.

"Suddenly there was this dark figure swimming through the surf," D'Onofrio told Alex Horvath (*SF Chronicle*, July 1, 2005). "It was this big dark creature—about 40 feet long."

And then the creature rose up and out of the water. It wasn't an eel or seaweed or anything else but a sea serpent, a monster so large that it pushed the ocean back.

And it had the head of a dragon.

D'Onofrio and his friend looked on in amazement as the serpent raised its head again, this time the dragon head was clear enough for both men to see.

D'Onofrio returned to his wood shop and worked for four days straight, desperately seeking to capture the image as completely and in as much detail as possible.

The mysteries of the sea may still hold secrets of creatures beyond our wildest imagination (*art by Bill Oliver*).

When he had completed the carving, his clients were extremely satisfied. Later, *National Geographic* displayed a photograph of the dragon table and D'Onofrio posing on a reef near the spot where he and his friend had sighted the sea serpent.

In August 2005, the National Geographic Channel featured D'Onofrio and the Rose Dragon Table in an episode of *Is It Real: Monsters of the Deep*. For the wood carver, the sighting had been a spiritual catalyst of sorts and provided the impetus for him to become a full-time artist.

Noel Dockstader of the Discovery Channel commented that D'Onofrio's encounter demonstrated that one can travel the world and the phenomenon of sighting sea serpents exists everywhere.

Giant Jellyfish Capsize 10-Ton Japanese Trawler

Out in our vast seas, there are many and diverse kinds of known and unknown monsters.

On November 2, 2009, a 10-ton Japanese fishing trawler, the *Diasan Shin-shomaru* was capsized off eastern Japan by a gigantic jellyfish. Creatures such as the Nomura jellyfish can weigh over 400 pounds, and the ideal breeding conditions off the coast of China has seen thousands of the huge blobs running afoul of fishing boats. In 2007, there were 15,500 reports of jellyfish damaging fishing equipment.

In the incident that occurred in November 2009, the crew of the *Diasan Shin-shomaru* was trying to haul a net that had become filled with jellyfish of all sizes. Some of the big jellyfish objected to such treatment and pulled back—and capsized the boat. The crew was thrown into the sea, and the vessel sank.

Unless you were one of the crew members tossed into the ocean by the big blobs, a jellyfish does not sound like the kind of sea monster that is really very dangerous. It must be pointed out, however, that the Nomura jellyfish can grow to be nearly seven feet across, can weigh as much as 440 pounds, and can deliver a very painful toxic sting.

The Akkorokamui Awaits Victims Off Hokkaido

In spite of the potential dangers of the Nomura jellyfish, the fishermen were probably grateful that they had not been capsized in Uchiura Bay, which is located in the southwestern portion of the Northern Japanese island of Hokkaido. According to decades of sightings by the Ainu people, it is here that the enormous squid-like monster the Akkorokamui awaits its victims. For generations, the Ainu have dreaded the creature, fearful of its inclination to swamp boats.

According to Brent Swancer writing from Japan and quoted on Loren Coleman's cryptomundo website (www.cryptomundo.com) the Akkorokamui is a huge octopus-like or squid-like monster that can reach sizes up to 110 meters in length. A bright red in coloration, the approach of the creature can be mistaken for the reflection of the sun on the water.

In his *The Ainu and Their Folklore*, John Batchelor, a nineteenth-century English missionary, told of a great sea monster with large staring eyes that attacked three men in a boat out catching swordfish. The men described the monster as round in shape and released a dark fluid and a noxious odor.

Swancer translated another nineteenth-century account of a Japanese fisherman's narrow escape from an enormous, red, undulating monster with massive tentacles "as big around as a man's torso." The sea beast, estimated to be at least 80 meters in length, stared at the fisherman with a "huge staring eye before sinking out of sight into the depths."

The Creature the Norwegian Scientists Call the Monster

The kind of massive creature that could pick up a good-sized fishing boat and crush it between its jaws sounds like the kind of sea monster that makes for good armchair adventuring. According to Richard Forrest, a plesiosaur paleontologist, a pliosaur was large enough to swoop up a small automobile in its jaws and bite it in half. A 150-million-year-old specimen was found on the Spitsbergen Island, in the Arctic chain of Svalbard in 2006. The Norwegian scientists who made the discovery named the creature "the Monster," as it measured 50 feet from nose to tail.

Now, if such a Jurassic-era giant should still be swimming around in the oceans of the world, that would unquestionably be a bona fide sea monster.

Paul Rincon, a science reporter for BBC News, explained that the pliosaurs were a form of plesiosaur, rather short-necked compared to some of the other marine reptiles. It had a large "tear drop" shaped body with two sets of powerful flippers that could propel it through the sea that reached enormous speed and made it an awesome predator.

If the pliosaur was about 50 feet in length, many ships have reported sighting sea monsters that long—and sometimes much longer.

The 140-Foot Visitor to Gloucester Harbor

According to old records, an enormous sea serpent inhabited the waters of Gloucester harbor for two weeks in August 1817 (**art by Ricardo Pustanio**).

According to old records, an enormous sea serpent inhabited the waters of Gloucester harbor for two weeks in August 1817. The many seamen and fishermen who saw the beast at fairly close quarters testified that the monster was nearly 140 feet in length. They contended that the sea serpent wriggled like a snake and possessed a row of coils that rose eight or ten inches above the water.

The behemoth appeared to have sought the sanctuary of the harbor in order to give birth to its young. One of the little beasties was killed on an island, and it was exhibited at the Essex Coffee House in Gloucester. The brown baby monster was reported to have measured three feet in length and was said to have had thirty-two humps on its back

The Sighting of the H.M.S. Daedalus

The crewmen of H.M.S. *Daedalus* reported sighting a sea serpent in 1848 that was longer than their ship.

"In a few moments it became more distinct, showing an apparent length of about 40 feet [above the surface of the sea], the undulations of the water extending on each side of a considerable distance in the wake. After passing the ship about half-a-mile, the serpent 'rounded to' and raised its head, seemingly to look up at us, and then steered away to the northward...." (From a letter to the *Illustrated London News* by James Guy, commander of the vessel *Imogen*, April 15, 1856.)

Cadborosaurus Makes Its Home in the Pacific Northwest

"Any fool can disbelieve in sea serpents," commented Victoria, British Columbia, newspaper editor Archie Willis in 1933. Willis' pronouncement came as a sharp rejoinder to the skeptics who laughed at the hundreds of witnesses who swore that they had seen a large snakelike creature swimming in the waters off the coast of the Pacific Northwest. Willis christened the sea monster, "Cadborosaurus," and the nickname stuck.

The creature with its long serpentine body, its horse-like head, humps on its back, and its remarkable surface swimming speed of up to 40 knots, has been a part of coastal lore from Alaska to Oregon for hundreds of years. While the waters of the Pacific Northwest border one of the deepest underwater trenches on the planet—where almost any massive sea beast could reside—the greatest number of sightings of Cadborosaurus have occurred in the inland waters around Vancouver Island and the northern Olympic Peninsula.

In their book *Cadborosaurus: Survivor of the Deep*, Vancouver biologist Dr. Edward L. Bousfield and Dr. Paul H. Leblond, professor of oceanography at the University of British Columbia, describe the creature as a classic sea monster with a flexible, serpentine body, an elongated neck topped by a head resembling that of a horse or giraffe, the presence of anterior flippers, and a dorsally toothed or spiky tail.

Dr. Bousfield, a retired cryptozoologist with the Royal British Columbia Museum, calls Cadborosaurus "a Mesozoic relic." In the Victoria, *B.C. Times* for August 9, 1997, Dr. Bousfield theorized that "the females come to shores of shallow estuaries to bear live young (similar to garter snakes)." Dr. Bousfield has collected many accounts of Cadborosaurus sightings over the years.

The Victorian Colonist (July 1997) carried the story of two university students who sighted a "snorting, 20-foot-long sea monster" off the shores of a Pacific coastal beach in Victoria, British Columbia. Ryan Green, 18, a Simon Fraser University business student, described the sea beast as a "twin-humped, round-bodied monster" that swam across Telegraph Bay near suburban Saanich. It was about 49 feet from the spot where Green and his friend, Damian Grant, were sitting.

"All of a sudden, this head comes up, like a whale with no spray. And then this hump, the size of an inner tube in diameter. And then another hump. It's nothing I've ever seen before," said Green.

Researcher Paul LeBlond, said about 160 recorded sightings of the swift-swimming monster have been reported. Dr. Bousfield interviewed the students and concluded that they had a sighting of Cadborosaurus.

The Cape Ann Sea Serpent—A Tourist for 340 Years

Offshore on the Atlantic seacoast of North America, there is a sea serpent that has been paying periodic visits to the Cape Ann area and Gloucester, Massachusetts, for more than 340 years. An Englishman named John Josselyn, who was returning to London, made the first sighting of the creature as it lay "coiled like a cable" on a rock at Cape Ann. Seamen would have killed the serpent, but two Native American crew members protested such an act, stating that all on board would be in danger of terrible retribution if the sea creature was harmed.

On August 6, 1817, Amos Lawrence, founder of the mills that bore his name, sighted the sea monster and issued a proclamation to that effect. Col. Thomas H. Perkins, one of Boston's wealthiest citizens, also testified to the reality of the great serpent, stating that it was about 40 feet in length with a single horn nine to twelve inches long on its head.

Then a serpent-like creature lifted its head from the surface, saw the fishing boat, and began to swim directly toward them.

On that same August day, a group of fishermen spotted the marine giant near Eastern Point and shouted that it was making its way between Ten Pound Island and the shore. They said later that they could clearly see the thing's backbone moving vertically up and down as it appeared to be chasing schools of herring around the harbor. Shipmaster Solomon Allen judged the serpent to be between 80 and 90 feet in length.

Generations of Gloucester residents and tourists have sighted the Cape Ann sea serpent, very often as they sailed the harbor and nearly always stating that they were frightened by the appearance of a huge snakelike creature at least 70 feet in length.

In April 1975, some fishermen saw the monster up close and personal and were able to provide one of the more complete descriptions of the monster.

According to Captain John Favazza, they had sighted a large, dark object on their starboard side, about 80 feet away, that they had at first thought was a whale. Then a serpent-like creature lifted its head from the surface, saw the fishing boat, and began to swim directly toward them. Favazza later told reporters that the sea serpent was black, smooth rather than scaly, with a pointed head, small eyes, and a white line around its mouth. It swam sideways in the water, like a snake. It was longer than his 66-foot boat, and he estimated its girth as about fifteen feet around.

Sea Serpent Spotted from City Island Bridge, Bronx

Late in March 1969, two fishermen angling off the City Island Bridge near the Bronx, New York, claimed to have seen a giant sea creature moving in the deep channel used by the oil tankers that travel up the Hutchinsou River. The fishermen described the monster as being slimy, black and gray, and bigger than anything that they had ever seen.

Harbor police who investigated the area found nothing, but they were soon called to Long Island Sound to look into a similar report from Little Neck Bay, Queens. It appears that something larger than a whale, something that could not be identified by longtime fishermen with practiced eyes, was exploring the bays of New York City.

Kai Kwai Sea Devil off Hong Kong

At about the same time, on the other side of the world, North American Newspaper Alliance reporters were writing the story told by fourteen Hong Kong university students who saw a "big black creature with green eyes" staring at them from only twenty yards offshore.

According to Benjamin Chae, the students had heard a crying noise from the sea. One of the girls had looked up and screamed. "I looked out to the sea, and about twenty yards from us, a big black creature was rising from the water. I yelled out *Kai Kwai* [sea devil] and all the others ran up and saw it too."

The students estimated that the monster was twenty to thirty feet in length and they insisted that the thing made a loud, crying noise. In their opinion, it was definitely not a fish.

Something Larger than a Whale Spotted off New York City

Early in 1969, something larger than a whale was seen churning about near New York City. Witnesses described it as a gigantic creature with green eyes and an eerie voice. Could either of these sightings—the monster near Hong Kong and the "whale" near New York have anything to do with the massive "something" that was washed up on a Mexican beach on March 7, 1969?

Mysterious Blobs or Decaying Sea Serpents?

At first, the huge blob was declared to be the remains of some prehistoric creature that had been thawed out of a drifting iceberg. Then two biologists at the Mexican navy's marine biology station at Tampico declared the hulk to be that of an oversized sperm whale. However, other scientists countered by pointing to the rare horn and shoulder blade as evidence that the creature could hardly be a whale of any kind.

The behemoth was dragged in with the aid of tractors and more than one hundred fishermen and soldiers tugging on cables tied to its carcass. An estimate of its weight was made difficult by the feeding of sharks and the mutilations of superstitious fishermen; but tests indicated that the unidentified monster had weighed somewhere between twelve and thirty-five tons.

The rotting hulk of some massive unidentifiable creature lay on a beach in Tasmania for at least two years before a representative of the Commonwealth Scientific and Industrial Research Organization decided to investigate. Three cattlemen had discovered the remains on the island's northwestern coast in August 1960, but their sketches and reports of the dead monster caused little excitement until Bruce Mollison, curator of vertebrate mammals, decided to trek into the rugged wilderness for a close look.

Mollison was surprised that the carcass had not deteriorated into nothingness over the two years that it had lain exposed to the elements. Although a good deal of the strange humped creature had rotted away, Mollison quickly became convinced that the thing he was studying was not of any known species of fish or mammal. He was certain that the twenty-eight-foot long eighteen-foot-broad beast had not been a variety of whale, squid, ray, or the like.

The creature's skin was hard and rubbery and covered with a greasy, straggly kind of hair. Several rows of spines, mounted on flanges, skirted its rear.

Experts at the Royal Prince Albert Hospital were unable to identify the flesh of the monster as belonging to any known species. A field expedition of the CSIRO went directly to the carcass itself to test Mollison's report and to hack off their own specimens. They reported that they were unable to identify the sea beast.

Then, as so often happens in such cases, a certain representative of officialdom issued the official word that since the flesh of the monster was something like the blubber of a whale, the creature must, therefore, be a whale.

Mollison expressed his shock at the official CSIRO report, and the ranchers who had discovered the rotting carcass fumed that they bloody well knew what a whale looked like and this had bloody well not been a whale.

Lobstermen Haul Up Sea Serpent Skeleton Off Maine

On Monday, August 7, 1967, the Gagne brothers, Richard and Peter, of Biddleford, Maine, hauled up a partial skeleton of the oddest looking thing that they had ever seen.

The Gagnes are lobstermen, and Richard pulled up the skeletal remains while he was searching in an outboard motorboat for one of his lobster traps off the southern Maine coast. What appeared to be the snakelike head and neck of some undetermined creature was over eight feet in length.

Peter remarked that the eye sockets on the head were so big that he could put his fist in each one of them. The eyes were on the side of the head, like a snake's. Bits of flesh still clung to some of the vertebrae. Many people who came to view the remains agreed with the Gagnes that the thing looked "just exactly like what a sea monster ought to look like."

Unidentified Sea Creature Off New Jersey Coast

The unidentified sea creature that appeared off the New Jersey coast on August 19, 1963, could not have had a more appreciative audience. As reported in the *New York Times*, the initial sighting was made by Dr. Lionel A. Walford, director of the Fish and Wildlife Research Center of the United States Department of the Interior at Sandy Hook, New Jersey.

Dr. Walford cautioned the reporter not to say that the scientist had seen a "sea serpent," but the expert did provide an excellent description of whatever it was he had seen: "It was at least 40 feet in length and about five inches thick and perhaps seven to eight inches deep—looking something like an enormously long, flattened eel.... I finally made a tentative identification of it as what is known as a Venus Girdle, a jelly-like creature. However, upon examining my scientific references, I soon and surprisingly determined that the Venus Girdle does not grow longer than a few feet. And no amount of research I could do provided me with a proper identification of this very strange creature."

Obviously Dr. Walford's sighting was of an unidentified sea creature of much less heroic proportions than many of the others we have reported in this chapter.

Sixty-Foot Monster Visits Nantucket Island

On May 12, 1964, three men aboard the Norwegian fishing boat *Blue Sea* reported that they had seen a 60-foot sea monster near Nantucket Island. Alf Wilemsen was the first to sight the strange creature and he yelled at his brother Jens and his partner Bjarne Houghan to look at the gigantic serpent swimming a few hundred feet away from their eighty-foot boat.

According to the Norwegian fishermen, the creature had an alligator-like head and a lobster-like tail. The body was dotted with black and white spots and the sea beast had a series of humps on its otherwise smooth back.

When the fishermen sailed into New Bedford harbor to report their remarkable sighting to the U.S. Bureau of Commercial Fisheries, a number of Coast Guard vessels and fishing boats set out to search for the huge serpent.

Three days later, the monster was spotted by the crew of the dragger *Friendship* in an area about ten miles from where the Norwegians had first seen it. The *Friendship* circled the massive creature twice so that the crew could get a good look at it. Captain Albert Pike gave a description of the alligator-headed serpent that exactly matched the one given by the Norwegians. The creature swam at a speed of five knots and did not bother to submerge once during the twenty minutes in which it was under observation by the *Friendship*. Unfortunately, the crewmen did not bring the sixty-foot sea beast back alive, but they did add another well-attested sighting to the history of sea serpent lore.

Are Sea Serpents Survivors of the Age of Reptiles?

Some scientists have entertained with a great degree of seriousness the popular speculation that the various sea serpents reported may be surviving members of one or more of the species of giant sea reptiles of the Mesozoic Age. The nineteenth-century naturalist Philip Gosse was an exponent of the plesiosaur theory to explain the sea serpent. Gosse argued that although the Mesozoic Age had ended tens of millions of years ago, there was not a reason why one of the descendants of the great sea reptiles could not have survived.

Our own century has produced evidence that makes it easier to give Gosse's theory added credence; for example, the discovery of crossopterygian fish off southeast Africa and India. The coelacanths, which are related to lungfishes and tetrapods, were believed to have been extinct since the end of the Cretaceous period. These fish that have survived almost unchanged for seventy million years—since before the Age of Reptiles—occasionally show up in local market places.

Other scientists champion the hypothesis that the sea serpent stories may be attributed to sightings of giant eels. Dr. Maurice Burton points out in his book *Living Fossils* that in recent years eel larvae three feet long have been discovered. If one compares the relative sizes of the larva and adults in eels of normal size, Burton states, there is no reason why such giant larvae should not attain a length of thirty-six feet when full grown.

At the beginning of the 1960s, Dr. Anton Brun of the University of Copenhagen, Denmark, announced the acquisition of an eel larva more than six feet long, with 450 vertebral plates. The only known eels have but 105 vertebral plates. Dr. Brun, once again working with the comparative sizes of larvae and adults in eels of normal size, reasoned that the larva might easily grow into a monster ninety feet long and weighing several tons.

A certain number of marine zoologists favor the existence of an as yet undiscovered aquatic mammal related to the whales as their candidate for the role of sea serpent. They contend that the hairy manes and flippers so often reported on the "serpents" would be most unlikely appendages for true reptiles. Also, quite convincingly, they argue that only a warm-blooded mammal would be able to survive in the icy waters of the North Atlantic where so many of the classic sea monster stories have had their origin.

Could sea monsters be species of plesiosaurs (ocean-dwelling dinosaurs) that survived whatever caused the mass extinction 65 million years ago (*Mary Evans Picture Library*)?

Other zoologists have expanded the theory of an unidentified giant sea mammal and combined it with another possible survivor of prehistoric times. They theorize that an ancient species of whale, the aeuglodon or basilosaurus, whose fossil remains are well known, would be well equipped for the role of sea monster. Basilosaurus is known to have been a huge beast with a slim, elongated body measuring over seventy feet in length. Its skull was long and low and the behemoth propelled itself by means of a single pair of fins located at its forward end. Basilosaurus is known to have survived into the Miocene Epoch, just over thirty million years ago. If crossopterygian fish have survived for more than seventy million years, it seems quite possible that such a comparative youngster as basilosaurus could still inhabit our seas.

The Sea Serpent Was Witnessed by Two Expert Naturalists

When the crew of the yacht *Valhalla* sighted a sea monster off Parahiba, Brazil, on December 7, 1905, it was fortunate to have among its passengers E.G.B. Meade-Waldo and Michael J. Nicoll, two expert naturalists, Fellows of the Zoological Society of Britain, who were taking part in a scientific expedition to the South Atlantic and

Indian Ocean. Meade-Waldo prepared a paper on the sighting, which he presented to the Society at its meeting on June 19, 1906. In his report, he told how his attention was first drawn to a "large brown fin … sticking out of the water, dark seaweed-brown in color, somewhat crinkled at the edge." The creature's fin was an astonishing six feet in length "and projected from eighteen inches to two feet from the water." Under the water and to the rear of the fin, the zoologist said that he could perceive "the shape of a considerable body. A great head and neck did not touch the [fin] in the water, but came out of the water in front of it, at a distance of certainly not less than eighteen inches, probably more. The neck appeared to be the thickness of a slight man's body, and from seven to eight feet was out of the water."

The head, according to Meade-Waldo's expert observation, had a "very turtle-like appearance, as had also the eye…. It moved its neck from side to side in a peculiar manner; the color of the head and neck was dark brown above and whitish below." Meade-Waldo also stated that since he saw the creature, he had reflected on its actual size and concluded that it "was probably considerably larger that it appeared at first."

Nicoll discussed the incident of the *Valhalla* sea monster sighting two years later in his book *Three Voyages of a Naturalist*: "I feel certain that [the creature] was not a reptile … but a mammal. The general appearance of the creature, especially the soft, almost rubber-like fin, gives one this impression."

A Harrowing Escape from a Sea Monster in Pensacola Bay

In the May 1965, issue of *Fate* magazine, Edward Brian McCleary told of his harrowing escape from a sea monster.

According to McCleary, he and four friends left on the pleasant Saturday morning of March 24, 1962, to go skin-diving at the sunken *Massachusetts* in Pensacola Bay, Florida. A sudden storm sent the boys into the ocean.

They clung desperately to their rubber raft. After the squall had subsided, a heavy, oppressive fog settled over the sea.

"The misty air became filled with the odor of dead fish," McCleary wrote. "Just then, about 40 feet away, we heard a tremendous splash. The waves reached the raft and broke over the side."

Whatever it was, the teenagers knew that no boat had made the sound. They heard the splash again, and through the fog they could make out what looked like a ten-foot pole with a bulbous head on top. It remained erect for a moment, then bent in the middle and dove under the surface. A sickening odor permeated the air.

From out of the fog came a strange, high-pitched whine. The five young men panicked, slipped on their fins, and dove into the water. They decided to keep together and try for the portion of the wrecked *Massachusetts* that remained above water.

In back of them, as they swam, they could hear "whatever it was" splashing and making a strange, hissing sound.

Then they heard a terrible scream. "It lasted maybe half a minute," McCleary remembered. "Then I heard Warren call, 'Hey! Help me! It's got Brad! I've got to get outta here.' His voice was cut off abruptly by a short cry."

The three remaining swimmers clustered together, not knowing how many feet of ocean separated them from whatever was down there waiting for them.

"Eric," McCleary gasped. "What happened to Larry? He was here a minute ago!"

The two boys dove for their friend, found nothing.

Then Eric got a cramp in his leg. McCleary wrapped his arm around his neck, and continued toward the wreck.

A wave broke and separated them. When McCleary surfaced, he saw Eric swimming ahead of him.

What happened next is the stuff of which lifelong nightmares are made.

"Right next to Eric that telephone-pole-like figure broke water," McCleary wrote. "I could see the long neck and two small eyes. The mouth opened and it bent over. It dove on top of Eric, dragging him under. I screamed and began to swim past the ship. My insides were shaking uncontrollably."

Somehow McCleary managed to swim the remaining two miles to shore. He remembers a series weird images—sprawling on the beach, stumbling to a tower of some sort, spending the night in a fitful slumber, then falling on his face before a group of boys. When next he awakened, he was in the Pensacola Naval Base hospital.

None of the journalists told all the facts of his escape from the hideous sea beast that took the lives of his four friends. Each of the various local newspapers carried the story of the tragedy, but they all attributed the boys' deaths to accidental drowning. The interviewing reporters told McCleary that the sea serpent was best left unmentioned.

McCleary wrote that he asked the director of the search and rescue units, E. B. McGovern, if he believed his story about the monster. According to McCleary, McGovern replied: "The sea has a lot of secrets. There are a lot of things we don't know about. People don't believe these things because they're afraid to. Yes, I believe you. But there's not much else I can do."

Ten-Foot Pickled Sea Serpent Head Was Reclaimed by the Sea

If the fickle and often cruel gods of the sea had been kinder to the whaler *Mononga-hela* the mystery of the sea serpent and its true identity might have been solved over 170 years ago.

On January 13, 1852, Captain Seabury, master of the whaler *Monongahela*, brought his telescope to bear on a monstrous creature thrashing about in apparent agony. The captain's immediate deduction was that they had come upon a whale that had been wounded by the harpoons of another whaler's longboats and was now dying.

Twentieth-century whalers sometimes told stories of running across sea monsters. On occasion, though, the sea creature may have been the victim of a harpoon (*Mary Evans Picture Library*).

Captain Seabury ordered three longboats over the side to end the beast's pain, and he was in the first boat as it pulled alongside the massive thing that he still believed was a wounded whale. The instant a harpoon struck home, a nightmarish head ten feet long rose out of the water and lunged at the boats. Two of the longboats were capsized in seconds.

Before the monster submerged, the terrified whalers realized at once that they were dealing with a sea creature the likes of which they had never seen.

Unfurling her sails to catch what little wind there was, the *Monongahela* managed to come alongside the capsized longboats and began to pick up the seamen who were bobbing in the water, fearing that the hideous beast might at any moment resurface and make a meal of them.

Captain Seabury made the harpoon line as fast as possible on the vessel, though he couldn't be certain that his monstrous prey was still impaled by the harpoon.

The *Rebecca Sims*, under the command of Captain Gavitt, pulled alongside her sister ship, and the crews of the two vessels began discussing the strange monster that they had encountered.

The next morning, the crewmen had pulled in only about half of the line when the massive carcass suddenly popped to the surface. It was much greater in length than the ship, which measured 100 feet from stem to stern, and it had a thick body that was about 50 feet in diameter. Its color was a brownish gray with a light stripe about three feet wide running its full length. Its neck was ten feet around, and it supported a grotesque head that was ten feet long and shaped like that of a gigantic alligator. The astounded crewmen counted 94 teeth in its ghastly jaws—and each of the three-inch, saber-like teeth were hooked backward, like those of a snake.

When the practical Yankee whalers tried to render the creature as if it were their usual prey, they were disappointed to find that the behemoth possessed only tough skin and no blubber.

Captain Seabury was fully aware of the ridicule accorded to sailing masters and their crews who claimed to have encountered "sea serpents," so he gave orders that the hideous head be chopped off and placed in a huge pickling vat in order to preserve it until they returned to New Bedford. In addition, he wrote a detailed report of their harpooning the sea monster and he provided a complete description of the thing.

Since Captain Gavitt and his crew were homeward bound, Captain Seabury gave him the report in order to prepare New Bedford for the astonishing exhibit that he and his men would bring with them upon their own return.

If only Captain Seabury would have transferred the grisly head to Captain Gavitt's vessel along with his report of the monster, the doubting world would have had its first mounted sea serpent's head over 170 years ago.

Captain Seabury's account of the incredible sea serpent arrived safely in New Bedford and was entered into the records along with the personal oath of Captain Gavitt. But the *Monongahela* never returned to port with its incredible cargo. Years later her name board was found on the shore of Umnak Island in the Aleutians.

SHADOW PEOPLE—
MYSTERIOUS ENTITIES
WITH MISSIONS UNKNOWN

The first time that I was asked about The Shadow People was in the late 1990s. I was appearing as a guest on a popular late night talk show. The host prefaced his question by saying that since I had been exploring the shadowy corners of reality for decades, I would be able to define a Shadow Person for the listening audience.

I immediately responded that Native American tribal traditionalists had many stories about such beings. I recalled the time when a medicine priest had asked me if I ever saw shadowy or blurry figures out of the corners of my eyes, in my peripheral vision. I replied that I had seen such figures many times.

"Over your right or left shoulder?" he asked me.

I gave his query a moment or two of thought, then replied that I had always seen these dark figures over my right shoulder.

He smiled and replied that was a good thing. "If you see such a being over your right shoulder, that may be your totem, your spiritual guide watching over you," he explained. "If you see the being over your left shoulder, that may be the Coyote Trickster or the death spirit. If it is the death spirit, then you may ask of him any question—and he must tell the truth. The death spirit will always answer all questions truthfully, because he knows that he will always have the final word."

Inadvertently, I had caused a small panic among the program's listeners, which I did my best to quell before the radio show ended. Dozens of people had been calling into the program to report their encounters with Shadow People—and many of them had seen the swiftly moving dark figures over their *left* shoulders. I spent the remainder of my time on the program assuring people that it was highly unlikely that they had seen the spirit of death, but they may have seen a rather ordinary spirit or one of an infinite variety of entities from the Shadow World.

Although there are many theories that seek to identify the mysterious Shadow People, I keep being drawn back to the many legends of the entities in Native American traditions.

The Three Sisters of Death are Shadow People who are harbingers of death among Native American tribes of the Southwest. This "portrait" was painted for this book by Apache Medicine woman Little Butterfly, a well-known artist, storyteller, and healer, who is also known as Priscilla Garduno or Sister Wolf.

In 1968, there were so many reports of Native American spirits appearing in homes in the greater metropolitan area of Los Angeles that the Los Angeles *Herald Examiner* assigned reporter Wanda Sue Parrott to write a special article on the phenomenon.

After describing a number of first-person accounts in an article for the "California Living" section of the newspaper, Ms. Parrott wrote that many area residents—men, women, and children alike—had shared in the ghostly Native American experience in their homes. Shadowy figures, yet identifiable as being dressed in traditional tribal clothing, had been sighted in bedrooms and living rooms at all hours of the day and night.

When one percipient found herself so unnerved by the manifestation of a Native American ghost in her home that she consulted a psychiatrist, she was told that there was nothing wrong with her; many of the doctor's patients had had similar experiences.

Nearly all the witnesses agreed that while their sudden appearances had been startling, the spirits seemed friendly and that they stayed for only a few moments before fading away.

In a number of cases, Ms. Parrott found that the percipients felt that the Shadow figures of Native American spirits had come to protect them and warn them of approaching danger.

There are, of course, reports of Shadow People manifesting all over the world. Perhaps one reason why so many individuals in the United States are encountering Shadow People lies in the oft-stated observation that the portals between the worlds of the spiritual and the material are becoming thinner.

Another reason may lie in the warning that Chief Seathe (Seattle) gave the white man when he learned that his people had been cheated out of their lands by the Treaty of Point Elliott in 1855. Chief Seattle knew that there was a higher law than that possessed by the white men who had stolen from his tribe. Calmly, but with enormous resolution of spirit, he pronounced a prophetic warning that the white conquerors would always have to deal with the red man—if not in the flesh, than as phantoms:

> Every part of this country is sacred to my people. Every hillside, every valley, every plain and grove has been hallowed by some fond memory or some sad experience of my people.
>
> When the last red man shall have perished from the earth and his memory among the white men shall have become a myth, these shores shall swarm with the invisible dead of my tribe.... At night when the streets of your cities and villages shall be silent, and you think them deserted, they will throng with the returning hosts that once filled and still love this beautiful land.
>
> The white man shall never be alone … for the dead are not altogether powerless. Dead, did I say? There is no death, only a change of worlds.

Perhaps a large number of Shadow People reports are spiritual embodiments of Chief Seattle's grim reminder to those who now occupy the land that once belonged to so many vanquished tribes—"these shores shall swarm with the invisible dead … for the dead are not altogether powerless."

The Ghost of Bear Lake

BY KEVIN THORSHEIM

North central Iowa is full of rolling hills, serene pastures, endless blue skies and restless spirits.

Our home lies three miles northeast of Forest City in a grove of ancient oaks. We are fairly isolated in our beautiful exile from town, but it wasn't always that way.

The white settlers came to this area and established a town in the early 1850s. The townspeople soon discovered a body of water outside of their new community. They called it Bear Lake and enjoyed its bounty of fish and lazy Sunday afternoons of row boating and town picnics. The local Indian population didn't mind these incursions of privacy as they only happened once or twice a week in good weather.

The storm lit up her room and framed a semi-transparent figure near her door. It was the same Indian woman she had seen the month before!

The lake was about three hundred yards from where our house now sits but it was drained during the Depression years to provide irrigation canals for the farm fields in response to the drought condition that plagued the rural areas of the time.

My parents built the house in 1973 and after twenty years sold it to us. Time went by uneventfully until a warm summer night in 1995.

Our daughter Jenna was ten years old and tired after a day of outside activity. It was around ten o'clock when she decided to go to bed. A few brief minutes later and she fell into a deep sleep.

All was quiet until 1:00 A.M. when she woke up from hearing the dog bark outside her window. Her eyes cleared from sleep just enough that she could make out the figure of an Indian woman by the foot of her bed.

Jenna pulled her knees to her chest and tried to scream, but her voice was paralyzed in her throat. The specter stood silent, staring blankly at her. She appeared to be about twenty-five years old, gaunt with hair tied back in a braid. She wore a tan deerskin dress with a small amount of beadwork on the front.

Jenna knew this was not a dream and reached for her blanket and pulled it up to her eyes as the uninvited guest faded away before her. She decided to keep this to herself and avoid ridicule from her younger brother. After several attempts she went back to sleep.

Days drifted by without incident until the middle of August. A storm had brewed that afternoon and unleashed its lightning later that evening.

It was past midnight when a loud clap of thunder woke Jenna from a sound slumber. The storm lit up her room and framed a semi-transparent figure near her door. It was the same Indian woman she had seen the month before! This time the spirit seemed to acknowledge her presence and appeared to be studying her features.

I worried that the storm had frightened her and quickly went to her room and opened her door. As soon as my hand touched the doorknob, the specter again vanished. Once more our daughter stayed silent on the episode.

It wasn't long until September came, and our children went back to school. Their time was consumed with study and sports during the day and homework in the evening.

Late one evening my wife and I were watching a movie on television when we heard Jenna yelling from her room. I thought she was only having a bad dream, but my wife sensed more urgency in her voice and went to investigate. As she opened the door she saw our daughter sitting up on her bed yelling "stay away from me!"

After several minutes of trying to calm her down she cried and related all three instances to us.

It took a long time, but I finally talked with one of the oldest residents in town and hesitantly described the happenings of the last few months. Instead of thinking we were crazy, he related that as a boy he frequently went to Bear Lake with his father and heard the stories of the Indians who lived by the lake year 'round. It didn't surprise him that we would come into contact with spirits as their tents were pitched on what is now our property!

Once he had asked his father how long the Indians had lived there. His father said an old member of the tribe told him, "We lived here forever; no one remembers how long. We live here, we die here, many stay here."

Some people believe there is only one reality, the here and now. They fail to realize there is more than one existing at the same time. To fully accept the concept of plural existence you need to experience it firsthand. Then you too will be a believer. Sometimes those from the other reality visibly step into our world.

Kevin Thorsheim is the author of Ten Tall Tales of the Old West *and an international award-winning poet. He lives outside of Forest City with his wife Maria and several other Spirits.*

Shadow Beings of the Dark

Since there are so many definitions of who or what a Shadow Being may be, I sought the opinions of the always well-informed Staff of Haunted America Tours, who provided the following insight into these creatures of the Dark.

Call them evil, or the work of the devil, but the inanimate comes alive in the black of night. The Darklings, the shadows, the dead sneak near to you as you breathe evenly and try to sleep.

Accounts of the essence of The Dark as individual beings typically describe Shadow People as deep non-reflective black humanoid silhouettes. Sometimes these beings have no discernible mouths, noses, or facial expressions, though at times those features might be all that you actually see in the darkness.

Many accounts also exist of these entities being child-sized humanoids or shapeless masses that sometimes change to more human-like forms or animals. The eyes are usually not mentioned as being discernible, but in some reports glowing red, white, or blue eyes are mentioned.

Movement is often described as being very quick and disjointed. Some witnesses describe this movement as though the shadow entities they have seen "danced" from one place to another.

Rarely, are Shadow People seen "standing" in the middle of doorways. Some accounts describe what appears to be the outline of a cloak, and in some instances the outline of a 1930s style fedora hat. This last type is referred as the "Dark hat-man" or "The Darkling King."

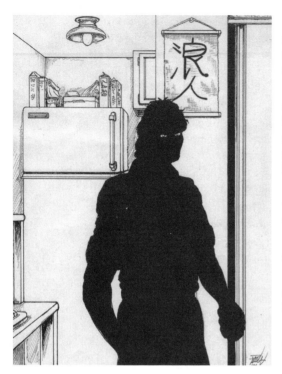

Some people who have seen them describe the Shadow People as non-reflective, black humanoid silhouettes. Sometimes these beings have no discernible mouths, noses, or facial expressions, though at times those features might be seen in the darkness (*art by Dan Wolfman Allen*).

The Dark has also been called "The Wight," from the Middle English word wiht, used to describe a creature or a living being. It is akin to Old High German wiht, meaning a creature or thing.

The evil of the Darklings over the centuries are based on supernatural shadow-like creatures of both modern folklore and traditional Native American beliefs. These creatures are known to attempt to pull you from your room your bed at night, perhaps to strangle or rape a victim.

The Darklings can also bite you, hit you, hurt you, and have been known to poke your eyes out as you sleep.

They have been known to kill infants as they sleep in their mothers arms or suckle at their breast.

They can scratch you to the bone, and there are tales of them even stealing kidneys, thought to be what they love to eat, from sleeping victims.

In the darkness they are the strongest paranormal entity you can encounter.

According to folklore, they may appear at first as dark forms in the peripheries of people's vision as they begin to haunt them. If they find no reason to haunt you, then they seem to disintegrate or move between walls, when noticed.

Reports of Shadow People occupy a similar position in the popular consciousness as ghost sightings, but differ in that Shadow People are not reported as having human features, wearing modern/period clothing, or attempting to communicate.

Witnesses also do not report the same feelings of being in the presence of something that was once human. A Shadow Person has never walked the earth as a human. Some individuals have described being menaced, chased, or in some rare instances, attacked by Shadow People.

Life in a Haunted House in Birmingham, Michigan

BY ALEX ZAVATONE

The house was painted yellow when I lived there in 1982. At that time, I was a sophomore in high school—I didn't drink, do drugs, and was a normal 15-year-old kid.

The first night my family lived in the house, all the lights went out in the house except in the garage below the small attic and the attic. The door to the small attic would slowly open with a creak and then within a minute, slam shut.

Often, when in the house and after standing still, I would get a feeling like someone cold was walking up behind me and putting their hand right over my shoulder. Quickly turning around would make the feeling go away, then it would settle in again. Like someone was right behind you and you turn around and they are not there.

When eating dinner, the sound of someone bouncing a ball would be heard over our heads. Like when you drop a ping-pong ball and it quickly speeds up its bouncing—but this would go on for several minutes.

Twice when entering the garage, a large rusty three inch nail fell out of a nailless, stucco ceiling, leveled out and zipped in front of me, hitting the garage divider, bouncing off a box and hitting the floor with a ping.

Then it disappeared.

The amazing thing was that the nail took exactly the same path both times it happened to me. There was no hole in the ceiling left by the nail either.

This happened to my father once, but he was able to pick up the nail.

Twice while sleeping, odd things happened in my room. One night, I woke up and saw my closet doors opening and closing. Realizing that there was nothing I could do to change things, I closed my eyes and went back to sleep.

The second incident was a simple "there is someone walking in my room." I could hear footsteps and boards creaking as if someone was entering my room. Again, I just went back to sleep.

While playing on the lake ice with my friend Kevin and his dog, we decided to play at my house. I warned him that it was haunted.

When we approached the house, it took some effort to get his dog into the front yard, but a taunting with a tennis ball eventually got the critter onto the grass. Finally able to grab the dog, we took him onto the front porch where he fought against us strongly. From there, Kevin took the dog by the collar and I opened the front door.

His dog froze, looked up the staircase inside, whimpered, backed off the foundation, taking us with him, almost dragging us off the lawn. We couldn't hold on, and the dog just stayed in the street, never coming close to the house or the lawn. Baffled and not seeing any spectres, Kevin and I entered the house and got cookies.

I had another friend named Justin who had a beer can collection like I did. I kept mine in the small attic and therefore did not go there much. Knowing that if I invited Justin over, the ghost would pay more attention to someone new, I told him about the haunted house and we went over to check out my beer can collection.

Justin reacted rather well. He often got a surprised look on his face and tried to brush something off his shoulder. Three times I asked him if he wanted to leave until he strongly told me that he would tell me when he wanted to go.

Three minutes later, he asked to leave.

As we went down the stairs, I asked him if he had felt the ghost touching his back. Abruptly, he turned to me and without answering my question, told me never, *ever* to take him back to that room again.

Years later, I described to him exactly what had happened to him that day, and he was amazed that I was exactly right: "It as if you're walking down a deserted road with no one near for thousands of miles—and yet you know there is someone right behind you."

Nonchalantly, I told him that I lived there for a year and was well accustomed to the feelings of that house.

When we moved to the house, we had a cat. The cat would normally be a "house cat" and stay around the house with a few late night jaunts. The critter's behavior changed, and it rarely spent time around the house—and it finally left.

Once, my father and I entered the room next to the room that went to the small attic and felt a presence. We decided to lighten up the atmosphere and started paying attention to the ghost and actively speaking about being nice to the ghost and maybe "take a ghost to lunch." One half-hour after we started, without a word, we stopped. An ominous hostile "stop NOW" was the general feeling that came about the room. We both got up and left. I asked my father, who was a former government agent and not a wimp, "let's never do that again. All right?" He quickly agreed.

Coincidentally, at the time that we lived in the house the motion picture *Poltergeist* (1982) was released to theatres. I definitely went to see that movie.

I asked my dad if anything happened to him that he hadn't told me about. He recounted a story of a few weeks earlier when a wastepaper basket flew across the room.

Up until that point, no one had seen our poltergeist, and we were set on staying in that house because it was ours. It's just what you do.

Late one night, I lay down to sleep for about ten seconds and then suddenly opened my eyes. What I saw could not exist in a three-dimensional world.

A gray object entered my room and flew up into the ceiling above it. I actually get chills just recounting this story. The object seemed to be a gray blob with enough "tv screen fuzz" so that it blended in with the background but was still visible. When it entered the room, it came inside about four to six feet, then went straight up into the ceiling. Strangely, it entered at two separate points. It did not stretch; it did not visibly separate: it just entered the ceiling at two separate locations at the same time without deforming itself.

Slightly stunned, I realized that I'd seen *it*. This was not a window reflection of car lights.

Realizing that there was nothing I could do about it, I went to sleep and told my parents about it the next day.

The final incident was the killer. I had left Justin's house across town where I had stayed while my parents were on vacation in Hilton Head. At the time I left, the weather was lovely and sunny. But in the driving five miles to our house, the weather turned sour. When we got to my house, large 40-foot trees were getting whipped around and the sky was gray. It just didn't make sense that the weather could change that much in five miles. I have never seen anything else like it since.

The strange and inexplicable events at the house in Birmingham, Michigan, led temporary resident Alex Zavatone to believe there was a shadowy presence there (*iStock*).

I expected to meet my parents, but to my disappointment they were late—and I was to face the house alone with this big storm brewing.

Walking up the gravel driveway to the back of the house, I could swear the house was looking at me.

Once inside, and to my horror, I found the same situation that had happened on our first night in the house was happening now. The lights were out in the majority of the house.

After 45 minutes and starting to panic, I began to feel the cold presence come up behind me—and all I could do was move about the kitchen to get it away from me.

If I left through the dining room, I would have to go out the front door—and I know I would have looked up the stairs to the second floor. Somehow, I was terrified that something was waiting up there and if I looked at it, it would be game over.

I could go out a window in the kitchen, but that was too difficult. The back door seemed like the only way out, and I would have to go by the green door down to the basement, open one door and then push open another.

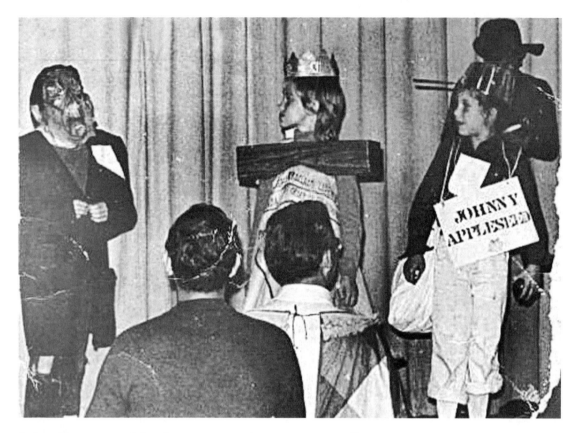

Robert Cheeseman said that this picture was taken in 1975 at a Halloween costume contest held in his elementary school. Robert is dressed as Frankenstein (far left). "One day, maybe ten years later," Robert said, "I came across it and as I was looking at it a little voice in my head said 'Hey, what is that?' I looked closer at the picture and saw that there was something behind 'Johnny Appleseed.' I got a magnifying glass and thought I saw eyes and a hand and what looked like a beam of light going into Johnny Appleseed's neck. I also saw that the 'person' behind Johnny had no legs. The curtains were not disturbed, so the person wasn't standing behind the curtain peeking out" (*photo courtesy Robert Cheeseman*).

It got darker, stormier, and I got even more scared. At this point I realized that I could call the realtor because she said if there was any problem living in the house, we should call (I suspected she knew something). Almost in tears, I called her and told her the situation I was in—wind whipping around the house, most of the lights out, and some cold spirit trying to walk up behind me alone without my parents. Hanging up the phone, I ran towards the back door, expecting the cellar door to burst open.

Fumbling with the internal door, I was able to pull it towards me. Then I ran again and pushed the second back door open as I ran outside.

The sky was a more violent gray, wind whipping more fiercely, and I swore the different windows of the house were looking at me. Cold and wet, I went back inside—unsure why I did. Inside, I yelled at the spirit to leave me alone, to stop following me.

I was in the kitchen for at least two hours before I heard my parents' car pull up.

Next day, the electrician said that we had partial voltage coming to the house. I asked him if that would have dimmed all of the lights instead of knocking half of them out in the house.

In any case, we moved soon after that to a house in the subdivision below the south course of the Oakland Hills Golf Club.

We had no bizarre occurrences as in the previous house, and we all realized just how foolish it was to stay in the yellow house. We wondered as soon as we left, just why the hell we stayed there. It seemed like someone wanted us to stay there to have someone on whom to vent its aggressions.

Once I went back to the neighbor who had always checked up on me. I asked him about the history of the house, if anyone died there or was buried in the backyard or whatever.

He told me that an older couple had lived there and had a rough and violent relationship. He told me that someone may have died or was murdered in the house.

I remembered a small patch of what seemed like fish tank gravel at the end of the driveway, and the solution occurred to me. "She's buried at the end of the driveway isn't she?" I asked the neighbor.

"Yes, I think she is," was his response. I really wished that he had told me this before.

All I can come up with is that the older family who lived there before us, had lived an abusive life, and no matter what happened, the wife hated men in general. She took that hatred to the grave with her and that grave was on the property. Her spirit was still in the house, and she influenced us to stay there while she took out her aggressions on all the men in the house or who would enter the house.

As a result of living in that house, I have a new saying. "You never know what it's like unless you've lived through it yourself."

The Ghost in the Hunters' Cabin

BY MARY CROFT

In October 1972, my friends, Suzanne and Jimmy, and I jumped into Jimmy's Datsun 240Z to drive 150 miles north to Huntsville, Ontario, to spend Thanksgiving weekend appreciating the autumn colors of the trees. I was stowed in the back of the car amongst the cases for most of the drive. Suzanne and Jimmy got to see where we were going and I got to see where we'd been. Due to poor planning, we didn't arrive at our tiny cabin in the woods until after dark and we were cold and hungry so we built a fire in the stove and ate everything we could get our mitts on.

Where each of us slept in the cabin is significant to our respective experiences of having been "haunted" by a ghost that night. I chose the cot between the door and the stove in the kitchen, Jimmy chose the bedroom down the short hallway, and Suzanne was in the bedroom at the end of the hall.

Nothing keeps me awake so I went off to sleep straight away, after we retired from our chatter that went on until eleven or so. The fire offered enough heat that I knew I wouldn't be cold, even after it died.

At 4:20 A.M., I was awakened by I don't know what. I heard myself answer "yes" as I supposed that Suzanne was standing beside my bed addressing me. When I saw that she was not there, I was surprised because I instinctively felt as if there were some-one standing there. I was not alarmed, yet, I was curious to know what could have awakened me. I am just not one to wake-up during the night. I noticed the fire was out so it could not have been crackling or burning wood which awoke me and I was not cold so I was in no discomfort. I just felt certain that I had felt someone's presence. My only concern was that now I was wide awake and I might lie awake for three hours waiting for my friends to rise before I could do anything. I didn't even have anything to read, not that there were any suitable reading lamps by which to read, if I did. I felt as if I might be in for a dreary two or three hours.

I was not sleepy. I looked at my watch again, which I could see by the modicum of light emitted by the smoldering embers. It was now 4:27 A.M. Seven minutes had passed. Seconds later I heard what is classically referred to as a "blood-curdling scream."

My breathing stopped; my heart pounded. It was Suzanne screaming from her room. I have never heard anything more frightening. I was too terrified to go to her so I yelled back at her, "Suzanne!", hoping that if she were having a nightmare, my call-ing her name would awaken her.

But, no. She was screaming, "Jimmy, come here! Jimmy! Quick! Jimmy!" Clear-ly, Jimmy was awake and also too terrified to go in because he kept yelling back to her, "Suzanne, what is it?"

I yelled at Jimmy to go to her because I was not capable of moving. After a moment, which seemed like a dozen, he ran into her room. All I heard from Suzanne was, "A MAN! A MAN!" and she was frantic.

Suzanne is no sissy. She's as rugged as anyone, not easily perturbed or scared. I was stunned by her carrying on like this, and I sensed that she had a right to be terri-fied so I felt terrified right along with her. Jimmy brought her out and we all curled up on my bed. She was closing in on calming down, yet, was still visibly shaken.

She described her horror. "For some reason I just woke up and looked out the door of my room. Silhouetted against the light from the embers, I saw the image of a stocky man standing in my doorway. I was certain that I was awake but I made a point of sitting up and rubbing my eyes because I was convinced that I must have dreamt it. He was still there. That's when I started screaming."

Jimmy looked as frightened as she did and I'm sure I, too, was pale.

"It's a good thing I was already awake. I hate to think how I might have respond-ed if I'd been *awakened* by your screaming. I probably would have leapt from that cot never to be seen again," I commented.

"Ditto!" added Jimmy. Both Suzanne and I looked askance at him.

Visibly shaken, she screamed frantically, "A MAN! A MAN!" (*iStock*).

"How long were you awake before you heard Suzanne screaming?"

"A couple of minutes."

"I was awake seven minutes, and I know this because I had been looking at my watch. Whatever it was that woke me, also woke you about three minutes later, and went on to scare the life out of Suzanne."

"You're making too much out of this," Jimmy scoffed.

"Well, why were you awake?" I asked.

"I had a frightful dream! I dreamt that an aeroplane went out of control and crashed through the trees and into our cabin. I woke up in a sweat. I never have bad dreams."

This was now becoming an adventure which began to intrigue me because I say that there are no coincidences and Jimmy's dream supported my contention.

We made tea and the sun began to lighten the room. While Jimmy made fun of me, Suzanne was encouraging me to come up with something that made sense of this episode. The more Suzanne referred to the "man" in her doorway as a "ghost," the more we lost Jimmy's participation in the mystery. I asked him if he had any faith in ghosts and his look of disdain told me that he had not.

Mary Croft (*photo courtesy Mary Croft*).

I asked Suzanne the same and she said, "Definitely, and if I ever saw one, it would scare the life out of me!"

I added, "Which it did."

I explained that I felt certain that after some people leave their bodies at death, particularly under duress or sudden circumstances, they hang around not knowing what to do because they don't even know what happened, let alone that they are dead. Maybe the man in the doorway was one of these unfortunates who just didn't have a grasp of his circumstances.

That's when Jimmy decided to go out for a walk.

As he was leaving, I asked, "Don't you think it was the 'man' who woke you up?"

"No, it was a bad dream," he called back.

I had not moved from my cot, and Suzanne was perched on one of those little, painted, runged, wooden chairs which people had in their cottage kitchens during the '50s. Her feet were up on the rungs and she held her tea in her lap.

Suddenly, she toppled from the chair, just catching herself by putting her feet onto the floor as her tea splashed all over her.

She looked at me as if she had been insulted and asked, "Did you see that?"

"How could I miss it. What happened?"

"I didn't move! Someone shook the back of my chair!"

I had been in conversation with her and can attest to the fact that I had my eyes on her the entire time. Without a doubt she had been shaken by an external force.

Quickly, she joined me on my cot, which caused me to query my *own* safety until I realized that I was in no danger based upon my thoughts about ghosts. As in *all* of life, experience is a result of *interpretation* of perception of events. Perception itself is a phenomenon influenced by a belief developed from a previous experience. It remains cyclic until we can perceive each as unique and 'now'. This can be done only by no longer referring to the previous experience. Typically, this takes a clearing of the emotion attached to the experience, since all perception is influenced by emotion—conscious or not.

My interpretation of ghosts happens to be that they are non-threatening, due to my investigation of information about ghosts and my conclusion that they are fascinating and benign, unless they're not, which would be a brand new perception for me. So, when I perceived the ghost, whilst I was asleep, my interpretation was that of "non-threatening."

This spirit of a man really did exist. It had probably been hanging around this area for many years. It ventured in, seeking either knowledge about its situation which it has been unable to understand since its untimely death and/or it was seeking companionship from us, or it was a poltergeist, which is just a confused, angry spirit that creates physical chaos due to frustration of being out of control of its existence. It entered the cabin at 4:20 A.M. I detected its presence, yet, had no fear because I thought it was Suzanne and also because I would have had no fear of one of these entities if I *did* encounter one.

I had previously given this some thought. It knew that I could not be provoked; in fact, I had compassion for it.

Unable to get any response from me, albeit, it seems as if its intent were to solicit fear and ultimately did, it moved into the next room. Its presence woke Jimmy about three minutes after it woke me. Jimmy interpreted the discomfort as a bad dream, not only because he has no faith in ghosts but also because he is certain he was dreaming of an aeroplane. The spirit did have an effect upon him, yet, probably not the effect it wanted.

Still bound by some sort of frustration, it then went to visit Suzanne who was only too willing to perceive it visually because she was adamant that not only did ghosts exist but also they would frighten her. Her declaration and her definition created her experience of this spirit. Suzanne corroborated my theory due to the timing and our respective attitudes about spirits and our subsequent personal experiences.

Jimmy came back in and we informed him of my explanation of the night's adventure. He continued to disagree that any of this was possible.

We packed up and … when the owner of the cabins appeared, I began to ask him some questions about the place. "Who owned the land before you?"

He replied, "No one; it was Crown land until I purchased it about twenty-five years ago (c.1947)."

"Any interesting stories about the woods or the lake?"

"When it was Crown land, it used to be a great hunting and fishing region. Fisherman used to fly in part way, then boat the remainder, and camp in this area. About forty years ago, an aeroplane with a couple of fishermen aboard flew in too far and crashed through the trees onto this very site."

As he said this, he glanced in the direction of our cabin.

I smiled at Jimmy who was now wide-eyed and pale. "Let's get out of here!" he muttered.

Eight months later, I moved into Suzanne's flat. The entire time I lived with her, she slept with her light on so, finally, I asked her why.

"I've slept with my light on, every night—ever since I saw that ghost in the cabin in the woods."

Mary Croft may be contacted at www.spiritualeconomicsnow.net.

The Ghost Walkers of Hawaii: A Conversation with Norma Joiner

Over the years, Sherry and I have become dear friends with Norma Joiner, a Hawaiian, who is extremely sensitive. Her granddaughter, Carissa, is very gifted and has been featured on a number of national television programs dealing with the paranormal. You may contact Norma at http://www.TheGuardianSpirit.com and also check their pages on Native Americans.

Brad Steiger: Native Hawaiian spirits are very powerful.

Norma Joiner: Yes, very powerful and through the years I've learned to respect all there is, to never go beyond boundaries. It's the culture thing where the Hawaiians believed in "good" and "evil." There are those who dwell in the dark side and when people deal with "evil" they just wreak havoc on themselves.

Brad: Once when I was visiting Honolulu, some construction workers moved a Pohaku stone for a new shopping center in Honolulu, and they severely suffered the consequences. Kahuna priests and priestess had warned them not to dig there, but they just laughed at native superstition. They weren't laughing after all their power machinery broke down day after day after day.

Norma: Oh, yes, there are many stories such as those. You grant respect no matter what.

By the way, Lori also has a story about a large Pohaku stone that was right in the front of their house. They were told *never* move that stone. Some workers had to do something in their yard and they moved the stone. Her mother was very upset about it. The next morning, the stone was back in its original spot—and today it is still there in the front yard!

Brad: What is your belief about the Night Marchers?

Norma: I believe in them even though I've not encountered them. I know these stories about such encounters are not made up. I truly believe there are souls who keep their old ways. I don't believe they are here to harm or hurt. They just want to keep their old ways as they know it. Same with the Native Americans. I feel that many times it's the humans "now" who interfere with their own thoughts and create the problems. They go beyond what is "common" sense. I guess my Japanese grandmother was influential in always telling me never to be afraid of ghosts. It's humans who will bring harm. Being "human" I can get pretty freaked, but it's because I get all the signals of tingly, cold sensation and the hair standing up on the back of my neck!!!

Brad: I have found similar "marchers" in a few other cultures.

Norma: Are they the Old Ones? Yes, I believe they are referred to as the "ancients."

Brad: Are they basically bad (I didn't say evil), good, or indifferent toward us?

Norma: You know, my sense of it all is that it all depends on the person. I don't know if I would use "indifferent," because I feel there's a reason they show themselves. I don't think we've even begun to tap into the mystery that is beyond the six senses. It's something we must seek out and be in awe of what we find. My journey through this life time has been one of inspiration and so much learning and opening up of my inner self.

Brad: What/whoever they are, they can be very frightening.

Norma: Yes, I believe "frightening," because it's touching an unknown … like sticking your hand out and it disappears into another dimension. Like what I said on that ABC special—and I believe it came from the guardians—we're here, accept us. Just because you cannot see us with your eyes, doesn't mean we don't exist. So what dimension are we talking about? It doesn't matter how many there are. We're not here to prove anything. We are here to share what we have experienced, because each person has to learn it all on their own. All I know is my journey is to share the fact that it is possible that there is something more than what we see as physical.

The stories of Hawaiian spirits can be quite unnerving, and there are many areas where they are very powerful.

My father also worked as a yardman at the famous Allerton Gardens. We used to take our picnic stuff to sit on the beach. Mr. Allerton used to let us in, and we would tour the gardens. I used to feel "spooked" whenever we toured the place. I always felt like "eyes" were watching us. My father told us to always stay on the path and not to wander off. When we got older, he told us that along the hillside were burial plots, old Hawaiian graves.

I felt the same way at the famous Waimea Falls park. Rudy Mitchell, the archeologist there back in the 1980s worked constantly to do digs. One time he told me to go to a certain area and walk a certain path. He took me there and waited at the bottom. I walked the path, and soon I was hearing sounds and conversations. I was getting spooked. When I got back to him, he laughed because he could tell that I heard and saw things. Not only that, I felt like I was being watched the whole time! There were several unmarked graves in the area, but spirits roamed there so there was a sign and barrier so people wouldn't go into that area and disturb them. Dr. Mitchell said he used to work late at night, and sometimes the security people would talk about seeing people and hearing voices. Aloha!

THUNDERBIRDS—GIANT BIRDS OF LEGEND THAT ARE REAL

The Chippewa have a tradition that in the time-before-time began there existed a bird of supreme majesty that descended to Earth, which was then only a vast expanse of water. The bird's eyes were fire; its glance was lightning; and the motion of its wings rippled the air with thunder. When its talons touched the water, the Earth Mother arose from the deep waters, bringing with her to the surface all manner of animals.

Many other Native American tribes have traditions that tell of birds as agents of creation, and the winged giants became objects of religious ceremony among many of the native people. The journal of an early Roman Catholic priest records that the first time the tribal members of the California mission that he served saw the representation of a dove over the altar, they asked if it was the Christian thunderbird.

For hundreds of years, it is not only the Native Americans who have claimed to have seen thunderbirds circling above them in the skies. Frontiersmen and settlers couldn't ignore them, and eventually, newspapers began to take these accounts seriously enough to begin to report them.

A Flying Serpent with a Forked Tongue

The *Bedford Times-Independent*, Bedford, Iowa, August 11, 1887, reported that a man named Lee Corder encountered a flying serpent "writhing and twisting, with protruding eyes and forked tongue. Great scales, which glistened in the sunlight, covered its huge body, which appeared to be flat and nearly a foot in width."

The newspaper described Mr. Corder as a man of "unimpeachable veracity," and goes on to state that he, and those with him, watched the flying serpent with "awe and

The Chippewa tribe has a tradition that in the time-before-time there existed a bird of supreme majesty that descended to Earth. The bird's eyes were fire; its glance was lightning; and the motion of its wings rippled the air with thunder (**art by Ricardo Pustanio**).

astonishment," as the creature landed in a cornfield, a few rods distant with a dull thud. As the witnesses observed the creature, they all professed to be so frightened that none of them wished to block its path. It was permitted to pass on its way "unmolested" and no one attempted to halt its wish to return to the sky.

A Winged Monster with Horns and an Alligator's Jaw

Three years later, in October 1890, citizens of Independence, Iowa, reported seeing a monster with "wings, a monstrous head with horns, a mouth like an alligator's. Its body was greenish in color and covered with shiny scales; its eyes glare like an electric arc light; and it yells in a tone that sounds like a combination of the roar of a lion and the scream of a wildcat."

A Green-Colored Flying Monster— Half-Giant Turkey and Half-Duck

According to the November 20, 1930 issue of the Cairo, Illinois, *Democrat* James Henry, of Mound City shot an unknown bird on the Kentucky shore, opposite that city, which was described as being larger than an ostrich, and weighed one hundred and four pounds. The newspaper went on to describe that "the body of this wonderful bird is covered with snow-white down, and its head is of a fiery red. The wings, of deep black, measured fifteen feet from tip to tip, and the bill, of a yellow color, twenty-four inches. Its legs are slender and sinewy, pea green in color, and measure forty-eight inches in length. One of the feet resemble that of a duck, and the other that of a turkey.

"Henry shot it at a distance of one hundred yards, from the top-most branch of a dead tree, where it had perched preying upon a full sized sheep that it had carried from the ground."

Experts speculated that the "strange species of bird," no doubt had "existed extensively during the days of the mastodon, is almost entirely extinct—the last one having been seen in the state of New York during the year 1812." The giant bird with the fifteen-foot wingspan was exhibited in an office in Mound City and drew hundreds of curious citizens, who had witnessed the creature on its flight across the town and river.

Thanks to Jerome Clark for the three newspaper clippings quoted above.

Did the Huge Pterodactyl
Come through the "Back Door" of the Universe?

On June 2, 2008, I received a brief, but fascinating email from Norma C. reporting a big bird sighting:

I don't remember the exact year, but my cousin and I were sleeping on a back porch early in the evening, and between two houses a "swish" sound like wings flapping were heard. We [rose] up out of our bed and viewed a large bird, but not distinctly, only knowing it was huge due to the swish of its wings. It flew between two houses and was never seen again.

The year was either 1940 or 1941. We immediately mentioned it to my parents and were told that we were "seeing things." I have never forgotten that evening, and when I studied history in school, the large bird resembled the pterodactyl in the pictures.

The memory has always persisted, and after reading other people's accounting of large bird sightings, I am certain that was what we encountered in our viewing.

I responded to Norma and inquired if she could provide any additional details. She replied immediately:

We were living in the house in Tulsa, Oklahoma. The time was early evening during the summer months, I think around June or July.

I don't know why, but this sighting has been etched in my mind for years. I am now 78 years old, but whenever any accounting about strange birds is mentioned, immediately I think of that swish of the wings and the enormous size of the bird. As I understand it, from time to time this huge flying creature has been seen in Texas as well. Sometimes I wonder if there isn't a "back door" to our Universe where things come and go, visibly and invisibly?

No one could have said it better than Norma: Perhaps there is a "back door to our universe where monsters come and go, visibly and invisibly."

A Monster Bird Larger than an Airplane

On April 9, 1948, a farm family outside of Caledonia, Illinois, saw a monster bird that they described as larger than an airplane. A Freeport truck driver said that he, too, had seen the creature on the same day. A former army colonel admitted that he had seen it while he stood talking with the head of Western Military Academy and a farmer near Alton. "It was a bird of tremendous size," he said.

Many individuals claim to have sighted huge birds larger than airplanes. Others have insisted that they have seen pterodactyls (*art by Bill Oliver*).

On April 10, several witnesses saw the gigantic bird in the skies over Illinois. "I thought it was a type of plane I had never seen before," one percipient said. "It was circling and banking in a way I had never seen a plane perform. I kept waiting for it to fall."

On April 24, back at Alton, a man described what he saw as an enormous, incredible thing flying at about five hundred feet.

A Bird the Size of a Cessna Put a Hole in His Roof

Author-Paranormalist Tina Sena reported in a personal correspondence (May 26, 2004) that she is quite certain that her great-uncle had an experience with a thunderbird in Brazil in 1960:

He was sitting in his house, watching TV when a mighty crack sent the shingles on his roof thundering to the ground. He thought someone had thrown something from an airplane, because in those days thieves would take small planes and abandon them enroute to make escapes and so forth.

He went outside to take a look and saw a huge bird circling over his head. He says that he will never forget it because it was the size of a Cessna. It left a huge hole in his roof, and it seemed to circle above his home for hours before heading off over the ocean.

A Scientist Told Him the Bird Tim Saw Was "Impossible"

Tim lives in western Clinton county, Iowa, about a mile from the Wapsipinicon River. Back in 1986, he was out hunting squirrels when he saw a really big bird. It stood over six-feet tall on the branch where it was perching. It was very bronze and black in color. In some ways it resembled a very large eagle. Eagles are quite common in that area, so he was certain that this was some kind of bird the like of which he had never seen.

One evening a few nights later, Tim was attending a campground event on "Birds of Prey in the Midwest."

"I described the giant bird in detail for the biologist," Tim said, "but the scientist told me that such a bird was impossible. There were no birds in the Americas larger than a condor, and there were no condors in Iowa."

From a personal correspondence, May 28, 2004.

Mom Has a Close-Encounter with Giant Bird while Driving Convertible Camero

John Carlson, co-host of The Paranomalists, www.theparanomalists.com, wrote to inform me that his co-host Ash Hamilton, had had a very interesting interview with Ash's mother regarding thunderbird sightings. Ash is originally from Illinois and his mother had a very close encounter with an enormous birdlike creature on a country road one night in 1995.

She was driving a convertible Camero, and she claims that the creature was at least seven feet tall when it stood erect and that the wings spanned the full width of the road. (The podcast, if you'd care to listen to it, can be found on the first page of the audio section on www.disclose.tv, titled "Illinois Thunderbird Sighting"). Interestingly, Ash's mother didn't get a clear look at the creature's face and didn't see a beak. She described the head as being low and kind of set between the shoulders, which sounded almost "mothman-like" to them. Whatever it was, it was an interesting, up-close account from a reliable witness. Ash said his mother didn't even speak of it to anyone for quite a while until she began hearing rumors of similar encounters by people in the area.

Aircraft-sized Birds Buzz Pennsylvania

Numerous reports of birds the size of small airplanes were reported in southwest Pennsylvania in the summer and early fall of 2001. On June 13, a resident in Greensville said that at first he mistook the huge bird for an ultra-light aircraft. He estimated the wingspan to be about 15 feet and the body to be nearly five feet in length. In July, a witness in Erie County claimed to have seen a large, black-colored bird with a wingspan of about 17 feet.

On September 25, a witness who said that he had a strong interest in ornithology, encountered a massive bird with a head about three feet long and a wingspan of 10 to 15 feet.

A Bird the Size of an Ultra-Light Aircraft over Bristol

On November 5, 2001, a resident of Bristol, Connecticut, who was out walking his dog at dawn, said that he had sighted a giant birdlike creature the size of an ultra-light plane flying over a community center.

The Pastor's Two Thunderbird Sightings in Pennsylvania

BY PASTOR ROBIN SWOPE

I think I saw a Thunderbird myself in July of 2001.

In 2000 I started working in a local graveyard in Erie County Pennsylvania. I had left association with denominational churches a few years prior because of the many abuses of power and people that I had seen over the years. Eventually I started my own independent non-denominational organization called Open Gate Ministerial Services to offer services that you would normally find in a church to those who did not belong to any church or religious organization. As an ordained clergyman of a small fellowship that acted as a church I preformed weddings, funerals, baptisms/dedications, and other services as needed to whomever needed them. But it didn't pay well. In fact I never asked for any fee, and lot of the time I never received one. But I liked that. It was very liberating. But I still had bills to pay and knowing that I went out into the workforce to support my family while still being able to minister to others through our organization.

I ended up working at the graveyard as a gravedigger. I started off as a salesman, but I couldn't make a sale for the life of me. I'm just not the salesman type—especially cemetery sales which is harder than most. But there was an opening in the maintenance department and it paid above the average wage at the time so I jumped at the chance. Most of the time it was pretty hard work—digging graves and burying bodies. Then there were the disinterments, taking a body out of a grave to move it to another location—the less said about those experiences the better. But then during the summer months came the times we mowed the grounds and tended the greenery. I was usually assigned to mow the grounds during the summer months and it gave me ample time to enjoy the outdoors and commune with nature.

It was one of those days in July of 2001. As I mowed the 23 acres of lawn between the mausoleum and the edge of the property dominated by a line of high tension wires, I saw something very odd. Obviously frightened by the sound of the mower, a gigantic bird had just launched out of the brush 25 yards to my right.

If it wasn't so large I might not have noticed it. The gigantic wings beat the air with dynamic effort and the avian was aloft and soaring over the brush and past the sprawling high tension wires and the pillar that supported them. The bird was absolutely humongous, and as it passed the support tower, I noticed that its wingspan as it reached its crest ran very close to the length of the towers upper supporting beam.

The creature quickly rose and then glided down past the treetops of the area where we dumped the excess dirt from digging graves and soon slipped out of sight.

It was strange, as a follower of all things Fortean I had heard of Thunderbirds since elementary school, but at this time I was betwixt amazement of what I had just encountered and actually comprehending what it was. As the realization of what I had just witnessed came to fruition upon my numbed mind I remember jumping off the mower and screaming "YES!" in jubilation.

I wanted to drive my mower back to the dumping ground to see if I could by chance catch another look at the strange bird that I had just beheld, to verify my adulation. But I knew that if I did so my boss (who worked us all like the Marines he once served with in Vietnam) would be very irate.

Anyway, the chances of actually finding the bird in the thick woods were going to be pretty slim. So restraining myself I went back to my mowing and glowed in the satisfaction of what I had just beheld.

But what had I just seen?

It was both similar to many large birds that I had seen in the area and yet very distinct. It looked downright primitive. It had no neck, a thin and very pointed beak and a long tail that ended with what looked to be a triangle. It was completely black or dark grey from head to tail with no visible markings on it except a small bulge of plumage under the neck that stuck close to the body.

Of all the workers in the field that day I was the only one to see it, which is no surprise since the others were scattered throughout the 90-acre property doing various

There are no birds in the Americas larger than a condor, and there were no condors in Iowa, where a huge thunderbird was seen (*art by Ricardo Pustanio*).

assignments which gave no reason to look up into the sky.

After work I took my measuring tape to the tower and measured the length of the upper support beam by comparing it to the base which was the same length—20 feet. So I estimated the wingspan of the creature to be anywhere from 15 to 17 feet in length.

The only local bird that comes anywhere near the size of the bird that I had just spotted was the Great Blue Heron. And to tell you the truth they do look similar in many ways.

The wingspan of a Great Blue Heron runs seven feet at the most. What I had just seen was at least twice that size. I had seen Herons quite frequently since a pair would often fly over our cemetery going to and from the various wetlands that encircled our property. In fact the year before when I first took the job, I had accidentally surprised one of the pair while it fished in the creek that ran by a military memorial. I was only five feet away as it suddenly jumped out of the water in fright and quickly flew off. I don't know who was more frightened by our close encounter though, seeing such a large bird pop out of nowhere was pretty unnerving. But the avian that I saw that July in 2001 was a giant compared to the Herons that inhabited our local woodland.

So with a possible Thunderbird sighting in hand I did what any good lover of the paranormal would do, I reported it. I sent a letter to *Fortean Times* and they published it in the August 2001 issue No. 148. Only later did I discover that there had been another Thunderbird sighting in June of that year only 50 miles south in Greenville, Pennsylvania. The similarities between the two creatures are striking.

Here is a description of the encounter as described by Stan Gordon in an October 1st 2001 posting at www.rense.com:

June 13, 2001—a resident of the town of Greenville, PA reported seeing a large bird the size of a small airplane from his living room. Greenville is a small town that lies near the border of Ohio and about half-way between Erie and Pittsburgh. The witness, Ray (Please note, the witness' actual name is not used as he has asked for anonymity) upon further inquiry during a phone interview on June 15, 2001, was able to flesh out the report. Ray described the bird as fully feathered a dark brown or black color. The back of the wings was a grayish-black. The body was not bulky and the overall appearance was not like any bird he had ever seen. As the house lies near Little Shedango Stream and the house overlooks a small pond and woodlands, Ray was extremely familiar with the birds and other wildlife in the area including bald eagles, vultures, and storks.

Ray stated that the bird flew in from the South at a distance of 200–300 yards from the window and landed on a large tree beside the small pond. As it flew in he saw a shadow first and thought it was an ultra-light aircraft that are used in the area by some neighbors. The bird landed and remained on the tree for 15 to 20 minutes, and then took off again to the South. Ray estimated that the wingspan was equivalent to some of the ultra lights he has seen in the area, around 15 feet of wingspan and upwards of five feet of body size.

Was it the same creature? If not then it had to be of the same species.

I worked for the cemetery for five more years after this sighting and I never saw the creature again while employed there.

However in April of 2009 while waiting for a paranormal investigative team to arrive at the cemetery for an investigation, I once again encountered either the same creature or one very similar.

In fact I was taking pictures of the high tension wire pillar for this article when the incident happened. I had just put the camera away in my car and was walking toward the mausoleum adjacent to the high tension wires when I heard a commotion from the swampy brush to the North.

The large bird came up from the brush and quickly gained altitude. It was being harassed by smaller birds that were circling and attacking. I estimated its wingspan to be almost 15 feet judging by the surrounding terrain.

I recovered my camera, but the batteries died as I tried to zoom in onto the bird, but I did manage to get one wide shot. By the time I had changed batteries, the bird had disappeared into the wooded area to the west of the cemetery and out of sight. Looking at the lone picture I took, I could see nothing. I assumed that I had missed it entirely.

The bird was exactly like the one I had seen before, and roughly the same size. It was black in color but I saw no white tuft as I did before. It was very similar to a Blue Heron but of course larger and the head was again slightly different.

A few days later I downloaded my photos, and to my surprise I saw a slight speck in the sky from that lone picture. Enlarging it you can clearly see a bird. The long tail is slightly visible, and I knew it was the large bird and not one of the smaller attacking ones.

A "Raptor-Like" Giant Bird Spotted by Pilot and Passengers

In October 2002, Alaskan villagers in Togiak and Manokotak reported seeing a huge bird larger than anything they had seen before. Pilot John Bouker, owner of Bristol Bay Air Service, said that he and his passengers sighted a large "raptor-like" bird with a wingspan that matched the length of his Cessna 207, about 14 feet. When Moses

Coupchiak, a heavy equipment operator from Togiak, spotted the monster bird flying toward him, he said that he thought it was a small airplane until it banked to the left and flew away.

Biologists in the region said that they believed the witnesses sighted a bird known as the Steller's sea eagle, a species native to northeast Asia, that occasionally shows up on the Aleutian islands and on Kodiak, Alaska. The Steller's sea eagle can have a wingspan of eight feet and is about three times as large as a bald eagle.

A Monster Hang-Glider Sized Bird Over Denver

Jason, a 32-year-old insurance salesman who lives in the Denver Metro Area wrote recently that "after an experience I had last night, I am hoping to find some reports that make me feel a little more sane. I am a skeptic of most things. I have an open mind and understand that there are things we do not know. For the most part I do not get surprised or excited about some of these reports." But now, after a most unusual occurrence, Jason said:

> *My best guess is that it had a 16 to 20 foot wing span. It glided effortlessly and flapped its wings a few times while I was watching.*

I have now had a personal experience I need to share with someone. At 8:05 P.M. last night I was standing in my front yard, and as I was looking around at my neighbors and their well-maintained lawns something in the sky caught my eye.

It was a bird, a very large very black bird. On occasion we will get a stray heron or other water bird around here that is pretty big, but when I say large, this bird was the size of a hang glider. It did not have the tell-tale legs dangling behind it like other large water birds and it was jet black. I had scrambled to get my phone out of my pocket and get it in camera mode, but by the time I was ready the bird was just a speck on my camera screen, but I could still see it. I had marveled at the bird too long before I got my camera out and thus do not have any pictures. I took some time to actually process what I had seen and was immediately convinced that I had not seen anything like it before.

My best guess is that it had a 16 to 20 foot wing span. It glided effortlessly and flapped its wings a few times while I was watching. It went from the east to the southwest in a lazy way. I watched it until I could not see it anymore, then went inside to tell my wife.

My wife and other family members chuckled and soon moved on to other topics, but the image of this bird is scorched into my mind and keeps replaying. What did I see?

UFO ABDUCTORS—SEEKING TO CREATE A HYBRID SPECIES OF ALIEN AND HUMAN

The night of January 6, 1976, will live long in the memories of three Kentucky women who were returning home from a late supper when they were abducted by a UFO crew and put through a torturous ordeal for more than one hour.

The three women, all reportedly of the highest moral character, were Elaine Thomas, 48; Louise Smith, 44, and Mona Stafford, 35. All live in or near Liberty, Kentucky. Two of the women were grandmothers, and Mrs. Stafford was the mother of a 17-year-old. None of the three could recall the full details of their experiences until they were placed under hypnosis by a professional hypnotist, Dr. R. Leo Sprinkle, a professor at the University of Wyoming.

It was 11:30 P.M. as the three women drove toward their homes from Stanford, Kentucky. They were about a mile west of Stanford when they noticed a large disc hurtle into view.

"It was as big as a football field!" stated Mrs. Smith, who was driving the car that night. She continued her description by stating that it was metallic gray, with a glowing white dome, a row of red lights around the middle, and three or four yellow lights underneath.

The UFO first stopped ahead of them, then circled around behind their car, at which point the car suddenly accelerated to eighty-five miles an hour. The others screamed to slow down, but Mrs. Smith found that she had no control over the car. Some force then began dragging the car backward. At that point the three women lost consciousness, and remained so for the next eighty minutes. The events that allegedly took place were brought out later under hypnosis.

The three women remembered vividly what had taken place during the lost eighty minutes that they were brought aboard the UFO to undergo physical examinations.

Elaine Thomas reported that she had been lying on her back in a long, narrow incubator-like chamber. The humanoids looked to her like small, dark figures, which she estimated at about four feet tall. She reported that a blunt instrument was pressed hard against her chest, causing much pain, while something encircled her throat.

Each time she tried to speak, she was choked. She cried softly under hypnosis as though reliving a horrible ordeal. It felt like hands pressing on her throat, and she could see shadowy figures passing around her. "They won't let me breathe—I can't get away!" she cried.

Under hypnosis Mrs. Smith said that she had been in a dark, hot place, and something had been fitted over her face. She begged the occupants to let her see, but when they did, she immediately closed her eyes, as what she saw was frightening! She could not describe the beings, however.

"Help me, Lord, please!" she cried. She told investigators that the interior of the UFO was very dark and that she was very frightened. She pleaded with the kidnappers to let her go, to let go of her arm.

She finally cried out, "I'm so weak I want to die!"

Still later she asked the beings if she could go, and the next memory she had was that of seeing a street light.

Mona Stafford's memory was of lying on a bed in what seemed to be an operating room, with her right arm pinned down by some invisible force while three or four figures dressed in white gowns sat around her bed.

Apparently Mrs. Stafford was not as overcome with terror as the others, but she did say that she seemed to remember being tortured, and that at one point her eyes felt as though they were being jerked out of her head. At another time, her stomach felt as though it had been blown up like a balloon. Next she reported that the humanoids were pulling at her feet, then bending them backward and twisting them. "I can't take any more!" she screamed, then lapsed into silence.

The next thing the three frightened women could remember was driving to Louise's home. They should have arrived about midnight, but they noticed the time was actually 1:30 A.M.—nearly one hour and twenty minutes were missing from their lives that night.

Louise reported that her neck hurt. When Mona examined it, she saw a strange red mark about three inches long and an inch wide, like a burn that had not blistered, Elaine's neck had the same type of mark on it.

The frightened women called a neighbor who lived next door to Louise. After hearing what they could recall of their adventure, he had the three women go into separate rooms and draw what they felt the strange UFO looked like. The three drawings looked very much alike.

Although the burn marks were gone in about two days, the three women still could not account for the time loss, nor could they recall anything from the time the car was pulled backward until they were driving about eight miles from where they first saw the UFO.

Following the hypnotic sessions, they were given polygraph tests by Detective James Young of the Lexington police department. Young, in a sworn statement, said, "It is my opinion that these women actually believe they did experience an encounter."

There are many reports from people who say they have been abducted by aliens who then performed breeding experiments on them (*Mary Evans Picture Library/Michael Buhler*).

Dr. Sprinkle stated that the three women, in his opinion, had specific impressions that indicated to them that they had been observed and handled by strange beings. He felt it would have been impossible for them to fake their reactions, and he commented that their experience during the time loss was similar to reports provided by UFO percipients who had had similar experiences.

Sheriff Bill Norris of Lincoln County, Kentucky, said that there had been a number of UFO sightings in the county that January.

In an article by Bob Pratt that appeared in the *National Enquirer* on October 10, 1976, Len Stringfield, a director of Mutual UFO Network, who investigated the whole incident, commented, "This is one of the most convincing cases on record."

The report of abduction by aliens, memory loss, missing time, and the shape of the UFO are all familiar to UFO investigators, for this is not an isolated episode. The three women were all known to be lifelong churchgoers with excellent reputations in their community. It is, in reality, but one more report of a physical examination of Earth humans by beings from other points in time or space.

Betty and Barney Hill: Prototype for the "Interrupted Journey"

The case of Betty and Barney Hill offers the prototype for the "interrupted journey," the classic case of humans abducted and examined by aliens from another world. On September 19, 1961, Betty, a social worker, and Barney, a mail carrier, then in their forties, were returning to their home in New Hampshire from a short Canadian vacation when they noticed a bright object in the night sky. Barney stopped the car and used a pair of binoculars to get a better look. As he studied the object, the illumination provided by the object showed a well-defined disk-like shape, moving in an irregular pattern across the moonlit sky.

Fascinated, Barney walked into a nearby field where from that perspective he could perceive what appeared to be windows—and, from inside the windows, beings looking back at him. The feeling that he was being watched frightened Barney, and he ran back to the car, got in, and began to race down the road.

Then, as if obeying some internal directive, he drove down a side road—where the Hills found five humanoid aliens blocking their exit. Suddenly unable to control their movements, Betty and Barney were taken from their car and, in a trancelike condition, led to the UFO by the visitors.

According to information later retrieved under hypnosis, Betty and Barney were returned unharmed to their car with the mental command that they would forget all about their abduction experience.

According to information later retrieved under hypnosis, Betty and Barney were returned unharmed to their car with the mental command that they would forget all about their abduction experience. The UFO then rose into the air and disappeared from sight, leaving the Hills to continue their journey home, oblivious to the whole event.

Perhaps the remarkable encounter would never have been brought to light except for two factors: they began to experience strange and disconcerting dreams that they could not understand, and they could not explain the unaccountable two missing hours in their journey home from Canada.

Betty decided to seek the help of a psychiatrist friend, who suggested that the memory of those lost hours would return in time, perhaps in only a few months. But the details of that unexplained "interruption" remained in a troubled limbo of fragmented memories until the Hills began weekly hypnosis sessions with Dr. Benjamin Simon, a Boston psychiatrist.

Much has been made of the Hills' alien medical examinations, and the skeptic could argue that their much publicized experience may have provided the prototype for thousands of other individuals who have claimed alien abductions together with their requisite physical and sexual exams. Their story was covered extensively by John G. Fuller in the book *Interrupted Journey* (1966), and presented in a made-for-television movie (1975) with James Earl Jones and Estelle Parsons playing Barney and Betty.

Barney died in 1969. Betty remained active as a speaker at UFO conferences until her death in 2004.

The Kidnappers from a UFO Did Not Return Telemaco

On September 16, 1962, Telemaco Xavier was taken away by what some witnesses described as alien beings. Xavier was last seen walking home along a dark jungle trail after attending a soccer match in Vila Conceicao in northern Brazil. A workman at a nearby rubber plantation told authorities that he had seen a round glowing object land in a clearing. Three smallish beings got out of the fiery vehicle and grabbed Telemaco, who was walking along the trail.

Rio de Janeiro newspapers quoted authorities who had discovered signs of a struggle where the worker said a fight had taken place between the man and his abductors. To the Brazilian newspapers it seemed evident that Telemaco Xavier was kidnapped by a flying disc, and some investigators suggested that the Brazilian had been added to a collection of Earth life which was to be scrutinized, evaluated, and analyzed in some alien laboratory.

Aliens Visit the Lieutenant Governor of Peru

In the Andean town of Santa Barbara, no less a personage than the lieutenant governor claimed to have seen two aliens about three feet tall walking through the snow near Lake Ceulacocha. The entities seemed to disappear in a brilliant flash after they had walked about for a few minutes. Hundreds of peasants in Huancavelica, Peru, were terrified later that same day when live UFOs buzzed their village for about three minutes.

Farmers and Villagers in Argentina Fight Off Six Kidnap Raids

From the village of Torren, Santo Time, Argentina, comes the story of UFO occupants who returned on successive evenings in February 1965 in an attempt to kidnap residents of the small farming community.

The first attack came on a very dark night, when a UFO landed in full view of a small group of terrified farmers. Two strange beings about six feet in height emerged from the craft and walked directly to a farmhouse, where they tried to drag off the farmer who lived there. Rallying to their friend's defense, the other farmers managed to thwart the aliens' kidnap scheme and drove them off.

On the next night, when the saucer crew landed to carry out their mission of obtaining human specimens, the farmers opened fire on them with their guns. Although the aliens' space suits seemed to protect them from the farmers' bullets, they seemed weak physically and were quite easily discouraged from further attempts at seeking quarry from the village.

No one on either side of the bizarre interplanetary brawl seemed to have been seriously injured; however, the farmer who had entered into prolonged physical contact with the celestial kidnappers did come down with a strange skin disease.

Two Sisters in Washington State Outran the Mysterious Strangers

On August 13, 1965, two Renton, Washington, sisters came to work at 7:00 A.M. to get an early start in Yas Narita's bean field near Kent. Ellen and Laura Ryerson had barely entered the bean field when they noticed that three "workers" were already walking in the area. The teenaged sisters had not been in the field long when they discovered that the three strangers were more interested in them than in gathering beans. Even more frightening was the girls' discovery that their three fellow bean-pickers were not human beings.

The three strangers had white, domed heads and protruding eyes. They were between five feet two inches and five feet five inches tall. The flesh of their expressionless faces had very large pores, and their complexions were "gray, like stone." The three aliens wore sleeveless purple V-neck jerseys with white shirts underneath.

Fortunately for the girls, the three strange "men" were easily outdistanced and appeared to be without weapons. Ellen and Laura were able to get back to their automobile, and they sped away to make their report to the Washington State Patrol.

Taken from a Fishing Dock in Pascagoula

October may be the month of ghosties, ghoulies, and long-leggity beasties, but it is often a very slow month for UFO activity. October 1973 proved to be an exception to all rules, starting with the report of two Mississippi fishermen who told authorities that they had been taken aboard a flying saucer that looked like a giant fish.

Charles Hickson, 45, and his fishing companion, 19-year-old Calvin Parker, were fishing from an old pier in the Pascagoula River, near the city of the same name in Mississippi. The men reported seeing a fish-shaped object, emitting a bluish haze, approaching from the sky. The craft landed, and the men allegedly were taken aboard by three weird creatures with wrinkled skin, crab-claw hands, and pointed ears. The men claimed to have been examined by the creatures aboard their craft, then released.

Sheriff Fred Diamond of Pascagoula told investigators that the two men were scared to death when they reported to him, and that he feared they might be on the verge of suffering heart attacks.

Their story was interesting enough to draw the attention of Dr. J. Allen Hynek of Northwestern University in Chicago, who had served as scientific consultant to the Air Force's Project Blue Book, and Dr. James Harder of the University of California, who had the men hypnotized. Once under hypnosis, Hickson and Parker revealed their traumatic experiences aboard the strange craft.

Harder commented, "These are not imbalanced people; they're not crackpots. There was definitely something here that was not terrestrial, not of the Earth."

"Where they are coming from and why they are here is a matter of conjecture, but the fact that they were here on this planet is beyond reasonable doubt," commented Hynek, who added: "The very terrifying experience of the two men indicates that a strange craft from another planet did land in Mississippi."

Hynek concluded that although the men could be hypnotized, their experience was so traumatic that it was necessary to progress slowly with them. This is the story the two men told:

Fishing buddies Charles Hickson and Calvin Parker claimed they were abducted by an alien with wrinkled skin, crab claw-like hands, and pointy ears (*art by Ricardo Pustanio*).

They were fishing for hardhead and croakers from an old pier near the Schaupeter Shipyard, a sun-bleached skeleton of a large drydock, at about eight o'clock the evening of October 11. Suddenly a UFO hovered just above them. "There was me and Calvin, with just our spinning reels," Charles Hickson said, "then Calvin went hysterical on me."

According to the report of the sheriff's office at Pascagoula, Hickson related that the luminous, oblong craft landed near them. Three creatures paralyzed him, floated him to their craft, placed him in front of an instrument that resembled a big eye, then put him back on the pier.

Calvin Parker was not able to add much to the report. He apparently fainted when the creatures approached the two men, and he said he did not know what happened inside the strange craft. After a couple of days, the two men refused further interviews with the press.

Following the report of Hickson and Parker, literally thousands of UFO sightings began cropping up from all over the United States, followed by more sightings from every corner of the globe. The October flap was underway!

More reports of UFO sightings came from other residents of Pascagoula that night of October 11, than from Gulfport, Mississippi. Over to Tallahassee, Florida, where two residents reported unidentified lights crossing the night sky of Leon County. North to Dayton, Ohio, where six more objects were spotted skimming over the Buckeye State. And on October 5, a week before the two fishermen had their experience in Pascagoula, a park ranger near Tupelo, Mississippi, reported that he had seen a saucer-shaped UFO with red, green, and yellow blinking lights.

Spanish Truck Driver Receives Four Visits from Alien Visitors

"**M**aximiliano Iglesias Sanchez does not seem very imaginative. If he is lying, he does it to perfection." Thus stated reporter Angel Gomez Escorial, writing in a Spanish magazine, concerning a young truck driver who reportedly witnessed UFOs on four separate occasions and had two close encounters with alien beings.

On the night of March 20, 1974, Sanchez, who was then 21, was driving his truck past the village of Horcajo on his way back to Lagunilla when he noticed a very strong white light some two thousand feet ahead on the highway. At first he assumed it was another truck, or perhaps a car. He switched his headlights to high beam several times, to signal the other driver to dim his own lights. The bright light remained almost blinding in its intensity. Its brilliance forced Maxi to pull his truck to the side of the road.

The bright light eventually dimmed to about the power of a 50-watt bulb. Maximiliano then continued to drive toward the light. When he was about six hundred feet away, Maximiliano discovered that the thing was indeed something very strange: Without warning, all the lights on his truck went out and the motor stopped. The area was illuminated only by the now dim light of the craft.

Sanchez described the object as having a metallic structure of either platinum or steel. It seemed quite solid, and it had smooth edges without rivets or openings of any kind. It was thirty to thirty-six feet in diameter and rested about five feet off the ground on three round landing pads.

"It was a light like I have never seen before" was how Sanchez described the light, which seemed to be uniform on all surfaces of the UFO.

He then noticed a second, similar "ship," as he called it, above and about fifty feet to the right of the first.

As if from nowhere, two beings appeared in front of the grounded UFO. They moved together, and began motioning to each other "like the tourists do." They looked at Sanchez, and one pointed at him. At that, one of the humanoids turned around and disappeared to the right of the first UFO, while the other remained to watch the young trucker.

Soon the other being returned. The two entities looked at each other; then both disappeared to the right of the ship. Soon, it slowly rose in the air with a slight humming sound.

Sanchez described the humanoids as about six feet tall and wearing close-fitting coveralls. The material of their coveralls was brilliant, like the ship, and appeared to be made of a rubbery material. The occupants' manner of walking was "normal," not like that of a robot, and their arms and legs seemed to be proportioned like a human's. As hard as Sanchez tried, however, he could not describe their facial features. The encounter had occurred at night, and he was never closer than six hundred feet to the entities.

When the first UFO reached the altitude of the second UFO, the two objects remained motionless in the air. Sanchez then decided to leave. His truck started right away, and the lights worked once again.

But he had driven only a short distance from the twin UFOs when curiosity got the better of him. Maxi Sanchez stopped his truck and climbed down from the cab to study them. He noticed that the illuminated ship had dropped down to the site where it had been before.

At this point, and for the first time, Sanchez registered fear. He took off as fast as his truck would carry him, and he drove straight to his home in Lagunilla, where he went to bed immediately without eating dinner.

The following day Maxi told the story to his neighbors, but he found that they did not believe him. However, the son of his employer told Sanchez that he gave his account credence, for it was similar to the experience a commercial traveler claimed to have undergone near Seville.

That afternoon, March 21, Sanchez drove to Pineda to deliver a load of construction material. While there, he made his customary visit to his sweetheart, Anuncia Merino. Maxi told her and her family what had happened the evening before. They insisted that he stay with them for the night and not continue his route until morning. It was getting late, and they were afraid for him to make the trip through that area again.

> *At this point, and for the first time, Sanchez registered fear. He took off as fast as his truck would carry him....*

He did not take their advice, however, but headed back home to Lagunilla.

At about 11:15 P.M. he arrived at the site of the previous night's UFO/humanoid sighting. Once again he saw a bright light ahead of him. Sanchez was convinced that the entities would do him no harm, as on the night before. Again, he drove to within about six hundred feet of the light. That night, however, the light was produced by not one but three UFOs.

As before, the truck lights went out and the engine quit—this time with a backfire! One of the UFOs was resting on the highway; the other two were just off the road to the right side of Maxi, one behind the other. All three were illuminated with the same soft light he had noticed the night before—or, rather, earlier that same morning.

Suddenly four humanoids appeared and walked to the center of the craft resting on the highway. The four looked at Sanchez as though studying him, communicating with one another through gestures. The beings pointed at Sanchez, then started walking in his direction.

Sanchez, fearing the motives of the four, began running along the highway. The four entities increased their pace. Sanchez started across country, with the four gradually gaining on him. When he came to a ditch, he jumped into it.

The metallic ship emitted lights that Sanchez at first mistook for headlights along the road (*iStock*).

The move to evade his pursuers seemed to work. They had lost him—for the time being, at least. He could watch them from his muddy vantage point as they circled in search of him. Although they were often as near as fifty feet, he could still not make out facial features—a matter that bothered him greatly when he reported the incident.

Finally the four strangers left, and Maxi felt it was safe to vacate his hiding place.

He started walking, and he was soon within sight of the lights of Horcajo, which he estimated at about a mile away or less. He sat down and smoked a cigarette to calm his nerves. He rested for perhaps ten minutes, then returned to the area where he had left his truck, feeling that by now the spot would be deserted. He was wrong, for the three ships were still there—although he did not see the four creatures.

As Maxi Sanchez reached the truck, something bothered him. The door was closed. He remembered that he had left it open when he departed earlier. His fear that someone might be inside was put to rest, however, when he found nothing and no one in the cab. He tried to start the engine but found it still wouldn't work.

As he shut the door, the four humanoids appeared in the middle of the road, as before, gesturing to one another. They went to the right side of the ship parked there and apparently entered it, just before it climbed to an altitude of about fifty feet. The same low humming sound was heard, but it stopped as soon as the UFO came to rest.

It appeared to Sanchez that the UFO was clearing the road so he could leave, just as it had done the night before. The truck started instantly this time, and the lights came on.

"And I buzzed out of there!" he told investigators. Apparently his survival instinct was not as strong as it had been nearly twenty-four hours earlier, for he stopped the truck about six hundred feet down the road, climbed from the cab, and walked back to the area where the three UFOs were located. The one that had lifted from the highway to let him pass was once again in place on the asphalt paving.

He hid in a clump of bushes about thirty feet from the four humanoids and observed the nearest ship to see if he could find some opening in it through which the beings had been coming and going, but all he could see were unbroken walls.

He watched the beings at work. They were using two tools that resembled a horseshoe and the letter T. They inserted the T into the ground at the embankment of the highway. Then they would withdraw the instrument and insert the horseshoe in the hole. They did not appear to be taking mineral or vegetation samples, however.

Even at close range Sanchez was not able to determine facial features on the foursome.

Not more than about three minutes passed before fear returned to Sanchez, a terror that was stronger than his curiosity. He later reported that the beings never looked in his direction or seemed aware that he was there, but he felt it was time to return to his truck and head for home.

When he reported the incident to his boss the next day, he was advised to contact the Civil Guard, which he did, accompanied by his employer's son.

The officer in charge contacted headquarters in Bejar, and after three days an officer arrived and filed a report, following an interview with Maxi Sanchez. Investigators went to the alleged landing site, where they found some strange tracks. On the highway where the craft had landed the investigators found a deep, straight groove, as if the asphalt had been scored by a very hard object. On the embankment the investigators found two scratches that seemed to substantiate Sanchez's story about the tools, but this was all the physical evidence the investigators found to indicate that the craft and its strange visitors had been there.

A few days later, two individuals from Madrid arrived in Lagunilla, stating that they were UFO investigators. They were equipped with instruments for making tests, including a Geiger counter. The team, trained in such investigative matters, was successful in finding three circles that appeared to have been caused by the craft resting there. The grass was pressed down, but no indentation from the landing gear could be found. Abnormal radioactivity in the area was recorded by the Geiger counter.

As a footnote, Maxi Sanchez added that although his truck started that night, the battery was completely dead the next morning. When he had it recharged, the garage mechanic could detect nothing abnormal about the battery.

The strange-craft sightings did not stop here, however. On March 30 Sanchez was once again with his girlfriend in Pineda. It was 12:45 A.M. when they saw what looked like two large spotlights in the sky at about twenty-eight hundred feet. The spots of very bright light were flying over the area, and they gave every indication of being similar to the UFOs witnessed by him earlier that month.

The fourth and final sighting took place in early May of the same year, while Sanchez was with his girlfriend and her uncle.

Sanchez had gone to the city of Salamanca, his hometown, to take a driving examination for a first-class permit. It was about 6:30 A.M. when Anuncia saw a strong, white aerial light, which soon disappeared.

A few miles down the road they saw another bright light—this one coming directly toward them at an extremely high speed. Anuncia feared that it was going to strike them head on, but about three hundred feet before impact, the light changed direction, passed over their car, and disappeared.

Sanchez reported no further sightings of UFOs or humanoids, and soon after these experiences he went into the Army. While curiosity at times may have overcome his fear of the unknown, he was quoted in a radio interview as saying, "There is no need to go on about bravery; before I did not know what fear was, but now indeed I know what it is."

An Interrupted Journey in France

Ms. Helene Giulana, a twenty-year-old French civil servant, was driving her car en route from Valence where she'd seen a movie to her home in Hostun on National Route 531 on the night of June 10, 1976, when, at 1:30 A.M., the headlights went out and the engine stopped. She was wide awake; the gas tank was not empty; but her automobile had inexplicably stopped running after she crossed the bridge of Le Martinet.

Then she saw a strange, luminous orange mass standing on the road about fifty feet in front of her car. Ms. Giulana locked all of her doors and, frightened, covered her eyes with her hands.

When she had recovered her courage enough to glance again at the road, the thing had disappeared. With some hesitation, she tried the ignition. The car started at the first turn of the key.

Relieved, fighting back panic, Ms. Giulana started for home. Because of her distraught condition, she took the longer way home, by way of La Beaume d'Hostun. But, even so, she should have been within the security of her own rooms within thirty minutes.

Ms. Giulana was astonished to note that it was 4:00 A.M. when she reached her home.

How had the thirty minutes become more than two hours? How long had she sat before the luminous orange mass in her immobilized automobile? What had occurred during those two hours of which she has no memory?

Ms. Giulana said that she was at first very reluctant to recount the details of her experience, for fear of being ridiculed. But she knew that she was respected quite highly in the town of Hostun, where she is employed at the Town Hall. Depending upon her credentials and her reputation to support her through the crisis of transient mockery, Ms. Giulana was determined to share her account of what may have been her very own "interrupted journey."

Did a Well-Known Paranormal Researcher Experience Abduction?

One cannot but wonder, are we as strange to the abductors as they are to us? Perhaps, but it is becoming apparent that while we continue to search for answers to UFOs and humanoids, they appear to have the technological advantage.

In the UFO abduction-examination account with which we are most familiar, the abductees informs ufologists or the communications media that he saw a vehicle on the ground and was either drawn to it, as if by hypnotic attraction, or was ushered into its interior by its occupants. The experience, though deemed by many people to be at best bizarre, at worst absurd, is nonetheless presented as a totally physical encounter.

"Not too long ago I had a strange thing happen to me," wrote my friend, and fellow paranormal researcher, Richard Senate. "I have had many odd events occur to me since I began to investigate the paranormal, but this seems to be the most mysterious. It seems I somehow managed to misplace a number of hours." According to Richard:

I was invited to a party in downtown Ventura (California). Those [who] know me understand that I am not a party person, but this time I felt compelled to attend. To make things worse there was a movie on the AMC channel that I really wanted to see, *How the West Was Won*. I had seen the film decades before in the theater, and I wanted to see it again. The film started at 9:30 that night.

I arrived at the party early. I guess it was about 6:30. I talked with old friends, ate the snacks, and sipped on a glass of wine. It was typical of many parties, the music was too loud, and the room became packed with people I didn't know.

I kept my eye on my watch, knowing it took about twenty minutes for me to drive to my house from downtown. About 8:30 I started to say my goodbyes and left the party at 9:00 sharp. I jumped in the car and drove home without stopping.

I noticed about half-way home, around the Ventura College, the traffic seemed to vanish. There just wasn't anyone on the road. I went right home, parked the car and rushed into the house. The first thing I did was turn on the TV and change the channel to AMC. I grabbed a snack from the refrigerator and took my most comfortable chair.

A detective film was on. I thought at first that I must have gotten home early and this was the tail end of a feature and my western would follow. It never came on. I checked the station and the TV guide and was mystified until I glanced at the clock. It was 4:30 A.M.! The detective feature was the one following *How the West Was Won*. My watch said 4:30, all the other clocks said that time. I even called time on the telephone to confirm the hour.

Even those who are not certain what exactly happened to them realize that they have no recollection of long stretches of time and no way of accounting for their whereabouts (*iStock*).

What had happened to me? Somehow I jumped forward in time from 9:00 P.M. to 4:30 A.M.

I have read about those who believed they have been abducted by aliens and subjected to alien probes. I did not feel different nor did I have any memory of any strange lights in the sky or large-headed Grey creatures. The only thing odd was the change in the traffic that happened when I was driving on Telegraph Road near the Ventura College. Maybe, if I was taken, it would have been there. I wasn't using any form of drugs and one glass of wine couldn't have affected me in such a way.

Not long after this curious event I noticed something peculiar about my left leg. There was a lump of something on my shin. It was as if there was a small pill embedded under my skin. Was this some sort of tracking device placed there when I was taken? I thought of having someone hypnotize me and try to recover that happened to me that night, but I wondered if I really wanted to know.

So I ask you, the reader, this question; has anyone ever had strange things happen with missing time on Telegraph Road? I can be reached at hainthunter@aol.com.

My friend Richard Senate is not a fantasy-prone individual, but he is also educated and well-read in the fields of the paranormal and UFOs. Because of his expertise, he would be well aware of people's stories of their encounters with UFO abductors and "missing time." Richard is not claiming to be an abductee, but he knows that something strange happened to him on this particular evening. Since he is an experienced researcher, he is careful to make such an assertion without additional evidence or proof. In the past few years, however, thousands of people swear on everything they consider sacred and holy that extraterrestrial aliens have taken them aboard their space vehicles and given them what appears to be some kind of medical examination.

The Coming of the UFO Abductors

Sinister aliens doing terrible things to humans didn't truly reach the general mass public consciousness until stories of men and women claiming to have been abducted by extraterrestrial crews for purposes of undergoing bizarre medical examinations were featured by UFO investigator Budd Hopkins in his book *Missing Time* (1981). In a later work, *Intruders* (1987), he continued to propagate the theory that aliens were abducting Earth men and women for the purpose of creating a hybrid mix of extraterrestrial and human DNA.

When Whitley Streiber published *Communion* in 1987, he transformed himself from a well-established horror writer into the world's most famous UFO abductee (or contactee, depending upon one's definitions of the terms). The author of such popular novels as *The Wolfen* (1978) and *The Hunger*, both of which were made into successful motion pictures, Streiber startled readers and researchers alike when he wrote a first-person account of his encounters with the "visitors" and detailed his personal abduction experience that had occurred December 26, 1985. The grim insect-like visage of the "Gray" staring out from the cover of *Communion* seemed to be an evil cousin of similar beings that had lovingly encircled and embraced Roy Neary in *Close Encounters of the Third Kind*. In 1989, Whitley Strieber adapted *Communion* into a motion picture with Christopher Walken portraying the author.

In 1992, Budd Hopkins' *Intruders* became a television miniseries starring Richard Crenna, Mare Willingham, and Susan Blakely. The television version of Hopkins's book chillingly portrayed military and political figures covering up the truth about alien abductions while issuing official denials that such events were taking place.

Once again, invading, threatening, abusive aliens and the entire UFO mystery were things to be feared, and thousands of people around the world, watching such films as these, began to recall abduction scenarios that they suddenly "remembered" that had been repressed until brought to conscious memory by such frightening scenarios as those depicted on the screen.

The UFO Abductors Have Been Here for a Long, Long Time

It may surprise many readers to learn that back in the early 1960s—long before Budd Hopkins's *Missing Time* (1981) or Whitley Strieber's *Communion* (1987), there were a number of serious researchers in the United States, Great Britain, Canada, Brazil, Argentina, France, and other countries investigating claims of UFO abduction. It will intrigue some readers even more to learn that the scenarios told by the experiencers, the abductees, have remained basically unchanged down through the decades. There truly are no new revelations to make concerning the abductee phenomena. The startling truth is that such abductions have been occurring for centuries.

Fellow writer John A. Keel (1930–2009) once told me how nonplussed he was to discover in reading through a number of old and rare books that these much earlier contactees and abductees were not only undergoing the basic elements which we have come to consider the classic pattern of alien abduction, but the contactees were receiving messages almost identical to the messages received today. Keel wondered if the slight alterations in the content are probably made in the percipients' minds to tailor the messages to contemporary situations. "There is a storage factor," Keel said. "Perhaps the original signal is stored in the collective unconscious, or perhaps there is some mechanism beyond our space-time continuum which is repeating an endless 'tape.' If all percipients in all ages have been receiving the same signals, then the actual transmission is not especially pertinent to any given period. The same source and process which inspired the Book of Revelation is at work in modern revelation."

Whatever this great UFO mystery is, it remains consistent, but it also continues to be flavored by popular culture. The challenge to the serious researcher remains always consistent: Be mindful of how difficult it is to truly differentiate between what is an actual experience sincerely reported and what is a deceptive mind-meld of Hollywood illusion and misinterpreted personal mystical experience.

As Wm. Michael Mott states in his excellent book *Caverns, Cauldrons, and Concealed Creatures* that the "Visitors," the "Abductors," the "Aliens," whoever they may be, always expend a great deal of effort to "convince abductees, contactees, experiencers, witnesses, and so forth that the UFO entities of various types come from somewhere else." "We come from Zeta Reticuli" they claim, "Orion, Epsilon Bootes, or some other star system."

Continuing with comments regarding the Great Deception, Mott writes:

> But the overwhelming evidence would indicate that the UFO phenomenon is localized to the region of the Earth, and this has been the case for thousands of years. Not just to the region of the Earth, but of the Earth. With the possible addition of our moon and Mars, the Earth seems to be the primary source of encounters with, and object of interest of, these beings. Earth is where the action is, where the genetic wealth is, where the various battles between different schools of thought, methods of interaction, religions, philosophies, and quite possibly the big mystery (spiritual truth or ultimate destiny) is to play out or to be revealed. In short, evidence simply indicates that this is the case. UFO entities are no strangers to manipulating human religious tendencies or belief-systems (All systems) and have done so repeatedly.

> To quote briefly from my own work "The Deep Dwellers" from the book *Caverns, Cauldrons, and Concealed Creatures*: "Yet the biology of all the different types or castes of abductors, as horrific as it might appear to superstitious human eyes, is essentially that of animal forms which are natural to the Earth: mammalian and reptilian. Obviously, it is very important to these beings that such a logical connection not be made. If there is even a shred of truth to UFO abduction accounts, then it is more than apparent that the abductors want their victims, and humanity at large, to believe that they are from "somewhere else." While humanity looks continually upward at enigmas in the sky, what is transpiring beneath our very feet? It should indeed be noted that an earthly vertebrate template is almost always in effect with such "alien" creatures: They tend to be bipedal, with two arms, two legs, two eyes,

one head, one central body or trunk, binocular (predatory) vision or ocular placement, et cetera. They are only occasionally insectoid, but these are probably vertebrates as well, since two arms and legs only are noted in these cases. Logic and numbers would indicate that this pattern would simply not repeat over and over throughout a universe as vast as ours. The range of forms would have to be more numerous. Despite the strangeness or outlandish nature of their initial appearances, UFO entities and abductors (humanoids) are not so dissimilar from human beings, with earthly animal characteristics often described.

After many years of researching these inter-related phenomena, it has become apparent to this writer that the modern abduction phenomenon is the same as the ancient, medieval, and all other abduction phenomena which have taken place over the centuries, and which seem to blur the lines between physical reality and various types of "altered states" of awareness. Shamanism's spirit abductors, alchemy's elementals, Christianity's demons, the fairies of rural folk traditions, the various abducting and seducing demons of Islam, Hinduism, Buddhism, and pretty much all other religious or mythical traditions exhibit the same types of behavior, preferences, similar appearances, and so on. In other words, the UFO abduction scenario is just a new mask for an old player, a new get-up for forces which have always plagued or hornswoggled us for their own selfish purposes.

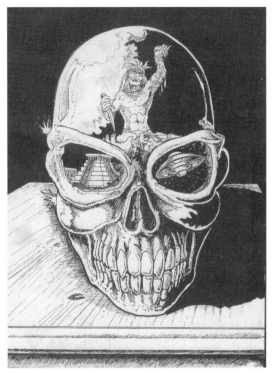

A crystal skull sent to the Smithsonian Institution anonymously in 1992 was purported to come from the Aztecs. The skull was so remarkably and perfectly designed that some speculated it had been left long ago by alien visitors (*art by Dan Wolfman Allen*).

A perfect example is the meaningless star-map, drawn on paper and hanging from a wall [in the spaceship they entered], which was shown to Betty and Barney Hill. Why would such technologically advanced beings be using a drawn or printed map, containing no recognizable star systems or constellations, and make a point of showing it to their captives, stating, in effect, "We come from here?" Where did they get the paper? Why not pull up a hologram or a screen?

COSMIC DISINFORMATION: This is identical behavior to the lack of use of anesthetic and so forth in their so-called medical experiments, which actually blend sadism and genetic theft activity. The Hill map scene, carefully contrived, was pure misinformation, given to captives who were in some sort of altered and highly-suggestive state of mind, so that they would retain the notion that their abductors came from a far-away star system, "cause they showed us a map." Meaningless in terms of the information it supposedly conveyed, but not meaningless in terms of the patterns of behavior exhibited which are indicative of an ongoing deception and manipulation.

We are dealing with a phenomenon which is very sophisticated, and which at times blurs the edges between what is considered to be reality, and the so-called supernatural. But this phenomenon is very real. Current advances in genetic engineering, talk of super-smart biochips which can be integrated into living brains or nervous systems, stealth technologies of various types—the group or groups under investigation here. They have been around in one form or another much longer than we have. They have a vast array of accumulated knowledge or technology, which for all practical purposes might as well be called magic. Maybe it IS magic, insofar as their understanding of what makes up reality might so vastly surpass ours that their science can affect the fundamental and underlying (quantum) laws which govern the universe as we know it. This would explain much. As Arthur C. Clarke's third law states so succinctly: Any sufficiently advanced technology is indistinguishable from magic.

This in no way negates or denies the more logical possibility that they "are from here and always have been (or they have been here for at least a very long time indeed), and may have themselves branched out to the immediate neighborhood of close planetary bodies." Instead of looking off-planet for the sources of many of the mysteries and terrors which have haunted us through the ages, perhaps it's time for humanity to take a logical look at an origin much closer to home ... beneath our very feet.

A Most Strange Abduction Case

Those readers familiar with my work know that I am quite skeptical regarding the vast majority of abductee reports. Listening to abductees tell about their having been taken up through ceilings, out through walls, levitated out windows and taken to an alien spaceship or medical laboratory seem more to me like bizarre paranormal occurrences. I have no doubt that something unusual, something very special, happened to these experiencers—but what?

I first began interviewing UFO contactees and abductees in 1966 and have included their accounts in a number of books. I have tried to consider their accounts in an objective manner, while, at the same time, wondering if the occurrences that they report might not really be personal mystical experiences that have taken place in dreams, visions, or out-of-body experiences.

With those introductory remarks, I have in my files the most incredible case of abduction which I have ever encountered—and there was physical proof of a most tangible kind. This is a remarkable account of an individual who had either discovered a doorway to other dimensions of reality, along with the ability to dematerialize his physical body, or he had been granted these unique talents through his interaction with UFO entities—or entities who identified themselves as such. If the following report were not attested to by a very matter-of-fact physician associated with one of the largest, most prestigious hospitals in the Midwest, I would be extremely hesitant about sharing it with the public.

I made contact with "Dr. William" through a correspondent who had taken a course in medicine with him. According to my correspondent, Mr. E. William had not mentioned the experience during the several weeks' duration of the course, but one day after a class session he had mentioned it over a cup of coffee. According to William, the following occurrence took place in a hospital in Hawaii in 1968. William was then about nineteen years old, serving in the medical corps and assigned to the military section of the hospital.

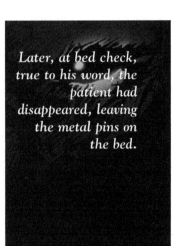

Later, at bed check, true to his word, the patient had disappeared, leaving the metal pins on the bed.

For obvious reasons I will not mention the name of the hospital in Hawaii. Neither will I give William's full name. He is a quiet, sincere man who wishes to continue his medical career and cannot see that his association with such an account would enhance his reputation as a doctor. Briefly, this is what happened:

A bedridden patient who was in traction and totally unable to move, with pins through his tibiae and femurs, told William that he would be gone that night for one hour to join his friends in a UFO. He said that William might accompany him if he truly believed in UFOs.

William indulgently told the patient that he would be unable to join him that night, as he would be busy.

Later, at bed check, true to his word, the patient had disappeared, leaving the metal pins on the bed. An extensive search of the hospital and the surrounding grounds by military policemen failed to produce any trace of the medically immobile man.

Here follows my questioning of Dr. William over the bizarre occurrence:

Brad Steiger: How old was this man, and why had he been brought to the military section of the hospital?

Dr. William: He was about sixty, a veteran of World War II.

BS: What was his name?

DW: It was a Spanish-sounding kind of name, something like "Espinia." He had bushy eyebrows, shoulder-length blondish hair, very large eyes. He had a round face, a flattened nose. His height was about five-foot-six and he was a bit chubby.

BS: Did you often engage Espinia in conversation?

DW: It was difficult not to. He was always talking about his weird techniques for meditation.

Espinia had a strange accent. By the time I was assigned to that hospital, I had already been around the world a couple of times, and I'm a bug on accents anyway; but I simply could not place Espinia's.

The night he disappeared, I was working the 11:00 [P.M.] to 7:00 [A.M.] shift. When I made the bed check, Espinia told me that he would be gone for about an hour, and he reminded me that I could come along if I wanted to. I chuckled and walked on to see about the rest of the patients.

Espinia was in a six-man room, but that night he was alone. My post was almost right across from his room. When I sat at my desk, I could survey the entire corridor. No one could get on or off the floor without my seeing them. And, of course, there were nurses, doctors, interns, and MPs walking around.

When I checked Espinia's room a bit later—maybe out of curiosity—he was gone. The traction weights were hanging there; the pins were on the bed; but Espinia was gone.

I put out an alarm, and MPs and other hospital personnel searched the place thoroughly.

Espinia was gone. No one had seen anything.

Some other patients said that they had seen a bright light, a very bright light, on that side of the building, and that would have been just before Espinia's disappearance.

BS: Is there any way that Espinia could have somehow removed the pins and the traction bars himself and crawled away?

DW: Well, first of all, a man would faint from the pain if he tried to pull those pins out. I mean, this guy was lying in that bed with both legs up, his femurs broken. Think of the terrible pain of trying to crawl under such conditions. It would be impossible!

After searching the hospital—and even the grounds—for an hour, somebody looked in Espinia's room, and there he was again, back in traction, pins in place. The patient had been gone for one hour. He told his interrogators that he had been with his "friends."

Every pin was in its place. A doctor on the floor said that while it might be possible for a man to pull the pins out, it would be impossible for anyone to shove them back in by himself.

Four MPs grilled him for hours, but Espinia wouldn't even reply to their questions. When they finally left him, he looked at me and told me that I could have come along with him, but his UFO friends knew that I didn't really believe in them. He said that he and his friends had spent a delightful hour flying over the Hawaiian Islands and chatting about metaphysics.

When I chastised him for having caused such a disturbance in the hospital, Espinia became a bit sheepish and said that the next time he went flying with his friends, he would leave his body there and just go with them in his mind.

William swears that this incident really happened. As I listened to him tell the story in his apartment, William's wife of a few months expressed her amazement. William had never mentioned the experience to her, and she said that she was hearing it for the first time that evening.

This account remains in my files as the strangest UFO abduction account that I have ever heard.

VAMPIRES—THEIR HUNGER FOR BLOOD IS ETERNAL

T here are five basic truths that one must acknowledge before engaging in the study of vampires:

1) Bram Stoker's inspiration for Count Dracula was not Vlad (the Impaler) Tepes, Dracul (Son of the Dragon, 1431–1476).

Vlad Tepes, King of Wallaschia, present-day Romania, was *not* a vampire. In present day Romania, Vlad Dracul is regarded as a national hero for his success in resisting the invading Ottoman Turks and for establishing at least a brief period of peace, independence, and sovereignty. Depending upon one's point of view, Vlad Dracula might be regarded as the Savior of the Western World by being the only leader to halt what seemed the unstoppable invading hordes from the East. In actual fact, Stoker came upon the name Dracul for his novel as he was flipping through some old books in an effort to come up with a more catchy title than *The Vampyr*.

Vlad's sobriquet, the Impaler, did not come from fangs that impaled the throats of his victims, but from the stakes that were driven though the warriors who had yielded to him in battle. He may not always have been the most pleasant fellow, but he was not a vampire.

2) The true, traditional, physical appearance of a vampire in European folklore is that of a grotesque, nightmarish creature with twisted fangs and grasping talons, rather than the current cinematic and literary portrayals of the undead as attractive, seductive male vampires and beautiful, alluring female night stalkers.

Nosferatu (1922) presented moviegoers with an accurate depiction of the traditional vampire. In this film, which was F.W. Murnau's unauthorized version of the Count Dracula saga, we see actor Max Schreck's loathsome bloodsucker, Count Orlock, moving from the shadows with dark-ringed, hollowed eyes, pointed devil ears, and hideous fangs.

The true, traditional, physical appearance of a vampire in European folklore is that of a grotesque, nightmarish creature (*art by Ricardo Pustanio*).

After Bram Stoker's novel *Dracula* (1897) became a popular stage play—and, in 1931, a classic horror film with Bela Lugosi portraying the Count as a sophisticated aristocrat—the image of the vampire as a hideous demon began to become transformed in the popular consciousness into that of an attractive stranger who possesses enormous sexual appeal—and a bite that, while fatal, also promises eternal life.

3) There are individuals who do seek to become real, blood-drinking vampires.

As a child, Richard Trenton Chase (b. May 23, 1950) was a bed-wetter, a fire-starter, and a killer of small animals. As an antidote for an imagined illness, Chase kept his blood flowing and his heart beating by killing and disemboweling small animals, mixing their organs with Coca-Cola in a blender, and drinking the potion.

In 1975, after he injected rabbit's blood into his veins and developed blood poisoning, Chase was committed to a mental asylum. Somehow, the hospital staff learned, Richard was able to capture small birds that landed on his window sill and eat them. After he had been found with blood smeared over his face a number of times, the staff began referring to him as "Dracula."

Chase was released to his mother in 1976 with a prescription for an antipsychotic medicine to be taken regularly. On December 29, 1977, he killed Ambrose Griffin, 51, in a drive-by shooting.

About a month later, January 21, 1978, Chase shot twenty-two-year-old Teresa Wallin three times. He dragged her body into the bedroom of her home where he stabbed her repeatedly, smeared her blood over his hands and face, and used a yogurt cup to catch some of her blood to drink.

Two days later, Chase bought two puppies from a neighbor, killed them, and drank their blood. He decided that animal blood did not give him the satisfaction that he gained from drinking human blood.

On January 27, Chase entered the home of Evelyn Miroth, 38, who was babysitting her twenty-two-month-old nephew, David. Her friend Danny Meredith, 51, had come over to keep her company. Evelyn's son, Jason, six, was getting ready to leave the house to go to play at a friend's. Within minutes, Chase had killed all four of them. Chase shot Meredith and Jason in the head, then forced Miroth into the bedroom where he stabbed her many times. He also removed several organs from her body and from Jason's body and drank his victims' blood from a cup.

While practicing cannibalism on Miroth, Chase was startled by a knocking on the door. It was Jason's friend, coming to check why he had not come to her house as he had promised.

Neighbors became suspicious, knowing very well that the family was home. While someone called the police to investigate, Chase made his escape.

When the police raided Chase's home, they were further disgusted to discover that the vampire had already eaten several of the baby's internal organs. It was also evident that he had brought home a quantity of blood to drink at his leisure.

Officers later said that the nauseating, putrid odor of Chase's residence was overwhelming. Nearly everything in his home was stained with blood. Plates, drinking glasses, eating utensils were thick with coagulated blood. When the refrigerator door was opened, they were horrified to find dishes filled with body parts. An electric blender on the kitchen counter was stained and clogged with rot. There were numerous dog collars scattered around various rooms, but no sign of any living pets.

Little David Miroth's body was not found until March 24 when a church janitor noticed a box among other stored items that he did not recognize.

Chase was subsequently examined by a dozen psychiatrists. He seemed to experience no real guilt for what he had done. He simply needed human blood to combat the many afflictions that he suffered. Blood drinking was therapeutic.

The trial for the Vampire of Sacramento began on January 2, 1979, in Santa Clara County. Chase was charged with six counts of murder. On May 8, the jury rejected the argument that Chase was not guilty by reason of insanity and found him guilty of six counts of first degree murder. It had taken them only four hours to decide that Richard Trenton Chase should die in the gas chamber at San Quentin Penitentiary.

On December 26, 1980, a prison guard found Chase dead in his bed. The Vampire of Sacramento had taken his own life just a few days short of the third anniversary of his rampage of death. A coroner determined that Chase had been hoarding his daily dose of Sinequan, a drug to combat depression and hallucination, and had overdosed.

4) There exists a subculture of humans who style themselves as Vampires but who do not wish to kill or to harm anyone.

"When a serious member of the vampire community describes themselves as a 'vampire,'" Merticus, a spokesperson for the community said, "they are not trying to tell you that they think they're a fictional character with supernatural powers, that they have trouble distinguishing between a role-playing game and reality, or that they hope you're gullible enough to believe that they're hundreds of years old and live in a castle. They're not even claiming kinship with the folkloric monster that frightened the people of Central Europe, and has them performing vampire-banishing rituals to this day."

Merticus is the administrator for Voices of the Vampire Community (VVC), basically the current leadership network for the modern vampire community with Michelle Belanger, Sanguinarius, SphynxCatVP, Lady CG, and others. As a vampire, Merticus explains that there is most certainly "a visible and vibrant community of people who are using the label to describe themselves, but to this day there is no functioning definition of a real vampire. This is primarily because no one knows what the cause

A subculture of modern-day vampire communities exists with members who wish no harm to non-vampires. What they mean, exactly, by "vampire" is subject to interpretation and personal preferences (*art by Ricardo Pustanio*).

of the phenomenon actually is, and the community has coalesced around a set of loosely shared perceptions and symptoms rather than a central organizing principle. Therefore, we can describe some common experiences involved in being a vampire, but these shouldn't be taken as a definitive vampire checklist. There are no known necessary and sufficient conditions to be met before you can be a vampire. Likewise, there's no single definitive sign that someone is not a real vampire."

Merticus went on to add that the most common experience that vampires share is the need to take in life energy or blood, from sources outside themselves, to maintain spiritual, psychic, and physical health.

"Blood-drinking, or sanguinarian, vampires have to consume small, polite amounts of human blood from willing donors," Merticus said. "The majority of sanguiniarians report taking only an ounce or less at a time; usually no more than once a week.

"Feeding is absolutely a health necessity; vampires have reported many negative physical symptoms when trying to ignore this need to feed. Psychic vampires, or psivamps, feed on psychic energy. Some psivamps enter into relationships with donors in the same way that sanguinarian vampires do, while others consciously train themselves away from human energy altogether, either for convenience or as a result of personal ethics. Some psivamps report a natural affinity for feeding on natural sources such as elemental or ambient natural energy. Others cultivate techniques for absorbing ambient energy from crowds and public places, so as not to take from any one source."

The Vampirism & Energy Work Research Study is a detailed sociological and phenomenological study of the real vampire community conducted by Suscitatio Enterprises, LLC. From 2006 to 2009 a combined response total (VEWRS & AVEWRS) reached over 1,400 surveys or over 650,000 individually answered questions; making it the largest and most in-depth research study ever conducted on the real vampire/vampyre community or subculture. Those who wish to contact the Vampire & Energy Work Research Survey and other aspects of Voices of the Vampire Community may visit them online at Vampire Community Resource Directory: http://www.veritasvosliberabit.com/resourcelinks.html

5) Real Vampires exist. They are ancient, multidimensional spirit parasites that have stalked humankind for its blood and its spiritual essence since pre-history.

Many researchers believe that a spirit parasite can seize the controlling mental mechanism of the host body of a human and direct the enslaved individual to perform horrible, atrocious deeds. The spirit parasite might implant murderous thoughts in a host's mind, such as the desire to taste human blood, to slash a victim's throat, even to eat portions of the person's flesh. After the crime has been committed, the vampiric spirit parasite is likely to withdraw into another dimension of time and space, thus leaving the confused human host alone, charged with murder, and having no memory of having committed the terrible deed.

Vampires Have Always Been with Us

The vampire legend has always been with us—from the shadows of the ancient Egyptian pyramids to the bright lights of New York City, the vampire's evil remains eternal.

Every culture has its own name for the night stalker. The word with which most of us are familiar rises from the slavonic Magyar—*vam*, meaning blood; *Tpir*, meaning monster.

In China, the *Chiang-shih* may appear as a corpselike being covered in green or white hair. The creature is equipped with long, sharp claws, jagged fangs, and glowing red eyes. The Chiang-shih may also possess a human body so that it can appear as a seductive woman or a handsome man to its unsuspecting victim. In some instances, the entity reanimates a recently deceased corpse, especially that of someone who committed suicide.

In the Shinto traditions, there are millions of *Kami*, nature spirits that can do either good or evil to humans. Although the Kami are by no means angelic, neither is it their sole purpose to harm humans. They can be brutal or benevolent, depending upon the intent or the purpose of the individual. Even the *Kappa*, generally considered the most evil of the Kami, a bloodsucking demon that haunts the night, can reverse its nature and single out individual humans to teach both medical and magical practices.

The seductive, blood-sucking Rakshasa of the Hindus is a beautiful nightstalker. The *Bhuta* haunts the wilderness and the wastelands and often signals its presence by an eerie display of glowing lights. The evil Rakshasas most often appear as beautiful women who drink the blood and feed off the flesh of men and women. The Rakshasas also possess shapeshifting abilities, and they take great delight in pos-

Many researchers believe that a vampiric spirit parasite can seize the controlling mental mechanism of the host body of a human and direct the enslaved individual to perform horrible, atrocious deeds (*art by Ricardo Pustanio*).

sessing vulnerable human hosts and causing them to commit acts of violence until they are driven insane.

In appearance, the Rakshasas are most often described as being yellow, green, or blue in color with vertical slits for eyes. They are feared as blood-drinkers and detested for their penchant for animating the bodies of the dead and stalking new victims.

The rapacious *Brahmaparush* is said to seize its victims by the head and drink their blood through a hole that it punctures in their skulls. Once it has had its fill of blood, the Brahmaparush eats the brains of those who have fallen into its clutches. When the gory feast has been completed, the vampire engages in a bizarre dance of triumph around the corpse.

The aboriginal people of Australia speak of the *Yara-Ma-Yha-Who*, a nasty shadow dweller who uses the suckers on the ends of his fingers and toes to feast on the blood of its victims.

In Arabian and Muslim traditions, the *Jinns* are evil demons who possess a wide variety of supernatural powers. Some scholars declare the Jinns a bit lower than the angels, because they were created of smoke and fire. Their leader is Iblis, once hailed as Azazel, the Islamic counterpart of the Devil.

> *The Jinns are accomplished shapeshifters, capable of assuming any form in their avowed mission to work evil on humans.*

The Jinns are mentioned frequently in the Qur'an, but the entities were known before the Prophet Muhammed wrote of their existence. In pre-Islamic Arabia, the Jinns were revered as godlike beings who inhabited a world parallel to that of humans.

The Jinns are accomplished shapeshifters, capable of assuming any form in their avowed mission to work evil on humans. On the other hand, Jinns may also, on occasion, influence humans to do good, and they may also perform good deeds for those who have the power to summon them. According to some traditions, King Solomon possessed a ring that gave him the power to summon the Jinns to fight beside his soldiers in battle. In addition, it is said, that Solomon's temple was constructed with the help of the Jinns.

Primarily, though, the Jinns are to be feared as creatures who exist for the purpose of tormenting humans. Some old beliefs affirm that a human dying an unrepentant sinner may become a Jinn for a period of time.

Many scholars of mysticism and the esoteric declare one type of Rakshasas as the Hindu equivalent of the Nephilim, the giants of the Bible, who declared war on the greater gods.

The ancient Persians and Chaldeans named those angels who fell to Earth the *Cadodaemons*. Cast out of heaven (another world, another universe) for rebelling against the prevailing order, their leader, Ahrimanes, was determined to rule Earth and the primitive humans who resided there. However, regardless of where he endeavored to establish his kingdom, the *Agathodaemons*, the representatives of universal law, prevented Ahrimanes from exploiting or interfering with the natural evolution of humans.

After attempting to wage a violent war of defiance on Earth against the Agathodaemons, Ahrimanes and his army were once again defeated. According to the Persians, the Cadodaemons were rejected from Earth and took refuge in the space between Earth and the fixed stars, a domain that is known as Ahriman-abad. It is from this dimension that Ahrimanes, resentful and revengeful, takes his pleasure in directing his daemons to afflict and torment human beings. Throughout all of history, these paraphysical beings, mimicking our human forms, have walked among us unnoticed, sowing discord wherever they wander, sapping our soul energy, invading host bodies whenever possible, causing vulnerable humans to seek the blood of their fellow beings.

Detecting Vampiric Possession

C ertain psychical researchers have created a kind of pattern profile of what may occur when humans have become the unwilling hosts of uninvited spirit guests.

The unfortunate human hosts may begin to hear voices that direct them to perform acts that they had never before considered. They may begin to use obscene and blasphemous language in situations that make their friends or relatives feel very offended or uncomfortable.

The infected hosts may frequently see grotesque images of the parasite spirit as it truly exists in its actual paraphysical dimension.

In the weeks and months that follow, the hosts may fall into increasingly extended states of blacked-out consciousness, times of which they have absolutely no memory.

On occasions, in the midst of conversations, the human hosts may find their conscious minds blocked and a trancelike state will come over them.

The human host may be observed walking differently, speaking in a different tone of voice, and acting in a strange, irrational manner.

Human hosts may begin doing things that they have never done before. Friends and family will remark that they are acting as if they are "totally different persons."

In the worst of cases, the parasitic spirit will completely possess the host's mind and body. The evil inhabitation may reach a climax with the host actually committing murder, suicide, or some violent antisocial act.

Ancient Evil Entities Whose Spawn Remain among Us

V enerable traditions state that such entities as Lilith first manifested on Earth at a time when the gods were said to walk freely among evolving humankind. To these godlike creatures of darkness, the primitive humans who regarded them with such awe and reverence were property, chattel from which to gain energy and sustenance.

The apocryphal book of Enoch tells of the order of angels called "Watchers," or "The Sleepless Ones." The leader of the Watchers was called Semjaza or Shemhazai (in other places, Azazel, the name of one of the Hebrews' principal demons), who led

Watchers manifest on Earth as angels, but their motives are just as blood-thirsty as those of corporeal vampires (*art by Jackie Williams*).

200 Watchers down to Earth to take wives from among the daughters of men. It was from such a union that the Nephilim were born.

Once in physical bodies, the fallen angels taught their human wives to cast various spells and to practice the arts of enchantment. They imparted to the women the lore of plants and the properties of certain roots. Semjaza did not neglect human men, teaching them how to manufacture weapons and tools of destruction.

The Nephilim are said in the Old Testament to have been the progeny of the "sons of god," whose union with earth women produced "giants ... men of great renown." Although often translated as "giants," the word Nephilim actually means "the fallen ones."

The plural form of "Lilith" in Hebrew is "lilim," which is found in Talmudic and Kabbalistic literature as a term for spirits of the night. Lilith is most often depicted as a beautiful woman with long, unkempt hair and large bat-like wings. According to the Midrash, Lilith preys not only on males as they lie sleeping, but also upon mothers who have just given birth, as well as their newborn babes.

Lilith quite likely was first feared in ancient Babylon as Lilitu, who, together with Ekimmu, wandered the night world in search of victims for their insatiable blood lust.

In Hebrew folklore, Lilith was Father Adam's wife before the creation of Eve, the true chosen mother of humankind. The terrible night creatures known as the incubi and the succubi were the children of Adam and Lilith. The incubi materialize before human women as handsome men, hypnotically seducing them and withdrawing from them their life force. Succubi appear to human men as lovely, sensual women, tempting and promising, disguising their thirst for human blood.

While those human males who consort with a succubus often meet an untimely end, drained of their life force, on occasion their interaction with the entity brings about a horde of demonic children, who will one day gather at the deathbeds of their human fathers, hail them as their sires, then scatter to capture as many human souls as possible.

The Watchers Exploit Humans for Their Blood and Spirit

Since the Watchers manifested on Earth as angels, the Watchers were beings of spirit essence, rather than flesh and blood. What these fallen ones invading Earth needed from the sons and daughters of humans was their blood and their flesh so that they might become corporeal beings. The Watchers and the Nephilim were the first real vampires to exploit humankind, and they continue today to feed on the life force of humans—both their blood and their spirit.

As Wm. Michael Mott has stated in his excellent work, "There is a definite need and thirst for blood and sacrifice among those of this mostly-unseen kingdom. As postulated previously in *The Deep Dwellers*, some types of creatures … which take blood and the sacrificial organs, particularly the livers, from pets, livestock and even human mutilation victims, may be on a mission to obtain these substances for their unseen, mostly amorphous or invisible (spirit or other-dimensional) masters in the traditional underworld, and/or another dimension. This would explain much in regard to the mutilation and exsanguination phenomena. By the same token, the incursions and predations of the incubus, succubus, fairy lover, or 'reptoid rapist' might be for the purpose of obtaining viable DNA and reproductive materials. In medieval esoteric tradition, the succubus was said to carry the seed of her victim to the underworld, where it would be put to use by the diabolical forces there…. All of these things are nothing new. The same forms— physical, spiritual, and archetypal—repeat, over and over again through the centuries."

The Duality of the Gods

It is interesting to note that all of the world's major religions speak of a duality of the gods or demigods that came to Earth—some to exploit; others to teach; some to enslave; others to free.

There are numerous ancient legends that refer to a great war that occurred in "heaven" before the defeated angels or demigods came to Earth; and, after the Nephilim had transgressed against the laws of God, there was another violent conflict that raged on Earth between the forces of light and darkness in humankind's prehistory. It was the defeat of the armies of darkness that forced them to return to their non-corporeal state and withdraw to other dimensions of time and space. Because of the dark forces' continued efforts to corrupt and to possess humans, some mystics argue that the warfare continues unabated and that the great prize is the spiritual essence of humankind.

Wm. Michael Mott has commented that "the The Nephilim (Annunaki) in particular, banished beneath the Earth's surface, were said in the Apocryphal Books to have performed a wide range of genetic experiments, combining different types of creatures and men, and creating many 'chimerical' forms (like El Chupacabras). The description of Mothman matches the bas-relief carvings of ancient Sumer and Babylon of UTUKKU, guardians and errand-runners of the underworld, who were humanoid yet reptilian and birdlike in form.

"Prolonged study reveals that there are paranormal aspects to all or most of these phenomena. The 'reptilian' aspect of many of these beings, even the spiritual or supernatural ones, may have more to do with their very ancient (pre-mammalian) time and place of origin, as well as with their ability to present glamour or illusion when they appear briefly in our surface world. The Tantric account is a perfect example of this. The description of the locomotion, distinctly, reptilian or serpentine, of the female entity holds many clues as to the origin of that being, whether physical, spirit, or something of both realms."

In his remarkable *Caverns, Cauldrons, and Concealed Creatures*, Mott makes the very important point that in the west, "demons are often wrongly thought of as 'fallen angels,' which they are not. They represent the restless spirits of what the Torah calls 'the people of old time,' destroyed during the rebellion of their fallen angelic masters yet still enslaved to the same masters, their previous civilization 'thrust down' beneath the ground: 'When I shall bring thee down with them that descend into the pit, with *the people of old time*, and shall set thee *in the low parts of the Earth*, in places desolate of old, with them that go down to the pit, that thou be not inhabited; and I shall set glory in the land of the living.'—Ezekiel 26:20"

Mott says that entities are the equivalent of the Asuras and Rakshasas of Hinduism, and perhaps to some forms of fairy-type beings. There is also a very strong relationship or kinship between them and the extant or physical forms, such as some so-called 'cryptids', or unknown humanoids, which circumstantial and anecdotal evidence would indicate are the descendants of the same ancient races or species which are "demons" in the spirit world. They are interrelated, representing two aspects of one unseen kingdom or force that has haunted and plagued mankind for thousands of years.

Vampires, Blood, and the Life Force

At some point and time, there came to early humans the realization that the shedding of a person's blood was connected with the release of the life force itself. And because it was required by the gods, blood became sacred.

After the gods in their various guises retreated to their other dimensional universe, some of their most devoted human servants recalled the power inherent in blood and the life force, and a large number of magical and religious rituals became centered around the shedding of blood. In an effort to become like the gods, many individuals began to practice the drinking of blood as it pulsed from the veins of their victims.

As civilization advanced and humankind began to free itself from the demands of the old gods and their priests who demanded blood sacrifice, the life force and the fluid that symbolized it demanded a new kind of respect. Blood became holy.

The Old Testament book of Leviticus [17:14] acknowledges that blood is "the life of all flesh, the blood of it is the life thereof."

Again, in Deuteronomy 12:20-24, the Lord warns, "Thou mayest eat flesh, whatsoever thy soul lusteth after.... Only be sure that thou eat not the blood: for the blood *is* the life; and thou mayest not eat the life with the flesh."

But clerical dictates and civic pronouncements hold no threat to those who heed the whispers of the old gods to satisfy their bloodlust with the vital fluid of others. Nothing can quell the hunger of the real vampires who crouch in the darkness and wait to drink the blood of men, women, and children and to drain them of their life force.

WEREWOLVES—SHAPESHIFTERS FOREVER AMONG US

- The villagers of Potingani, near Hunedoara, Romania, began placing crosses near their homes to protect them from Gheorghe David, a 50-year-old Wolf Man with fangs and who howled at the full moon. In addition to the night terror that Gheorghe brought, people feared him for the power that he commanded over packs of wolves.

- In October 2000, a group of werewolf hunters broke into the Wolf Man's home and set fire to his vast collection of books about Black Magic. Ever since, each of the people involved in the burning of the books was visited by wolves that howled outside their windows throughout the night until dawn.

- A Queensland, Australia, social worker tried his best to answer cries for help from parents whose teenaged sons had become ensnared by a Werewolf Cult. In 2003, numerous parents discovered that their sons had been lured into the practice of lycanthropy or werewolfism and that the boys had been drinking blood and eating raw meat.

- In May 2006, two friends of 23-year-old Jeremy Allan Steinke, a man accused of a triple murder, testified in Medicine Hat, Alberta, Canada, that he had told them that he was a 300-year-old werewolf who liked the taste of blood. Steinke's friends said that he wore a necklace that bore a small vial of blood and that he identified himself as a "Lycan," a werewolf.

- A woman in Fond du Lac, Wisconsin, had allowed a friend to stay at her apartment until he began claiming that he was a werewolf. When the police answered her call to have him evicted in March 2007, the Lycan began speaking in what sounded to the police like some kind of medieval language. He threatened the officers that he had the power to turn into a werewolf and could attack them in his other form.

- Inhabitants from the rural area of Taua, Ceara, Brazil, endured an attack of werewolves in July 2008. The wolfmen carried off a number of sheep and broke into several homes in the area. Witnesses reported the figure of a "half-man, half-wolf" that they sighted in the light of the New Moon. Many testified that the creature was very ugly and smelled of sulfur.

The Werewolf Has Always Been with Us

As Linda Godfrey tells in her book *The Beast of Bray Road*, late one winter's night in 1993, Lorianne Endrizzi was driving down Bray Road in Elkhorn, Wisconsin, when she saw what she at first thought was a man crouching at the side of the road. Curious as to what he might be doing on the shoulder of the road, she slowed down to take a closer look. Within the next few moments, she was astonished to see that the being spotlighted in the beams of her headlights was covered with fur, had a long, wolf-like snout, fangs, pointed ears, and eyes that had a yellowish glow. The thing's arms were jointed like a human's, and it had hands with humanlike fingers that were tipped with pointed claws.

In July 2008, inhabitants from the rural area of Taua, Ceara, Brazil, endured an attack by werewolves (*art by Ricardo Pustanio*).

Lorianne sped off, thinking that the creature was so humanlike that it had to be some kind of freak of nature. Later, when she visited the library, she found a book with an illustration of a werewolf. She said that she was startled to see how much the classic monster of legend resembled the beast that she had seen that night on Bray Road right there in Elkhorn, Wisconsin.

Doristine Gipson, another Elkhorn resident who sighted the creature on Bray Road, described it has having a large chest, like that of a weightlifter's. She was certain that she had not seen a large dog, but a humanlike creature that had a wide chest and was covered with long, brown hair.

A twelve-year-old girl said that she had been with a group of friends walking near a snow-covered cornfield when they sighted what they believed to be a large dog. When they began to call it, it stared at them, then stood upright.

As the children screamed their alarm, the beast dropped back down on all fours and began running toward them. Fortunately for them, the monster suddenly headed off in another direction and disappeared.

Not long ago, Linda Godfrey and I had an opportunity to discuss real monsters and real werewolves.

Brad Steiger: When you began your interviews with the witnesses, what struck you most about their encounters?

Linda Godfrey: What impressed me most about the first witnesses was their almost visible sense of deep fright that was still obvious as they recounted what they saw. They didn't act like people making something up, and in fact, they could hardly bring themselves to tell their stories. I was also impressed by the fact that they all noticed a certain jeering cockiness from the creature as it made eye contact with them. This is a characteristic that has continued to be present in every sighting reported. Even when the witness is some distance away, he or she reports feeling almost more like the observed than the observer. And that is very unnerving to even the most macho, outdoorsy of the witnesses. I was also struck by the fact that the creature apparently was more interested in getting away than in harming anyone.

Linda Godfrey, author of *The Beast of Bray Road* and many other books exploring werewolves and the paranormal.

Officially, I don't eliminate any sightings that are reported in good faith, as long as the witness felt there was something very strange about it. In much Native American lore, "spirit" animals are visually indistinguishable from ordinary creatures. So if witnesses think there is something different enough about what they see that they are compelled to report it, I just put it down exactly as they tell it. I feel the more information we have, the easier it will be to see patterns.

It's worth noting that people do see ordinary dogs, coyotes, bears, wolves, etc. all the time and the reaction is just, "hey, there's a coyote" ... not, "heaven help me, there's something so unusual it's scaring me to death." So I tend to trust people's instincts when they say there was something not right about what they've spotted, whether it was size, speed, posture, or even as some have reported, telepathic communication!

Steiger: Did you ever entertain the idea that the witnesses might have, indeed, seen a real werewolf?

Godfrey: The tough part about answering that question is defining "real" werewolf. Most people entertain the Hollywood notion of the slathering, tortured soul who transforms bodily under the full moon and must be killed with silver bullets. Others might consider the word to signify a shamanistic shapeshifter who is able to summon the very realistic illusion of another creature.

Or perhaps you are talking about the medieval notion of a human who is able to project an astral entity that looks like a wolf (usually while the person is sound asleep) that is able to roam the countryside, kill and eat people and which, if wounded, will transfer the wound to the corresponding area of the human body.

There are other versions, too. Statements by witnesses such as "I thought it was a demon from hell," or "it was something not natural, not of this world," have indeed made me wonder if something other than a natural, flesh-and-blood animal is roaming the cornfields around here.

A few witnesses that I detail in my second book, *Beyond Bray Road*, claim to have seen the creature either morphing or materializing. This points to the supernatural, but still doesn't prove that an actual human has changed bodily structure, grown fur and fangs, and then sneaked out for a midnight possum dinner. However, I do consider the possibility. And while I know there are self-proclaimed lycanthropes who insist they do transmute, I haven't yet found the evidence to prove it occurs.

Steiger: Could any of the sightings have been of Bigfoot?

Godfrey: Several of the sightings, especially some of those which have come in since the first book was written, do sound more like a Bigfoot or Sasquatch than a wolfman or dogman. A few witnesses sketches have borne this out. They are still greatly in the minority, however.

It's interesting to me that every witness who has had a good look at the head has been adamant that it was either dog/wolf-like or ape-like. But since there do seem to be two separate types of sightings, we have to grapple with the unsettling fact that perhaps we have two different anomalous creatures in the vicinity. If natural animals, they would probably compete with each other for territory, water and some food, and it's hard to believe a lot of them could exist in this relatively small area. If supernatural, though, there is no reason that one creature couldn't appear in different forms, and that would explain the creature diversity very neatly.

Steiger: I think you are familiar with the Native American legends of the Windigo, a monster of the woods. Could there be a link between werewolf accounts, Bigfoot sightings, and some of the ancient Native American traditions?

Godfrey: That's a very rich possibility and one I've been exploring with some of the native tribal people of Wisconsin. The Windigo is often mentioned as an explanation for the Beast of Bray Road, but if you explore the many Windigo legends, this particular story does not fit witness observations or the southern Wisconsin terrain very well. The Windigo legend is more related to starvation-related cannibalism in the northern forests, and varies widely in size and description from tribe to tribe. It's often composed of ice that melts down to reveal a human or animal. There are better fits, such as the Canadian Cree Hairy Heart beings that I talk about in my first book. The Hairy Hearts also sound like Bigfoot. But so far, the Native Americans I've talked with lean toward more of a "spirit being" explanation.

Linda Godfrey tempts the Beast of Bray Road with a chicken in an attempt to establish a clearer identification of the wolf-like being.

Steiger: Shape-shifting is an acknowledged and an accepted device of tribal shaman. Could someone have mastered the craft of shape-shifting that has been an element of magick for thousands of years? Could ancient European magick traditions and practitioners have blended with the Native American legends to have created a hybrid monster?

Godfrey: This is another area I explored in my second book. But I'm not sure it would be necessary for ancient North American shamanic practices to blend with European magick to create this hairy creature—according to their own traditions, either society would be capable of such conjuring. In both medieval Europe and among our Native American medicine societies, it has been an accepted belief that animal forms could be created or summoned to our corporeal world by certain rituals and disciplines. Of course, these days there are various occultic groups blending what they know of native shamanism and other practices, sometimes with the involvement of psychotropic drugs, so it's hard telling what can be cooked up!

Steiger: What about some ghost ... spirit ... or multidimensional visitor having been responsible for the werewolf sightings?

Godfrey: Various paranormal researchers and writers have suggested that Wisconsin is a key "window area" with many portals from other dimensions. The latest super-string theories of quantum physics have posited that there must be at least eleven dimensions in our universe. Although we have no way of knowing whether "creatures" from one dimension could function in another (or if the other dimensions have anything we could recognize as life), it does make the idea that things could be popping in and out from other places a bit more plausible. And it would help explain the many sightings of UFOs, Bigfoot, over-sized birds, ghost-like visions, light phenomena, and of course wolfmen, that keep paranormal researchers in this state hopping.

A Brief History of the Werewolf

Sometime around 140,000 years ago wolves and primitive humans formed a common bond and evolved together in one of the most successful partnerships ever fashioned. The wolf's strength, stamina, keen sense of hearing, and extraordinary sense of smell helped humans to hunt prey and to overcome predators. Because we humans teamed up with wolves, we became better hunters and thus supplanted our rival species of Homo erectus and Neanderthal.

Humans and wolves share a similar social structure. Both species employ a cooperative rearing strategy for their offspring with both parents participating in the feeding and rearing process. In most mammals, the care of the young is left almost exclusively to the mother. Wolves practice fidelity and mate for life, thus setting an early model for the family structure. Wolf packs also have dominant members, like any tribe or community, and humans probably began the domestication process by assuming the role of the dominant wolf and achieving acquiescence from the lupine leader.

The human species greatly depended upon wolves for its continued existence and modeled much of their behavior, especially in the area of survival skills, upon the wolf. As these prehistoric "wolf men" learned over time to hunt in packs and, with the assistance of their wolf allies, to subdue much larger predators, then certain elements of lupine savagery may well have been "inherited" along with the more noble aspects of a sense of community and mutual support.

In the beginning of our bonding with the lupine, all men and women wanted to be werewolves—Man-Wolves. However, after a few centuries of "civilization" the human community reached a time when it would be considered improper, antisocial, and criminal to behave like a wolf. Still, there remained the sorcerers and those on the fringes of society who believed that one could attain great power by maintaining those lupine links to a more savage past. They believed that they had the ability to shape shift to werewolves—wolf men and women.

The Werewolf and Sorcery

According to the ancients, any skilled sorcerer who so chose could become a werewolf. Throughout history, self-professed werewolves have mentioned a "magic girdle," which they wear about their middles, or a "magic salve" which they apply liberally to their naked bodies. Others tell of inhaling or imbibing certain potions.

Magical texts advise those who wish to become a werewolf to disrobe, rub a magical ointment freely over their flesh, place a girdle made of human or wolf skin around their waist, then cover their entire body with the pelt of a wolf. To accelerate the process, they should drink beer mixed with blood and chant a particular magical formula.

Some werewolves claimed to have achieved their shape-shifting ability by having drunk water from the paw print of a wolf. Once this had been accomplished, they ate the brains of a wolf and slept in its lair.

One ancient text prescribes a ritual for the magician who is eager to become a shape-shifter. He is told to wait until the night of a full moon, then enter the forest at midnight. Then, according to the instructions:

> Draw two concentric circles on the ground, one six feet in diameter, the other fourteen feet in diameter. Build a fire in the center of the inner circle and place a tripod over the flames. Suspend from the tripod an iron pot full of water. Bring the water to a full boil and throw into the pot a handful each of aloe, hemlock, poppy seed, and nightshade. As the ingredients are being stirred in the iron pot, call aloud to the spirits of the restless dead, the spirits of the foul darkness, the spirits of the hateful, and the spirits of werewolves and satyrs.

Once the summons for the various spirits of darkness have been shouted into the night, the person who aspires to become a werewolf should strip off all of his clothing and smear his body with the fat of a freshly killed animal that has been mixed with anise, camphor, and opium. The next step is to take the wolf skin that he has brought with him, wrap it around his middle like a loincloth, then kneel down at the boundaries of the large circle and remain in that position until the fire dies out. When this happens, the power that the disciple of darkness has summoned should make its presence known to him.

If the magician has done everything correctly, the dark force will announce its presence by loud shrieks and groans.

Later, if the would-be werewolf has not been terrified and frightened away by the Dark One's awful screams, it will materialize in any one of a number forms, most likely that of a horrible half-human, half-beast monster. Once it has manifested in whatever form it desires, the Dark One force will conduct its transaction with the magician and allow him henceforth to assume the shape of a wolf whenever he wears his wolf skin loincloth.

In the classic accounts, once the transformation into wolf has occurred, it is difficult to detect any differences between the werewolf and a true wolf without careful examination. The werewolf that has undergone a complete shape-shifting process is somewhat larger than a true wolf, very often has a silvery sheen to its fur, and always has red, glowing eyes.

The werewolf of ancient tradition runs on all fours and has discarded all vestiges of clothing before the process of transmutation begins. If the shape-shifter should be killed while in the form of a wolf, he or she would return to human shape and be found to be naked.

Those who became werewolves of their own choice and who sought the power of transmutation through incantations, potions, or spells, gloried in their strength and in their ability to strike fear into the hearts of all who hear their piercing howling on the nights of the full moon.

Famous Werewolves in Ancient History

Apparently, this technique must have worked very well for some individuals.

- In 400 B.C.E. Damarchus, a werewolf from the Greek city state of Arcadia, is said to have won boxing medals at the Olympics.
- In about 85 B.C.E. the great Roman poet Virgil speaks of the powers of the werewolf Moeris, from whom he claims to have learned many secrets of magic, including the raising of the dead.
- In 175 Pausanias, a Greek traveler, geographer, and author visited Arcadia and met the Lycanian werewolves.
- In his *City of God* (c. 410) the great Roman Catholic clergyman St. Augustine relates the account of certain sorceresses in the Alps who give their unsuspecting victims a special kind of cheese that transforms them into beasts of burden.
- In 435 St. Patrick arrives in Ireland and discovers that among his flock are many families of werewolves.

The Church Declares War on Werewolves

By 906, werewolves were becoming too numerous and Abbot Regino of Prum condemned as heretical any belief in witchcraft or in the power of sorcerers to change people into animals. If anyone believed they had the ability to transform a human into a creature of another species, they were being deceived by Satan.

At this time the Christian clergy was more interested in stamping out all allegiance to the goddess Diana and regarded as primitive superstition any suggestion that witches or sorcerers possessed any kind of magical powers or that men and women could be transformed into werewolves. Unfortunately, in 1233, the Church smothered all such rational thinking with the thick black smoke of the Inquisition.

How Does One Distinguish a Vampire from a Werewolf?

It was not as easy detecting werewolves among the human population as it was to hunt down the vampires lurking in the shadows. Perhaps the most essential difference between the two creatures of the Darkside is the fact that the werewolf is not a member of the undead. When werewolves were not in the throes of transformation precipitated by the rays of the full moon or the wearing of the magic wolf belt, they walked about the bustling streets of the city or the pleasant country lanes appearing as any normal human.

Werewolves have no need to scamper off to a coffin before the rays of the rising sun begin to burn welts into their hide. Werewolves can freely walk in sunlight.

Mirrors offer no problem for werewolves. They can straighten their collar or comb their hair without worrying if they are casting a reflection.

Crucifixes are of no concern. Werewolves might even wear the sign of the cross themselves, attend church services, and perhaps even serve as members of the clergy.

How to Detect a Werewolf

The werewolf hunters did have some clues when it came to detecting the werewolves among them. As early as the seventh century, Paulos Agina, a physician who lived in Alexandria, described the symptoms of werewolfism for his fellow doctors:

- Pale skin.
- Weak vision.
- An absence of tears or saliva, making the eyes and a tongue very dry.
- Excessive thirst.
- Ulcers and abrasions on the arms and legs that do not heal, caused by walking on all fours.
- An obsession with wandering in cemeteries at night.
- Howling until dawn.

Other traditions insisted that the hands may provide the biggest giveaway. Check the palms of a suspected werewolf, and if his palms are covered with a coarse, stiff growth of hair, you had better avoid his company on the nights of the full moon.

Another certain sign of the werewolf, according to a vast number of ancient traditions, lies in the extreme length of the index finger. If you should notice a man or woman with an index finger considerably longer than the middle finger, you have quite likely spotted a werewolf.

Then there is the matter of the eyebrows growing together. If they should meet in the center of the forehead, there is cause for genuine concern that you have encountered a werewolf.

A good many traditions regard the pentagram, the five-pointed star, as a symbol of witchcraft and werewolves. Some werewolf hunters of old believed that the sign of the pentagram would be found somewhere on a shape-shifter's body, most often on the chest or the hand. It was also an aspect of that belief structure that the shadow of the pentagram would manifest on the palm or forehead of the werewolf's next victim and would be visible only to the monster's eyes.

And while the eyes of the werewolf appear normal at all other times, when the curse is upon them, their eyes glow in the dark, most often with a reddish hue.

The Inquisition and Its Torture Machines

Werewolves most often attack their victims for the sheer joy of the slaughter, the ripping and biting at the flesh, tearing at the jugular vein with claws or fangs. Its strength is superhuman.

Since there is no time when a werewolf is really vulnerable in its animal form, over the centuries werewolf hunters learned to wait until the creature had shifted back to its human shape. That was when the foot soldiers of the Inquisition seized werewolves for its torture machines and death by burning at the stake.

In 1257, the Church officially sanctioned torture as a means of forcing witches, werewolves, shape-shifters, and other heretics to confess. Some judges at the various Tribunals insisted that those suspected of being werewolves be executed by beheading with a double-edged sword, for that was the only certain way to dispatch a werewolf.

Such a decree of torture and painful death inspired testimony from those who swore that they had been transformed into werewolves against their will.

According to ancient tradition, by far the most familiar involuntary manners in which one becomes a werewolf is to be cursed for your sins by a priest or someone you have wronged or by being the victim of a sorcerer's incantations.

Another involuntary means of becoming a werewolf, according to some old traditions, is to be born on Christmas Eve. The very process of one's birth on that sacred night, so say certain ecclesiastical scholars, is an act of blasphemy since it detracts from the full attention to be given to the nativity of Jesus. Thus, those born on that night are condemned to be werewolves unless they prove themselves to be pious beyond reproach in all thoughts, words, and deeds throughout their lifetimes.

When those individuals who became werewolves against their will are not under the power of the curse that forces them to become ravenous

According to the ancients, any skilled sorcerer who so chose could become a werewolf (**art by Ricardo Pustanio**).

beasts, they experience all the normal human emotions of shame and disgust for the deeds that they must commit under the blood spell. They may long for death and seek ways to destroy themselves before they take the lives of more innocent victims.

- In 1407, dozens of werewolves were tortured and burned during witchcraft trials at Basel.

- In 1521, three werewolves of Poligny, accused of having eaten children and consorted with wild she-wolves, confessed to having achieved their transformation from a magic salve. They were burnt at the stake.

- In 1555, Olaus Magnus recorded his observation that the werewolves of Livonia put on a girdle of wolf skin, drink a cup of beer, and uttered certain magic words to accomplish their transformation from humans to wolves.

- The infamous Gilles Garnier was burned as a werewolf in 1573, and the notorious Peter Stubbe was executed as a werewolf at Cologne in 1589.

- Roulet, The Werewolf of Chalons, a tailor accused of eating children in his shop, was executed in Paris in 1598, and in that same year, the Gandillon family was burned as werewolves in Jura.

The Vicious, Mysterious Beast of Gevaudan

In the 1760s, residents of southern France were terrorized by a werewolf that allegedly killed hundreds of people during a bloody three-year reign of bestial butchery. What or who was the Beast of Gevaudan has puzzled students of unexplained mysteries for more than two centuries. Le Gevaudan is a barren, seventy-five-mile stretch of hills and valleys in the rugged mountain range that runs along the edge of the Auvergne plateau. Although Lyons and Toulouse are populous cities, the outlying area is sparsely settled.

Loup-garou! "Werewolf!" became a cry that terrorized the whole of Le Gevaudan. Outlying farms were abandoned as the monster preyed upon the peasants. Entire villages were deserted as the beast moved boldly into these communities in search of new victims.

The creature was described as a hairy beast that walked upright on two legs. Its face was sworn to be like that of Satan, and its entire body was said to be covered with dark, bristly hair. Those who were fortunate enough to escape the beast's clutches always mentioned an "evil smell" that emanated from its foul hide. Deep claw marks on the bodies of its victims indicated that the monster sucked blood from the corpses. One eyewitness described the werewolf's eyes as glassy, like those of a wild animal; and its dark face was covered with hair.

Some said that the beast looked like a man running in an animal's skin. Others told investigators that it could run on all four legs or upright, in a loping, humanlike movement.

Dragoon Captain Jacques Duhamel scoffed that such creatures as werewolves were nothing but superstition and old wives' tales, but Portefaix carried a petition from the villagers directly to Louis IX at Versailles, and the King ordered a detachment of dragoons to search the mountains of Le Gevaudan. After the soldiers had left the region, the murderous rampage of the beast increased with savage fury.

The years of 1765, 1766, and 1767 are spoken of as the "time of the death" in the mountains. Parish records reveal daily attacks by the monster, who seemed to choose housewives and children as its principal victims.

A Marquis organized a posse of several hundred armed men, and after tracking the beast for many days they succeeded in surrounding the creature in a grove of trees. As dusk deepened into darkness, the monster charged its pursuers and was shot down. Jean Chastel was given credit for the kill.

According to Chastel's testimony, he had prepared himself according to certain ancient traditions. His double-barreled musket was loaded with bullets made from a silver chalice that had been blessed by a priest.

Since that dramatic final encounter with the Beast of Le Gevaudan there has been constant debate concerning the type of creature slain by the Marquis' posse. Some researchers have argued that the beast was some type of rare leopard; others a wild boar with deadly tusks and tough, dark bristles. Chastel himself described his trophy as possessing peculiar feet, pointed ears, and a body completely covered with coarse, dark hair. The general consensus among the members of the hunting party claimed that the beast was a true werewolf, half-human and half-wolf.

It is known for certain that the carcass of a large wolf was paraded through the streets of several villages in the area as proof that the terrible beast had truly been killed. Municipal records attest to the hundreds of people who were killed by the murderous monster—whether werewolf, wolf, or whatever.

Science Discovers Lycanthropy

Contemporary medical professionals have sought to offer rational explanations for the werewolves that have scourged the past and haunted the present. The term "lycanthropy"(from the Greek, literally, wolf-man) was used by Reginald Scot in his *The Discovery of Witchcraft* to denote an extreme form of violent insanity in which the individual may imitate the behavior of a wild beast, especially a wolf. Scot argued against the Church and the Inquisition and its institutionalized program of torturing and burning of witches, werewolves, and other shape-shifters; and he nearly ended up bound to a stake for his heretical efforts on behalf of reason. Scot used the term in the same manner as a modern health professional when referring to the mental disease that manifests itself in ways applicable to werewolfism.

The term lycanthropy was also applied to those individuals afflicted with a form of dark melancholy, a deep depression that gave rise to a violent form of insanity. In his *Anatomy of Melancholy*, Robert Burton writes that those men and women who are suffering from an advanced form of melancholy that graduates into werewolfism lie hidden throughout the daylight hours, then "go abroad in the night, barking, howling, at graves ... they have unusually hollow eyes, scabbed legs and thighs, very dry and pale."

Dr. Mary Matossian, professor of history at the University of Maryland, viewed such statistics as those from France which proclaimed that 30,000 individuals were condemned as werewolves between the years of 1520 to 1630 and wondered how such a mental aberration could possibly have been so widespread. As she researched the phenomenon, she derived a theory that the peasants were eating a rye bread that was contaminated by a fungus that acted as a powerful hallucinogenic. In essence, Dr. Matossian suggested that thousands of men and women were suffering from "bad trips" from a potent fungus that caused them to have delusions that they were magical beings capable of transforming themselves into werewolves.

According to Dr. Matossian: The fungus was ergot, a parasite that attacks rye. The ergot produces sclerotia which grow on the rye plant, taking the place of its natural seeds. The wind blows and the fungus latches onto other rye plants.

During harvesting, the ergot was collected along with the grain and became part of the bread. Since ergot is like today's LSD, some individuals suffered bad trips and imagined themselves being transformed into animals, such as wolves.

Others saw themselves with special powers, like flying on a broomstick. They were the witches. The ergot caused them to act in other bizarre ways, even committing murder and injury. As a result, numerous victims of ergot poisoning were tried as wolves and werewolves—and executed.

In the Canadian Psychiatric Association Journal in 1975, psychiatrists Frida Surawicz and Richard Banta of Lexington, Kentucky, published their paper, "Lycanthropy Revisited" in which they presented two case studies of contemporary werewolves.

Their first case, that of Mr. H., obliquely supported Dr. Mary Matossian's hallucinogenic hypothesis in that he had ingested LSD before he saw himself changing into a werewolf. He saw fur growing over his hands and face, and he craved flesh and blood. Even after the effects of the drug had supposedly worn off, Mr. H. still believed himself to be a werewolf. He was treated as a paranoid schizophrenic, treated with antipsychotic medication, and after about five weeks, released from a psychiatric unit.

Surawicz and Banta's second case study was that of a 37-year-old farmer, who, after his discharge from the Navy, began allowing his hair to grow long and began sleeping in cemeteries and howling at the moon. Although there was no indication of drug

The werewolf of ancient tradition runs on all fours and has discarded all vestiges of clothing before the process of transmutation begins. The beast is not a Wolf Man, but a wolf created by the Dark Arts (*art by Ricardo Pustanio*).

abuse or misuse in Mr. W.'s case, he was freed from his delusion after treatment with antipsychotic medication.

Psychiatrist Harvey Rosenstock and psychologist Kenneth Vincent discussed their case history of a forty-nine-year-old woman who underwent the metamorphosis into a werewolf in their paper, "A Case of Lycanthropy," published in the *American Journal of Psychiatry* in 1977. Although she finally was admitted to a locked psychiatric unit and received daily psychotherapy and antipsychotic drugs, she still beheld herself as a wolf woman with claws, teeth, and fangs and believed that her werewolf spirit would roam the earth long after her physical death. Medical personnel would manage to get the woman under control until the next full moon. At that time, she would snarl, howl, and resume her wolf-like behavior. She was eventually discharged and provided with antipsychotic medication, but she promised to haunt the graveyards until she found the tall, dark, hairy creature of her dreams.

In his *Bizarre Diseases of the Mind*, Dr. Richard Noll lists the traditional traits of the lycanthrope:

- The belief that they are wolves or wild dogs.
- The belief that they have been physically transformed into animals with fur and claws.
- Animal-like behavior, including growling, howling, clawing, pawing, crawling on all fours.
- The desire to assault or kill others.
- Hypersexuality, including the desire to have sex with animals.
- Use of a hallucinogenic substance to achieve the metamorphosis of human into a wolf.
- A desire for isolation from human society (stalking the woods, haunting cemeteries).
- The belief that "the devil" has possessed them and provided the power that causes the transformation from human to wolf.

When the Moon Is Full and Bright

Since the very earliest accounts of werewolves, those who would seek to explain the onset of such frightening behavior have stated with authority that it is the light of the full moon that serves as the catalyst for the transformation of human into wolf. The ancient Greeks and Romans associated the moon with the underworld and those human and inhuman entities who used the night to work their dark magic. Witches, werewolves, and other shape-shifters received great power from the moon—and just as the moon changed its shape throughout the month, so could these servants of the underworld transform their shapes into bats, wolves, dogs, rats, or any creature they so chose. In addition, they could also change their hapless victims into animals.

There have been a number of studies which indicate that the full moon does make people more violent. In 1998 researchers observed prisoners in the maximum-security wing at Armley jail, Leeds, England. Claire Smith, a prison officer on A wing, carried out the psychological study of all 1,200 inmates for more than three months, and the researchers found that there was a definite rise in the number of violent and unruly incidents recorded during the first and last quarter of each lunar cycle, the days on either side of a full moon.

Ms. Smith expressed her opinion that she believed her study to have proved that there is a link between the moon and human behavior. "The best theory I have heard to explain why this happens is that we are made up of 60 to 70 percent water," she commented. "And if the moon controls the tides, what is it doing to us?"

The Werewolf Attacks Hollywood

For millions of contemporary men and women, the word "werewolf" immediately conjures up images of the actor Lon Chaney Jr. in *The Wolf Man* (1941), creeping through the mists of the moors, a good man tortured by the knowledge that the bite of a werewolf has caused him to endure a monthly metamorphosis into a monster during the full moon. Although a wolf, we still recognize Chaney as a man, fully clothed, walking upright in a peculiar loping movement.

In later motion pictures, such as *The Howling* (1981), *An American Werewolf in London* (1981), and *An American Werewolf in Paris* (1997), vastly improved visual effects allow us to witness the complete transformation of man into wolf. The most recent treatment, *The Wolfman* (2010) with Benicio Del Toro, shows the audiences more aspects of a transformation from man to beast than its 1941 inspiration, but Del Toro still remains a Wolf Man, a creature we recognize as half-wolf, half-man, not truly a werewolf. *The Wolf Man* created a number of traditions that truly became cinematic werewolf dogma in many horror films to follow.

On September 2, 2000, at the age of 98, the true "Wolf Man" died. On that date on his ranch in Three Rivers, California, Curt Siodmak, the screenwriter of *The Wolf Man*, passed into the mists of time as the man who really created most of the werewolf traditions that movie-makers still honor today:

- People become werewolves after being bitten or scratched by a werewolf.

- Upon the rising of the first full moon after surviving the attack by the werewolf, the victims are themselves transformed into werewolves. Such shall be their fate forever.

- The process of transformation causes fangs and claws to grow, hair to sprout all over the body, and human compassion to be clouded by blood lust.

- Werewolves retain an upright, two-legged human body shape and continue to wear the clothing in which they were attired before the transformation began. Shoes are the only items of wearing apparel discarded before the lycanthropes terrorize the moonlit countryside.

- Wolfbane is very effective at keeping a werewolf at bay. Garlic is also a good werewolf deterrent, and a pentagram (the five-pointed star) might save your life if it is made of silver.

- An object made of silver is the only thing that can kill a werewolf. (A silver bullet in the heart would be added by Siodmak in *Frankenstein Meets the Wolf Man*, 1943.)

With these rules for lycanthropic behavior, manners, and mores firmly established in *The Wolf Man*, Universal Pictures reconstructed and revised centuries of werewolf lore and legend. Even the famous old Gypsy folklore, "Even the man who is pure at heart/And says his prayers at night/May become a wolf when the wolf-bane blooms/ And the moon is clear and bright," was composed by Curt Siodmak for the film.

We All Bear within the Seed of the Werewolf

While most of us have become "domesticated" and listen to the inner voice of conscience that has been strengthened by moral and spiritual values and cultivated over centuries of civilized behavior, those individuals who have succumbed to the more vicious seed of the wolf within them walk among us today as those sadistic sex criminals who slash, tear, rip, rape, mutilate, and cannibalize their victims. When one compares the details of the offenses charged to alleged werewolves during the witchcraft mania of the Middle Ages with the offenses attributed to such sex criminals as the Chicago Rippers, Harry Gordon, Richard Ramirez, Henry Lee Lucas, and Jeffrey Dahmer, it becomes clear that there exists a true werewolf psychosis that can cause people to believe that they are transformed into wolves or can cause them to commit cruel and vicious crimes as if they were wolves scratching, biting, and killing their prey.

The werewolf of tradition is the deliberate creation of a human who, motivated by a desire for power or revenge, has sought to release the beast within....

While the werewolf as sex criminal constitutes a very grim reality and a serious physical threat to unsuspecting members of society who are its potential victims, the werewolf as a creature of superstition poses a psychic threat to those who may trespass beyond the boundaries of logic and reason into the dangerous and uncharted regions of the supernatural. The werewolf of tradition is the deliberate creation of a human who, motivated by a desire for power or revenge, has sought to release the beast within and accomplish the transformation of human into wolf.

Since prehistoric times the bloodline of the wolf has blended with that of our own species, and each one of us bears the personal responsibility of honoring the noble aspects of our lupine heritage and, at the same time, keeping the savage bloodlust under control.

The Loup Garou

F ew people have the courage or lack the common sense to laugh at the stories of the Loup Garou, the werewolves of the Louisiana swamp country. Gators and panthers are easy to deal with, but the werewolf has a power that has followed the Cajun folk from France to Acadia (Nova Scotia) and then to Louisiana when the British drove the exiled Acadians out of Canada.

Taste for Nutria: A Cajun's Tale of the Loup Garou

by Alyne A. Pustanio

A t the end of a long day's work of emptying traps along the water's edge throughout the shadowy, winding labyrinth of the bayou, the trappers were gathered together near the camp of one man where they all planned to spend the night. No one wanted to be caught out in the dappled darkness so the little fishing camp known as the "Tide Over" was picked for the overnight stay.

With the boats and traps secured at the camp's makeshift dock, and the nutria (a large herbivorous, semi-aquatic rodent) safely stowed in an old metal ice chest near the back door, the trappers settled in for the night.

Soon the screened windows were aglow, casting feeble yellow light into the near-impenetrable darkness of the surrounding swamp. Insects buzzed against the window screen and now and then a large moth fluttered in the light before the night sucked it up again. Amid the comforting chirping of the crickets and katydids, the familiar snuffling of the raccoon and the possum could be heard; every now and then a little "plunk" from the still bayou water meant a fish was jumping or a frog had caught a meal.

The men made a quick dinner of some catfish they had caught earlier in the day and washed it down with ice-cold beer. Soon the lights were dimmed and the tired trappers contentedly took to their beds. Surrounded by the all-encompassing darkness and the symphony of the swamp, they were soon asleep.

Baudier was the first to wake up, jolted, all of a sudden, but by what he did not know. Blinking in the darkness, he listened. He sat up. He listened some more. And he sat straight up because he heard—nothing. Absolutely nothing.

Not a cricket, not a katydid, not a snuffle or a plunk. He heard nothing.

"Chotin!" he whispered to the man on the cot next to him. "Chotin! Wake up, man! Dere's sometin' wrong out dere!"

Chotin, a large lump of a Cajun man, sleeping shirtless but in his pants and white shrimp boots (it was these that Baudier saw move first), sat up and looked into the darkness toward Baudier's voice.

The wild, heavy forested regions of Minnesota, Wisconsin, and Michigan have also produced many reports of "Dogmen" (*art by Dan Wolfman Allen*).

"Maannn! What is wrong wid you?" Chotin droned. "You waked me up from a good sleep, I tell you. Dis better be good!"

"Shhh!" said Baudier. "Listen!" He peered into the darkness until he could make out Chotin's wide face. "Hear dat?"

Chotin listened. He heard nothing. "Hear what?" But even as he said it, he became aware that he, too, was hearing nothing and he let out a low whistle. "Chere! Dere ain't notin' out dere!"

Nearby, Tirout and Gaspard, hearing Chotin whistle, sat up too.

"Maannn, what is you two doin'?" said Gaspard.

"Shhh!" came a hoarse little whisper from Tirout, then, "Listen! What's dat?"

All together they heard it, a THUMP, then another THUMP, followed by a couple of splashes, then two more THUMPS.

In each of their minds the terrified trappers could envision, by the approach of the sounds, just where they were coming from. THUMP and THUMP were on the little spit of land where the traps were set; the splashes put the sound near the boats; the two last THUMPS on the bank near the boats.

Waiting, sweating, not understanding what had them so frightened, but too scared to ignore their gut, the four trappers sat petrified, listening to something approach in the absolute stillness of the night.

THUMP. THUMP.

"Gawd!" Baudier choked and in the darkness the round, white eyes of his friends turned to him. "Dat sounds like FEET to me!" The white eyes grew wider and all turned away toward the screened windows and the night beyond.

Just then came three THUMPS in succession followed by the definite sound of something stepping onto the wooden porch alongside the camp. Though they thought they had been scared before this, the terror level inside the little fishing camp hit a peak as a sniffing, snuffling, snorting kind of sound filled the air. SOMETHING was out there and it was SMELLING for them!

Beads of sweat broke on Baudier's forehead and dripped down into his eyes. He glanced at the windows, illuminated by the faint starlight glinting down from the canopy of cypress and moss; he could feel the others were looking this way, too. That is why there never was any debate on what Baudier must have seen before he passed out, because three other men saw it right along with him!

A huge animal head went past the windows then: like the head of a big dog, blown up to enormous size. The three men who did not pass out saw it in vivid profile against the shimmer of the night beyond. Long, dog-like ears stood straight up to hear every sound; the glassy yellow of monstrous, watery eyes that, had they turned inside, would surely have caused the shaking Cajuns to die on the spot! Drool hung in long, sinuous strings from grisly teeth, and, perhaps worst of all, was the scraping and skittering of what could only be long nails scratching along the outside wall.

Suddenly, the creature bent down, probably to walk on all fours because the next sound was like a big dog scampering on the wooden porch planks. The thumping led away to the rear of the camp and suddenly there came a loud metal "CLANG!" The beast had found the old cooler!

With growing terror and disgust the Cajun trappers sat in the darkness of that camp and listened while the horrible Loup Garou devoured every single one of the nutrias they had trapped that day. Guttural gulping and the horrible cracking of skulls and bones filled the men with dread, but they dared not move so long as the Loup Garou was feasting.

Long moments passed that seemed like hours, then suddenly, to their horror, Baudier began to awake and he was groaning loud enough for the Loup Garou to hear!

Now all the wide, white eyes in the pitch-black room turned upward and each man began to pray, while Baudier continued to groan.

Suddenly, the horrible eating stopped. The Loup Garou was listening!

A limp, sad little thump sounded and the men knew the beast had dropped a nutria to the deck; a rustling and clicking noise meant the beast had surely heard Baudier's pitiful groaning.

> *A limp, sad little thump sounded and the men knew the beast had dropped a nutria to the deck; a rustling and clicking noise meant the beast had surely heard Baudier's pitiful groaning.*

Chotin, Tirout, and Gaspard thought about all the things they would miss in life—boudin sausage and Miller Lite beer, bingo and deer hunting, their boats and watching Saints football, their mommas and their wives—when suddenly, from out in the swamp, they heard a sound that made the hair on their bodies rise and stand straight on end!

"CAAWWWW!!" came the horrible noise. "CAAAWWW! CAAAWWWW!"

The noises from the Loup Garou stopped instantly. The thing was wary now, listening. Maybe its yellow eyes were big, too, and peering at the swamp. Stillness descended. Then, suddenly, a cacophony of unearthly screeching and squawking and flapping and howling filled the night air.

In the tumult Gaspard, the Cajun closest to the outside window, now summoned up a courage that would become legendary in the swamp, talked about at crawfish boils and fais-do-dos for years to come. He rose stealthily from his cot and sneaked over to the screened window. Looking out he saw an amazing sight: The huge shaggy Loup Garou was covered with angry black crows, all flapping and pecking at the creature.

Suddenly, with a howl, the Loup Garou broke free and in a flash of thumps, snorting and splashes, it bounded away from the little camp, into the pitch darkness of the swamp with the birds, a cloud of soot and feathers, following. The trappers now clung together, drenched in sweat and shivering with fear in the uneasy silence. They sat like this, holding on for dear life, fearful that the beast might return, until the pale grey light of day could be seen illuminating the sky beyond the moss-hung canopy of the swamp. Then, all together in a group, like a turtle or a doodlebug with many legs working in unison, they moved toward the back door and opened it.

What greeted them was such a feast of horror that none would soon forget it! Nothing was left of their trapped nutria but some brown fur, some bones and a lot of blood. The men moved around, inspecting the area and found huge prints, like the footprints of a huge dog, all around the camp. It was Baudier who nervously pointed out the bloodstained scratches near the handle of the camp's door.

But suddenly, Tirout stopped. "Listen!" he called out in a hoarse whisper. They all listened.

Out of the silence they heard a single croak, the "caw" of a big black crow perched at the very top of a ragged cypress tree. They watched as the crow spread its wings and flew away, and as it did so, it seemed to the men, that the swamp came alive again. Birds chirped, frogs were croaking, and the incessant song of the katydids started up again, as if on cue.

"You know what dey say, don' you?" said Tirout looking thoughtfully up at the crow. "Dey say dem old swamp witches dey go around like big black crows and dey is the only thing what scare de Loup Garou to an inch of his life!"

Chotin whistled again, as was his habit. "Maaannn! You tink dere's sometin' to dat?"

Just then a cackle, almost like a hoary laugh, trickled down to them from the crow. The men watched as the black bird became a small speck moving in the distance; it wheeled once and fluttered down to be lost among the moss-shrouded trees and grey morning haze.

This last was a sign to the men that it was now safe to move on. Needless to say, not nobody nor nothing had to tell them twice!

And this, they say in South Louisiana, is a true story of the Loup Garou.

ZOMBIES, VOODOO, AND THE UNDEAD

Paranormal Investigator Chantal Apodoca told Paul Dale Roberts, Haunted Paranormal Investigations General Manager (www.hpiparanormal.net) that she once she met a zombie in San Francisco. It was a wintery night and Chantal went into a Mystic/Metaphysical type of shop and started browsing around.

The store clerk came out to greet her and asked if he could help her. Chantal immediately thought that the clerk looked bizarre. His eyes were glassy and his movements were somewhat robotic. When he wasn't helping customers, he was reading a book about Voodoo.

Chantal also noticed that on his cloth belt, there were attached three small, brown, primitive-looking dolls.

Chantal asked the clerk what the dolls represented. The clerk looked at her with his foggy drippy eyes and said they were "good dolls." He would not elaborate further.

As Chantal was leaving the store, the strange-looking clerk blew a powdery substance in the air and mumbled something under his breath that sounded like chanting. Chantal felt uneasy and left the store quickly.

To this day, she wonders if the clerk of this store was some type of zombie or if he practiced the Voodoo arts.

Chantal would find out soon through a vision. One month later after encountering this zombie clerk, as she lay on her bed, she felt as though she was suddenly wide awake.

She looked toward the closet of her bedroom. The closet door slowly opened—and to her surprise there stood the store clerk. The man's eyes were as black as coals, and he stared at Chantal for a long period of time. No longer did he have the foggy drippy eyes. His eyes now were black and intense.

Chantal was frozen to her bed. She felt as if she was paralyzed. She couldn't move her arms, and she couldn't even scream for help.

As she watched the zombie clerk in her closet, a maniacal look came upon his face. His chest cavity opened up. For a period of five minutes his chest remained open and he stared down upon Chantal. After a few more moments, small black animal heads began staring out of the man's chest cavity.

Chantal was confused and kept looking and wondering what the small animal black heads were. Then to her revulsion, she realized that they were the small black heads of rats.

About 30 rats came out of the zombie clerk's chest. They started climbing onto the bed where Chantal lay. They climbed all over Chantal. Chantal felt like they were gnawing on her. She felt like her skin was being ripped apart. She tried to scream, but couldn't.

Her bed started shaking. Strange light beams came ripping through the walls. The zombie clerk started moving slowly toward Chantal. His outstretched scaly hand reached for Chantal's face.

When the zombie clerk finally lay his hand on her face, it felt as though he had ripped Chantal's face apart. When this happened, Chantal was finally able to scream and at that moment passed out.

When she finally awoke, everything was normal in her room. It was now daylight.

After sitting on her bed and thinking about the incredibly real dream or vision, she decided to tidy up her room to get her mind off the incident.

As she was dusting and cleaning out her closet, she discovered a small baby dead rat in her closet. She screamed immediately.

It made her wonder if the visitation from the zombie-like man was not a dream and if the dead baby rat had somehow manifested from her nightmare and entered her reality.

Whenever Chantal now watches a zombie movie, she gets a little "creeped out," because she will always think of that zombie clerk she met in San Francisco who later appeared in her darkest of dreams.

Zombie Madness

Who could have predicted the enormous popularity of the zombie in today's culture when George Romero brought the monster into contemporary consciousness with his motion picture *The Night of the Living Dead* (1968)? Large numbers of our current population have gone "Zombie Nuts," which has extended far beyond films and has lead to mass numbers of men and women role-playing and gathering in large groups to dress, dance, and act like the zombies do. You can never predict when you may encounter large numbers of pseudo-zombies dancing at your local mall—even on days other than Halloween.

The enormous popularity of the zombie in contemporary times has no doubt confused and frightened many individuals who don't know whether or not to take this horror seriously.

Is it possible that millions of people could become "zombified" after a great apocalyptic event? In the great majority of current motion pictures, books, games, and other media expressions, the zombies are themselves initially the victims of a great biological warfare, a mysterious virus, or some kind of mass pandemic that first kills them, then resurrects them with the uncontrollable desire to chomp on all humans who remain uninfected.

Real Zombies Live in an Eternal Twilight Zone

A *real* zombie is not the victim of biological warfare, a blast of radiation from a space vehicle, or a unknown virus that escaped a secret laboratory. A real zombie is a reanimated corpse who has been brought back to life to serve as slave labor. Originating in West Africa as worship of the python deity, Voodoo was brought to Haiti and the southern United States, particularly the New Orleans area.

As Lisa Lee Harp Waugh, a noted Necromancer, writer, and student of Voodoo put it, "A Zombie is a soulless human corpse, still dead, but taken from the grave and endowed by sorcery with a mechanical semblance of life. It is a dead body, which is made to walk and act and move as if it were alive."

For those who embrace the teachings of Voodoo, the zombie, the living dead, are to be feared as very real instruments of a Priestess or Priest who has yielded to the seduction of evil and allowed themselves to be possessed by negative forces and become practitioners of Dark Side sorcery.

Lisa Lee said that some Southern zombie-making-rituals consist of digging up a fresh corpse from its tomb or deep grave.

"The body is then fed strange potions and whispered to in strange chants," she explained. "Many individuals who have witnessed the evil, dark deed say that it is disturbing to view. You stand frozen in the shadows as a voyeur to some devil dark secret spell. You see a recently deceased man being made into a zombie before your eyes.

"Picture the image of a beautiful Voodoo Queen riding a rotting corpse like a wild banshee,

According to Lisa Lee Harp Waugh, "A Zombie is a soulless human corpse, still dead, but taken from the grave and endowed by sorcery with a mechanical semblance of life" (**art by Ricardo Pustanio**).

having dark magical sex in a graveyard," Lisa Lee continued. "Certainly this would be a sight that you will never forget. Imagine the strange image as candles flair, and mosquitoes bite hard into your skin. Then the spell comes to a conclusion as the zombie corpse comes to life. At that moment the Voodoo Queen takes him into what seems to be a deep kiss—and bites off his tongue to make him her eternal slave."

Most contemporary experts on New Orleans Voodoo and zombies agree that the legendary Dr. John, the ultimate "simplifier," created the perfect zombie juices and powders to make a living, breathing zombie that will not die, age, and become truly immortal. Marie Laveau, the most famous of all Voodoo Queens, fed her zombies a fine gumbo made with fish heads and scales and bones.

Some historians of Voodoo suggest that the origin of the word "zombie" may have come from *jumbie*, the West Indian term for a ghost. Others scholars favor the Kongo word *nzambi*, "the spirit that has resided in the body and is now freed" as filtering down through the ages as "zombie." Although the practice of Voodoo and the creation of zombies was familiar to the residents of Louisiana before 1871, a number of etymologists believe that year is about the time that the word "zombi" entered the English language. The word that was originally used by the Haitian Creole people, these scholars maintain, was *zonbi*, a Bantu term for a corpse returned to life without speech or free will. There are others who argue quite convincingly that *zombi* is another name for Damballah Wedo, the snake god so important to Voodoo. In other words, a zombie would be a servant of Damballah Wedo. A common ritual that creates a zombie requires a sorcerer to unearth a chosen corpse and waft under its nose a bottle containing the deceased's soul. Then, as if he were fanning a tiny spark of fire in dry tinder, the sorcerer nurtures the spark of life in the corpse until he has fashioned a zombie.

In Haiti the deceased are often buried face downward by considerate relatives so the corpse cannot hear the summons of the sorcerer. Some even take the precaution of providing their dearly departed with a weapon, such as a machete, with which to ward off the evil sorcerer.

There are many terrible tales of the zombie. There are accounts from those who have discovered friends or relatives, supposedly long-dead, laboring in the fields of some sorcerer.

Paul Dale Roberts, told me of his interviewing a man who claimed to have been turned into a zombie:

> Pete claims that when he was vacationing in Haiti, he had a fling with a Haitian girl, whose father is a Voodoo Shaman of the island. When the Haitian girl saw him [Pete] with another, he was a marked man.
>
> One night in a disco, he was stabbed in the arm with a hypodermic needle. He passed out and awakened in a coffin. He was buried alive. He was paralyzed, but aware of his surroundings. Later, he was dug up from his grave and used as a slave, picking sugar cane for six months. He somehow managed to get out of his comatose state of mind and escaped the island back to California. He claims to this very day that he has skin lesions on his arms, legs, and torso, because of his zombie transformation in Haiti.

Voodoo is a name attributed to a traditionally unwritten West African spiritual system of faith and ritual practices. Like most faith systems, the core functions of Voodoo are to explain the forces of the universe, influence those forces, and influence human behavior (*art by Ricardo Pustanio*).

The connotations of evil, fear, and the supernatural that are associated with Vodun (also "Voudou" and, popularly, "Voodoo") originated primarily from white plantation owners' fear of slave revolts. The white masters and their overseers were often outnumbered sixteen to one by the slaves they worked unmercifully in the broiling Haitian sun, and the sounds of Voodoo drums pounding in the night made them very nervous.

Vodun or Voudou means "spirit" in the language of the West African Yoruba people. Vodun as a religion observes elements from an African tribal cosmology that may go back as many as ten thousand years—and then it disguises these ancient beliefs with the teachings, saints, and rituals of Roman Catholicism. Early slaves—who were abducted from their homes and families on Africa's West Coast—brought their gods and religious practices with them to Haiti and other West Indian islands. Plantation owners were compelled by order of the French colonial authorities to baptize their slaves in the Catholic religion. The slaves suffered no conflict of theology. They accepted the white man's "water" and quickly adopted Catholic saints into the older African family of nature gods and goddesses.

When Vodun came to the city of New Orleans in the United States, it became suffused with a whole new energy—and a most remarkable new hierarchy of priests and priestesses, including the eternally mysterious Marie Laveau.

Some Voodoo traditions maintain that the only way that people can protect themselves from a zombie is to feed it some salt.

Lisa Lee Harp Waugh said that the story of not feeding salt to a zombie is actually over-rated. "Yes, it can destroy a zombie," she said, "but if given to them in moderation, it tends to keep a zombie frozen for a few years until its services are once again needed. A full dose of pure white salt—and that's about a full teaspoon today—would put an end to an animated corpse in a minute or less. They usually fall to the ground with violent convulsions and all the fluid drains from their bodies."

Voodoo is inspired by the worship of the python god, Damballah, who created the world. He stretched out his 7,000 coils to form the stars in the heavens and to mold the hills and valleys of Earth. His mighty lightning bolts cooled to fashion metals, rocks, and stones. When he perceived that water was necessary for life, he shed his skin and allowed it to melt into all the oceans, rivers, lakes, and waters on the planet. As the foam was settling from the life-giving deluge of water, the sun shined through the mist and a lovely rainbow was born. This rainbow was Ayida Wedo. Damballah fell instantly in love with her beauty, and the serpent and the rainbow became one: Damballah Wedo. Damballah Wedo's color is white and his day is Sunday.

Damballah Wedo, a loa (spirit) of peace and purity, speaks only to humans by possessing a follower of Voodoo, Santeria, Macumba, or one of the other African religions. This possession most often takes place during the dancing that follows other ritual observances. Damballah's image is that of a very large snake.

January 10 is National Voodoo Day

According to many authorities, it is in Benin City in southwestern Nigeria that Vodun began about 350 years ago. In 1996, Vodun, Voodoo, won state recognition. January 10 was inaugurated as National Voodoo Day, and the religion that is practiced by 65 percent of the 5.4 million Beninese took its place alongside Christianity and Islam.

Voodoo (Vodou, Vodoun, Vudu, or Vudun in Benin, Togo, southeastern Ghana, Burkina Faso, and Senegal; also Vodou in Haiti) is a name attributed to a traditionally unwritten West African spiritual system of faith and ritual practices. Like most faith systems, the core functions of Voodoo are to explain the forces of the universe, influence those forces, and influence human behavior. Voodoo's oral tradition of faith stories carries genealogy, history, and fables to succeeding generations. Adherents honor deities and venerate ancient and recent ancestors. This faith system is widespread across groups in West Africa. Diaspora spread Voodoo to North and South America and the Caribbean.

Numerous practitioners of Voodoo insist that the practice developed a more sinister side only after the advent of the slave trade shipped millions of West Africans to Haiti, Cuba, and the Americas. The Old Gods followed their captive people to help them survive and to cast evil spells upon those who would enslave them. At the same time, the people who were carried far from their home villages cleverly began to use the names of Catholic saints to disguise the ancient ones in their pantheon of gods under the names of those whom their captors deemed holy.

At the center of more traditional African tribal religions is the concept of a universal force of life that finds its expression in all things—humans, animals, vegetable, and mineral. The conviction that there is a oneness of all life forms, that both humans and everything else in the environment draw spiritual nourishment from the same sacred source is now known to be a common expression of shamanism and the teaching of tribal spirit "doctors."

Hoodoo

As defined by the knowledgeable staff of *Haunted America Tours*, Hoodoo refers to African traditional folk magic. This rich magical tradition was for thousands of years indigenous to ancient African botanical, magical-religious practices and folk cultures. Hoodoo was imported to the United States when mainly West Africans were enslaved and brought to the Americas.

Hoodoo is used as a noun and is derived from the Ewe word *Hudu* which still exists today. Hoodoo is often used in African American vernacular to describe a magic "spell" or potion, the practitioner (hoodoo doctor, hoodoo man, or hoodoo woman) who conjures the spell, or as an adjective or verb depending upon the context in which it is used.

The word can be dated to at least as early as 1891. Some prefer the term hoodooism, but this has mostly fallen out of use. Some "New Age" non-Diaspora practitioners who have taken up Hoodoo as a hobby employ such synonyms as conjuration, conjure, witchcraft, or rootwork. The latter demonstrates the importance of various roots in the making of charms and casting spells.

It is important to note that in traditional African religious culture, the concept of "spells" is not used. Here again, this Afro-botanical practice has been heavily used by the New Age and Wiccan communities who have little understanding of "Hoodoo's" spiritual significance as it is traditionally used in Africa.

An amulet characteristic of Hoodoo is the mojo—often called a mojo bag, mojo hand, conjure bag, trick bag, or toby—a small sack filled with herbs, roots, coins, sometimes a lodestone, and various other objects of magical power.

Santeria

Santeria originated in Cuba around 1517 among the slaves who were mostly from West Africa and who were followers of the Yoruba and Bantu religions. The African slaves were at first greatly distressed when they were told by their masters that they could no longer pay homage to their worship of the *Orishas*, their spiritual guardians, and that they would be severely punished if they did. But their resourceful and attentive priests quickly noticed a number of parallels between Yoruba religion and Catholicism. While appearing to pay obeisance and homage to various Christian saints, the Africans found that they could simply envision that they were praying to one of their own spirit beings. A secret religion was born—*Regla de Ocha*, "The Rule of the Orisha," or the common and most popular name, Santeria, "the way of the saints."

> *While the rites of Santeria remain secret and hidden from outsiders, a few churches of that denomination have emerged that provide their members an opportunity to practice their faith freely.*

This sort of religious substitution was also practiced by followers of the Old Religion, the Witches, in Europe when the Pope and his clerical minions began to punish Witches who claimed to interact with their animal "familiars." In those regions where the country folk and rural residents persisted in calling upon their familiars, the Church decreed the spirit beings to be demons sent by Satan to undermine the work of the clergy. All those accused of possessing a familiar or relying on it for guidance or assistance were forced to recant such a devilish partnership or be in danger of the torture chamber and the stake. In similar manner to the practitioners of Santeria, the Church actually provided saints and their symbols as acceptable substitutes for the ancient practice of asking favors or help from the witches' familiar. Many of the saints of Christendom are identified by an animal symbol, for example, the dog with St. Bernard; the lion with St. Mark; the stag with St. Eustace; the crow with St. Anthony; and the much-loved St. Francis of Assisi was often represented symbolically by a wolf. Perhaps the most remarkable of all, the celebration of the fertility goddess Eostre (Ostare, Eustre) provided the Church with a ready-made festival that commemorated the resurrection of Christ, which was named Easter.

While the rites of Santeria remain secret and hidden from outsiders, a few churches of that denomination have emerged that provide their members an opportunity to practice their faith freely. The Church of the Lukumi Babalu Aye was formed in southern Florida in the early 1970s and won a landmark decision by the Supreme Court to be allowed to practice animal sacrifice. Each celebration usually begins with an innovation of Olorun, the supreme deity. Dancing to strong African rhythms continues until individuals are possessed by a particular Orisha and allow the spirits to speak through them.

Possession in Haitian and New Orleans Vodou and Santeria is described as a god seizing a horse (the human being) who is ridden, sometimes to exhaustion. The all-powerful god is both distant and close, but too great to concern him/herself with humans, instead delegating the mediating task to the spirits (the law or loa). There are hundreds of lwa, who may be the protective spirits of clans or tribes from Africa or deified ancestors.

While Santeria's rites are controversial in that they may include the sacrifice of small animals, it is essentially a benign religion, and it continues to grow among Hispanics in Florida, New York City, and Los Angeles. Some estimates state that there are over 300,000 practitioners of Santeria in New York alone. Although it was suppressed in Cuba during the 1960s, lessening of restrictions upon religious practices in the 1990s saw the practitioners of Santeria in that country increase in great numbers.

Macumba

The Macumba religion (also known as Spiritism, Candomble, and Umbanda) is practiced by a large number of Brazilians who cherish the ages-old relationship between a shaman and his or her people. In its outward appearances and in some of its practices, Macumba resembles Voodoo ceremonies. Trance states among the practitioners are encouraged by dancing and drumming, and the evening ceremony is climaxed with an animal sacrifice.

Macumba was born in the 1550s when the West African tribal priests who sought to serve their people with their old religion were forced to give token obeisance to an array of Christian saints and the God of their masters. As in the cases of Santeria, Voodoo, and other adaptations of their original religious expression, the native priests soon realized how complementary the two faiths could be. The African god, Exu, became St. Anthony; Iemanja became Our Lady of the Glory; Oba became St. Joan of Arc; Oxala became Jesus Christ; Oxum became Our Lady of the Conception, and so on. The Africans summoned their Orishas with the sound of their drums and the rhythm of their dancing. In that regard, the West Africans were more fortunate than those slaves in the States, whose masters forbade them to keep their drums.

Macumba resembles Voodoo ceremonies, and trance states among the practitioners are encouraged by dancing and drumming (*art by Ricardo Pustanio*).

From the melding of the two religious faiths and the Africans' passion for drumming and dancing, the Samba, the rhythm of the saints, was created. The Samba became a popular dance, and even today is recognized in Brazil as a symbol of national identity. The dance, synonymous to many as a symbol of Brazil and Carnival, has also become widely accepted throughout the world. One of the Samba's derivations is the Bossa Nova.

King and Queen of the Undead

Baron Samedi is the most famous and the most frightening of the loa spirits. The Baron is the infamous master of the dead who escorts souls from the graveyard to the underworld.

However, the Baron does not concern himself only with the dead—he can enter the realm of the living and force people to do his terrible bidding.

Baron Samedi (Baron Saturday, also Bawon Samedi, or Bawon Sanmdi) is one of the loa of Haitian Vodou. Samedi is usually depicted with a white top hat, black tuxedo, dark glasses, and cotton plugs in the nostrils, as if to resemble a corpse dressed and prepared for burial in the Haitian style. He has a white, frequently skull-like face (or actually has a skull for a face). He is the head of the Guédé (also Ghede) family of loa, those gods concerned with death and resurrection.

Many call Baron Samedi the ruling loa or god of New Orleans. He and his bride, The Great Maman Brigitte, are sometimes referred to as the King and Queen of The Zombies. Voodooists believe that only through his power can a soul be forced from a living body and placed between life and death.

On Halloween night, Baron Samedi stands at the Crossroads, where the souls of dead humans pass on their way to the gate to Guinee, the astral counterpart of the ancient homeland in Africa. Samedi is a sexual loa, frequently represented by phallic symbols, and he is also noted for disruption, obscenity, debauchery, and having a particular fondness for tobacco and rum. As he is the loa of sex and resurrection, he is often called upon for healing by those near or approaching death. It is only the Baron who can accept an individual into the realm of the dead. Samedi is considered a wise judge and a powerful magician.

He as well as Ghede, the most benevolent loa of the dead, often possess individuals whether they are practicing Voodoo-Hoodoos or not. Many have experienced and documented such possession.

As well as being master of the dead, Baron Samedi is also a giver of life. He can cure any mortal of any disease or wound—if he thinks it is worth his time to do so. His powers are especially great when it comes to Voodoo curses and black magic. Even if somebody has been inflicted by a hex which brings them to the verge of death, they will not die if the Baron refuses to dig their grave. So long as this mighty spirit keeps them out of the ground they are safe. What he demands in return depends on his mood. Sometimes he is content with his followers wearing black, white, or purple clothes, and offering a small gift of cigars, rum, black coffee, grilled peanuts, or bread. On other occasions, the Baron will ask for a Voodoo ceremony in his honor. If he is in a bad mood, he may dig the grave of his supplicant bury him alive or bring him back as a mindless zombie.

The spiritual children of Baron and Maman Brigitte are the Ghede loa, the protectors of the dead. A New World loa, Maman Brigitte is probably traceable back to the Irish Saint Brigid. The Ghedes are powerful, and will prophesy the future, heal the sick, give advice, or perform magic of all descriptions. They also exert control over those who become zombies.

At Voodoo ceremonies, the Ghede possess the Voodooists and dance the banda, which is a wildly suggestive dance miming sexual intercourse. And in the midst of all this winding and grinding, these loa keep perfectly straight faces. They have reached such a deep trance state that it is as if they are cadavers and feel nothing.

Papa Legba (also Papa Ghede) is considered the counterpart to Baron Samedi. If a child is dying, it is Papa Legba to whom the parents pray. It is believed that he will not take a life before its time, and that he will protect the little ones.

Papa Ghede is supposed to be the corpse of the first man who ever died. He is recognized as a short, dark man with a high hat on his head, a cigar in his mouth, and an apple in his left hand. Papa Ghede is a psychopomp who waits at the Crossroads to take souls into the afterlife.

Although he was one of the most revered loa in Haitian Voudun, he was eventually transformed into the figure of a gentle and loving old man, who stands at the Guardian of the Centerpost, the Opener of the Gates to any who communicate with the loa.

Lisa Lee Harp Waugh, a Voodoo reactionary, has many times been in the company of the Baron Samedi. She suggests that many people in the paranormal field fear or have not investigated the sacred rites of Voodoo and the many spirit and ghost contacts that occur.

Waugh was called upon to help discover if a young Haitian woman in Miami, Florida, was actually possessed. Her case drew a lot of local attention in early 2009. The young woman had been held—or "ridden"—by the spirit since Halloween 2008. The case has been documented and will be featured in a forth-coming documentary on Voodoo-Hoodoo possession and exorcism.

BIBLIOGRAPHY

Armstrong, P.A. *The Piasa or the Devil among the Indians*. Morris, IL: 1887.

Astuya, Juan Carlos. "Chile Homeowner Terrified by Chupacabras." Translated by Scott Corrales. *La Estrella de Valparaiso*, October 14, 2001: http://www.rense .com/general15/chu.htm.

Barker, Gray. *They Knew too Much about Flying Saucers*. Kempton, IL: Adventures Unlimited Press, 1956.

Beckley, Timothy Green. *MJ-12 and the Riddle of Hangar 18*. New Brunswick, NJ: Inner Light Publications, 1989.

Berlitz, Charles, and William L. Moore. *The Roswell Incident*. New York: Grosset & Dunlap, 1980.

Booss, Claire, editor. *Scandinavian Folk & Fairy Tales*. New York: Gramercy Books, 1984.

Byrne, Peter. *The Search for Big Foot: Monster, Myth or Man?* Washington, DC: Acropolis Books, 1976.

Carrington, Richard. *Mermaids and Mastodons*. London: Arrow Books, 1960.

Clark, Jerome, and Loren Coleman. *The Unidentified*. New York: Warner Paperback Library, 1975.

———, and Loren Coleman. *Creatures of the Outer Edge*. New York: Warner Books, 1978.

Coleman, Loren. *Curious Encounters*. Boston and London: Faber & Faber, 1985.

———. *Mysterious America*. Boston: Faber & Faber, 1985.

———. *Mothman and Other Curious Encounters*. NY: Paraview Press, 2002.

Corrales, Scott. "How Many Goats Can a Goatsucker Suck?" *Fortean Times 89*. September 1996, pp. 34–37.

———. *Chupacabras and Other Mysteries*. Murfreesboro, TN: Greenleaf Publications, 1997.

———, and Colin Bord. *Unexplained Mysteries of the 20th Century*. Chicago: Contemporary Books, 1989.

Dash, Mike. *Borderlands*. New York: Dell Books, 2000.

Del Valle, Fernando. "The 'Goat Sucker' Legend Claws Its Way into Texas." *USA Today*. May 15, 1996.

Dinsdale, Tim. *Loch Ness Monster*. 4th ed. Boston: Routledge & Kegan Paul, 1982.

DuBois, Pierre. *The Great Encyclopedia of Fairies*. Illus. by Roland and Claudine Sabatier. New York: Simon & Schuster, 2000.

Eisler, Robert. *Man into Wolf*. London: Spring Books, n.d.

Ellis, Richard. *Monsters of the Sea*. New York: Alfred A. Knopf, 1994.

Fodor, Nandor. *The Haunted Mind: A Psychoanalyst Looks at the Supernatural*. New York: New American Library, 1968.

———. *Between Two Worlds*. New York: Paperback Library, 1967.

Friedman, Stanton T., and Don Berliner. *Crash at Corona*. New York: Paragon Books, 1992.

Froud, Brian. *Good Faeries, Bad Faeries*. New York: Simon & Schuster, 1998.

Gordon, Stan. "Additional Pennsylvania Thunderbird Reports," *FarShores Crypto News*, October 1, 2001: http://www.100megsfree4.com/farshores/ctbird.htm.

Gordon, Stuart. *The Encyclopedia of Myths and Legends*. London: Headline Books, 1994.

Green, John. *On the Track of the Bigfoot*. New York: Ballantine Books, 1973.

Henderson, Mark. "Team 'Find Traces of Sumatran Yeti.'" *London Times*, October 29, 2001.

Heuvelmans, Bernard. *On the Track of Unknown Animals*. New York: Hill & Wang, 1958.

Hurwood, Bernardt J. *Vampires, Werewolves, and Ghouls*. New York: Ace Books, 1968.

Jones, Alison, ed. *Larousse Dictionary of World Lore*. New York: Larousse, 1995.

Keel, John A. *Strange Creatures from Time and Space*. Greenwich, CT: Fawcett Publications, 1970.

————. *The Mothman Prophecies*. NY: Tor Books, 2002.

Keightley, Thomas. *The World Guide to Gnomes, Fairies, Elves, and Other Little People*. New York: Random House, 2000.

Larousse Dictionary of World Folklore. New York: Larousse, 1995.

Mack, Carol K., and Dinah Mack. *A Field Guide to Demons, Fairies, Fallen Angels, and Other Subversive Spirits*. New York: Holt, 1999.

Mackal, Roy P. *The Monsters of Loch Ness*. Chicago: The Swallow Press, 1976.

————. *Searching for Hidden Animals: An Inquiry into Zoological Mysteries*. Garden City, NY: Doubleday, 1980.

————. *A Living Dinosaur? In Search of Mokele-Mbembe*. New York: Brill, 1987.

"Man-Beast Hunts in the Far East." *Fortean Times 83*, October/November 1995: pp. 18–19.

Martyr, Deborah. "An Investigation of the Orang-Pendek, the 'Short Man' of Sumatra." *Cryptozoology 9*, 1990: pp. 57–65.

Masters, R. E. L., and Eduard Lea. *Perverse Crimes in History*. New York: The Julian Press, 1963.

Melton, Gordon J. *The Vampire Book: The Encyclopedia of the Undead*. 3rd ed. Farmington Hills, MI: Visible Ink Press, 2011.

Ocejo-Sanchez, Dr. Virgilio. "Eyewitness Describes Flying Chupacabras." Translated by Mario Andrade. Miami UFO Center: ufomiami@prodigy.net. Accessed September 21, 2001.

Otto, Steve. "Absolute Kinda Irrefutable Proof of Skunk Ape." *Tampa Tribune*. http://news.tbo.com/news/MGACIN7J3JC.html. Accessed February 13, 2001.

Porco, Peter. "Southwest Alaskans See Bird They Say Is Super Cub-sized." *Anchorage Daily News*, October 15, 2002: http://www.adn. com/ 1962481p-2066841c.html.

Randle, Kevin D., and Donald R. Schmitt. *UFO Crash at Roswell*. New York: Avon Books, 1991.

————. *A History of UFO Crashes*. New York: Avon Books, 1995.

————. *Conspiracy of Silence*. New York: Avon Books, 1997.

Rose, Carol. *Spirits, Fairies, Leprechauns, and Goblins: An Encyclopedia*. New York: W.W. Norton & Company, 1998.

Sanderson, Ivan T. *Abominable Snowmen: Legend Come to Life*. Philadelphia: Chilton Company, 1961.

Simek, Rudolf. *Dictionary of Northern Mythology*. Translated by Angela Hall. Rochester, NY: D.S. Brewer, 1993.

Spence, Lewis. *The Fairy Tradition in Britain*. London: Rider & Company, 1948.

Steiger, Brad. *Worlds before Our Own*. New York: G.P. Putnam's Sons, 1978.

————, ed. *Project Blue Book: The Top Secret UFO Findings Revealed*. New York: Ballantine Books, 1995.

————. *The Werewolf Book: The Encyclopedia of Shape-shifting Beings*. Farmington Hills, MI: Visible Ink Press, 1999.

————. *Real Vampires, Night Stalkers, and Creatures from the Darkside*. Canton, MI: Visible Ink Press, 2010.

————. *Real Zombies, The Living Dead, and Creatures of the Apocalypse*. Canton, MI: Visible Ink Press, 2010.

————, and Sherry Hansen Steiger. *The Gale Encyclopedia of the Unusual and the Unexplained*. Farmington Hills, MI: Thomson-Gale, 2003.

INDEX

Note: (ill.) indicates photos and illustrations.

X, Y, Z